THE WRITER'S WORK

DEAN MEMERING
Central Michigan University

FRANK O'HARE
The Ohio State University

Guide to effective composition

SECOND EDITION

PRENTICE-HALL, INC.
Englewood Cliffs, New Jersey 07632

THE WRITER'S WORK

Library of Congress Cataloging in Publication Data

MEMERING, DEAN, (date)
   The writer's work.

   Includes index.
   1. English language—Rhetoric.   I. O'HARE, FRANK.
II. Title.
PE1408.M463   1984   808'.042   83-21266
ISBN   0-13-971739-0

THE WRITER'S WORK: Guide to Effective Composition, second edition
DEAN MEMERING/FRANK O'HARE
© 1984 by Prentice-Hall, Inc., Englewood Cliffs, New Jersey 07632

Editorial and production supervision: Joyce Fumia Perkins
Interior design: Lee Cohen
Drawings: Eric Hieber
Manufacturing coordination: Harry P. Baisley

Printed in the United States of America.

10   9   8   7   6   5   4   3   2   1

ISBN 0-13-971739-0

Prentice-Hall International, Inc., *London*
Prentice-Hall of Australia Pty. Limited, *Sydney*
Editora Prentice-Hall do Brasil, Ltda., *Rio de Janeiro*
Prentice-Hall of Canada, Ltd., *Toronto*
Prentice-Hall of India Private Limited, *New Delhi*
Prentice-Hall of Japan, Inc., *Tokyo*
Prentice-Hall of Southeast Asia Pte. Ltd., *Singapore*
Whitehall Books Limited, *Wellington, New Zealand*

PREFACE

Composition instructors of the 1980s are heirs to a complex history and stewards of an uncertain future. The 1960s were a decade of unrest and experimentation; in many schools where it had been traditionally taught as a mechanical skill, composition became self-expressive writing, a change some found refreshing and others disturbing. In the 1970s there has been much public and professional concern about an alleged loss of direction in composition and a presumed deemphasis of basic skills in composition courses. As SAT scores have fallen, critics of the profession have insisted that composition has become dichotomized, divorcing content from style, invention from expression, the larger issues of composition from the lesser. The skills of writing have always been difficult to teach, more difficult to learn, and—especially when divorced from more creative aspects of writing—they are often the least rewarding components of the writing process. Yet writers themselves seldom view the skills as trivial. The dichotomy between ideas and skills of expression does not exist in the work of experienced writers, most of whom hold that the quality of an idea is limited by the writer's power of expression. The notion that style and substance are separable creates a hardship for our students if this notion means that they are being offered a choice between ideas and language skills: between

v

large, important matters in one composition course and small, un-important matters in another composition course. Because we be-lieve this split between form and content is false, and contrary to both the theory and the practice of good writing, we have continued to present both and to show the interaction between them in this second edition of *The Writer's Work*.

Chapter by chapter, as they move through a progression of in-creasingly formal writing tasks from personal to informative to criti-cal to persuasive to research writing, students will see how these choices of style and substance work together regardless of the writ-ing task. The nonfiction writer's commitment to truth, accuracy, and integrity in writing requires not only factual honesty but dedi-cation to accuracy of expression. Even such mundane matters as spelling and punctuation are seen not just as a writer's tools, but as important means of achieving the writer's overall purpose. Because of the special nature of the relationship between the writer and the reader of nonfiction, all accidents of expression both interfere with the intended message and send another, negative message about the author's view of self and attitudes toward the reader and the subject. After more than a decade of controversy over form and sub-stance, it is time to replace the dichotomy with a unified theory of composition.

Part of the impulse behind *The Writer's Work* has been the dis-covery that inexperienced writers are capable of dedication to their craft. We have discovered, for example, that students can move from the inherently rewarding pleasures of personal writing and autobiographical narratives to the more demanding work of other kinds of writing. The "term paper," or research paper, is not be-yond inexperienced writers and need not be a routine and unin-spired collection of footnotes. Class testing of the materials in *The Writer's Work* has demonstrated that students can succeed at aca-demic writing. Leading students through increasingly more de-manding writing tasks and building into those tasks an accumulation of skills that develop into formal and impersonal kinds of writing, the text provides a natural bridge from free writing to research writ-ing.

Part One: Writing

In the second edition of *The Writer's Work,* Part One, Writing, puts much greater emphasis on the *aims* of discourse, on the writ-er's overall purpose, and on the recursive nature of the composing process itself. Emphasizing the need for several drafts of a paper, Part One reflects our conviction that writing is *re*-writing.

Chapter 1, The Composing Process, first presents the writer's choices and then describes the stages of writing in which the choices operate. All writing is governed by the writer's purpose, but having said that, we must go on to explore the choices a writer makes as a part of that purpose: choices about audience, experience, self, and especially choices about code—the language a writer selects. These elements must unite in the writer's overall design, either through conscious decision or writer's intuition, to produce the concept and the expression of that concept, which we call composition. Decisions about each of these aspects must be made during the writer's initial draft, working draft(s), and final draft. Chapter 1 explains and illustrates the composing process with both student and professional writing, offers activities to help students understand the process, and, finally, provides students with the initial, working, final, and proofread drafts of a real student paper for discussion.

Chapter 2, Personal Writing, begins by offering students an opportunity to express the self by means of a series of free-writing and journal-writing experiences. Students then move to more structured personal-experience writing, where they learn to shape their experience into narrative form for a reader. The chapter, which contains student and professional examples, activities, and principles for effective personal writing, has been enriched by the expansion of the section on journals and by the addition of a section on description. Student examples show a greater range of maturity than in the first edition.

Chapter 3, Informative Writing, begins with a discussion of the important role that informative writing plays in college and in the real world, moving students from the purely personal to a focus on subjects in the world outside the self. The chapter introduces more formalized invention procedures than those in Chapter 2: students are shown several ways to find material and analyze subjects for expository writing they'll be doing in chapters 3 through 5, including Burke's *pentad*, brainstorming, and the journalistic formula. In this chapter, students are assigned a number of informative papers—comparison and contrast, classification, process, definition—and are encouraged to use a variety of these strategies of exposition in their informative writing. Interesting new student examples help to strengthen explanations of the principles of informative writing.

Chapter 4, Evaluative and Persuasive Writing, begins by having students write objective and critical summaries and then critical reviews. The section on evaluative writing is followed by a full treatment of logic, including syllogistic reasoning and the common fallacies. The section on argumentation and persuasion has been expanded to include a fuller treatment of audience analysis. In addition to new student papers, there are specific suggestions for a variety of writing activities.

Chapter 5, Writing with Sources, introduces a powerful new instrument for dealing with the research paper—*the search strategy*—a systematic procedure for finding and refining an interesting, relevant research question and for accumulating information to answer that question. The chapter includes a detailed sample search as well as an introduction to the library that will help students familiarize themselves with the contents and organization of their college library. The chapter presents documentation formats in MLA style, as well as generic coverage of APA style. The chapter also includes a new model paper and a selection of popular research topics. Chapter 5 is the culmination of the progression from unstructured, informal, personal writing to structured, formal, impersonal writing. In their research papers, students are encouraged to use all the strategies—to express self, to inform, to evaluate, to persuade—they have been exposed to in Part One.

Part Two: Skills

Chapter 6, Effective Paragraphs, presents principles of paragraph composition and demonstrates the application of topic sentence, development, unity, and coherence in mature paragraphs. The chapter introduces a number of approaches to paragraph structure, including Christensen's generative rhetoric of the paragraph. The chapter includes various approaches to such problem paragraphs as the introductory and concluding paragraphs of formal nonfiction. Effective Paragraphs is illustrated with student and professional writing and contains many suggestions for writing activities at the paragraph level.

Chapter 7, Sentence Combining for Effective Sentences, combines two chapters from the first edition of *The Writer's Work*, Sentence Combining and Effective Sentences. The chapter contains exercises based on the signal system developed by Frank O'Hare, as well as new unsignaled and creative exercises in exploring prose. While we view sentence-level problems as just one of many difficulties in writing, students often view sentence problems as the chief difficulty in writing. Students who tediously write one word at a time (like those who read one word at a time), students who labor to produce a sentence and then discover that the sentence is incomprehensible—students who lack syntactic fluency—are often not able to attend to larger problems of composition. The sentence-level barrier is absolute for them. As most instructors know, efforts to drill grammar into these students have usually failed. But the new research incorporated into *The Writer's Work* should make this kind of language handicap a thing of the past for most students. O'Hare's work, *Sentence Combining: Improving Student Writing without Formal Grammar Instruction*, NCTE Research Report No. 15, 1973, demonstrated that syntactic fluency is a discrete skill and that most students can acquire an ease with sentences characteristic of mature writers. Based on O'Hare's research, sentence combining makes possible the dedication to skills required by the view that composition is a union of thought and expression. With periodic exercises throughout a semester, students will first lose their "scribal stutter," and second, acquire something of the grace and maturity of the professional writers whose prose illustrates this chapter. The sentence-combining exercises have been combined with rhetorical and stylistic considerations of effectiveness in sentence structure based on principles of clarity, economy, emphasis, and variety. The chapter demonstrates flaws to be avoided or revised, as well as the many options available to writers. This comprehensive treatment of sentence options allows teachers flexibility in determining how much of each they wish to emphasize with students. In addition, this chapter describes and gives students experience with the chunk—a unit of discourse longer than a sentence, shorter than a paragraph. Practice with the chunk allows students to wrestle with the sentence boundary, the most common error (run on sentences and fragments) in student writing. The chapter contains professional and student examples of effective prose contrasted with less effective writing.

Part Three: Conventions

Chapter 8, Effective Diction, highlights the vocabulary choices writers make, as well as those they avoid, based on the overall purpose and stance of the writer who is interested in clear, concise, and accurate writing. This chapter contains a dictionary section discussing entries and connotative and denotative definitions. The choices are presented in pairs exemplifying effective diction contrasted with less effective writing. The chapter uses many examples of professional and student writing and contains review exercises to help students distinguish between effective writing and poor.

Chapter 9, Usage, describes grammatical choices and problems. As we use the term, "grammar" is retricted to such things as agreement of subjects and verbs, the reference of pronouns to their antecedents, and so forth—what is frequently called "usage." Since usage questions can involve minority dialects, linguistic prejudice can become a real problem in any classroom in which instructors teach a "standard English." But the nonfiction writer's task is to affect his or her audience; the reader-writer relationship is created and controlled through the language the writer uses. The writer cannot ignore the usage expectations of readers. Educated readers expect subjects and verbs to "agree," pronouns to refer clearly to antecedents, and so forth. Thus, for the writer, usage choices become a means of fulfilling the expectations of the reader. The more intimate and self-expressive the writing is, the less the reader expects the writer to conform to conventional usage; but as the writing becomes more formal, less focused on self, readers have greater expectations of conventional usage. Chapter 9 explains and illustrates with effective prose the usage choices typically found in formal writing today. The chapter includes a Dictionary of Usage Problems and abundant exercises, to help students familiarize themselves with conventional usage.

Chapter 10, Mechanics, provides a reference guide to punctuation, spelling, and capitalization. Mechanics rules and principles are explained and illustrated, as are significant options and variations. The spelling section contains a guide to trouble spots in spelling.

The Glossary of Language Terms amounts to an eleventh chapter—an extensive glossary of grammatical, linguistic, rhetorical, and lexicographical terms that students may encounter in *The Writer's Work* and elsewhere, as they study composition and undertake research for writing assignments. This glossary and the comprehensive index complete the text and make of it not only a classroom guide but a reference work for students, writers, and others who may have questions about nonfiction writing.

TO THE STUDENT

There is little about writing that all writers will agree to, except perhaps that all writers are different. You may approach writing one way; your friend may do just the opposite. Some writers compose standing up, some make endless notes and preliminary outlines, some work very fast, others are very slow. Despite these differences, many writers—especially inexperienced writers—share a common fear: the fear of writing. You may be one of those who feel writing is too complex, too subjective, too mysterious to learn. There are even some writers who fear that writing requires a special talent or genius they lack.

Our experiences with writers have shown that these fears are usually unfounded. Most people can learn to write. Writing is not mysterious. We cannot promise that you can learn to write with the artistry of a great author, but we do promise that most inexperienced writers can learn to write well. We are certain you will be able to understand what effective writing is. We believe that anything important to writers can be explained in simple language, and we rely on examples to help explain and illustrate every concept and problem in writing. We have drawn on the work of many published authors—some famous, some not so famous—to demonstrate the power and variety of modern writing. All the writing assignments are illustrated with student examples, many of them papers students wrote in response to the writing assignments in the first edition of *The Writer's Work*.

Through these examples and plain-English explanations, we have attempted to focus on the work of the writer. The nonfiction writer uses data, information, facts. These have to be collected and arranged. While work is not necessarily easy, most work has procedures and guidelines you can follow. The key to work is practice; the more you do of it, the better you get at it. Writers too have methods and techniques in their work, and for writers too, practice is the key. We have tried to show how writers do their work, and for that reason we have titled our book *The Writer's Work*.

Because writers are different, some need to start with free writing and journal writing to help themselves gain confidence and a degree of fluency before moving on to more structured assignments. Most writers enjoy personal writing and gain insight into their writing techniques through it. In both fiction and nonfiction writing, story-telling is very popular. But in nonfiction writing there are other forms the writer should explore too. Beyond narrative writing there are equally rewarding forms of expository and critical writing. Eventually nonfiction writers should be able to use any form or technique appropriate to their purpose, including research writing. How much you do of any one kind of writing depends a lot on you. Some writers need a good deal of work in personal writing before they feel ready to move on. Others may be ready to start immediately with informative or critical writing. Some inexperienced writers have felt that research writing is too difficult to attempt at all. But sooner or later, research becomes a primary tool for the nonfiction writer, and we have attempted to go beyond mere footnote advice to show you, by means of a search strategy, how to find data, how to evaluate evidence, and how to put together a research paper. Research writing needn't be mechanical or uninspired. Since few nonfiction writers can get along without research, we have attempted to show some of the interest, the challenge, and the reward of research writing. Still, how much research any given writer is ready for depends on the writer. Some may be ready for it immediately; others may need preparatory work first.

A writer must have ideas to write about, of course, and the first part of *The Writer's Work* is devoted to the writing process and invention procedures that will help you find your own ideas. To further help you, we have included many of the ideas students have suggested, including students who used the first edition of *The Writer's Work*. But a writer must have skills, too. Very few professional writers are indifferent to spelling, punctuation, grammar. To help you review your skills, we have provided many exercises. We don't mean to imply that Part Two and Part Three should be used like a workbook, nor even that you should wait until you have finished Part One before turning to Skills and Conventions. Some writers need to review when problems come up in their own writing. Others may need to do some of the exercises. In some cases your instructor may wish to go over some of the exercises in class. We do not think writers learn the skills and conventions of English merely by drilling away at them, and we have not provided exercises for that purpose. Our experience has been that limited, periodic review of skills is most effective with inexperienced writers.

Nothing in writing can be approached in a mechanical and unthinking way, and nothing in writing can be seen as too trivial to bother with. Some writers make the most improvement in the quality of their writing when they gain control over the skills and conventions of English. Sometimes it is the lack of skills that gets in the way and prevents a writer from finding his or her ideas: "I know what I mean; I just can't say it!" It is as if a barrier to expression is formed at the skills level, and it is this barrier that is removed when students improve in skills. It is true that when you have your ideas clearly in mind, writing is easier than when your ideas are not clear. It is also true that when you can express yourself clearly and easily, your ideas will flow with greater ease.

Our students have been pleased to discover the relative ease with which they have been able to turn their sentences into mature and effective writing. One of the best techniques of untangling sentence problems is sentence combining, a creative exercise in which writers experiment with different ways to write sentences. With sufficient practice in generating well-formed and effective sentences, most writers gain surprising strength and effectiveness in their writing. The aim of sentence combining is to give you flexibility and control at the rewriting stage so that you can easily produce long, short, simple, complex, or any other kind of sentences that suit your purpose, and without struggling with grammar or traditional advice about when to do what in writing.

The Writer's Work is a complete guide to the craft of writing. There are two attitudes about modern usage. One is that there are correct and incorrect language choices. (Most of us were taught that "ain't" is incorrect.) The other is that there is no such thing as "correct" or "incorrect" language. All language must be judged on its suitability to the author's purpose. Language should be appropriate to the context. We think appropriateness is the best guide for language choices. But we also think that inexperienced writers need more guidance and more to hang on to than the concept of appropriateness. Therefore, throughout *The Writer's Work* we have attempted to specify the contexts of appropriateness. In general we suggest a middle-level style stressing clear, concise, and accurate English. And we show the changes in appropriateness as writers move from informal, personal writing to formal, impersonal writing.

To make it easier to find answers to your questions about how best to express what you want to write, the pages of Chapters 6 through 10, are colored—one color for Chapters 6, 7 and 8, in which the larger issues of paragraphs, sentences, and words are discussed; and a different color for Chapters 9 and 10, in which you will find guidelines on usage and mechanics.

You may wonder, as others have, whether writing is worth the effort it requires. What is the point of writing anyway? There are two very good answers to that question. Nonfiction writing is a salable skill. Business, science, law, medicine, education—all modern careers have heavy demands for writers, and that demand is growing. Reports, proposals, letters, speeches, and dozens of other writing tasks arise today in all sorts of jobs. Try to imagine the numbers of writers required in a visual and oral medium like television: everything you see and hear on television must first be written by someone. Quite an astonishing percentage of the work in our so-called oral world is conducted through the written word.

But the best answer is that, for many writers, writing is fun. Writing is a totally involving and demanding activity, calling upon all your inner resources. It is a means of self-expression and a means of communication. Even for the nonfiction writer, writing is creative work. It can produce something meaningful and artistic like a nonfiction novel. Nonfiction writing today need not be mere drudge work, pointless exercises in formula writing. As you can see from the examples throughout *The Writer's Work*, the people with whom we have worked over the years have enjoyed writing (even though there may have been a lot of hard rewriting and polishing to produce the final version). And from the many enjoyable pieces our students have provided for examples, we believe you can see that there can be a tremendous feeling of satisfaction in writing. Like other forms of self-fulfillment, writing leaves many writers pleased and proud of a job well done. Our students have said so. We think you will agree with them.

ACKNOWLEDGMENTS

As in the first edition, we have received generous suggestions and helpful criticism from many people. Special thanks to the following: Sister Margaret Camper, C.S.J., *Fontbonne College;* Elouise Bell, *Brigham Young University;* Bonnie Braendlin, *Florida State University;* Betsy Brown, *The Pennsylvania State University;* Michael A. Dockery, *Harrisburg Area Community College;* John Harwood, *The Pennsylvania State University;* Lynne M. Kellerman, *Rutgers, The State University;* Fredric Koeppel, *Northwest Junior College, Mississippi;* Jerry Olson, *Middlesex County College;* Peter C. Page, *University of New Mexico;* Ronald Primeau, *Central Michigan University;* Jo Ann Seiple, *University of North Carolina at Wilmington;* M. Beverly Swan, *University of Rhode Island;* Joan Weatherly, *Memphis State University;* John T. Wolfe, Jr., *Fayetteville State University, North Carolina;* Laura M. Zaidman, *University of South Carolina.*

DEAN MEMERING
FRANK O'HARE

CONTENTS

SKILLS

THE WRITER'S WORK

PART ONE

WRITING

CHAPTER ONE

The Composing Process

I suffer as always from the fear of putting down the first line.

It is amazing the terrors, the magics, the prayers, the

straightening shyness that assails one.

JOHN STEINBECK, *The Journals of a Novel: The East of Eden Letters*

GOOD WRITING

As a beginning writer, you should be aware of one important fact about writing: *good* writing isn't the same as *great* writing. It is possible to have a well-written children's story, a well-written humor piece in a magazine, a well-written editorial in a newspaper; but none of these is necessarily "great" writing. Masterpieces of literature are well written, but they are also significant and beautiful and a number of other things that we call "great." Naturally, we would all like to turn out writing that is both well written and great; however, it is important to remember from the start that the two things are not the same.

You are bright enough and educated enough to become a good writer. Good writing can be learned, and there is nothing very mysterious about it. Writing is a craft, and those who practice it enough can become good at it. And nearly everyone of average ability and experience can tell the difference between something that is well crafted and something that isn't. For example, which of the following two paragraphs is well written?

Somebody asked Picasso why did he choose to be an artist but he got mad and said that if he would have to ask a question like that he would stop being one. I asked some scientists the same thing. They didn't get mad, but they didn't really give me reasons why. They just said they liked it. They couldn't describe it any better than why a young guy falls in love with some girl but not with another one. Most scientists know they won't get rich. They know they won't be successful, really. So why do they do it?

Picasso, when asked why he chose to be an artist, lost his temper and retorted that when a man finds himself asking why he is doing what he is doing, it is time for him to give it up. The men of science whom I questioned kept their tempers; still, what they gave me were not reasons at all but only statements of preference. These highly analytical men were no more able to describe precisely what had captured their minds than is any young lover able to explain why he is deeply in love with a particular girl and not with her sister. They knew there would never be wealth as the world measures it, nor even success in the popular sense. Why, then, do they do it? They don't know.

Most people would agree that the second paragraph, which is by Mitchell Wilson ("On Being a Scientist," *Atlantic Monthly*, Sept. 1970), is well written and the first is not so well written. Both passages are about the same idea; the information in them is quite similar. Yet almost any reader can see that Wilson is expressing it better.

Wilson handles language better; he expresses himself better; and this is what is meant by "well written." Wilson's paragraph has no difficult language, no hard words, and the idea itself is quite simple: neither artists nor scientists know why they choose their careers. Good writing, therefore, can be crafted from very humble language and simple ideas. What is good about such writing lies precisely in the craftsmanship, the skill with which the writer puts together words and ideas. And this skill can be learned.

Learning to write well means becoming fluent in written English. All native speakers of English are, by definition, fluent in spoken English. But these same fluent *speakers* have shown a surprising tendency to "stutter," falter, become inarticulate when they write. It is specifically, and *only*, in the process of writing English that people tend to lose their natural fluency with language. Therefore, your goal should be to express yourself in writing as fluently as you do in speech. It is very easy to say that good writing comes from one *or* the other—good ideas or good language skills— but few things in life work on this either/or principle. Ideas without language skills are apt to sound like the paragraph that tries to express Wilson's ideas without his command of language: inarticulate, immature. On the other hand, smooth-sounding language that doesn't say anything is just as bad, and thinking people will not accept it. Thus, there really is no choice; there is no either/or to it. Good writing must have both: good ideas and good language skills.

Fortunately, another fact about writing—perhaps the most important one—is that although writing is difficult, you are equal to the challenge. If you continue to think of "real writing" as something you will have to do *after* you've completed your education, that assumption will work against you. Students can and do become skilled writers *while* they are in school, as the following paragraph reveals:

> As he sat tightly strapped to the chair, the young man listened while the warden read the execution order and then asked the condemned man if he had anything to say. The riflemen who were to be his executioners were hidden from the man, behind a dark-colored curtain, and he gazed for a long moment at the ceiling and then back at the warden, uttering a brief sentence. There was a loud explosion, and the five bullets that tore through Gary Gilmore's heart ended not only his life, but also the uneasy moratorium on the death penalty that had begun nearly ten years before.
> MICHAEL G. KNAPP

This is good writing by adult standards, and it was written by a student *in* college.

Moreover, much of this book is the result of important research in composition showing that students can write mature sentences without relying on traditional grammar systems. The writer in the preceding example has learned the art of combining short sentences into longer ones. His first sentence, for example, could be composed of several shorter sentences such as the following:

> The young man sat tightly strapped to the chair. He listened. The warden read the execution order. Then the warden asked him a question. Did he have anything to say?

It doesn't take knowledge of grammatical terminology or great talent to revise these sentences into one longer, more mature sentence. What used to take years of complex grammar study can now be accomplished relatively quickly through sentence combining, and this means you can soon be writing the sentences of an experienced writer—even if you are one of those people for whom "English was always my worst subject."

SPEAKING AND WRITING

You already have a skill that will help you learn to write well: your ability to speak. Writing developed as a means of recording speech. Ancient peoples evolved methods for keeping records of the seasons, harvest yields, who owed what to whom, and so on. From these beginnings grew the world's writing systems.

Nearly every child learns to speak his or her native language almost without effort. Many people who find writing quite difficult have no difficulty communicating orally. Perhaps we should not be surprised that most people are better at speaking than writing; still, if writing is only a way to record speech, it is not clear why people who speak fluent English should have so much trouble writing the language.

Part of the answer lies in the fact that written languages are not identical with spoken languages. We can only imperfectly record speech. The written language is voiceless; it does not very well convey *tone* of voice, rising and falling *pitch*, loud or soft *volume*, rapid or slow *pace*, nor other things we can do with our voices. We attempt to make up some of the deficiencies in written language through punctuation and other conventions of print.

But speakers take shortcuts with the language. They speak in fragments and silences that cannot be translated into written English. They are able to do so because, in addition to the words of the language, speakers have nonverbal feedback systems that supplement their words. A nod of the head, a lift of an eyebrow, a gesture or facial expression, or a snort, sniff, or chuckle—with these, speakers and listeners have the means to understand messages that would appear incoherent in print. Thus, in addition to differences between voiced and unvoiced communication, there is an important difference between communicating directly (talking) with a present audience and communicating indirectly (writing) with an absent audience. Facial expressions as well as outright complaints indicate to a speaker that the audience isn't understanding the message. The speaker can immediately repeat or rephrase and keep on doing so until the audience does understand. As a writer you have no such opportunities. Once the words are written and sent on to readers, there is nothing more you can do.

If all writing were only simple, factual communications—How many cows are in the meadow? Whose turn is it to go to market? When must we plant corn?—you might be less concerned with audience. Simple information can be given on a take-it-or-leave-it basis. In most cases, such information-dominated writing is reader-initiated. That is, the reader starts the communication process by requesting or seeking information. In these situations, your task is straightforward: to write the facts when readers ask for them.

But most of the world's writing is initiated by the writer, not the reader. Letters, stories, news accounts, advertisements, business documents, and so on, are writing tasks undertaken when a writer perceives the need to reach out to a reader. The need to reestablish lines of communication with a friend, the wish to share a story or an experience, the compulsion to involve others in a crusade—writing happens most often because a writer wants or needs to create some response in a reader.

For most writing, then, you aren't just supplying requested information. Indeed, in some cases you may be offering *unwanted* information, and the written word may actually be received with hostility, contempt, or indifference. The telephone, television, radio, recorded music, and films—not to mention the demands of family, friends, and work—all vie for people's attention. Imagine the task, in that case, of trying to get people to donate money to your favorite charity by means of what you are able to write in a letter or brochure. How can you get anyone to pay attention instead of just throwing your writing into the wastebasket? Effective writing is writing that moves your reader to react in some way you intend. Written communication is very much a transaction between reader and writer, and in most cases the transaction is aimed at getting the reader to do something: to learn, to share, to laugh . . . to react in some way.

You can *control* every aspect of writing except the reader's reaction. Fortunately, though you may not always know who will read your words, you can *imagine* an audience and aim your writing at an *intended* audience. And to the degree that you can imagine *speaking* to such an audience, you can take advantage of the speaking-writing relationship. In short, you can use your fluency in oral English to help yourself become equally fluent in written English, as long as you use your imagination to make up for the lack of audience feedback in writing.

THE WRITER'S CHOICES

Writing involves a series of interrelated choices. Think of what happens when you write. Sometimes your *purpose* is to entertain; at others to argue or persuade; at others to discover what you think ("How do I know what I think until I see what I said?"). Your *audience* is just as variable; it may be your closest friend on one occasion, a group of nameless, faceless strangers on the next. To these, add choices (conscious and subconscious) about your *experience*, about the *self* you project in your writing, and about the structure and language, which we call *code*, you use to convey your written message. Writing *is* choice. The thinking you do about each of these elements, together with the decisions you make about each of them, shapes and controls your writing. Your message grows from all these choices, and that is the creative delight of the writer's work.

Most of the ills of writing can be traced to underemphasizing or overemphasizing any of these elements. A finished piece of writing appears to the reader as one thing, a unified composition. In order for all these elements to blend together so that nothing appears to be missing and nothing sticks out and draws too much attention to itself, you must consider each of them and orchestrate them all into the finished product, just as notes, rhythm, pace, and lyrics must be blended together to make a pleasing song. A closer look at each of these components will help explain why this is so.

The Writer's Purpose

The word *purpose* means, in part, the writer's intention, *why* the writer is writing. It also means the unifying principle of any written work: not only what the writer is attempting to do, but what the composition is attempting to do.

If the question is, What prompts you to write? you may give reasons such as to entertain, to inform, to persuade, to impress, to evaluate, or to express yourself. There are many possibilities. Quite possibly, you may not always have a clear notion of why you are writing when you start out. And it can happen that you sometimes have more than one motive.

If you ask yourself, What is my purpose? you will realize that you must think about all the components of the writing process before you can answer. A good writer will not settle for mere surface analysis. What are your *true* motives? Furthermore, if you have a purpose, it must be a purpose aimed at the reader, at least in any writing that someone is actually going to read. Some analysis of the audience you are writing to is inevitable. And if you are selecting elements from your experience to write about, you must be aware that your selection is not random. Analysis of your experiences, your audience, and your view of self all become factors in your purpose. Even the code you use—whether you use street slang or formal English, for example—depends on all the other factors.

We can summarize purpose as the overall controlling set of decisions in a piece of writing. It includes your view of self and your motives; your attitudes and decisions about your experiences; your decisions and attitudes toward audience or projected audience; and your decisions about the code to be used to carry the message to the reader. All these factors interrelate and are mutually dependent upon each other, like the pieces in a design. The harmony among them or the pattern among them becomes the unifying principle of the written work. Change any one of them and you change all of them.

Writing that is directed at no one in particular usually fails. A keen sense of audience helps you refine your purpose, view your self, and select from your experience. You will discover that who you write to powerfully influences what and how you write. Is your audience the instructor? What does the instructor expect? Is your audience the "general reader"? Can you imagine anything about such a person? Are you your own audience (as in a diary that only you may read)? Must you adapt yourself to the audience? Or can you make the audience accept you "as you are"? What do you know about the audience? What do they know about you? What do they know about the subject of your paper? How do they feel about this topic? Will they react favorably to your point of view? Will they be persuaded more by emotion than cold fact?

Answering questions like these creates an audience model to whom you can write. You can assess whether you need to define your terms for this audience, whether they will understand a comparison you want to draw, whether you need to quote other people to be believable. In short, what you decide about your readers influences the writing strategies you choose.

For most college writing, it is a good idea to imagine a composite general audience, such as the people in your composition class. You can assume that such a group will probably understand and appreciate many of the things you know and enjoy. And if you're ever in doubt as to their opinions on a particular subject, you can always ask them.

The Writer's Self

Every writer's attitude toward self and outlook on life in general are fundamental to his or her motives. And every writer must try to *find* his or her self. Only when you've developed a sense of self can you begin to communicate with your audience. People are complex, multifaceted, many layered. Are you an optimist or a pessimist, a mystic or a realist, a believer or a nonbeliever? Your view of self is part of your point of view.

When you consider your attitude toward your self and your subject, you have an important decision to make: how do you want to appear to your reader? Suppose you've been assigned a serious paper for an academic audience. You are very interested in the topic, but you realize that you are easygoing and very informal. Your "natural" writing style (as in letters to friends) is also informal, sprinkled with slang. Suppose you tend to be short-tempered, however, and sometimes sarcastic. Realizing that lack of control, informality, and inappropriate language may cause you to offend your audience, you must project an appropriate self-image, one that is genuinely serious about and interested in the topic. You decide a fairly formal style and tone are right to help persuade your audience of the reasonableness of your position.

It is important to project an appropriate self-image when you write. There is no way to avoid *having* self and no way to avoid expressing it, either. Consequently, it makes sense to project the writing personality best suited to your purpose.

Aristotle said, "The unexamined life is not worth living." We should add to this, the unexamined life is not worth writing about. Once you begin questioning yourself, be prepared to be surprised. Within your many-layered personality you can find a self for most writing purposes.

Writing activity

Write a paragraph or two in which you project a character who is trying to persuade a particular audience to act or think in a certain way. Try to project a self who will be viewed sympathetically by the audience. Then, in a paragraph or two, project a second self whose purpose is the same but whose writing personality will almost certainly alienate the audience.

What effect did the change in self have on the piece of writing? How did you show the two different selves? Describe each self in a sentence or two.

The Writer's Experience

The word *experience* means every instant of your life—everything you have done, everything that has happened to you, everything you know, everything you remember. Suppose you have been asked to write a story or an essay about a subject of your own choosing. You think over your experiences, or maybe you go to the library and start looking for something that sparks your interest. Thus you begin to explore subject matter. Finally, you decide to tell about wrecking the family car. What can you tell about it? It was all over in a flash; how can you fill up two or three pages? You must try to understand the subject just as you try to understand yourself. In fact, the subject and your view of it should fuse so that your writing does more than report the facts. Why *this* story? What does the subject mean to you personally? It is not a good idea just to start numbering the different details of a car accident. (If that's what your readers wanted, they'd read the police report.) What happened means nothing until it interacts with the human nervous system to which it

Need to give reality a new shape or structure — something unique

happened. We learn very little from a chronological analysis of an accident. It isn't just the *what* about anything that people care to know but also the *so what* about it—the way the accident entered and affected your store of experience.

You may feel that your experience is limited at this stage in your life. It's not. Count as experience all the incidents, events, people, places, and objects you've seen; all the books, journals, magazines, and newspapers you've read; all the films and television programs you've watched; all your daydreams and daily existence. The section called Stages in the Composing Process later in this chapter will show you that your experience is a far richer store than you may imagine.

The Writer's Code

Having interesting ideas is only a beginning; writers must be able to present these ideas clearly and efficiently. Knowing what to say is not enough; you must also know *how*. This *how* skill, the language writers use to express their ideas, we call *code*. Code includes not only the language—words, phrases, and sentences—but also the overall structure of a composition, including the coherence among sentences, paragraphs, and the whole work. Also involved in code are style, tone, and the various methods of developing a piece of writing. We will have more to say about these elements of code throughout this book. For now, it is enough to say that code signifies the relationship between language and idea in writing.

Any writing you do creates a set of expectations you must fulfill for your readers. If you start out to prove a point, the reader expects you to try to prove it. If you set out to be logical, you aren't free to use faulty reasoning, propaganda, or emotional language. If you address a learned audience on a formal topic but use a very informal tone and style in a rambling, ill-organized paper, you won't establish much credibility with that audience. All these matters of language and form and thought comprise code. And decisions about the code you choose become part of your decisions about purpose.

Writing activity

Recall or imagine a brief incident in your life: a car accident; an argument with your boss; an upsetting encounter in school or on a trip; the time when you came home in bad shape; and so on. Write about the incident in different styles: very formal language; street slang; childlike simplicity; newspaper style; telegram style; *Time* magazine style; and so on. How do the changes in code affect the meaning of the message?

Do writers decide their purpose, determine their audience, select a self, choose an experience, and then use a code to express it all? In the real world of writing, things aren't that simple and orderly. Indeed, for many writers, writing—especially the initial stages—is confusing, disorderly, even chaotic. How are the choices we've been talking about really made? Here is what can happen when you have to write a typical college paper.

Suppose that you have just heard a lecture given by a renowned scientist on the future of organ and limb transplants. You decide that this topic might make an interesting paper for assignments you have in both your biology class and your composition class. You begin jotting down informal notes from past experiences—what you know about people who have lost limbs and about organ donors and recipients—from books, magazines, newspapers, scientific journals, films, and radio and television programs. Next, you skim through several articles from *Time, Redbook,* and *Harper's;* two or three from scientific journals recommended by your biology instructor; and the relevant sections of Alvin Toffler's *Future Shock.* You take detailed notes, especially from the scientific journals, because they cover unfamiliar territory. A quick look at all your notes shows you that they're sketchy, unorganized, and that there are striking differences in the level of formality of these notes. Some summarize scientific concepts in complex language; others, like the ones about your grade-school classmate who had a kidney disease, are short anecdotes.

At this point, perhaps, you decide to write the paper for your composition course, partly because you have a paper due in that class and partly because you are more interested in the human side of your topic than in its scientific aspects. You select the composition class as your audience and decide that your purpose will be not only to inform but to entertain them. You may even impress them with your scientific knowledge. A too formal tone will be forbidding and dull, so you decide to try for a relaxed, reasonable tone, somewhere between the familiar and the formal.

You begin making careful notes, most of which expand on the jottings you have about your classmate. You quickly write out a page and a half describing how difficult it was for her to keep up in school when she spent so much time in the hospital undergoing dialysis treatment. As you reread these pages, you realize that focusing on your classmate's school problems has turned out to be depressing, not entertaining. What you've written sounds too personal and emotional when you had intended to sound relaxed and informative. And with this emphasis, you haven't a way to include any of the

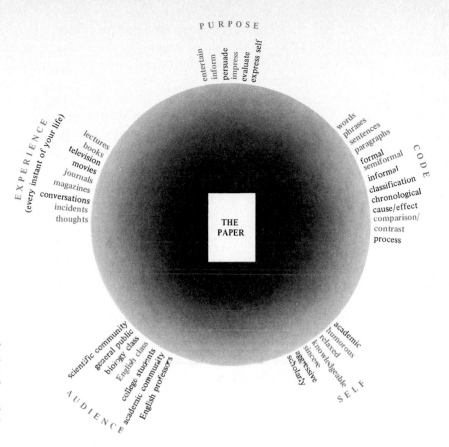

PURPOSE

entertain
inform
persuade
impress
evaluate
express self

E X P E R I E N C E
(every instant of your life)

lectures
books
television
movies
journals
magazines
conversations
incidents
thoughts

words
phrases
sentences
paragraphs
formal
semiformal
informal
classification
chronological
cause/effect
comparison/
contrast
process

C O D E

THE
PAPER

scientific community
general public
biology class
English class
college students
academic community
English professors

A U D I E N C E

academic
humorous
relaxed
knowledgeable
sincere
aggressive
scholarly

S E L F

FIGURE 1.1
IN THIS DIAGRAM OF
THE COMPOSING
PROCESS FOR THE
PAPER ON ORGAN AND
LIMB TRANSPLANTS,
THE ITEMS IN COLOR
SHOW THE CHOICES
ACTUALLY MADE.

ideas you heard at the lecture that got you interested in the subject in the first place.

As you look back over all your notes, you become convinced that a better approach is to use a historical perspective. You'll compare and contrast today's techniques for kidney transplants, about which you've become fairly knowledgeable from your reading, with treatment for kidney disease in the past. You'll illustrate the situation in the past by bringing in two or three anecdotes about your classmate's experience with dialysis. You'll then connect these perspectives with your sense of the way kidney disease will be treated in the future, as described by the lecturer. You sketch out a rough outline to keep your ideas straight, then begin to write a first draft.

Figure 1.1 is a model of the choices made from a range of possibilities for the paper on organ and limb transplants. You should be aware, though, that a diagram cannot show the way one choice influences others, or the way that each aspect of the thinking and planning and writing you do involves you in a continual process of reevaluation and re-vision.

It should be clear now that we are not describing a sequential process like baking a cake, in which each step follows in prescribed order and, once completed, need not be thought about again. Disorder, during which multiple purposes, audiences, selves, experiences, and codes have to be sifted and selected, weighed and evaluated, reconsidered and reworked, is *normal*. Writing is like painting or sculpting or composing music; all evolve from a complex of decisions that must mesh together and contribute harmoniously to an outcome that you may or may not have foreseen at the start. The stone lion that is the sculptor's finished product may have started simply as an exploration in stone. The outcome is ultimately determined by an ongoing process of decisions, choices, reconsiderations, and changes. So too the compositions you write.

Writing activity

Select a real or imagined event—a news report, a family incident, a sports report, a fashion show—and relate the incident in a paragraph or two to a particular audience. Your purpose should be to present the event in a favorable light. Then, using the same incident, write a paragraph or two in which your purpose is to present the same incident in an unfavorable light. Compare the results; what happens when you change purpose?

STAGES IN THE COMPOSING PROCESS

There is no single right way to write well, no magic step-by-step formula or procedure that will guarantee you success. Sometimes writing is very difficult. Many modern writers have attested to the fact that writing can be an agonizing, painstaking process. William Styron said, "Let's face it, writing is hell" and went on to describe the struggle he had getting his ideas on paper. Sometimes writing can come easily too. A celebrated example of a work flowing onto the page is that of "Kubla Khan" by the British poet Coleridge, who vividly described how the poem wrote itself. A number of writers have remarked on the same phenomenon. Sometimes their writing goes with surprising ease. These professional writers have obviously done a great deal of planning, prewriting, and preliminary drafting in their heads.

However, less experienced writers need a systematic way to approach the task of writing. We have, therefore, divided the writing process into several stages: the initial draft, the working draft(s), and the final draft. Each of these drafts is a target to aim at as you develop a composition.

Most writers find it difficult to get started because experience has taught them that the initial stage of writing—often referred to as prewriting—is disorderly, even chaotic. It is a time of intense creative work as the mind sifts and sorts and rearranges the various components of writing, until finally—sometimes suddenly—things begin to fall into place and the vague outlines of an initial draft begin to appear.

Tapping your experience is a good way to begin the composing process. Here are some possibilities.

1. *Memory*   Look back over past experiences; search through your life for incidents, events, people, places, and things to write about. Your memory is a vast repository of data concerning all your experiences. And you can go searching in this repository, forcing yourself to remember and bring back, in surprising detail, your past life.

2. *Observation*   Examine the world around you; analyze the events and issues of your daily life. You may include in this the viewing of television and films and the reading of books, magazines, and newspapers. With modern communications systems, anyone can have a wealth of material to observe, think about, and write about.

3. *Participation*   Your daily experiences—talking with friends, going on dates, participating in sports—may not be extraordinary (few are), but they are all grist for the writer's mill. You may include in this vicarious experiences, such as the intense involvement that is possible with great literature and, occasionally, good films. The entire inner world of subjective responses—emotions, sensations, feelings—can become the source of your writing.

4. *Imagination*   Project yourself into situations and even into others' minds and bodies. This is the major technique of the fiction writer, but the nonfiction writer too may speculate and hypothesize. You may invent (speculate on), for instance, a crisis in which China and the U.S.S.R. confront each other along the Sino-Soviet border, in order to imagine (hypothesize) what course of action the United States might take in such an event. Even if you are going to attempt to describe an object, you will discover how much imagination can aid observation if you project yourself into the object and imagine how the object must appear to someone not familiar with it.

5. *Research*   Conduct experiments, seek out answers and data, use the library, interview sources. Using the skills of researching, you

can become very knowledgeable quickly about practically anything. And this is one of the major prewriting techniques for academic writing.

Once you have discovered a topic that interests you, prewriting lets you dig into it, approach it from every conceivable direction. If there is to be anything new or effective in what you write, you must come to know the subject at least better than your readers know it. (You'll learn several prewriting techniques in coming chapters.)

In the early phase of the composing process, you may—probably will—take notes, formal ones as well as scribbles and jottings. You will also make decisions—and mental notes or written reminders—about audience, purpose, code, and so on. You may or may not make an outline, formal or informal. At the prewriting stage, you collect, sort, and begin to arrange material into coherent form.

The Initial Draft

At some point, you will attempt an initial draft, one that is essentially exploratory in nature. This draft should be written fairly quickly, without letting attention to matters of correctness slow you down or stop you. Think of the initial draft as something you have to get off your chest, not something you should agonize over.

A useful bit of advice is, *don't* write and edit at the same time. Laboring away over every word and sentence, crossing out and rewriting, and later returning for further changes all add up to a very discouraging and laborious procedure. A far better procedure is to work out the design and substance of your composition in the initial draft, leaving the polishing for later drafts. The crumpled-paper syndrome is evidence of an author stuck at some point and unable to go on. It is far better to skip over the sticking point; force yourself to go on and return later to the problem spot rather than spend hours laboring over a sentence or paragraph of the composition that won't "write." Unfortunately, sometimes a problem spot means the design of the composition is faulty; in that case you need to return to prewriting. In either case, it is wisest to resist rewriting until you get to the end of your initial draft; otherwise, you may not *get* to the end.

When you have completed the initial draft, it's a good idea to let it cool for at least a day. Then you can approach it with a more objective eye. E. M. Forster said, "How do I know what I think until I see what I said?" The initial draft lets you see what you know and what you don't know about your topic. Your next task as a writer is to examine this draft to see if it is saying what you intend it to say. Then the real job—that of *rewriting*, of re-visioning—can begin.

The Working Draft(s)

Rewriting is when playwriting really gets to be fun. . . . In baseball, you only get three swings and you're out. In rewriting, you get almost as many swings as you want and you know, sooner or later, you'll hit the ball.
NEIL SIMON

Quite often an initial draft doesn't reflect your planning. Don't be discouraged; you should view this second phase of the process as an opportunity to produce a draft that better fulfills your purpose. Initial drafts tend to be written from the writer's standpoint. Working drafts should concern themselves more with the reader. The more critical and thorough your analysis of the initial draft, the more likely you are to achieve your purpose in a working draft.

Ask the following questions as you analyze a working draft. Are your ideas clear? Considering the aims of your composition, are these the most effective words? Which of them need to be changed? Can you think of improvements? Does each of the sentences carry the information and maintain the reader's interest? Should any of the sentences be deleted? Rearranged? Substituted for? Expanded? Are the paragraphs well constructed and coherent? Which of them should be rewritten? Redesigned? Does each paragraph advance the argument? Should any of the paragraphs be deleted? Expanded? Does the composition begin and end well? Where in the composition have you failed to project the writing personality you planned? Have you captured the appropriate degree of formality? Does this draft handle the audience well? What strategies might better reach your readers? How can you make this draft more nearly achieve your overall purpose?

The Final Draft

You may compose several working drafts before you come up with one that satisfies you. Again, we recommend that you let any draft cool off for a day or two in order to see more clearly what it conveys. As you work on the final draft, keep in mind that two very important sections of the composition are worth all the effort you can put into them: the beginning and the ending. Furthermore, the body of your essay will benefit from a highly critical examination and revision. Would the composition improve if you rearranged the paragraphs? Added to them? Subtracted from them? Substituted for them?

One of the chief problems with many papers by beginning writers is that they lack sufficient evidence; they don't have enough information. Give the final draft a reading in which you concentrate only on the evidence; become a reader who doesn't know the topic as well as you do. Will that reader need additional data, more examples and reasons, more or different illustrations and details?

In the final draft you also need to think of a critical reader who will respond not only to the information in your paper but to your style of writing as well. This is the place to cut excess verbiage, prune clichés and jargon, and in general clean up the English. In the final draft you need to look at your sentences and paragraphs the way a critic would. Can they be made more accurate? Can they be made more readable? By combining some and deleting others you can improve the style and tone and efficiency of your writing.

I believe a story can be wrecked by a faulty rhythm in a sentence—especially if it occurs toward the end—or a mistake in paragraphing, even punctuation. Henry James is the maestro of the semicolon. Hemingway is a first-rate paragrapher. From the point of view of ear, Virginia Woolf never wrote a bad sentence. I don't mean to imply that I successfully practice what I preach. I try, that's all.
TRUMAN CAPOTE, *Writers at Work*, Malcolm Cowley, ed.

It is in the final draft that you must use the real skill of an artisan. This means seeing that a word you've used is not exactly right. It means seeing that changing the punctuation of a sentence changes the emphasis and gives new meaning to the sentence. Far from being merely finishing work, this final draft is the one most writers say is the draft that counts, and the one you should give your maximum effort to.

I rewrote the ending to *Farewell to Arms*, the last page of it, thirty-nine times before I was satisfied [. . .] Getting the words right.
ERNEST HEMINGWAY, *Writers at Work*, George Plimpton, ed.

As your final draft nears completion, you'll find it useful to review the five components of the writing process—purpose, audience, experience, self, code—and the decisions you made as these components interacted in your head and on paper. This review should help you to make last-minute improvements in your final draft.

Proofreading   After rewriting, re-visioning, it is time to move to proofreading—finding slips of the eye and hand in your final draft. The purpose of proofreading is to make sure that the composition says what you think it says. Check spelling, punctuation, grammar, and other things that tend to go wrong of their own accord. Proofreading means examining the finished copy that is to be handed in to a teacher or editor and finding and fixing errors. Errors must be neatly painted out with correction fluid, and then the pages must go back into the typewriter, if that is possible, or the correction penned in. You may cross out neatly with a pen and write the corrections above the errors, provided there aren't too many of them.

THE COMPOSING PROCESS
IN ACTION

Here is the work of a writer making the choices and using the process described in this chapter. As you study these materials, think about two things: (1) the choices Terese Mowry made at each stage and (2) the ongoing process of creation and change from first notes through final draft.

Prewriting Notes

"Old Bible	New Bible
worn	new, crisp
marked up	impersonal
stained	no markings
memory-filled	to "clean" to touch
torn	uninviting
faded	mother bought
unique personality	younger brother
binds family together	new version, new translation
binding is worn	Bible history
grandfather reads	changes in Bible
Christmas	new ideas on religion
Easter	changes in family
finger prints, marks	personality
family history	renewal, begin again
when bought, why	pages slick, noisy
cost, money problems	stiff
family life then	church
old ideas	credo
heavy, big	Christianity
emotions	favorite verses
on book case	end table, sofa

*Both have same message, same version --
the <u>meaning</u> of the two, importance.
Mostly description -- the bible and our
family, show old bible is better.*

Study these notes carefully. Can you see any pattern in Terese's prewriting? Can you find any places where one idea seems to have triggered another? What evidence is there in these notes that she is thinking of purpose, audience, code, self, experience?

The Initial Draft

Two Bibles

*One is new -- has no bent corners, stains, thumb
prints, tears, yellow, red, or pencil markings, tear
stains, tears, faded cover, scratches. It is
impersonal 'til opened and marked.*

*The other is used, marked up, fingerprints, coffee
stains, tear stains, endless use, etc. Has family
history inside, is more valuable. To know what
each person feels is meaningful at the time
their reading book. May help another person
from your own feelings, ideas, or markings.*

*Old one is more precious because it has a little of
each family members personality in it.*

*Though markings and the years of use take away
the appearance of being new and beautiful, in
reality the wear and tear makes the Bible more
precious than the new one because, through the
use, or from just picking the ragged one up, a
person's life will be changed in some way
because of the unique personality it possesses.*

*New one sitting on sofa end table. Old one put in
the bookcase. Old one should be with new one*

so strangers can gain insight to my family's personality and a pencil or marker should be available for anyone to write their thoughts or underline meaningful verses also. So instead of one precious Bible another can be started.

Though rough, this is a fair beginning. Like many students, Terese has begun her work by following her English assignment (to write a comparison). Her initial draft may suggest that the comparison is the *point* of the assignment (versus a *technique* for thinking about experience). But she is struggling to make order out of her ideas. Compare her initial draft with her notes. Has she used all her prewriting ideas? Has she added anything to the initial draft that wasn't in her notes? Terese lists physical differences in the old and the new Bibles. Can you see any promise of a controlling *idea* in her rough draft, something more than this simple, physical description? Was there any hint of this idea in her notes?

The Working Draft

The Family treasure

Flipping through the endless many chapters, red, black, and yellow markings leaped from the pages, showing its many years of avid intense use. Next to it, the new bible is spotless and perfect. It's strange how to Bibles, containing the same version and the same message, will be so different from each other.

The new Bible's cover is shining in the sunlight, absent of marks, and the gold letters sparkle on its black, background. The Bible gave and appearance of being too clean and new to touch.

The old Bible's cover was faded and cracked, it's gold lettering is dull or missing from the cover and frayed bindings portrayed signs of its years of use and warned readers to handle with care. Also, stains from various beverages spotted its cover. An inviting air surrounded this book, urging others to pick it up and look at its pages.

Picking up the new Bible, its crisp, new pages were flipped through, searching for familiar verses. Without any markings, the pages appeared cold, uninviting, and impersonal. They even cracked loudly as if in protest to every turning motion rendered to them.

I replaced the new Bible on the table again and gently lifted the old one onto my lap. It's pages, now worn from years of usage, precariously opened to expose a page filled with black, red, and yellow markings. Familiar passages leaped from the page, each high-lighted in the various colors which represented different family member's and times the markings occured. By reading the many familiar notes and underlined verses I again wondered and ultimately could only guess from the verse what feelings, thoughts, and moods promted my family to leave their unique mark upon this and the many other pages of this book forever. Besides multi-colored markings and notes, turning the pages and closer observation revealed smudged prints, torn pages, and tear stains.

The new Bible had none of these traits, but I think that's why my mother purchased it. I beleive she felt it was time to begin the search for new meaning to the old, but ever-precious verses and allow my younger brother an opportunity to experience the same joy we did in marking a verse that had a personal meaning for the first time. By the time he was old enough to read the bible was pretty marked up.

Though no names were recorded by the marked verses of the old bible, each knew someone else found special meaining in that particular verse, through this a spritual bond was created within my family. I can still remember my grandfather reading from the worn Bible's pages the Christmas and Easter stories. Yes, many memorys are stored within its yellow pages.

The bible tells us of the church and of the life of a Christian. Both the old and the new bible carry this timeless religious message.

Though markings and the years of use take away the appearance of being new and beautiful, in reality the wear and tear makes the Bible more precious than the new one because, through the use, or from just picking the ragged one up, a persons life will be changed in some way because of the unique personality it posseses.

Compare the working draft with the initial draft. Would you agree that the working draft is an improvement? Can you suggest any explanation for the changes? Would you say that some of them were made because of Terese's view of audience (her English class), purpose, self, experience, or code?

Point out specific changes. Where does the working draft differ from the initial draft? Can you "find" the first draft in the second, or has it disappeared entirely? Look back at the prewriting notes.

Does the working draft contain anything from these notes that the initial draft doesn't?

The Final Draft

The Family Treasure

Sitting in the sunlit living room, contemplating what my paper would be about, my eyes fell upon the new, family Bible. On impulse, I rose from my comfortable rocking chair, crossed to the dust covered bookcase, and scanned the shelves until I found the desired object of my search. Returning to my rocker, I placed the precious, family Bible in its original position beside the new Bible and then leaned back to gaze intnetly upon the two, now side by side. It's strange how to Bibles, containing the same version and the same message, are so different from each other.

The new Bible's cover glistened in the sunlight, absent of any scratches or stains across its front cover, and the gold-inscribed lettering sparkled from its black, textured background. The Bible gave and appearance of being too clean and new to touch.

The old Bible's cover was faded and cracked, its once-gold lettering was now dulled or missing from the cover, and frayed bindings portrayed signs of its years of ouse and warned readers to handle with care. Also, stains from various beverages dotted its cover, spilled from the hands of famly members, both young and old. An inviting air surrounded this book, urging others to pick it up and look among its pages for what was and still is of importance to me and my family.

Picking up the new Bible, I casually flipped through its crisp, unmarked pages, searching for familiar verses. Void of any markings, the pages appeared cold, uninviting, and impersonal. They even crackled loudly as if in protest to every turning motion rendered to them.

I replaced the new Bible on the table and gently lifted the old one onto my lap. It's pages, now worn and supple from years of use, precariously opened to expose a page filled with black, red, and yellow markings. Familiar passages leaped from the marked page, each high-lighted in the various colors which re-presented different family members and times the markings occured. By reading the many familiar notes and underlined verses, I again wondered and ultimately could only guess from the verse what feelings, thoughts, and moods prompted my family to leave their unique mark upon this and the many other pages of this book forever.

Besides multi-colored markings and notes, turning the pages and closer observation revealed smudged finger prints, torn pages, and tear stains. Each page contained a segment of every family member's personality and life. Though no names were recorded by the marked verses, each knew someone else found special meaining in that particular verse. Through this, a spritual bond was created within my family which still has remained after members moved from home, got married, or died. Even with the pages closed, I can still remember my grandfather reading from the worn Bible's pages the Christmas and Easter stories. Yes, many memorys are stored within its yellow pages.

The new Bible had none of these traits, but I think that's why my mother purchased it. I beleive she felt it was time to begin the search for new meaning to the old, but ever-precious verses and allow my younger brother an opportunity to experience the same joy we did in marking a verse that had a personal meaning for the first time.

Someday, I'm sure the new Bible will become worn, yellowed, and dirtied like the old one. The binding will fray, and multi-colored markings and notes will cover its many pages. But for now, the treasured, old Bible will resume its place on the end-table until the new Bible has acquired a unique personality of its own, and the old one is held together only by its threads. For I've heard it said before that a good Bible is a well-used Bible, and I have proof to that.

Compare the third draft with the first and second drafts. Where are the changes? Look for large, organizational changes as well as changes in sentences and diction. (Note that Terese has replaced both the introduction and conclusion.) At this point, some students might feel satisfied enough to turn in the paper; it is not bad as it is. But here and there you can see a mistake; some of them are simple to correct, some not so simple. Then too, even in the "final" draft, writers often spot something that is not quite as they want it. The word *draft* comes from an ancient word for fish net, or the act of catching fish in a net. And the writer's "draft," too, is an effort to "catch" meaning. Therefore, the "final" draft is usually the final phase of that process in which writers are still looking for material and ideas, the overall shape of their composition.

However, there is still work to do, as any fisherman knows, once the catch is in. The clean draft or proofreading draft is the real end of the writing process. In this draft authors correct errors of spelling, punctuation, grammar. Almost always the clean draft contains some minor editing and polishing. Because this is the draft that will be given to readers, most authors read and reread carefully and critically—it is the writer's last chance to make sure the composition says exactly (not approximately) what he or she intends. Most writers say this is the draft that counts and is the one that calls forth all their critical skills and art as writers. Your sense of language and your image of what you want to say must guide you here as you try to make words on paper communicate with your readers.

The Proofread Draft

The Family Treasure

TERESE MOWRY

Sitting in the sunlit living room, I contemplated the new family Bible. On impulse, I rose from my comfortable rocking chair, crossed to the dusty bookcase, and scanned the shelves until I found what I was looking for. Returning to my rocker, I placed our precious, old family Bible in its original position beside the new Bible and then leaned back to gaze intently upon the two, now side by side. It's strange how two Bibles, containing the same version and the same message, can be so different from each other.

The new Bible's cover glistened in the sunlight, free of any scratches or stains across its front, and the gold-inscribed lettering gleamed from its black, textured background. The Bible looked almost too clean and new to touch.

Next to it, the old Bible's cover was faded and cracked, its once-gold lettering now dulled or missing from the cover. Frayed bindings showed signs of years of use and warned readers to handle with care. Also, stains from various beverages dotted its cover, spilled from the hands of family members, both young and old. The book had an inviting air, urging others to pick it up and look among its pages for what was and still is of importance to me and my family.

Picking up the new Bible, I casually flipped its crisp, unmarked pages, searching for familiar verses. Void of any markings, the pages appeared cold, uninviting, and impersonal. They even crackled loudly as if in protest at every turn.

I replaced the new Bible on the table and gently lifted the old one onto my lap. Its pages, now worn and supple from years of use, limply opened to expose a page filled with black, red, and yellow markings. Familiar passages leaped from the marked page, each highlighted in the various colors which represented different family members and times the markings occurred. Reading the many familiar notes and underlined verses, I again wondered, but ultimately could only guess from each verse, what feelings, thoughts, and moods prompted my family to leave their unique marks upon this and many other pages of the book.

Besides multicolored markings and notes, turning the pages and closer observation revealed smudged fingerprints, torn pages, and tear stains. Each page contained a segment of every family member's personality and life. Though no names were recorded by the marked verses, each knew someone else found special meaning in that particular verse. Through this, a spiritual bond, which has remained even after members moved from home, got married, or died, was created within my family. Even with the pages closed, I can still remember my grandfather reading from the worn Bible's pages the Christmas and Easter stories.

The new Bible had none of these traits, but I think that's why my mother purchased it. I believe she felt it was time to begin the search for new meaning to the old, but precious, verses and to allow my younger brother an opportunity to experience the same joy we did—to mark for the first time a verse that had a personal meaning.

Someday, I'm sure the new Bible will become worn, yellowed, and soiled like the old one. The binding will fray, and multicolored markings and notes will cover its many pages. But for now, the treasured old Bible will resume its place on the endtable until the new Bible has acquired a unique personality of its own, and the old one is held together only by its threads. For I've heard it said that a good Bible is a well-used Bible, and I have proof of that.

Look closely for the changes in the proofread draft; some of them are very small and simple. Would you say that the proofreading helped, that Terese improved even her "final" draft with proofreading and last-minute polishing? Looking back over all the changes from her notes to her proofread draft, would you be willing to say that most of the changes were useful?

Can you suggest an explanation for the changes, especially the last ones? Either in writing or as a discussion: assume the clean (proofread) draft was the student's aim from the outset—assume she was trying to write what she eventually did write, or that she was trying to discover the composition that eventually emerged. Examine her five components of purpose, self, experience, code, and audience: explain how each of them, in your opinion, may have affected her choices.

Writing activity

1 *Prewriting* Think of a subject that interests you and begin to investigate its possibilities. You can use the strategy of old and new, as in Terese's paper, or look through the following chapters if you need an idea to get you started. Jot down ideas, details, the materials of your experience. Then, after letting the ideas generated by your notes percolate

for a time, decide what your purpose and audience will be: what are you trying to write, and for whom?

2 *Writing* Write an initial draft of the paper. In your mind, try to imagine how the reader will react to you, your personality, the kind of self you are projecting. What kind of language will best suit this self? After a day or two, look at the initial draft. Enrich it with details from your notes and from your additional prewriting. Then write a working draft.

3 *Rewriting* After letting the working draft sit for a while, write a final draft. Read it carefully to make sure you've accomplished what you want concerning your purpose, audience, self, experience, and code.

4 *Proofreading* Proofread and polish the final draft. Prepare a clean copy.

CHAPTER TWO

Personal Writing

> It is enough if I please myself with writing;
>
> I am sure then of an audience.
>
> HENRY D. THOREAU, *Journal*

THE WRITER'S VIEW OF REALITY

Personal writing emphasizes *self*. How do *I* see the world? What does *my* life mean? Some of this writing can be private, such as a diary; but most of it is written to share personal views with others. The familiar essay, the memoir, the personal-experience story, sometimes even fiction can be seen as an author's personal view of reality.

Personal writing is concerned with the details of everyday life and usually includes the author's reactions to people, places, and events. The common theme of such writing is that the life of a single individual counts for something. Instead of focusing on extraordinary people and unusual events, personal writing reveals the significance of common events, the strength, humor, sorrow, and vitality of human life. For example:

KEVIN STOTTS

He was *my* dog.

He came to the house one warm, late, summer afternoon.

I thought at first he was a pup. But when he finally let me get close to him, I could see the gray hairs and cracked, calloused pads.

His tan and white short hair, barrel-round body, too short legs, and desperate stare made me love him.

Dad said I couldn't keep him. ("Don't feed him or he'll stay.") Mom helped me sneak him food.

I called him Brownie.

He followed me on my bike rides.

I remember once he carried off a little stale cookie and buried it. He always buried a part of his food. He must have done it because he was never sure that food would be there the next day.

My cousin, Miles, still teases me about the time I watched Brownie run back home from his house, down the tar-bubbly gravel road and said, "Brownie's going home. I'll have to go, too."

And when I needed somebody just to listen to me, Brownie was always there. He never laughed at the wrong time or yawned from boredom. Instead, his cinnamon eyes gazed at mine, almost as a lover's do.

He was my dog and everybody knew it.

My best friend in high school was Mike Barnes. When juniors, Mike and I and our new Argentinian friend, Jorge, spent a hot, wet, laughter-filled day at Cedar Point. I got home at about midnight—exhausted, dirty, and still thoroughly excited about that day. Mom was still up. That struck me as a little unusual, since she had always "trusted me" and staying up for me was not something she did.

She was very quiet. Solemn. I knew something was wrong. That awful feeling grabbed me. My neck went stiff, my ears buzzed, my breath quickened, and a fine film of perspiration burst over my entire body.

"Brownie's dead," she said.

The word hung there in the air—above and in front of my face. An invisible barrier was keeping those words from actually passing by my ears into my head. But the words had been spoken and they had sunk into my brain. I guess I was only pretending I hadn't heard them and was only acting like I could keep from hearing them.

I didn't say anything . . . but Mom knew that I wanted to know how it happened. And God, I wish she had lied. My dad and brother, Randall, were cutting the grass in my uncle's orchard with a tractor and side-arm mower. They hadn't seen Brownie running beside them. The scissorlike blades had caught Brownie's front legs and nearly severed them. Dad and Randall stopped their work immediately and tried to save him, Mom said, but he was hurt too badly. Dad put him out of his misery with one shot from his .22.

Mom found out how it happened, she said, when she came home from the grocery store and found Dad and Randall crying. She thought that while working together, they had gotten into their usual fight.

She told me more than just about Brownie's death. She told me that Dad and Randall felt so bad about what they had done, that I was not to say anything to them. But damn it, he was my dog and I didn't want to pretend that the whole thing hadn't happened. I was angry and in shock and her request made my chest hurt even worse. But I agreed not to say anything and shrank into bed—the one I still shared with my older brother—and lay there, awake.

The next morning I avoided my father's and Randall's eyes. After two weeks or so we could talk to each other almost normally. And now, fourteen years later, I still haven't talked to them about it. I love them—they are, after all, my father and my brother. But a little part of me hates them.

They killed my dog.

GEORGE PLIMPTON, *Paper Lion*

From the beginning I had trouble getting into the helmet. The procedure was to stick the thumbs into the helmet's earholes and stretch the helmet out as it came down over the head, a matter of lateral pull, easy enough if you practiced isometrics, but I never had the strength to get my ears quite clear, so they were bent double inside the helmet once it was on. I would work a finger up inside to get the ears upright again, a painful procedure and noisy, the sounds sharp in the confines of the hard shell of the helmet as I twisted and murmured, until it was done, the ears ringing softly, quiet then in the helmet, secure as being in a turret. Then I would look out beyond the bars of the nose guard—the "cage" the players call it—to see what was going on outside, my eyes still watering slightly. It was more difficult to get the helmet off.

These examples of personal writing succeed to the degree that we identify with the author. We may not have actually experienced the same thing before, but if the author has written convincingly we can share in the experience through the words on the page; to a degree we can step into the author's shoes. The writer has extended a bridge to us; for a moment we can share in the life of another human being.

In personal writing the author illustrates and exemplifies, rather than proves, our common humanity. It's the difference between going to a lecture and going to a play. The one tells you the facts; the other shows them in action. For example, have you ever had an accident?

NANCY MYERS

I walked up to the bar and gave it a couple of hard pushes. Then while it was swinging, I ran back about ten feet from the set and began to run towards the bar. Back and forth it went. I watched it as I picked up my speed. The bar was just on a downward swoop when I caught it. I flew up into the sky. The roof was under my feet. Then I went higher. The kitchen was in my eyesight. All I could see was the ground coming up at me. I put my hands out to stop my fall. I hit the ground and pain came. I couldn't breathe. I rolled over onto my back, experiencing a momentary panic as I fought for air. I wanted to catch my breath and scream at the same time.

After what seemed like five minutes, I got my breath and yelled. Unfortunately this did nothing to relieve the pain. My brothers had seen the terrific swing and came running. The first thing I heard was, "Look at Nan's arm!" I knew something was really wrong. When I looked at my arm, even I could tell that it was broken.

Have you ever complained about doing your taxes?

CAROL BROWN

"Taxes." That conversation-stopper ends the long-distance call from Jan. Ten-thirty Monday night—what a time to remember the taxes! (We filed an extension April 15; they're due tomorrow, June 15.) Furthermore, Jim, having met a client for several hours at Clem's Other Place, is passed out in the chair.

My taxes are simple, but we file a joint return. "You louse," I mutter to the form in the chair. "You should be doing this." Yet here I am, dutifully pulling out his business records, reconciling his day-timers with his receipts, and pawing through an endless stack of bills. My thoughts begin to wander as I punch the buttons on the TI–30.

There was a time when we worked on our taxes together. That was before Jim went to night law school. Before the first class met, Dean Clapp called the wives of the new students together for tea and a lecture. (He called it orientation.)

The dean reminded me of my father as he told us firmly but sincerely that our lives would have to change. Our husbands were in the big time now. They would certainly flunk out of law school (not an unlikely occurrence since the freshman class of seventy-five dwindled to nine by graduation four years later) if they were burdened with or bothered by trivia. If the toilet runs, call the plumber. When a bill is due, pay it. If we can't pay it, *we* should figure out what to do about it. If a child is sick, call the doctor. But, above all, don't disturb this overburdened man who is working full-time, going to law school from 6:00 to 10:00 three nights per week, and studying full-time in between. Give up your social life. Expect to be mother and father to your children. And so he spoke, on and on . . . .

How young I was then. I had always obeyed my father so, of course, I would follow the advice of this wise, kindly gentleman. I tried to make life flow smoothly for Jim during those four years. I succeeded—his life was untroubled, and he was graduated from law school at the end of the four years.

The devastating results of Dean Clapp's advice are still evident, even though I have attempted to effect a change—to direct our relationship to the sharing of the PLS (pre-law school) days. I think fleetingly of the other law students and their wives. Of the nine who graduated, we are the only ones still married. I wonder how many of the original seventy-five survived the wonderful advice of Dean Clapp, the educator. Jim and I still love each other, and we're still married, but here I sit at 3:00 A.M., still working on the taxes.

A loud snore interrupts my reverie. Are you listening, Dean Clapp?

Have you ever seen people starving?

EMMANUEL RINGLEBLUM, *Notes from the Warsaw Ghetto*

A special class of beggars consists of those who beg after nine o'clock at night. You stand at your window, and suddenly see new faces, beggars you haven't seen all day. They walk out right into the middle of the street, begging for bread. Most of them are children. In the surrounding silence of night, the cries of the hungry beggar children are terribly insistent, and, however hard your heart, eventually you have to throw a piece of bread down to them—or else leave the house. These beggars are completely unconcerned about curfews, and you can hear their voices late at night, at eleven and even at twelve. They are afraid of nothing and no one. There has been no case of the night patrol shooting at these beggars, although they move around the streets after curfew passes. It's a common thing for beggar children like these to die on the sidewalk at night. I was told about one such horrible scene that took place in front of 24 Muranowska Street where a six-year-old beggar boy lay gasping all night, too weak to roll over to the piece of bread that had been thrown down to him from the balcony.

Ever been pregnant?

PAMELA SCHOLZ

I loathed my pregnancy. Having fought to keep pounds off all my life, pregnancy was my personal nightmare. Not only did my waistline expand, but my arms, legs, and face puffed out, too. Cursing my shortness every step of the way, I waddled cumbersomely through those last four months, disgusted with my rotund condition. Those around me were sweetly sympathetic and strongly supportive. To me, I was the first and only short woman who had ever become pregnant.

The birth was no picnic either. In spite of careful attention paid to a six-week Lamaze childbirth course, when the moment arrived I was emotionally and mentally stymied. During the last evening of the Lamaze class, during the final simulated practice of labor, my water broke. Water, water everywhere, no time to think; the reality of the impending events hit me with the force of a torrential downpour. The Lamaze instructor took advantage of the "teachable moment," using me as the perfect model while the other pregnant women lumbered over to get a good view, smell, taste of my very own amniotic fluid. I sat in a pool of disbelief, listening to squeals of delight and congratulations. I wanted to drown in humiliation. Hadn't the instructor said just last week that *nobody* loses their water in public?

LINDA LOHR

It's always the same. I approach the door oblivious to the name of the highly trained professional within. My mind freezes on the three initials which follow the name: DDS The two *D*s are irrelevant; *S* is obviously an abbreviation for *Sadist*.

The institutional Muzak enters my consciousness as I open the door. Even while acknowledging to myself that the music should relax me, I succumb to the same uneasiness I feel when elevator doors close and I am alone with a stranger. Here the stranger is the receptionist, who greets me with an expensive smile as if she's delighted that at last it's my day to be here. I wonder if she has paid with pain, caps, and braces for her toothsomeness.

The waiting room is not large, and it becomes increasingly smaller, closing me in, threatening me with the awareness that they know I'm here and it's too late to back out. Earthy browns and beige have replaced the cheery yellow of a few years ago; straw fans on the wall and effusive Boston ferns are evidence of the work of trendy decorators. The standard rectangular aquarium has been supplanted by an elaborate fish pond in the center of the floor, its extravagance reminding me that my agony is not just physical or psychological, but financial as well. I sit with my back to the preposterous pond, resenting its presence here as much as I do my own. I am appropriately well-behaved, self-assured, even calm. Behind me the Loch Ness Monster surfaces in the water.

Halfway through last summer's *People* magazine, I am pulled to consciousness when the smiling one asks, "Do you want to come back now?" In monumental dedication to self-restraint and my mother's etiquette lessons, I don't answer. Instead I smile stupidly and follow her into the inner chamber. Once again I am invited—I react as if .357 magnums are trained on me—and slide meekly onto the long tan chaise, a curious mix of hair salon furniture and electric chair. No matter how the leering young woman adjusts the mechanism, the chair doesn't bend where I do, and I wait for someone to sympathetically place a hood over my head.

When he enters, silently totaling the value of his stock portfolio, I try to look relaxed. He suggests that because I need only one filling today, perhaps I'd rather not bother with Novocain. I beg for general anesthesia. He thinks I'm kidding.

He stands behind me so I can't see what he's up to, and I wonder if he's reading the instructions on the dental instruments or glancing over a *Cliff's Notes* on molars. With a vacuum tube hanging from my mouth, I recite the last stanze of "Thanatopsis" in a final attempt at death with dignity.

His work is quick, but it is still too late for me. The receptionist, smiling no longer, grimaces in a futile effort to unclench my cold, steel fingers from the arms of the chair.

In these excerpts the authors have invited you into their lives to laugh with them at their frustrations and silliness, to empathize with their pain, to forgive them their anger, to share their love and hate and joy. The incidents created by these writers are all different. The thread that unites them is their humanity.

FREE WRITING

When confronted with a writing task, many beginning writers say, "I just can't write. My mind goes blank. I can't think of anything to say." They are surprised to hear that this feeling of hopelessness is common among experienced writers too. But experienced writers know this fear is only a writer's hang-up, not a sign that they can't write. Getting started is often the hardest part of writing, and experienced writers have discovered that one solution to the problem is to force themselves to begin writing immediately.

If you allow your mind to go blank each time you sit down to write, you may develop a kind of writer's paralysis, in which you are permanently conditioned to freeze up when you have to write. To overcome this fear of the blank page, practice *free writing*—sitting down and writing anything at all, without interruption. Free writing is "free" in the sense that there are no rules to follow. Spelling, punctuation, and grammar are ignored; you don't even need an idea or plan. The only thing that *is* important is not stopping. Let the words pour forth spontaneously, from your mind onto the paper.

Free writing is designed to sharpen your ability to think on paper. You may believe that professional writers think out in detail what they are going to say, make an outline, and then sit down and dash off the finished work. Very few writers can do that. Most writers say that their writing begins to take shape *after* they have struggled with their ideas *on paper*. Writing itself is an act of discovery. Instead of first thinking and then writing, you need to learn to think with a pencil or pen in your hand.

Here is the free writing of a writer whose mind is blocked. He is convinced that he has nothing to say until he forgets that he is writing and begins to think on paper:

CARL WINSLOW

Nothing, nothing, nothing, nothing, nothing, nothing, nothing, nothing, nothing, I have nothing to say, nothing, blah, blah sounds like a duck blah blah, quack quak what is this anyhow? What a rut nothing I thought this was suppose to be college? Free writing, free writing FREE WRITING. How can I write if I din't have nothing to say. Let your hand do the writing the man says—let your fingers do the walking just like in the yellow pages, everybody is doing it, write, write, write. The guy next to me is drawing doodles—like this ~~~~~ wonderful. I paid a fortune for this? or my dad did anyway. Why? This is how I get to be an engineer, sitting here trying to unfreeze my mind. My minds set in cement, maybe that's the point—too much mind cement, a mind set. Don't let the ink dry. Isn't ten minutes up yet, forgot my watch. Something, something, something.

Writing activity

Try a ten-minute free writing. Start writing as fast as you can. Instead of thinking about what you are saying, let your hand copy whatever is going on in your head—words, pictures, emotions, physical sensations, anything at all. Don't censor your mind: let it range freely. If your mind truly is blank, just write "nothing" or "blank" over and over again. Remember, don't stop; don't let the ink dry before you write the next word. Keep practicing free writing until you have proved to yourself that you have conquered your fear of the blank page.

Focused Free Writing

When you are confident that you can write freely, you'll discover that there is little difference between thinking and writing. When you reach the point where your hand automatically records what your mind is thinking, you can set your mind in any direction you like and produce free writing on specific subjects. Here are two examples of free writing. The writers aren't controlling their minds consciously; they are focusing on specific topics but allowing their thoughts to flow freely.

My legs ached like crazy. I had just run past the four mile mark of a ten mile race. In my mind kept running the workouts that I have had before and how this distance seemed so difficult to reach. Sweat started to break all over my body especially on my forehead where it would run down into my eyes. The sweat contained salt which would make my eyes hurt. I reached the 5 mile mark. Where in hell am I? There are cornfields all around me, I hope I can make the whole distance because it is so embarrassing if I didn't. Oh no another runner passed me. I keep telling my body to relax do not tighten up on me. It is important for a runner to keep all his muscles loose so they do not tighten up on you. My heart is pounding against my chest so hard I think it just might pop out. All this for a lousy breakfast run which I haven't even trained for. Ugh there is the drink truck if I drink anything now I think it might come up as fast as it went down. Oh who cares boy does that taste good. Splish-splash I can feel the water bouncing around in my intestines. 3 more miles to go and I can rest. I never dreamed 3 miles could be so long. My legs are taking smaller and smaller steps. There is the coach and here I am the last of the 22 runners in the annual breakfast run. Maybe I will have better luck next year.

CAROL BROWN

If I had my life to live over again, I'd live it as an Irish Setter. What beautiful, total, blissful freedom. Not really bright enough to perceive the fence that limits her freedom, the Irish Setter races across the yard, chasing a bird, an insect, a dream. The goal is not important. The chase is. The *wind blows just enough to enhance her full feathering, her coat glistening red in the sunlight. No responsibility for this animal; she knows joy. Joy is catching a ball, romping in the grass, wading along the river's edge, being told she's loved. Sometimes, just for a moment, I'd like to exist in that unthinking world of hers.*

Writing activity

Try a focused free writing. Set your mind to thinking about some subject that interests you. Write about the weather, your goals, a person you saw on the bus, a problem you're having—anything at all. If you begin to day-dream or wander from the subject, let it happen. If your mind doesn't want to stick with the subject you have chosen for it, find out what your mind does want to think about, and write about that.

JOURNALS

If you decided to become a ballet dancer, an artist, a pianist, a tennis or racquetball player, you would spend a great deal of time—some enjoyable, some tedious—practicing these skills. You could not become proficient by practicing only once a week. Like any other worthwhile skill, writing also takes practice.

Most good writers write almost daily. Hemingway set aside the morning hours to do his daily quota of writing. Balzac is said to have had a servant chain him to his writing desk every day for at least six hours, with strict instructions not to set him free. The story is surely exaggerated, but Balzac knew what all writers know: nothing is easier than *not* writing. Television looks interesting, visitors drop by, a headache starts, the bathroom needs cleaning. There are dozens of excellent reasons for postponing writing, and you have to resist each one. A writer isn't just someone who can write; a writer is someone who can and *does* write.

To get regular practice in writing, keep a journal for at least two weeks. Keeping a journal is not only a good way to get daily practice in writing, it also gives you the opportunity to practice specific writing skills. The journal allows you to describe objects, people, events from different perspectives, to zero in on a subject, to practice noting details, to *focus*. The journal is a place where you can discover what you really think of some issue or person. Sitting down to write in your journal can give you a break from your daily responsibilities and problems; it can help you slow down and focus on your life. These minutes can be a time for self-examination, reflection, introspection, a time for remembering. The journal can also be a notebook of your ideas, a source for essays and stories you might want to write later, even a soapbox where you can expound on life, art, the latest fashions, politics. See, for example, what these journal writers have done:

MARY ELLEN TYUS

Ugh. 6 o'clock already. Did I sleep?
Pain. Killer muscles. Stiff. Stretch. Unkink neck aaagh.
Can't find C. R. pictures. 10 minutes wasted.
Pick up donuts for group feed. $5.68.
Bagels would be nice. With cream cheese. Journals are a drag. The class on the other hand, it could be worse.
I had *lots* of good ideas this morning while washing my face. Need a tape recorder to get that stuff down.
Stapler looks like alligator jaws.
Well! Time to split
I've gotta *read* tonight. Also Jazz class. Sleep? Of course!

ANNE MOODY, *Coming of Age in Mississippi*

I worked for Linda Jean throughout my seventh grade year. But that spring and summer Raymond tried farming again, and I was only able to help her on weekends. When I entered eighth grade the following fall we were poorer than ever. Raymond had worse luck with the farm than the year before, so we weren't able to buy any new clothes. I had added so much meat to my bones that I could squeeze into only two of my old school dresses. They were so tight I was embarrassed to put them on. I had gotten new jeans for the field that summer, so I started wearing them to school two and three days a week. But I continued to fill out so fast that even my jeans got too tight. I got so many wolf whistles from the boys in class that the faster girls started wearing jeans that were even tighter than mine. When the high school boys started talking about how fine those eighth grade girls were, the high school girls started wearing tight jeans too. I had started a blue jeans fad.

DEAN FOWLS

After having already written for a good four hours today, I am beginning to suffer from sure signs of writers' exhaustion. There are certain symptoms which definitely signal the onset of this affliction:

—I find it hard to direct my attention away from the television where Benny Hill is performing the same comedy routine I have seen him do at least three times already.

—I develop a craving for Haagen-Dazs ice cream, which means a quick trip to Gordons on campus.

—The slightly crooked painting on the wall suddenly resembles the Leaning Tower of Pisa. (It takes me at least five minutes to get it just right.)

—The dog's coat appears to be a little matted and must be brushed at once.

—After months of realizing that the clock is 2 minutes slow, I get the compulsion to correct it. (This, of course, means a call to time and temperature to get the exact time.)

—The plants seem a little droopy and will undoubtedly wither entirely if not watered immediately.

—The hum of the refrigerator becomes a major source of noise pollution.

—The moonlight shining through the window becomes blinding.

There are literally thousands of other symptoms associated with this malady, but really only one cure.

How To Write a Journal

How you handle your journal is your decision, but the following hints may help you get started:

1 Write every day. Regular, specified periods of writing are better than fewer and longer sessions. Don't try to cram a week's worth of writing into one night; you'd get the same effect as if you tried to cram a week's worth of jogging into a single session.

2 Discover the time and place best for you to write, and then don't let anything interfere with your schedule.

3 Write at least a page a day, even on the days when you'd rather not. (Especially then.)

4 Write anything you want, any way you want, but remember that a journal is *not* a diary or a private, intimate document for your eyes alone. A journal is a record of your thoughts that others should be able to read. Your instructor may want to check your journal to see your growth as a writer.

5 Do not treat your journal as if it were merely a record of your activities:

Got up early. Studied for test. Went bowling in the afternoon. Nothing much happened today.

Entries like this are a waste of time because the writer is *avoiding* his thoughts and recording only actions. Instead, the writer might have written about why he studied for the test. Was he worried about failing? Is he chasing grades? If so, why? Did he enjoy the bowling? What is the significance of "Nothing much happened today"? Is he bored? Disappointed? A journal should be a record of what your *mind* is doing.

Keep a journal for two weeks. Write in it at least once a day for the fourteen days. If you can find the time, write in it more than once a day. On days when you can't think of anything to write, you may want to start your reflective writing with a topic from the following list:

The present . . . today, this week, this year

The past . . . high-school days, home life, friends

The future . . . yours, the country's, the world's

The ideal . . . life, day, place to live, car, form of government, partner

An open letter to . . . a politician, minister, civic leader, bigot, old friend, the world at large

Advice . . . to anyone about anything

Please repeat! . . . places and people you'd like to see again, things you'd like to do again

Never again! . . . things to avoid, places not to visit

People . . . what they look like, think about, their interactions with you

Moods . . . feeling sad, lonely, happy, silly, coping with moods

Problems . . . money, health, sex, fears, studies, appearances, drugs, smoking, too fat, too thin, too short, too tall

Philosophy . . . what life is all about, good and evil, personal identity

Discussion activity

Select one of the following journal entries and discuss its strengths and virtues. Is the person who wrote the entry getting anything out of journal writing? What can you tell about the journal writer as a person?

TERRY KUNST

Your wrist is bent almost at a 90° angle as you open all the way. The tachometer is climbing rapidly. Your left hand is gripping the other side of the handle bars. The vibration from the machine is hitting your body from many different positions. Your fingers and hands have a numb, tingling feeling in them as the tach needle reaches the red line. Your left hand automatically reaches forward, grabs the handle in front of it, and pulls; simultaneously your right hand rolls the throttle back, and your foot hits the gear lever. Your foot's back, lever forward, and throttle open again. Thundering down the hill. The trees flashing by so fast that it is a constant blur on either side of you. Your eyes fixed upon the trail ahead. The wind hitting your face with the impact of a tornado. Blinking eyelids, trying to keep the airborne debris from the main part of seeing.

There's a small knoll up ahead. Taking a tighter grip on the handle bars, until you feel the increased vibrations running through your body, you raise slightly off the seat, let the machine take most of the shock. You hit the knoll, the front wheel leaves the ground, the back tire struggles to carry the entire load itself. Throwing large parts of grass and dirt into the air. Just at the top of the knoll you are standing straight up on the machine, the front wheel off the ground as high as you can handle. Gravity starts to do its thing with the front wheel. The front hits hard. The shocks bottom out and the rest of the shock is absorbed through your body. Your head snaps forward. You struggle to keep your eyes on the trail ahead. What trail? All you see in front of you is a big oak tree. Its limbs reaching out to gather you in. Right hand rolls off the throttle, left hand pulling the lever, right foot and right hand pushing the two levers. Right foot pushing so hard that it becomes numb. The tree is closing in for the kill. Decisions and ideas race through your mind. The bike slows down, a little. The back tire is plowing up the earth as it seeks to find a good hold on the earth. Rear tire is not turning at all, front wheel's turning some, but the bike is still going faster than both tires together.

Leaning to the left, the bike is at a 10° angle as your left foot makes contact with the ground. Before you realize it you are hitting the ground with your whole body as the bike slides on its side toward the tree. You look up. The bike is on its side, engine is running wide open and back tire is spinning. You jump up and run to your bike with a limp. Reaching down you struggle to pick up four hundred pounds of dead weight. Looking it over with a trained eye, you are satisfied. Everything seems to be all right. Hopping back on, you again take the controls in hand. Once again you are free. Nothing out here but you and mother nature.

HENRY DAVID THOREAU, *Journal*

April 16, 1852

His tail was also brown, though not very dark, rat-tail like, with loose hairs standing out on all sides like a caterpillar brush. He had a rather mild look. I spoke to him kindly. I reached checkerberry leaves to his mouth. I stretched my hands over him, though he turned up his head and still gritted a little. I laid my hand on him, but immediately took it off again, instinct not being wholly overcome. If I had had a few fresh bean leaves, thus in advance of the season, I am sure I should have tamed him completely. It was a frizzly tail. His is a humble, terrestrial color like the partridge's, well concealed where dead wiry grass rises above darker brown or chestnut dead leaves—a modest color. If I had had some food, I should have ended with stroking him at my leisure. Could easily have wrapped him in my handkerchief. He was not fat nor particularly lean. I finally had to leave him without seeing him move from the place. A large, clumsy, burrowing squirrel. *Arctomys*, bear-mouse. I respect him as one of the natives. He lies there, by his color and habits so naturalized amid the dry leaves, withered grass, and the bushes. A sound nap, too, he has enjoyed in his native fields, the past winter. I think I might learn some wisdom of him. His ancestors have lived here longer than mine, he is more thoroughly acclimated and naturalized than I. Bean leaves the red man raised for him, but he can do without them.

MARY ELLEN TYUS

June 23, 1982

Gak! is a highly evocative exclamation. It gets right to the heart of the emotion.

Coffee poisoning is setting in. Glug glug. Onomato-poison.

*words words words words words words
words words words words words words words words
words words words words words words words words
words words words words words words words words
words words words words words words words words
words words words words words words words words
words words words words words words words
words words words words words words words
words words words words words words words
words words words words words words words words
words words words words words words words words
words words words words words words words words words
words words words words words words words words
words words words words words words words words
words words words words words words
words words words words words words words words
words words words words words words words words
words words words words words words words words
words words words words words words words words
words words words words words words words words
words words words words words words words words
words words words words words words words words words
words words words words words
words words words
words words words*

—I'm drowning in words,

Get me out!

LINDA LOHR

June 20, 1982

Father's Day. Wonder where my father is? Guess he's at the cabin with his new family. I harbor such a curious mix of sentiments about the whole thing. When Mom died, Dad was at his best, it seemed to me. He was devastated but at the same time so caring and gentle. He gave us all so much. And it was heartbreaking to see him get lonelier and lonelier. So when Dolores came along, I for one was really happy for him. I was absolutely willing to share him. I didn't know I'd have to give him up. And I still don't know why things are the way they are. Did we "let him go" to make his life easier with Dolores? Did she snatch him away? I wish I knew how Dad felt about it. I can see Peggy giving Dad a present today as they all cook out. Does he realize *we* are his kids—not Peggy? Does he like our presents too? Why doesn't he tell us? Will he think of us today? Humbug.

ANNE KING

Monday, June 28, 1982

On Sunday we made the 10 o'clock Service rather than the 8. I was glad that I didn't grumble at Matt about wearing a jacket. A large number of young men and older men were just wearing a shirt with a tie. Time certainly has changed our church services. I can remember wearing a hat, gloves, and hose to church. I wouldn't have been caught without gloves. Now gloves are for keeping the hands warm. A hat causes heads to turn. Maybe we're better off not being so formal. I am glad to see the move away from faded cut off shorts for church wear. Even when that was acceptable, I privately felt that it wouldn't kill a teenager to look a little more dressed up on Sunday, but that fad passed too.

SUE HAWLEY

September 6, 1977

When I found out the news, all I could feel was shock. I feel bad now for at the time I couldn't cry, shout out or anything. All I could do was stand with my mouth agape, like a piece of rock. I just couldn't believe it could happen. It seemed like I was walking in a fantasy world and it remained as such for the next week.

It all started on Sunday night or really Monday morning at twenty to one. I remember because I was just coming home from the Hall and Oates Concert and was undressing for bed. The phone rang and I felt a sensation of dread as if something terrible had happened. As I picked up the phone the dread turned out to be real. The voice was a familiar one, the son of my parents' good friends and the brother of my very closest girlfriend. When he talked, it was a very quiet, well-controlled voice which came over the receiver. My stomach was churning with anticipation, as Bob asked to speak to my father. My brain was racing with ideas as to what could be wrong. I walked to my parents' room in a trance and shook my father awake without speaking, for something was freezing my mouth. My movements were that of a mechanical robot, hearing what my father said into the receiver but not comprehending. When my father hung up the phone my face had gone quite pale and before I could get my wits back together, he was rushing to his room. I followed automatically without realizing it. My father was talking rapidly now and I heard what he said from a fuzzy distance. What was happening, what I was hearing couldn't possibly be true. Terri was in a car accident and severely hurt, she had been taken to the hospital, but how? What happened? When I floated back to some sort of sanity, my parents were rushing out the door. For the next five hours I lived in a state of dreamlike chaos. I couldn't sleep so I walked. The night air was soothing against my hot cheeks but it could not help the turmoil that was passing through my brain. My mind was spinning, never touching down on one coherent thought. When I walked into the house my body could have dropped from pure exhaustion but my brain kept racing on. The phone was ringing and I walked to it with a steady calm which was surprising. It was my mother who was at the other end, saying words I couldn't bear to hear, didn't want to bear them. Terri was dead. A one-car accident with her boyfriend at the wheel, stone drunk, she was sound asleep. The car skidded and slipped. Terri was thrown out and cracked her skull. She was killed instantly. All was over, all was quiet.

The realization of everything that happened that night is finally beginning to sink in. It was a time of total bewilderment. I still to this day can't remember everything that happened after my mother's phone call. My mind was numb, devoid of emotion. In a way I think I knew what had happened when Bob had called, but I couldn't accept it until it had been confirmed. Even then I don't think I fully comprehended the full extent of what had happened. Terri Lynn, my best friend, dead at the age of eighteen, just four days after we graduated. I didn't even cry for days afterward, I couldn't, it seemed as though something held me back. I did cry though and tears still prick my eyes when I think about the first two weeks of June. The days when a beautiful girl's death shook the hearts of many and whose laughter will remain in the memory of those who loved her.

VOICE IN PERSONAL WRITING

Free writing and journal writing help you learn to think on paper. They build your confidence as a writer. When you become completely at ease with your writing, the *voice* on the paper will begin to "sound" like you. If you look back at the examples in this chapter, you will see that each one sounds different; each has a different voice. Of course, we can never be sure whether the voice in a paper is really the writer's own or an imaginative creation. Fiction writers often create stories whose narrators have totally different personalities and attitudes—different selves—from the writers'. Such literary selves, or *personas*, are masks the writers put on for their narrative purposes. But in nonfiction writing, most readers assume that the voice they hear represents the writer's true self.

Composition textbooks often warn against trying to sound too academic or phony, advising writers to "try to sound natural; sound like yourself." This is good advice, but there is a snag to it. As we pointed out in Chapter 1, the self is very complex; thus, you have many voices. When you talk to your family, you use your family voice. And you have more than one of those too, depending on whom you are talking to and why: there's the voice you use when you want the family car or some other favor, the voice you use when you are explaining why you didn't take out the garbage or something else you should or shouldn't have done, and several others. Then there is the voice you use with friends—different voices for different friends and different situations. And there is the voice you use with strangers and unfamiliar situations: the one for the judge in traffic court, the one for a personnel director during a job interview, and so on.

The problem in college composition is, which voice should you use when you write? There is no such thing as a "nonvoice." Your writing will have a voice even if you are trying to sound bland, objective, and toneless. Which of your many voices is appropriate for college writing? The voice you have been developing in your free writing and journal entries comes close to it. In college, you can write more formally in this natural, "journal" voice simply by avoiding things that will distract readers who expect a certain degree of formality. The end product should still sound like you, minus some of the informalities (slang, abbreviations, nonstandard spelling or punctuation) you would allow in your free writing. In short, your writing voice should be your natural voice modified by your purpose and audience. If you are telling a story to fellow students, street slang may be appropriate. If you are explaining a problem in forest conservation to the Sierra Club, on the other hand, street slang wouldn't be appropriate, but the writing should still sound like you, writing naturally but tailoring your language to fit this more formal situation.

You may think your college writing should sound very learned and formal. That assumption usually leads to difficult writing and forces the reader to pay more attention to *how* you are writing than to *what* you are saying. For example, here is a paragraph about a student's first impressions of college. The writer has made some assumptions about what the composition teacher expects, and these cause some problems. Why is the student writing this way? Is this an effective way to write? What would you tell this student to do to improve her writing?

Being that I am a freshman at this university, which I just enrolled at, I feel I have some authority for the assertions which I am about to elucidate. This institution is one of higher learning, and one could suppose that its intentions were of the highest academic merit. But this is not the case in actuality. In fact the conditions are such that just exactly the reverse is true. The average freshman here, of which I count myself as one, soon discovers that instead of serious contemplation of scholastic matters, a rather casual attitude is prevalent concerning the acquisition of progressive knowledge. The real function of this university is as to promote the social development of the individual, which is essentially a high-school orientation of education.

The student has used a dollar's worth of language to convey a dime's worth of information: she is unhappy because she finds college too much like high school. Because she is criticizing the college, she feels that she must adopt the very formal voice of someone intelligent and well educated. (We know this is an adopted voice because no one talks like this naturally.) The student assumes her subject is very important, and she assumes the professor will enjoy a display of big words. The true motive behind such writing is to impress the reader with the writer's intelligence. But the outcome sounds unnatural and pretentious, and most readers come away with a negative reaction to the writing and the writer.

Dialogue

One way to focus on *voice* in writing is to practice writing dialogues. Dialogues enliven writing, make it seem more realistic, more immediate. They let the readers hear exactly what went on and participate as if they were there. Dialogues also let the writer practice "sounding like" different people, using different voices. In the following short episode with dialogue, the writer is trying to sound like himself and a police officer. Does he succeed? Does the writing sound "natural"?

DAN NIELSEN

"Stop that bike and hop your fanny off 'afore I pull it off, boy!" the police officer hollered brazenly through the open window of his police cruiser.

"Whaa?" I turned my head and sure enough, my ears hadn't failed. I was staring eyeball to eyeball with one of the thickest-skinned rhinos on the force.

After wrestling my bike over to the loose gravel shoulder and calming down a certain female passenger who was alternately screaming and scolding me for the minor confusion I'd created, I climbed off, immediately putting on my give-me-a-break face. I actually didn't even know what I had done.

"Do you know you're riding that bike with an out-of-date license?" the cop hollered while climbing out of his vehicle.

I managed to glance at the man before reaching for my wallet. He would have made a good-sized refrigerator freezer. I pulled out my driver's license and gave him probably one of the most confused looks he has ever gotten.

"It says here it's good until 1981."

"No, you smart-assed kid, not driver's license, license tags, boy, the metal things you get from the state every year to put on the back of your bike."

I felt like a real dummy as I walked around to the back of the bike and looked at the muddy, bent-up, year-old license plate. Then I remembered, "Oh yeah, those, well you see sir, this is my brother's bike and, uh, he didn't have current registration or something, but he's got all the papers that say he's legal."

"Well, where's he keep all these so-called documents, boy?"

"In his boot."

"And where's his boot?"

"Well, to tell you the truth, he's wearing them, but he said it was okay to ride his bike."

"He did, did he? Well that's real nice o' yo' brother, boy, but I'm afraid he didn't ask the police department if it was okay. Why don't you go sit in my police car, son."

So, giving my girlfriend a please-excuse-me-for-a-moment look, I waddled over and sat in his car while the cop got a real important-looking notebook out and wrote a bunch of stuff in it. Then he came over to his car.

"Okay, so this bike belongs to your brother, huh? What's your brother's name?"

Dave, David Nielsen." The cop picked up his microphone and called it in. "Car nineteen to dispatch."

"Dispatch, go ahead."

"Registration for South Carolina motorcycle tag, M–Y–1–0–2."

After a pause, the dispatcher came back on: "Bike registered to Robert Marion."

"Oh my lord," I whispered.

"Sixty-seven West Fourth Street."

My brother had forgotten to change registration.

"Virginia Beach, Virginia."

I was in heap-big trouble. The cop, misunderstanding the whole problem, glared at me a minute with eyes that would knock Dracula cold, and then, very quietly, spoke: "You stole that bike, dinja, boy?"

"No sir, you can take me home and ask. . . ."

"Ain't takin' you nowhere, 'cept the police station."

Some problems to avoid in dialogues:

Bravelys   Try to let the words of the dialogue show your readers what the speakers are feeling. "Bravely," "kindly," "hopefully," and "cheerfully" are descriptive overkill in this example:

"I'm all right, doctor," she said bravely.
"Of course you are, my dear," he said kindly.
"I know I'll walk again," she said hopefully.
"Without a doubt," he said cheerfully

Stilted English   Try to capture the sound of real people talking about real things. No one really talks this way:

"Good evening, Mother dear; I am home for dinner!"
"How nice to see you, Lester; we are having pot roast!"

Too Many Speech Tags   "I said," "she retorted," and so on keep your reader constantly aware that a writer is present:

"Hi," I said.
"Hi yourself," she retorted.
"What's new?" I inquired.
"What's new with you?" she countered.

In good dialogues, the writer fades into the background. Use speech tags *only* to tell the reader things that aren't clear from the words of the dialogue itself. Realism is the goal. In spoken English, people tend to use contractions and informal English. And if a dialogue is meant to be read aloud, too many speech tags will overwhelm the speakers' words.

Writing activity

Try a dialogue or a story with dialogue. You can make it all up, but it will be easier just to remember and write a real dialogue or one close to it. Conflict situations usually make for easy dialogues because they have built-in tension. Without tension, dialogues tend to sound like two people trying to talk to each other when they have nothing to say. Try to recall a conflict between you and your parents, you and a close friend, you and the police, you and a teacher, and so on. Put yourself in the other person's role for a moment; try out the other person's *voice*. (You can have three speakers, if you like.)

Discussion activity

Read the following dialogue. Does it sound realistic? Describe the different voices you hear.

GORDON PARKS, *Born Black*

"Do all of you sleep on this one mattress?"
"That ain't nothing, brother. There's a poor fella livin' down the hall what's got six children and their place ain't no bigger'n this. There was eight of 'em till two of the young'uns got drafted in the army a month or so ago."
"Where's your toilet and bathroom?"
"Take him down the hall and show him, Lil. Show him good." Lil, his

wife, nodded toward me and I followed her down a dark corridor, where she opened a door and pointed in. There was an old bathtub with most of the enamel broken off and a filthy toilet. The seat next to it had rotted and fallen apart, lying in a heap of other decaying boards and fallen plaster. The foul air was unbearable. "Would you wash your child in that mess?" she asked. I didn't answer. I knew she didn't expect me to. I just took a picture of it; and we went back to her husband and children.

"Well, how'd you like it? It's a dog, huh?" I nodded, and he went on, "Eight families use it, brother. See that baseball bat over there in the corner? Well, my boy there don't play ball with it. We kill rats with it."

DESCRIPTION

Description is an important skill for writing about personal experiences, as well as for more objective writing, even laboratory and clinical reports. Practicing descriptions can help you make effective choices of words and details, so that a reader will see as you saw.

A good description is seldom an accident—it has to be consciously crafted—but there are no iron-clad rules to follow. In describing a scene, one writer might move from left to right, another from top to bottom, another from the center outward. The important thing is to *have* a plan of attack. One good technique is to imagine as you prewrite that you're a portable movie camera with audio capability. First, record every detail you can remember. Then, *select* only the sights, sounds, smells, tastes, and textures that will help create the sense of significance—the point you want your reader to get. Describing all the people, actions, physical details might recapture the scene for you, but it would probably confuse and bore your reader.

Read the following description. What plan of attack does the writer use? What dominant impressions do you get from this description? What words and phrases create those impressions? Are there too many descriptive details? Too few?

Winter Echoes   PAM ROTHROCK

A few short months before, it had been the hub of sweltering summer afternoon activity. Now it lay cold and desolate, the blue-gray of the outer shell matching the steely clouds as they rushed through the sky ahead of a frigid north wind. The thin arms of the abandoned crab apple trees in front of the building clacked together in the wind, and their leaves lay piled on the yew-bordered walk that barefoot youngsters had padded carelessly up not so very long before. Cars cruised by slowly on Mill Street, but none stopped to pull into the lot any longer. The wind whined through the barbed-wire fence that herded in a lonely group of green picnic tables. I tightened the scarf that was wound around my neck and leaned down to rub a hole in the winter dust on the window and look inside. It was dusky, but a barrage of old memories came hurtling at my senses as I stopped there in the biting wind.

There was the sound of a radio, blaring tinnily the unrefined lyrics of either disco or rock, depending on who was assigned to work in "The Cage," as the teenage workers called the wired-in lobby of the building. The floor was slimy with wet footprints of all sizes tracking across it. From the boys' side of the locker room came the sound of screechy adolescent voices in the midst of a war or a game of tag. Three damp teenagers were looking around at the wooden counter that was scarred with the names of past and present employees, their boyfriends, girlfriends, and acquaintances. They went boringly about their job: one deeply engrossed in a sensual romance novel; the second staring into space, trying to find a new dimension of living; and the third brandishing a homemade flyswatter, trying to beat out last week's champion in the flyswatting contest. Every so often a waterlogged lifeguard would wander in on break, whipping a towel and carrying a Diet Pepsi.

The way outside was through a dusty, musty-smelling locker room that was similar to a cave deep in the bowels of the earth. Outside, the pavement was hot and slightly sticky on the bottom of the feet. Kids were racing around like little daredevils in flashy bathing suits, their hair spiky, tousled, and dripping. It was almost impossible to take a step without nearly being plowed over by a swarm of six-year-olds.

The water looked clear, cool, and crisply blue. In the three-foot end, little kids splashed and screamed while their mothers looked on from the side of the pool. Little boys dolphined around close to the four-foot diving board, wiggling their bodies in pantomime of a swim and coming to the surface with a high-pitched laugh. Standing along the edge of the five-foot board was a cluster of junior-high girls, hugging their bodies with their skinny, tanned arms and giggling, not yet quite sure how to get into the cold water. Their problem was solved by the inevitable group of junior high boys, who attacked from behind and dumped them in without mercy.

The grass to the right was nearly covered by a colorful assortment of beach towels and blankets, folding chairs and umbrellas. Those mothers not inclined toward the water sat in a well-oiled semicircle and gossiped behind large tinted sunglasses. Small children lay belly-down on their towels and played game upon game of Old Maid, sloshing down endless sodas, and chewing on half-frozen Zero Bars. Teenage girls lay back for some serious tanning and talked lazily of parties, watching the boys clowning on the dives. A deeply tanned lifeguard with white sunscreen on her nose twirled her whistle on a blue-and-white macramé string and watched over her domain with an eagle eye.

A long line of impatient youngsters clutching cold quarters and slightly soggy dollar bills extended from each of the two windows at the refreshment stand, affectionately known as "The Pit" by the teenagers who worked there. Inside the low building, teenagers screamed and swore at each other, got in each other's way, burned themselves on the ovens, and prayed that the crushed ice would give out so that they would not have to make any more of those abominable snow-cones. The person whose schedule called for work in "The Pit" usually went home that night to dream of salty soft pretzels, Charlie Chips Bar-B-Cue Potato Chips, rubbery hot dogs, and frayed nerves.

On a hot, sticky day in the middle of August, the Quakertown swimming pool was the center of a well-timed yet chaotic ballet of confusion, splashing, screams of delight and laughter. The parking lot would inevitably be filled to the brim with cars, the bicycle racks packed with bikes of every race, color, and creed, the pool filled up with children both young and not so young. The sounds drifting through the wire fence from within were just a part of the lazy summer afternoon scenario in the middle of town. Now the sound of the wind rattling the links in that same fence brought me harshly back to the cold and the winter, the summer gone. I pulled back from the window clouded with my breath, and my eye caught the red-lettered sign that proclaimed the pool would open again on Memorial Day as it has always done, when the big red door would swing open, ushering in the heavily scented breezes of summer and scattering the dusty ghosts of a mid-November's day.

Pam contrasts the swimming pool as winter is setting in with the pool of her memory: full of the noises, sights, and smells of summer vacation. She begins by peering through the window into the lobby and then "walks" the reader from the interior of the lobby to the pavement outside, to the pool itself. She then directs the reader's eyes and ears across the pool itself to the sunbathers on the grass to the right, then to the "The Pit," and finally to the sights and sounds of the parking lot. Pam uses a number of directional cues: "in 'The Cage,'" "the way outside," "Outside," "In the three-foot end," "along the edge of the five-foot board," "at the refreshment stand," "Inside the low building." These directional signals help Pam to control her reader's experiences, by creating a sense of order and coherence in the scene she describes.

Discussion activity

In groups or as a class, discuss the following pieces of descriptive writing. What were the authors' overall purposes? What dominant impressions do the writers convey? Do you think you responded the way the writers wanted you to? How did the writers try to control your reactions?

The Room   JOYCE SERETNY

The walls of the room were covered with faded green and gray striped paper. "Why don't they ever paint these places a bright cheerful orange?"

I thought. Directly opposite the doorway were two large windows, but tightly closed venetian blinds shut out the fresh air and sunshine. The room was dim and oppressively hot. The potted red geraniums on the windowsill were wilting from the extreme heat and lack of care.

In the far corner stood a white portable commode. The attendant must have forgotten to empty it because the stench was so acrid that I had to swallow again and again to keep from vomiting.

Against the other wall, like silent partners, stood a hospital bed and night table. Strewn across the top in disarray were vitamin pills, thread, salt, camphor, brush, comb, epsom salts, and a glass with false teeth soaking in water. Within reach of her possessions an old woman rested in a wheelchair. Her fine white hair was cut too short, giving her a masculine appearance. "It used to be down to my waist," she whispered as she tugged at the uneven strands, as if the pulling would make them grow again. The skin on her face was soft and almost wrinkle-free. "Never used any of those fancy lotions, or make-up. Ain't good for the skin," she confided.

She wore a blue print cotton dress with two buttons open around the middle. "Got so fat. Nothing fits anymore. Maybe I'll get to play Santa Claus this year." She laughed at her own little joke and then repeated it several times.

With great effort she held one hand up in front of her and started rubbing it with the other. The fingers were misshapen. Dark, puffy veins covered the backs of both hands. The fingernails were long, brittle, and yellowed. "Can't cut them myself anymore," she said. She sat quietly for a moment and then inched the wheelchair even closer to the night table and slowly opened the drawer. It was crammed with greeting cards, letters, and yellowed pictures. Her hands shook as she piled them all in her lap. Her blue eyes teared. "The heat always did make my eyes water," she said. "They never forget me. Look at all these cards. Had ten children. Most of them gone now, but lots of grandchildren and great-grandchildren left. They're always sending cards . . . pretty to look at. They never forget."

JAMES BALDWIN, *"Previous Condition"*

The room I lived in was heavy ceilinged, perfectly square, with walls the color of chipped dry blood. Jules Weissman, a Jewish boy, had got the room for me. It's a room to sleep in, he said, or maybe to die in, but God knows it wasn't meant to live in. Perhaps because the room was so hideous it had a fantastic array of light fixtures: one on the ceiling, one on the left wall, two on the right wall, and a lamp on the table beside my bed. My bed was in front of the window through which nothing ever blew but dust. It was a furnished room and they'd thrown enough stuff in it to furnish three rooms its size. Two easy chairs and a desk, the bed, the table, a straight-backed chair, a bookcase, a cardboard wardrobe; and my books and my suitcase, both unpacked; and my dirty clothes flung in a corner. It was the kind of room that defeated you. It had a fireplace, too, and a heavy marble mantelpiece, and a great gray mirror above the mantelpiece. It was hard to see anything in the mirror very clearly—which was perhaps just as well—and it would have been worth your life to have started a fire in the fireplace.

Writing activity

Describe some person, place, or situation you know very well. Try to recapture the experience for your readers, carefully choosing details that will allow readers to see what you want them to see. Try this technique: mentally explore the scene or object you are going to describe, one sense at a time. First jot down everything you can see, then everything you can hear, and so on with taste, touch, and smell. After you've explored with your five physical senses, try using your sixth sense. What kind of emotional vibrations do you get? Any intuitions of mood, atmosphere, mental imagery?

Decide the overall impression you want to convey, and then select from the dozens of details you have in your notes those that will help recreate the experience for your readers.

PERSONAL-EXPERIENCE NARRATIVES

Once you have conquered the blank page and have some control over your writer's voice and descriptive skills, you are ready to move on to more unified kinds of writing. Personal-experience narratives are a first step in learning to structure your writing to a specific end. Shaping your materials so that they come out the way you want them to is what *composition* means. Rather than start with something complex like an argumentative essay, you'll find it simpler to start with something you know very well: a personal experience.

Look at your own life to find something that had particular meaning. Your goal is to show the reader what the experience meant. You may say, "But I've led a dull life; I've never done anything unusual or extraordinary to write about." Few of us have anything extraordinary to write about, but you can try to show the meaning of commonplace events. Indeed, great writers have already written about every aspect of human existence, again and again. The only thing new in the world is each individual. *You* are new; your perceptions, your understandings, your own experiences are new, unique to you. Almost every human being has had a love affair, or will have sooner or later; yet writers never tire of writing about love, and people never tire of reading about love. Why? Because each story is slightly different; each writer gives the story an individual interpretation.

For example, here is a story that narrates a very simple event—taking a canoe ride down a river. Is the writing good? What is there in the story that is new, that only *this* person could have known about and written? Would you say the writer is being honest about her experience? Can you tell that she is selecting details to include or leave out of this story, shaping her materials?

My Personal Poseidon

LAURIE STEWART

From that first moment we launched our canoe, I knew it would be disaster.

"Which end do you want?" I asked my partner, Merry, who had never touched a canoe in her life.

"Oh, I don't know, what's the difference?"

"Well, do you want to steer or just paddle?"

"I guess I'll steer," she said, heading towards the front of the canoe.

"If you want to steer, you go in back." I turned her around and headed her to the rear. Boy, listen to me, the voice of experience. I had only been canoeing twice, but in this case I guess I was the expert of the crew.

We launched it into the river and we both clambered in. Using the same side for leverage, we immediately leaned the canoe to its brink, spilling all its contents into the river.

We were both frantically reaching for our possessions—the sandwiches, lemonade, and bag of dry towels. Of course the canoe was whirling down the river and we lost our balance, practically tipping ourselves over, as our belongings went sailing along the river.

"Oh brother," I moaned. We were starting out well.

"Well, at least we didn't fall in," said Merry cheerfully. With that happy, reassuring note, we were off. Boy, were we off. The second we got caught up in the current, we were both hanging on for our lives. The canoe rocked and swayed precariously, and suddenly I realized it was time for some definite action: we were headed straight for a fallen log.

"Hey back there, steer this damn thing!" I screamed.

"But I don't know how!" she answered with rising hysteria. Great, I thought, just great.

"Just stick the oar in the water like we're going to pivot around it!"

"Okay," she said, but I didn't feel us veering in any other direction—just straight for that ominous log.

"Push the oar in farther!" I yelled.

"Okay . . . Oh! . . . Oh! . . . Oh, *help!*" she screamed. Definite hysteria. And the canoe came to a halt, the water rushing past us. We were docked.

"What the hell's going on?"

When I looked behind me, all I could see was Merry's rear conspicuously staring at me, as the rest of her was standing, leaning over our vessel and hanging onto the oar, now stuck in three feet of muck.

"I can't get it out!" Merry's pitiful wail.

"Well, don't let it go, for heaven's sake, that paddle cost us six dollars!" Boy, would good old Jerolim's Canoe Rental make a haul on our venture.

"What do I do?"

I was just asking myself that same question, actually. I thought about telling her to jump out, grab the oar and then swim like hell back to the canoe. Unfortunately, the river is a bit faster than Merry. I also thought of telling her to jump out and wait, perched up on the oar, for the Coast Guard to show up. Man, I'd do anything for six bucks.

"Need some help?" a friendly voice called. That was quite the understatement.

"Yah, we sure could use some of that," I said.

A young man and his dog, paddling down the river, came to our rescue. Skillfully pushing alongside our canoe, he gave the paddle a swift yank, washed off the mud, and handed it to Merry, all the while keeping our canoes side by side.

"Thanks a lot!" we yelled, relieved and thankful. With a smile he was off, his dog riding along contentedly. Thank heavens for heroes!

Well, we were a little bit more warmed up by this time. We sort of made our way down the river, crashing and rebounding from bank to bank. After about an hour of bumper-canoe, we decided we needed a little rest.

The next problem was how we were going to pull over. We decided our best bet was to just let ourselves glide over to the bank, then stop and get out. But of course that was our worst possible choice.

I didn't see it until we were right up on it. We had both stopped paddling and were floating along peacefully when I saw it—it was a giant underwater rock, with the current dancing deceptively over it. I swear to God it was the size of a buried volcano. Man, we were dead.

"Oh, my God! Oh, my God! Hang on, Merry!" I screamed. We both clung to the sides like we were glued to them, but to no avail. We hit it full force—sending the canoe over on its side and finally completely turning it over, dumping us into the ice-cold river.

"Why didn't you steer, you stupid moron?" I came up sputtering at Merry.

"Me? Why didn't you warn me it was there? You're in front!" she said, teeth chattering. We stood in the middle of the river, dripping, shivering, and bickering until I suddenly spun around. Oh man, we were in trouble!

"The canoe!"

We both started running after it, while it just went along its merry little way—upside down and all. We were like two clumsy buffaloes—running, slipping, and crashing heavily through the water. We finally managed to catch up with it, after it had conveniently gotten tied up in some branches. We both staggered up to it and leaned on it, breathless.

"God, we lost the paddles," I moaned despairingly.

"No, we didn't. I managed to grab them when we were running up here," said Merry, smiling.

"Wow, Merry, you life-saver!"

"How do you like that? And to think only a minute ago I was a stupid moron!" We looked at each other, and then at our beat-up dented-in canoe, filled with water, and we burst into laughter. We plopped right down onto the dirty, muddy bank and stayed for a long while—two freezing, wet, dripping girls with stringy, tangled hair and faces covered with mud; two cold, bruised, tired bodies—and we laughed until we cried.

Laurie narrates her story with humor and enough details to allow the reader to participate. Notice her use of dialogue. It is the dialogue that gives the reader a you-are-there kind of participation.

Laurie's story illustrates an important principle in narrating personal experiences. You can't just *tell* the reader what happened—you must *show* the reader. The idea is to re-create, dramatize the event so that the reader will see, hear, and feel your experience.

You can avoid many problems with personal-experience narratives if you will remember to *limit your story to one specific incident*. Pick a moment in time, an hour or less of your life that had some meaning for you. Then tell what happened in that moment, in detail. If you try to write about something that took longer to experience, you will find yourself summarizing, just hitting the highlights, being general when you should be specific. If you try to write "My Trip across the Country" or "My Day at the Grand Canyon," the reader will fall asleep long before you get to the important part. So will you.

Here is the beginning of the final draft of a personal-experience narrative. Is it an interesting beginning? Has the writer supplied you with enough details? Should the writer have started at a different point?

SHIRLEY MICHAELS

We stood there alone, the pale green windowless walls ensuring our privacy. No one could see us. Still, I glanced nervously around, stunned by the request. No, stunned by the demand to remove my clothes. Nothing like this had ever happened to me—never. Now don't get the idea I'm a young naive girl. Not at all. In my thirty-odd years I've been around; I know the score. I read the newspaper daily and *Time* weekly. In fact, I had been here before. Although others had been apprehensive, maybe even frightened, when we had come here, I had never felt so. I had an easy familiarity with the place. But, this time was different.

I played for time, repeating the command: "Take off my clothes?" Maybe if I questioned I could avoid compliance. The answer was a slight but imperative nod of the head. Disbelief flooded my consciousness. I've had my share of fantasies imagining disrobing in front of others, especially at their insistence—maybe even delighting a little in showing off. This certainly wasn't playing like one of my fantasies. I joked that my fantasies had always involved men. The response was an impersonal, perfunctory "Place them on the bench behind you." Did I have an alternative? No. I awkwardly started undressing. Should I start with my blouse or with my slacks? Did I have to take all my clothes off? Could I leave my panties on? My mother's dictum about the necessity of always wearing clean underwear in case of an emergency flashed through my mind. But, one look at her face and the flippant mood and questioning died in my throat.

My breasts—my very being was shrinking, shrinking as she commanded me to sit. She seemed more concerned with separating my toes, unaware of my ashen, anemic body. Later as I stood there naked, awkwardly exposing myself to her further scrutiny—her searching, relentless examination, I thought, "What's a nice girl like you doing in a place like this! . . . For forgetting to pay a fine for doing 37 in a 25-mile-an-hour zone."

Shirley's beginning keeps readers in suspense: Why is she being asked to take off her clothes? Where is she? Shirley has consciously shaped her narrative to gain her readers' attention, to engage her readers in the experience, to make them feel as naked and vulnerable, as dehumanized, as she did.

The initial draft of this story was very different. Shirley began at the beginning of the day, recounting how she got ready for work, what she thought about on her way to work, how busy her day was going to be, how she wouldn't have time to take care of that business errand. She described two problems at work and how she solved one of them. She recounted how she drove to the police station and had trouble getting anyone to answer when she knocked on the door, how she joked with the officer as she tried to pay her overdue fine, how no one responded to her jokes and her friendliness, and eventually how she was fingerprinted, stripped, and searched.

In the initial draft, Shirley told her readers too much. She summarized *every* incident in her day, instead of showing her readers what was important. In the final draft, Shirley's beginning re-creates the event; she dramatizes the incident so that her readers can see, hear, and feel, can relive the experience with her. She does not begin at the day's beginning. Instead, she focuses on what she is really interested in writing about—the event that started with "Take off your clothes." The initial draft was a simple act of memory. The version you read is *composed,* its incidents and details selected and shaped.

The following story narrates a commonplace event—going home by bus. Is it interesting? Has the writer included every detail of this experience? How has the writer shaped her materials? What incidents has she left out of the story? Why?

Mr. Princeton   ANNE CONNERS

Bounce, rattle, jolt—I sleepily perceive that the Greyhound bus is pulling to a stop. The dim yellow lights flicker on as the driver drones, "Portland." I bury my head in the plastic upholstery and try to go back to sleep—after all, it is 3 A.M. Soon I dimly realize that someone is standing near me.

"Excuse me, is this seat taken?" Yes, by me, I crossly think as I pull my sprawled body into a sitting position and my new seatmate plops down beside me. The bus resumes its journey but not for long as we stop in front of a garishly lit Dunkin' Donut shop. "Fifteen-minute stop here," the driver bellows.

"Translated—the driver wants a doughnut," my companion wearily chuckles.

"Come on," I mutter beneath my breath, "who needs cynicism at this hour?"

I stumble down the aisle and enter the doughnut shop, the sickly-sweet smell of greasy doughnuts assailing me as I make my way to the ladies' room. Peering into a mirror, I see a tired, disheveled face—is that me? I make some feeble attempts to straighten my hair and put some color into my wan cheeks. "Who the hell really cares?" I wonder aloud as I trudge back to the bus. Only three hours and forty-five minutes to Bangor, I quickly calculate—maybe I can sleep the rest of the way.

After boarding the bus, I take my seat, resenting the stranger who'd deprived me of the opportunity to comfortably sack out on two seats. My "friend" reboards the bus, carrying an orange plastic bucket of Munchkin doughnuts.

"Would you like one?" he politely offers as he sits down.

"No," I abruptly snap, recoiling at the greasy ball of calories.

Our conversation dies as the bus resumes its journey into the darkness. Pulling out a tattered copy of Kurt Vonnegut's *Breakfast of Champions*, my companion begins to read. From my vantage point, I study my new seatmate. His large, muscular shoulders strain the fabric of his green flannel shirt. A pug nose protrudes sharply from his solid face, and boyish curls bounce up and down as the bus bounces over potholes. Not bad looking, I surmise. Maybe the last leg of my journey won't be as boring as I thought.

Trying to sound casual, I take the plunge—"Where you headed to?"

"Bar Harbor, to camp out with some friends." He closes his book (ah, I've snared him), and we begin to exchange pleasantries. Soon I've found out that he's from California. "California—you mean where everyone goes to find himself?" We laugh as he tells me he hasn't been lost lately.

"So, you going to school?" I inquire.

"Yeah, Princeton," he casually replies. Princeton—I'm sitting with a real live preppie? Do I need to act any differently?

Temporarily losing my composure, I fumble for the next standard question. "What's your major?"

"International law," he suavely replies. My, a sophisticated lawyer. I swallow nervously.

"Uh, what year are you?"

"A junior." Hmm . . . an older man. Now what do they like?

Plunging on to the next question, I ask, "What'd you do this summer?"

"Oh, I led a bicycle tour through France—and Switzerland." France and Switzerland?! Just your average, lower-middle class vacation spot, I ironically note, remembering my excursions to Niagara Falls and Cedar Point.

Soon the conversation swings my way. "Where you from?" he asks.

"Uh, uh, Erie—you know, the mistake by the lake in northwestern P.A."

"Oh, yeah."

"Nobody comes to Erie to find himself," I feebly joke.

"Where are you going to school?"

"Well, Penn State—you know the farmers' school in the hills of central P.A."

"Oh yeah, I think I've heard of their football team."

"What's your major?"

"I really don't know yet," I meekly reply. Oh no, indecision and bumpkintry in the face of suaveness and sophistication—my stomach sinks.

"What year are you?"

"A freshman," I mutter into the cushion.

"A what?" he asks.

"A freshman," I humbly squeak, feeling more and more insignificant. Whose idea was it to start a conversation anyway?

Mr. Princeton turns and calmly regards me for a few seconds. Thank God it's dark—I hope he can't see my eye twitching. "You know," he begins, "one thing you have to keep telling yourself during your freshman year is—this is funny, this is funny, this is so funny." Wow, he's not going to disdain my lowly station in life? I relax somewhat—the twitching in my eye stops. Maybe preppies are people too.

Soon weariness overtakes both of us; our conversation trails off as the steady motion of the bus lulls us to sleep. Ouch—my head strikes a metal bar, jolting me into consciousness. Once again I'm comfortably reclining on two seats—Mr. Princeton is gone. Peering around I finally locate him—stretched out on the hard, dirty bus floor, sound asleep. What in the hell is he doing there?

The headlights illuminate a green highway sign which proclaims: "Bangor, next exit." That's me! I excitedly begin to gather my belongings. "Mr. Princeton, Mr. Princeton—hey, wake up—I have to get off soon," I whisper to the prone figure on the floor. "Uhh, huh, uhh," groaning and grunting, Mr. Princeton very ungallantly hoists himself into the seat.

"Just for curiosity's sake, what were you doing on the floor?"

"I just decided to sleep there," he curtly responds.

"Well, to each his own," I nonchalantly reply. (Maybe preppies are weird after all.)

"And besides," he continues, "a little while ago you decided to put your head on my shoulder."

A paralyzing vise tightens around my throat and my cheeks turn scarlet. After a few seconds, I plead, "You're joking?"

"Naturally," he assuredly replies, "no."

Sinking into the cushions, I thank someone that I'm getting off at the next stop. We pull into Bangor just as day is breaking. My flushed cheeks and flustered manner are clearly visible as I grab my belongings and stutter goodbye. Clutching my suitcase, I walk off the bus mumbling, "This is funny, this is funny, this is so funny."

Anne has taken a chance by using the present tense—"I sleepily perceive . . . I wonder . . . He closes his book . . . I stumble off the bus"—to tell her story. Most stories are easier to tell in the past tense. Has she succeeded?

Notice her use of dialogue to give readers a feeling of "being there." What other ways does Anne *show* rather than *tell* the reader what is happening?

Writing activity

Write a two- or three-page paper narrating a personal experience of your own. Limit your story to one specific incident, an hour or less of your life that meant something to you. Tell what happened during that incident, in detail. If you are writing about a car wreck, condense the preliminaries— where you were going, road conditions, and so on. Spend most of your time describing—re-creating—in great detail the actual instant of the crash. Use all your senses: what did you see, hear, feel, smell, taste? What thoughts went through your mind? Finally, when you get to the end of the story, stop. Don't tack on a moral: "I've learned never to take Deadman's Curve at fifty miles an hour again." The reader should be able to learn the moral, if there is one, just as you learned it, by experiencing the wreck with you. If you have to tell the reader what it meant, there is something missing from your story. For this paper a good rule to follow is, the more details the better, even though you know it is possible to have too many details in a story.

DISCUSSING YOUR WRITING

One of the best ways to get a sense of what your readers need and expect is to share and discuss your writing—especially early drafts—with your classmates. Form groups of five or six and take turns reading the papers out loud. Here are some noncritical, non-threatening things you can say or ask:

1 Effective use of details. They let the readers (listeners) feel they are right there with you. Tell me more (or less) about . . .
2 Good words. Sounds like you really know what you are talking about. You didn't settle for general terms but picked just the right words for the story.
3 Nicely put together. Doesn't waste too much time on preliminaries. Ends where it should, doesn't tack on an unnecessary ending.
4 I had a similar experience; I know just what you mean and how you felt.
5 Why do you suppose things like this happen? Did you feel it was all your fault?
6 Your voice comes through good and strong, sounds very realistic and natural, shows your personality.
7 Good title, fits the paper well, interesting and lively.
8 Had anything like this ever happened to you before, or to anyone else you know? Was it different this time? Were you surprised?
9 What happened afterward? How did your parents, friends, relatives feel, react?
10 The best part of your paper was . . . . It really makes the point stand out, shows how you felt, makes me see what you meant.
11 How did you prewrite this? How did you get your idea, start your paper?
12 Was it hard to write? Did you have any difficulties, or did it write itself?

Try to pick up from classmates' comments whether they are getting from your writing what you think you are putting into it. Don't be afraid to ask specific questions: "Should I write more (or less) about this? Is this word (phrase, sentence, idea) as clear and good as I think? Does the paper start and end in the right places?" and so on.

Discussion activity

In groups or as a class, use the list above as a guide to help you discuss the following personal-experience essays.

Stealing Apples—
No Fun, No
Profit

BILL PILCHAK

"And don't anyone holler about a dog unless it's chewing on your leg!"

Wow! I had been drifting along in a daydream until the words brought me back. And there we were again, once my head focused: five guys, a girl, and a dog—a puppy—all crammed into one tiny Fiat humming along M–20 to a well-known local apple orchard. It was three o'clock into the Saturday morning; an apple feast would end the night's activities.

"Did someone say something about a dog up there?" I finally asked. I'd hoped they were part of my daydream.

"Yeah," Lucci turned to face me from the crowded front seat. "Every time we go to this place, we hear dogs. Eric thinks he has seen bloodhounds around, but we think they have some kind of record with a timer. So don't yell unless you get bitten." Lucci turned around and squeezed back between the shoulders beside him.

"Don't worry, if I get bitten, I'll yell. These farmers get pretty serious about this, eh?"

"Bill, we're really stealing apples." He emphasized "stealing." The way it sounded it was every man for himself. The trick was to get into the orchard, pick two grocery bags of apples, and then scram. If you get caught—tough. I was worried, but it wasn't nearly as dangerous as I then believed. Bloodhounds? If someone said that they had bloodhounds today, I'd say they were nuts. There probably aren't two bloodhounds in the whole state. But on that Saturday night, I would have believed that the whole Russian army was lurking behind those trees.

Irony, I pondered, was hitting home. Wasn't it I who supported this idea in the first place? Weren't Pendergrass and I the only ones who really wanted to go? Yeah, I thought with remorse, and now everyone is so dead-set that my only alternative was to get out and pay my respects to that raccoon that John just ran over, and wait until they got back, if ever. After a while, I just settled into the seat and became absorbed in the music.

When the tapedeck was turned down below the audio-destruct level, I knew something was up. "There's the farmer's house," Eric said to everyone, although I was the only one who didn't know.

"Hey, all the lights are on. Every single one." A spark of panic had been ignited. Voices started coming all at once.

"Man, that's not cool."

"What do you suppose it means?"

"They're probably catching apple-snatchers out there right and left."

"Sure, on a Saturday night with all the stars and no moon."

"Would you guys shut up!" It was Lucci again. He was staying cool, keeping organized. "That farmer always parties his brains out on Saturday nights, and besides, the trees that we hit are a mile from his house." Lucci really knew how to steal apples.

In another minute we were turning off the highway onto a gravel road. John cut the lights and at the same time yanked the small car into a tight circle until it again faced the pavement. The whole maneuver seemed pretty snazzy to me.

The six of us started tumbling out of the car while at the same time stuffing shopping bags under our arms. John made it out first, then Pendergrass, and finally me. As soon as I got out, I walked to the back of the car and noticed how quiet the night was, and how dark. The sky was covered with stars, but there was no moon; it was very much three o'clock in the morning. And then suddenly, although I could see nothing, there came a definite rustle from a distance in the grass. "Pendergrass, your dog's loose. You'll never see him again," I warned.

"Ziggy is still in the car."

Oh, I thought, then said, "Well there's someone out here besides us then," very calmly.

"Come on now, who can be out here at three o'clock in the morning? Quit being paranoid."

That's right, I thought. And I had recently alluded to being a definite paranoid anyway. Sure, there was no one out there. I believed that for about two seconds, until I heard a second rustle in the grass. "I heard it again." I was running the risk of becoming monotonous.

"Right," was all I got.

Seeing John run down into the small valley separating the orchard from the road, I decided to be second from last in line. Safest spot, I thought. As he started up the other side, I was glad I had.

"Oops," John said; "Excuse me. What the hell?"

"Damn right 'oops,' I live here."

"Let's get out of here."

We must have resembled volunteer sardine fillets once we heard the farmer. When we were all finally back in, and Eric had jumped over the front seat into our laps, we all noticed one conspicuous absence: we had no driver. The farmer still had John.

"John's still out there," Lucci said. I could tell he was thinking heavily, making decisions. "To hell with him. I'll drive and we'll come back for him later, maybe Monday." But as he slid over and took the wheel, he found the keys were gone. They were in John's pocket. We all knew at once.

The car flooded with embarrassment and guilt. There was nothing we could say; no one even thought to turn off the overhead dome light so the farmer couldn't see us worrying. Someone finally broke the silence. "If anyone can talk us out of this, it's John."

Soon he returned and entered the car, his face a blank.

"He's gonna let us go, eh John?"

"Well," he began, "first off, that wasn't the farmer. That was his son. Turns out he hates his old man. He's taking us to the best apples." He turned and grinned, "He's gonna help us steal his own apples!"

The little car pitched and rocked with the convulsions of five guys laughing and carrying on. For a while we were completely satisfied with ourselves, until the reality of the situation hit us. In fact, we had been caught. As of now we were not stealing apples, merely taking them. The group was subdued. The farmer had won. Our simple victory rang only in the crunch of bitten apples and echoed in no one's ears.

Coming Up   MARY ELLEN TYUS

I climbed to the top floor through the murky gloom of the steep stairwell. Dust motes swirled around me, and the ancient stairs creaked ominously. After the sharp cold of the lakeside air, the building felt especially hot, dry and oppressive. Beyond the second landing my arms began to ache from the bundles which shifted precariously in my grasp. My thick coat hung heavily from my shoulders and flapped around my knees, impeding my progress up the stairs. Beneath it my clothes began to cling moistly to my body.

My face was flushed from the effort of the climb, and I could feel the tight lines along my cheeks where the tears had dried. My head throbbed slightly as a headache sought to take hold. My eyes were dry and stung. The passage was as arid as the chalk dust which lightly powdered its walls.

I reached the summit and paused, surveying the expanse of empty, dust-filled rooms opening one onto another. Once these rooms had fairly hummed with activity. For nearly one hundred years myriad feet had trod down these halls, wearing paths into the wood—deep trails, like old auto grooves in forgotten woodlands—paths now filling with the dust of the wood itself, with the dust of time.

I crossed the hall and climbed over the barricade into a wide, dusky room lighted only by the diffused Northern glow filtering through the dirty panes of a pair of French doors. The floor bowed deeply at the center, and here and there the light and shadows revealed sunken areas in the aged wood. I wondered if it would crash to the cellars beneath my feet, and I stepped in silently.

The floor did not creak as I crossed it, but there was a feeling of tentativeness in the atmosphere as though I, and the room, and the moment were caught in some delicate, timeless balance. I stopped at the windows and looked back. The dust had absorbed my foot-falls and smoothed itself as if I had not passed. I held my breath and listened. Nothing.

I turned to the windows and looked out. The stark, cold, February forenoon winds wafted no voices to my ear, no hurrying footsteps on the pavement far below. No birdsong. I turned the latch and stepped out. The rusted fire escape swayed ever so slightly from its weary moorings. Perhaps another step would send it crashing down. I peered over the rail at the small square of brickwork six flights below.

Flights. If I leapt from the balcony, would I fly? Would I plummet groundwards, veering at the last second and rising—arms spread—in a graceful soar?

The balcony shifted again under my weight and I felt the sudden rush of tears against my lashes. They would find me on those faded bricks, their worn surface new-red with the liberal glazing of my blood.

Then what? I thought of faces pale with alarm; horror. People turning away, stomachs lurching, as the blanket was spread. He'd be sorry then. The bastard. Let him look at that!

A tear fell down the six long flights, invisible as it passed the rail. I watched, unseeing, imagining its path as it spiralled earthward. Would my passing, too, be so unmarked? I turned and stepped back into the gloom.

"Hell, nobody's worth *that!*" I said, and walked swiftly through the dust and shadows, through the webs and memories, down the stairs and out to life.

CHAPTER THREE

Informative Writing

Choosing, defining, creating harmony,

bringing that clarity and shape that is rest and light

out of disorder and confusion—

the work that I do at my desk

is not unlike arranging flowers.

Only it is much harder to get started on writing something!

MAY SARTON. *Plant Dreaming Deep*

Once you've gained some confidence and fluency from personal writing, you can move on to *informative* writing, where you will learn to *analyze* an issue and *explain* to your readers what you think about it. You will continue to use the skills you developed in personal writing, but you will learn to use them in new ways.

In your personal-experience narratives, your purpose was to recapture a significant experience, and you invited readers along to share it. Expository writing involves you in a more complex transaction with your readers. You may have to teach a reader how to change a tire, explain why he or she should buy a personal computer, define *chauvinism* for your political-science class, compare and contrast the semester and trimester systems for the student-faculty council. You must gather convincing evidence and then shape and explain the information so that it is useful for your readers. Your purpose is to help your readers find their way through a complex situation. To do so, you must anticipate where they will have questions and guide them so that they understand what you have explained.

INVENTION

In Chapter 2, you used free writing and journal writing to help you generate subject matter for your personal narratives. You relied mainly on *memory* to provide details for your stories. But for informative writing, memory won't always provide you with enough material—facts, details, examples, reasons—to convince your readers. You need to develop more systematic methods of invention. Invention—derived from the Latin word *invenire*, "to find"—involves searching to find both the material you'll need to inform your readers and the strategies you'll use to organize and present that material.

Try out all the invention techniques described in this chapter, from free-association *brainstorming*, which taps into your subconscious mind, to the more structured *journalistic formula* and the *pentad*, which probe every aspect of a topic with exhaustive sets of questions. One of these techniques may feel intuitively right to you, a method you already use; or you may be most successful combining techniques. The only real rule is to develop a system that gets you started and keeps you going. You need to have several techniques to draw on in case any one isn't adequate in a given writing situation.

Brainstorming

Brainstorming is a popular and easy-to-use invention technique; many professional writers claim brainstorming is the only method they use to generate and organize subject matter. In reality, these writers have unconsciously assimilated more formal strategies of finding and shaping what they want to say, though they call it brainstorming. In either case, free association or formal, brainstorming is an excellent way to begin to explore a subject.

Assume that you have just seen a tobacco commercial or read an article on the tobacco industry and you have decided this might be an interesting topic for an informative paper. To begin brainstorming, write down everything that comes into your mind that is related in any way to the tobacco industry and smoking. Approach the subject from every conceivable angle and write every thought that enters your mind. Write down each fact, opinion, statistic, or idea in a single word, a phrase, or even a complete sentence. As you keep working at your subject, one of two things will happen. You may realize that this subject is not for you; it may bore you or you may not know enough about it and don't care to find out. (This rarely happens.) More likely, your mind will begin to generate a flood of information about the subject. Facts, opinions, counterarguments will begin to appear in chaotic fashion on the page. Your mind will probably run ahead of your hand. Don't sift and analyze at this stage. Keep writing. Even if you suspect a fact or idea isn't relevant, write it down; you can delete it later. Surprisingly, many seemingly irrelevant facts turn out to be useful later as you develop your paper. Figure 3.1 shows a page of brainstorming that you might come up with on the general subject, the tobacco industry.

Try to do your brainstorming over a period of two or three days—perhaps a half hour at a time—to allow your unconscious mind to work over the topic, to incubate. Your best ideas often come when you allow the evidence to simmer for a while in your subconscious. Previously unconnected ideas suddenly come together, providing you with new insights and attitudes toward your subject. New angles develop as your mind wrestles with the topic. You often begin to see the problem you are trying to solve in an entirely new light. Counterarguments come to your attention, and the simple solution you had in mind becomes more problematic. The other side might not be wholly wrong; some of your arguments aren't as effective as you first thought. You'll probably need to take a more balanced, more judicious approach than you first planned. You need more evidence to support your argument.

As you examine your brainstorming sheet, (Figure 3.1), you can see that your experience has yielded a rich harvest. You have a great deal to say on this subject, but naturally it all looks confusing and disorganized.

Focusing   It is now time to *focus*, to zero in on your topic, to find out if you have a workable idea to develop into an interesting paper. As you think about the ideas you've accumulated, you begin to realize that the subject was too broad. What really interests you is the effects of smoking, and you have fairly strong feelings about this subject.

The next step is to select the words or phrases that are relevant to your new, more focused subject, the effects of cigarette smoking. It is obvious from your brainstorming sheet that most of your data either favor or attack cigarette smoking, so you decide to make two lists, each in no special order. (You'll find, though, that like things will tend to drift together. The mind instinctively tries to organize experience.) Figure 3.2 shows these lists, one headed *Against Smoking* and the other *For Smoking*.

Expanding Within the Focus: The Journalistic Formula and the Pentad   This new list may make you feel a little uneasy. Moving from the more general subject, the tobacco industry, to the more focused one on the effects of cigarette smoking caused you to discard many facts and ideas. You have a more manageable subject, but have you exhausted all the possibilities? Are there areas within this

Fires and deaths when smokers fall asleep with
cigarettes burning - how many house & hotel
fires caused this way?

Tobacco Industry
Huge, lots of people have jobs in it - economic problems if
it folded
Would it fold? There will always be people who smoke no
matter what surgeon general says

Economic benefits to all other industries, though - fewer days
missed because of smoking - related illnesses
If we banned everything bad for us - diet drinks (saccharin)
fast foods, junk foods, beer, etc. - life boring. We're going
to die anyway.

Dr. St. G. said it was better for Aunty
Re to smoke moderately than to weigh an
extra 25 lbs.

Eases hunger pangs
Settles your nerves
Keeps Mary Lee from biting
her nails

Expense - price - poor teenagers
but easier to get money for a
pack of butts than for something more expensive

Helps people diet

A way to feel more at ease
socially

Leaves smell on hands, clothes,
skin (not nice to kiss a SOME PEOPLE
ALLERGIC TO
SMOKE
smoker)
Irritates eyes & throats of others
Stains teeth and fingers
Cigarettes burn holes in clothing
& furniture

Gives hands something
to do

Psychological crutch

Looks cool, classy

In-group - if peers smoke,
so will you

Chew tobacco instead -
stains teeth, chewers
really gross

Linus's blanket not so bad to
have a psychological crutch
Habit not worth breaking - I can't stop anyhow.

Health

Cancer - surgeon general warning
on pack
Emphysema (sp?) Dan's father
coughed like crazy, had to lie in
bed with oxygen - dust in house
always had to be vacuumed up, etc.
Heart attacks, circulation problems
Lung cancer
Cancer of mouth - tongue and lips, especially pipe smoking -
but pipe smokers look distinguished like col. professors with
leather patches on elbows - not gross like chewing -
baseball players always have a wad in their cheek -
Hate to see people spitting

A woman refused to sit
beside her husband on
plane because he smoked
cigars.
BAN IN PUBLIC - NOT
ENOUGH - BAN COMPLETELY!

But then would there
be illegal sales - like
pot? Black market?

FIGURE 3.1

70

AGAINST SMOKING	FOR SMOKING
Causes lung cancer	Constitutional right – smoke if
Should ban smoking	you want to
Ban smoking in public	Economic disaster
Ruins teeth	Kids get started smoking to be cool
Causes emphysema	Settles your nerves
Poor circulation	Stops hunger pangs (temporarily)
Heart trouble	A way to communicate socially
Causes early death	A habit not worth the effort of
(males and females)	breaking
Nonsmokers nauseated	Can't stop
by fumes	Life boring if we banned every-
Cancer of lips & throat	thing bad for us (saccharin,
Economic benefits – fewer	fast foods, beer). We die
days missed from work.	anyway.

FIGURE 3.2

focused topic that you have not explored or discovered? At this stage in the process of invention, it's useful to examine the facts and ideas of your more focused subject in a more systematic way by using two complementary invention devices: the journalistic formula and rhetorician Kenneth Burke's *pentad*.

The journalistic formula consists of asking Who? What? When? Where? Why? How? News reporters are trained to use these six questions as they learn to produce news copy. If you use the questions creatively, you will discover many aspects of your subject that did not occur to you during the initial brainstorming. The *pentad* restates the journalistic formula in a more revealing way, one that stresses the possibilities for interaction between different elements in this scheme:

Action: What is happening?
Agent: Who is causing it to happen?
Agency: How is it being done?
Scene: Where and when is it being done?
Purpose: Why is it happening?

Although not all these questions will generate useful information for every paper, they are designed to cover most of the possibilities, especially if you use the basic questions in a variety of ways. Instead of simply asking the *Who?* or *Agent* question—"Who smokes?"—you can ask "Who does not smoke?" One possible answer: people who suffer eye and throat irritation and/or infections. Isn't most of the statistical evidence that is cited to support a ban on cigarettes based on data from people who smoked cigarettes with a high tar and nicotine content? What if they had smoked cigarettes with low tar and nicotine content? A question like "Who has a stake in the cigarette industry?" might generate economic arguments against banning cigarettes. "Why do people smoke?" might generate a number of productive responses. What effect would a ban on cigarette smoking have on individuals? Would it result in diet problems or in nervous disorders? Why *do* people smoke? As you ask these questions while examing your *For* and *Against* lists, you might generate notes like the ones shown in Figure 3.3.

The *pentad* is especially useful when you begin investigating your topic in magazines and journals. If, for example, you were examining an article that was pro-tobacco-industry (*Action*), it would be sensible to ask who wrote the article and check on the author's background (*Agent*). Why does the writer favor the tobacco industry (*Purpose*)? You might be swayed by the statistics used in the article only to discover they were supplied by the cigarette industry, which solicited the article in the first place.

The journalistic formula and the pentad have almost limitless possibilities for generating information, especially when you go beyond the simple "Who did it?" or "When did he/she do it?" to ask more complex questions. For example, the *Who?* or *Agent* question can also be "Who could have . . . ? Who should have . . . ? Who

FIGURE 3.3

Irritates eyes and throats of others

Cigarettes expensive — an unnecessary luxury

Psychological crutch

*** NEED STATISTICS ON HEALTH HAZARD — CHECK MAGAZINES

But smokers seem <u>unrelaxed</u> especially when they're dying for a cigarette

Nail biting

Economic disaster for huge tobacco industry — thousands would be out of work

Psychological crutches may be necessary — like Linus's blanket

Social acceptance, especially teen in groups

Helps you relax (say smokers)

will have . . . ? Who must have been . . . ? Who has . . . ? Who is . . . ? Who might have . . . ? Who will have been . . . ?" This approach to generating information can also be expanded by combining different *kinds* of questions. For example, if you combine agent and purpose, you might ask "Who objects to cigarette smoking and why?" or "Who is defending cigarette smoking and why?" Don't be discouraged if some of the questions you come up with produce information you cannot use. Learning to recognize and reject irrelevant information is as important a skill as selecting arguments and facts to support your thesis.

As you examine the latest version of your brainstorming sheet you will have further questions. Articles have to be read, statistics checked. But you will also be pretty confident. You have strong feelings toward your topic—ban cigarette smoking—and you have facts and details to back this assertion. It is now time to begin writing the paper. During the writing of your initial draft, don't hesitate over details. Formulate an overall plan of attack and go on. Rely on your *intuition* to guide you. Writers often refer to intuition as a mystical event. They struggle with a section of their writing, abandon it in frustration, and later inspiration strikes—a solution to their writing problem appears, seemingly from nowhere. Take advantage of such flashes of intuition happenings; they often prove to be the richest ideas in your paper.

Writing activity

Brainstorm a subject that interests you and create a brainstorming sheet. Then focus on your evidence, using a combination of the journalistic formula and the pentad. Using this second brainstorming sheet, organize your paper and write an initial draft. At the end of this initial draft, write down what further steps you would need to take to develop a substantial and interesting paper on this topic. You may want to choose one of the following general subjects:

capital punishment	**pollution**
crime	**poverty**
new-wave music	**small cars**
dormitories	**sports equipment**
jewelry	**women in the military**

THE INFORMATIVE PAPER

In college and in much writing done outside of college, the most common writing task is the *informative paper*. *Information*—facts, details, examples, statistics, reasons—is at the heart of expository writing. You have been learning to generate information from your experience, to focus on a topic, and to expand within the focus to develop a rich base of information. But information organized in lists or notes is not enough. You must also learn how to arrange that information, to develop an overall plan or strategy that lays the information out in an interesting and coherent way for your readers.

The basic strategy used in informative writing is the thesis and support formula. The word *thesis* means "main idea," the point, the guiding concept your paper sets out to develop. What we are talking about in this section, then, is a paper that presents a main idea, a point, a guiding concept (the thesis) and then develops, explains, or substantiates it (support).

The Thesis Statement

If you look back at the writing you did in Chapter 2, you may find that you never actually stated a thesis. But each composition you wrote had a guiding *idea* behind it. As you write more formally, a useful strategy is to turn your thesis idea into an explicit thesis statement.

The following informal introduction to a paper implies a thesis, though the writer doesn't come right out and state it:

I was never much for pulling pranks, breaking minor laws, or being plain mischievous. But, the Halloween of my junior year I upset my straight life and went out with the gang, equipped with filled water balloons, two-week-old eggs, and red, ripe tomatoes.
LANA EMBERS

There can be little doubt in the reader's mind that we are about to hear the tale of pranks and so forth that occurred on that Halloween. Lana doesn't have to come right out and say that is what she is going to tell us; she has raised the *expectation* of a story in our minds and that is all a storyteller has to do. However, in the somewhat more structured paper that follows, the writer introduces an argument, and comes much closer to stating his thesis outright.

In these days of women's liberation, with women screaming about being oppressed in a man's world, I would like to bring to light that, at least in one situation, women are definitely favored over men. It particularly bewilders me because they are favored in an area in which, from six years of personal experience, I have found them to be hopelessly inferior to men: driving an automobile. (I can just hear the protests now.)
ED PLATO

Ed's thesis illustrates the chief quality of a formal thesis statement—it is a statement that someone *could* disagree with or take exception to. Ordinarily, the main idea of a story is not referred to as a thesis for this reason: no one is expected to agree or disagree with a story (which is not the same thing as liking or disliking the story). The true formal thesis, then, is an arguable proposition, and Ed has stated clearly in his first sentence that women are favored over men in one area. However, Ed is not writing a completely objective, formal paper. He is giving a personal opinion, and so his thesis is informally stated. The reader needs both Ed's first and second sentences to discover that Ed thinks women are favored over men in the "area . . . of [driving]." At this point, most readers would want to know exactly what he means. It takes the next paragraph of Ed's paper for the reader to discover that Ed thinks women get out of traffic tickets more easily than men do. At this point, the reader has a full, formal statement of Ed's thesis, although Ed scattered the information through two paragraphs of his personal-opinion paper. Though Ed's thesis is not stated as formally as it could be, it is more formal than Lana's, which is not stated at all.

The full, formal thesis statement, then, is a single sentence that contains an arguable proposition and clearly states the author's position on the issue. In the following example, the full statement of the thesis appears in one sentence. Which one?

I grew up with the problem, and I never got used to it. Too many meals were ruined when my dad puffed smoke into my face, for me to forget. I'm happy that I survived the smoke-filled cars and stuffy rooms. A problem? Yes, tobacco smoke bothers me and I resent having to breathe it. For the good of everyone, cigarette smoking should be outlawed.
PETER GRANTZ

In Peter's introductory paragraph the formal, arguable thesis statement is, "For the good of everyone, cigarette smoking should be outlawed." And Peter's argument is a real one; very few people are unaffected by the smoking problem. The "formality" of the thesis is somewhat reduced because Peter is starting with firsthand, personal information, but the rest of his paper relies on facts and figures he has found in his reading. "Formal" here means that the thesis is stated in a certain form, namely, a single sentence containing an arguable proposition. When we say a paper has a formal statement of thesis, we are saying only that there *is* a thesis statement and that it is complete, versus the implied thesis or the scattered thesis.

As in the thesis, there are degrees of formality in the informative essay as a whole. When we talk about the informality or formality of an essay, we're talking not only about the thesis but about the kinds of ideas and the words and sentences used to express them, about the relative presence or absence of the author's voice, and so on. Informative essays can be quite informal, such as the paper about women drivers, or they can be rigorously formal, such as a research report on a scientific experiment. The thesis statement itself can be implied, presented informally, or fully and formally expressed.

For most college writing, you should strive for the semiformal paper, one that has a fully stated thesis (though that may sometimes be optional) but that is not as rigidly structured and impersonal as a government report. Until you become very confident of your writing, it's hard to write totally formal papers without sacrificing interest level. In fact, it takes high art to write both interesting and formal papers on complex subjects. Interesting writing isn't just a matter of picking "lively" words and adding anecdotes to your writing. A mature and well-crafted style certainly helps; nothing good can come from a paper in which the writer can't make his or her sentences behave. But as you move away from purely personal subjects, the amount and quality of the information itself will carry much of the interest.

Supporting the Thesis

Once you have a fair notion of your thesis, you can begin trying to structure your informative essay. This doesn't mean starting in on a rough draft yet, though you can try that if you are very confident of your subject; instead, it means putting together notes or a working outline. Not every writer uses outlining, and those who use the technique may not use it all the time. Very short and informal pieces probably don't need outlines, but as you work into longer and more formal writing, you may find that the outline—be it ever so rough and sketchy—is a very useful tool for getting over a hard problem: organizing your essay. Even if you are extremely confident that you have the whole essay in your head, it won't hurt to jot down a few key ideas; doing so may well show you some unexpected possibilities for your paper. A basic outline for the paper on smoking by Peter Grantz might look like this:

Outlaw Smoking
  I. **Smoking is harmful.**
 II. **Smokers suffer coronaries and lung cancer.**
III. **Nonsmokers suffer from passive smoking.**
 IV. **Everyone will benefit from a smoking ban.**

But this looks pretty skimpy. This outline is more harmful than helpful because it seems to say everything Peter wants to say and leaves nothing for the essay. It represents the main *ideas* in his essay, but it doesn't offer much structure for the essay. Worse, it doesn't generate any new ideas or information for Peter to use in his essay. We have to ask, "What do you mean? Where's your evidence?" When Peter asks those questions himself, and begins to think in terms of the essay he is going to write—as a composition that has an introduction and that proceeds in a certain fashion to a conclusion—he explores each of these ideas, breaks them down into smaller components, and produces a more detailed outline, one with additional information in it, like this:

Outlaw Smoking
I. Introduction
   A. Personal connection with topic
   B. Thesis statement: outlaw smoking
II. Why smoke
   A. For pleasure and status
   B. Ignore dangers
III. Dangers real for smokers
   A. Medical evidence
      1. Coronaries
      2. Lung cancer
   B. Smokers' acknowledgment of danger
      1. Men
      2. Women
IV. Danger to nonsmokers
   A. Passive smoking
   B. Carbon-monoxide poisoning
V. No escape for smokers or nonsmokers
   A. Need for nonsmoking areas
   B. Total ban most effective solution

Peter is being very careful to follow the "rules" of outlining he learned in high school. He has a Roman numeral for each of his major points. He has both an *A* and a *B* for each of his points. When he is using a sentence outline, as he did the first time around, all the statements are full sentences. And when he is using a topic outline, as he did the second time, he is consistent there too. Of course, if you are just making a scratch outline for your own benefit, you needn't be so neat and tidy. The point is not to see how attractive you can make your outline but to see whether your outline can help you put your paper together.

In this case, Peter probably could have written his paper without an outline, either planning in his head or revising from a rough draft. But it is also clear, in this case, that the outlining procedure can serve as a way to *find* the components of a thesis. And it is through this rough- or working-outline stage that you can begin to see the shape and substance of your essay—a necessary step to discovering whether you have enough supportive material to write the essay your thesis requires. The well-known student procedure of outlining *after* a paper is written is mostly part of an academic tradition in which students were forced to write outlines whether they needed them or not. Even after the paper is written, the outline might show you what kind of order and material your paper does have and might suggest areas where you need to shore up the composition with additional material.

The Thesis on Trial

In an informative paper, the most common way to support your thesis is with examples and reasons. Nothing is quite so effective as concrete evidence; in fact, if you think of your thesis as being *on trial* and yourself as the prosecuting attorney, you will have a very good image of the situation a thesis paper requires. You say your roommate is a savage? Very well, present your evidence: "His personal habits are filthy! He has no sense of order or neatness!" In any court of law, the attorney for the defense would shout, "Objection! You are stating opinions, drawing conclusions!" The jury (your audience) needs to see the evidence on which these opinions are founded: "He never washes, shaves, or changes his clothes. He never makes his bed. He dumps books, clothing, trash at random on bed, table, floor." Now we are getting closer to concrete reality. If you continue in this manner, *you* won't have to convince the jury; the evidence will do it for you.

In informative papers dealing with less personalized subjects, you may have to rely on the testimony of others: "My friends who speak Spanish tell me . . ."; or rely on observation: "We all watched as Benny jumped on the window ledge shouting that he was Captain Marvel . . ."; or rely on research: "The Pollution Control Board found . . . ." Wherever your information comes from, it is the concrete evidence the reader needs to see more than your generalizations, opinions, and conclusions. Concrete evidence is the one indispensable aspect of the informative paper.

Read the following informative paper. What is the thesis? Where is the thesis stated? Is there enough concrete detail to make the point? In other words, is the thesis adequately supported? What would you say this writer is doing right? Does the author analyze and explain his facts and examples in enough detail to show how they support his thesis?

MICHAEL KNAPP

A metallic hum, growing louder as it echoed off unseen walls, shattered the silence of my room. This hum was soon joined by the machinegunlike staccato of drums, and the effect was completed a moment later when a raspy voice wailed unintelligible words as if in pain. This senseless din was soon replaced by the sounds of car engines and tires squealing, accompanied by an obscenely husky voice and high-pitched cries of "Ooh-wah-oo" and "Sh-bop, sh-bop." This strange menagerie of sounds finally surrendered to the monotonous droning of violins and a long, sad moaning dripping with tears.

All of these, believe it or not, are examples of what is known to millions of Americans as rock and roll, or simply rock, which not only outsells every other kind of music, but has emerged "from a fifties teen subculture phenomenon to its present status as the dominant force in entertainment and the performing arts," according to John Burke in "A Look at 1973" (*American Libraries*, May 1974). This musical revolution has come to exert a powerful and far-reaching influence on the youth of today, an influence I fear is not as harmless as many seem to think; though the radical sixties are gone, rock has not yet released its all-encompassing hold on our society.

Surely one of the most obvious features of this influence is the tremendous amount of money generated by rock: over $2 billion was spent on pop music per year in the early 1970s, making this part of the recording industry quite lucrative. But the tremendous boost that this revenue gives to the economy is offset by other characteristics of a successful market: cutthroat competition and shady deals emerge in a trade that can supply a recording conglomerate with as much as a third of its total profits for a year. And an environment where such enormous profits are to be made inevitably attracts the criminally inclined, from the petty ripoff artist to organized crime, which controls an ever-increasing part of the scene.

Rock has also influenced quite strongly the way in which teens spend their money; rock music sells not only records and tapes, but also guitars and stereo equipment, and provides ample opportunities for the status seeker. Cars, the ultimate possession for a teen-ager, are being challenged by the complete stereo system and a massive record collection. Naturally, these stereo rigs, some of which would dwarf a computer in complexity, are providing many foreign companies the chance to saturate the market with their lower-priced components, giving them an edge on the homemade "Made in U.S.A." products.

Netting quite a sizable share of the action are the rock concerts, which, if the group is on tour, can gross as much as $9 million. These appearances give additional exposure to rock groups that otherwise would have to depend on the radio stations to sell their music; competition is fierce, and air play can make or break a song's chances for success. This risk is offset, however, by the possibilities of rapid stardom, with some performers attracting cults greater than those of Sinatra or Monroe in the forties and fifties. They are the new aristocracy of the entertainment world, and live much the way the Hollywood movie stars did, with real-estate investments and pension plans.

Because of the seemingly endless diversity of record styles, rock attracts many different kinds of listeners, and this has led, some critics argue, to a cheapness and theatricality that didn't exist before. Concerts have become mere light shows, with many groups dedicated more to out-sickening their opponents than to out-playing their music. With more and more performers bought and paid for, manipulation of them by the record companies has become common, resulting in "packaged" groups having no appeal other than that manufactured by promoters to "sell" the group to the public.

Rock brought more with it than mere commercialism, however. It gave a voice and the means for a whole new lifestyle to the dissatisfied antiwar generation. The key to understanding this movement, one author suggests, is in the music itself: the overamplified volume, electronic distortion and pulsing, driving beat create "passionate excitement" that carries the listener right into the music.

Rock also brought with it, through this total participation in the music, acceptance of drug use. Though there is the possibility of overdose, which can be fatal, the fear of this is lessened by the fact that both the musicians and one's companions are "high" so as to enjoy the experience more. One good thing about this is that there is relatively little trouble at rock concerts, as everyone is too doped up to care about anything around them other than the concert itself.

Musicians at these concerts increase the excitement by their antics on stage, and by their outlandish costumes. The nonconformist clothes and long hair signaled these people as the vanguard of the protest against society's standards. Also part of this protest was the notion of sexual freedom; words in songs mention love not between a man and woman, but a universal, brotherly love.

Rock, above all else, is a means of communication among today's younger generation. It unifies them and provides a means of relating not only to one's peers but to the world itself. As such, rock music has given teens a whole new culture of heroes to look up to, much different from those of their parents. Violence and money-grubbing pettiness are traits passed along by the modern supermen of the rock world. The subtleness of its influence is the most frightening aspect of rock, as it is seen to be desensitizing teens into adults bent on personal gratification above all else.

Rock music, because of its all-encompassing nature, poses not only mental issues, but physical ones. Because of its electronic aspects, rock music must be amplified many times, rock fans say, to be adequately appreciated. But continued exposure to these high-intensity sounds, according to research studies, causes irreversible hearing damage. A typical rock concert produces sound levels higher than those of a jet airliner on takeoff, and interestingly enough, it is not the electronically enhanced instruments themselves that pose the risk of ear damage, but the excessive sound pressure levels produced by the electronic systems. Rock concerts are not the only source of this damage, however; stereos blaring continually at top volume also produce similar pressure levels, which can eventually deafen the listener who gets used to high volumes.

This has proved to be a serious problem on college campuses where, in many places, rock obliterates "conversation, reason, and even genuine emotion," according to Russell Kirk in "Cacophony" (*National Review*, 12 Nov. 1976). Students can't concentrate to study, an exception being the quiet-study dorms, reserved for the exceptional student. Loud rock is addictive; some students find they cannot study without a stereo drowning out all other sounds. After all, they can't help it if they were raised that way.

It is clear that though rock music is beneficial to our society in a number of ways, its all-powering presence and the changes it has brought with it are of doubtful merit. Whether or not the teens of today really are being adversely affected by this music is hard to say, but the evidence certainly would seem to indicate that society is being led astray by the recording industry, which is concerned only with how much it can take. Let us hope that rock is the art form it is hailed to be, rather than another means to our own demise.

Michael's paper raises an interesting question about rock music. His thesis statement is in the second paragraph: "This musical revolution has come to exert a powerful and far-reaching influence on the youth of today, an influence I fear is not as harmless as many seem to think . . . ." You may not agree with Michael, but that is one of the requirements of a good thesis; it should raise an issue about which reasonable people could disagree.

As soon as readers know what the thesis is, they expect to hear some evidence. On what grounds can rock be seen as harmful? Michael immediately begins to illustrate with examples: the involvement of organized crime, the exploitation of teen-aged consumers, the "packaging" and "selling" of performers by record companies, and other things, not the least of which is the possible physical impairment caused by the deafening volume of the music.

The paper ends with a concluding paragraph in which Michael reiterates the thesis and the compelling nature of the evidence. About his evidence we can say that some of it many readers would challenge but that on the whole the argument gains believability because Michael quotes from some of his reading; there is more evidence here than just personal opinion. The key to Michael's success is the amount and quality of the information he supplies his readers.

Note the introductory paragraph. Many readers prefer to have the thesis statement appear in the first paragraph of the paper. Others will enjoy Michael's "dramatic incident" as a means of capturing reader interest. (See Chapter Six for interesting and effective ways to begin an essay.)

There are trivial and nontrivial ways to approach the informative paper. Putting together a thesis on the basis of the available examples is usually a trivial approach. A writer who quickly comes up with three or four pet peeves and then creates a thesis like "I Have a Number of Pet Peeves" is making weary work for him- or herself and for the reader too. The best approach is to assume that you and your readers are taking part in a transaction of *reason*. To understand that statement, you should think about the motives behind your writing. What is the *purpose* for a reasoned approach to readers? Generally, the writer perceives some wrong, some deficiency, or some problem that affects not only the writer but the reader as well. The thesis can be worded in terms of a good or a benefit ("There Are Many Benefits to Be Gained from Going to Church"), but the implication is that people are not taking advantage of the good or not appreciating it enough. At the invention stage for an informative paper, consciously set up a search procedure to find a subject you think your readers will benefit from.

The intention of the informative paper is to *analyze* and *explain* the problem. Your objective is to convince your reader that the problem is as you say it is; and the way to accomplish that is to explain without seeming either to argue with the reader or to bias the evidence. You should back up your ideas with clear, concrete evidence so that your reader will not only understand the problem but will trust in your ability to present it objectively.

And last, but most important of all, your thesis should pass the "So what?" test. If you were to say to your readers, "I'm thinking of writing about *X* and I plan to defend the following thesis . . . ,"and they answered "So what?" then clearly you don't have a topic or thesis worth writing about. If, on the other hand, some agree and others disagree with your thesis and most seem to be interested in the topic, then you probably have the makings of a worthwhile informative paper.

Read the following paper. Does it pass the "So what?" test? Does the author support her thesis adequately? Does her evidence seem to be both reliable and convincing?

Dial O—for Service?

SUSAN ADAMS

An issue that may seem quite minute to most people is becoming increasingly important to me . . . with the loss of every shiny nickel. The issue to which I am referring is my problem with public pay phones and telephone operators. The rising amount of trouble I am having has made it necessary for me to try to express my argument on paper, possibly to decide whether I have an argument at all.

I would like to start off by saying that I realize that the job of an operator is bound to be extremely hectic, with all the customers they serve every hour. They are expected to calmly handle just about any emergency that may arise. I give them full credit for all the lives they have undoubtedly helped to save. I do not hold them at all responsible for any breakdown of the public pay phones, because they too are victims of the machine and the "telephone system." Their fast thinking and patience, I'm sure, have saved many a day. They've had to deal with all types of people and more than likely a million prank calls. They deserve much admiration and respect for a job such as theirs.

Being at Central has created the need for me to be in more contact than ever before with telephone operators. Unfortunately, I've had several unpleasant encounters with these people recently. One of these happened a few weeks ago when I unsuccessfully tried to call home to Saginaw, Michigan. I was excited to call and I rushed down to the pay phone in the Beddow Hall lobby. After secluding myself in the booth, I placed my platinum coin into the slot and dialed O. It *rang* and *rang* and *rang* and no one ever answered! I almost laughed out loud because I've never heard of the operator not being home. The idea was absurd! I replaced the receiver, thinking that I must have done something wrong, and was decidedly thankful I didn't have a fire or some type of emergency. I couldn't understand it—my quarter wasn't coming back to me either. I pressed the coin return a couple of times. Nothing happened, and tension was starting to mount. Oh well, be patient, I decided; you can't win 'em all. I inserted another quarter and dialed the O again, and finally after at least eight to ten rings someone answered.

"Operator," a woman's sharp voice stated.

"Yes. I just called you and no one was home."

"No one was home!" (tee hee)

"What I mean is that no one ever answered and I let it ring a good number of times, and also I never received my quarter back."

"That's impossible, Miss. Besides, if no one answered you, as you claim, your money would have been automatically returned to you. I'll try the coin return from here. Nope, sorry ma'am, no money was put in on your end," she replied very dryly.

I was starting to feel like I was in a sinking ship, and I was just too tired to try and bail out. Somehow from the way it looked, I didn't stand half a chance anyway.

"Well, I guess I'll just place a long distance call to Saginaw, Michigan, then. . . ."

After the connection was made, some fool had to be on the line at my house, gabbing, I'm sure. Exasperated, I went back to my room, and a short while later I called my folks collect, right from my room, hassle-free, but thirty cents more per minute than if I had called direct. (You can't call long distance directly from the dorm rooms.) I was never one to think that one *bad apple* spoiled the whole bunch, but situations of this nature have been happening so frequently as of late that it is close to the point of being ridiculous.

Another example to which I would like to refer points specifically at the phone company, not at the operator, because she has no control over this aspect. Last week, on a chilly, drizzly, dark evening, I went down to the lobby, maintaining a positive attitude to make another call. Shoot! This phone was OUT OF ORDER! Well, at least that meant that people wouldn't get rooked for a little while, but I also found out that the phones in Thorpe, Merrill and Sweeney were out as well. These were the three closest phones to me, and venturing out across campus into the vast darkness, alone in the pouring rain, didn't sound exactly appealing. It has been a week now, and all four of them are still not fixed! I asked the girl at the desk if she had any idea when they might be in use again and she replied, "Who knows? With the run-around we've been getting from the phone company, it might be Christmas."

One other quick example I would like to mention is another time when an operator was somewhat rude to me. First of all, I had to repeat to her three times the number that I wanted her to dial for me. 1–517–5552041, 1–517–5552041, 1–517–5552041. When the call had been completed, she came back on the line and commanded, "Stay on the line for your charges!" After she told me what I owed for the call, I immediately deposited the correct amount of money into the slot and I nicely thanked her for her assistance. Without even a "You're welcome," she just hung up on me, like it was a headache for her to even serve me at all.

Altogether now I've lost about $2 to $3 and I feel somewhat bothered every time I think of these numerous incidents. I've talked to a lot of others who have had just as much trouble, if not more, with making outgoing calls. I realize that a lot of these difficulties are completely out of the control of the operator, and it would not be fair or right to blame her for any failing of the mechanical end of the "system." I must say, too, that I have talked to some very nice operators who seemed fully competent. There really is no definite party in the "wrong" in this case. There are faults on both sides, and I know I'm much too impatient; but sometimes I just feel that we "well-paying" customers deserve more satisfying service.

Writing activity

For your first informative paper, think about wrongs, problems, faults, and so on, that need correcting. You may immediately think of starvation, health problems, energy shortages, or any of the other major problems in the world today, but these are all very big problems and require very big papers to deal with them satisfactorily. For a paper of three to six pages, restrict your thesis to something much less comprehensive than the whole energy crisis. The "size" of any thesis is determined by the amount of evidence needed to illustrate it. If you were in court, how much evidence would it take to convince the jury that international oil interests were ma-

nipulating the oil supply to create artificial shortages? The thesis is too big and too complex to attempt without a great deal of evidence. On the other hand, how much would it take to convince your readers that the price of gasoline has gone up at an extremely high rate of increase?

The key to the informative paper is working out a clear thesis, one you can illustrate with a few examples that you can analyze and explain in a short paper. You may want to choose a topic from the list that follows. Some of these topics can be used just as they are worded. Others can be further broken down to even more restricted statements. For example, "TV Commercials Create Distorted Views of Life" could be focused even further to "TV Commercials Create an Unnatural Concern about Body Odors."

College is Expensive
College is Not Barrier-Free for Handicapped Students
Lawn Care Is Not Easy Work
Attack Dogs Do Not Make Good Pets
It Takes Know-How to Buy a Used Car
Co-ed Dormitories Do Not Promote Sex
TV Dramas Depend on Stereotypes
TV Commercials Use a Variety of Appeals to the Viewer
TV Commercials Create Distorted Views of Life
Film Violence Has Become Excessive
It Is Easy to Make a Bad Film
Dress Reveals Personality
Punk Rock is Junk Rock
Reading Fiction Is a Great Pleasure
Discrimination Is Not Dead in Our Society
Factory Work Is Boring
Taking Care of a Two-Year-Old Is Not for Amateurs
Newspapers Have Become Too Commercial
Young Adults Do Not Care about Politics
The Dentist's Office Is Itself Intimidating
Superheroes Act Out Our Adolescent Fantasies
Campus Crime Is on the Rise

STRATEGIES OF EXPOSITION

If you were to examine a number of informative essays, you would discover that they were *developed* in a variety of ways. Writers use different *strategies* to support their theses. One writer might have spent time carefully defining key terms; another might have found it necessary to classify different attributes; another might have explained a process in some detail, and still another might have found it useful to compare and contrast two ideas or objects. Some writers may use two or three of these strategies or methods of development in one essay. To *classify, define, compare,* and/or *contrast* are important strategies in writing because they reflect the way the human mind works. These are the systems of thought we use to make sense of what we experience.

Although you'll learn about and practice these strategies of expository writing separately, it is important to remember that much writing involves a *combination* of strategies. For example, if you were to write a paper comparing flagella and cilia, you might define each term first, then describe physical characteristics, then classify the functions of each, and compare on the basis of physical characteristics and function. Your paper's overall purpose should determine the strategies you use.

COMPARISON AND CONTRAST

A basic skill in writing and thinking is the ability to compare one thing to another. To compare means to show both similarities and differences, and the purpose of comparison is *discovery*. Often we do not realize how much we value something until we compare it with something else. Sometimes we discover something surprising through comparison. Confronted with just one object, we can learn a lot through dissection. If you take a cuckoo clock apart, you will discover how that cuckoo clock works. But if you compare a cuckoo clock with an electric clock, you may discover not only information about clocks but something about science and civilization as well.

There is no limit to the application of this skill. On the physical level, comparisons bring new insights to descriptive writing. On a higher level, the comparison of points of view, evidence, and arguments is fundamental to argumentative, philosophical, and research writing. We would not have advanced as far in technology as we have without the ability to compare one thing to another, new information with old, one experiment with another.

Observation is a significant aspect of the process of comparing and contrasting. To the casual observer, two chairs, two flowers, even two cats look very much alike; to the skilled writer, tiny differences may reveal a story or an idea. Notice in the following paper how observation brings out details and turns something as commonplace as a quilt into a study of contrasts.

Something Special

TRACY ROOT

Neatly folded and tucked up into the top shelf of my closet lies my old quilt. Evenly spread out over my bed lies my colorful new quilt. Both are very beautiful but their uniqueness is quite different.

My new quilt is very colorful. Yellows and blues, greens and pinks are evenly printed over it in shapes of diamonds. Inside the diamonds are printed flowers and polka dots.

My old quilt is also colorful, but it isn't because of the printed colors on it. Little green bows peek out of it in certain spots. It's colorful because of the different patches of materials on it. There are checkered and plaid patches. Some of them have Raggedy Ann dolls printed on them. One of the green patches has a snag on it from my dog jumping off my bed. There's a faded pink stain on another part of it from the time I spilled my Kool-aid on it. I wasn't even supposed to be drinking it in my room!

On my old quilt, each patch on it was cut and stitched by hand, my mother's. I remember watching her take some of the clothes I had outgrown and carefully cut them apart in neat little squares. I wasn't very happy about it then, but now I think it was a very neat idea. I can lie down on it and study the different patches, remembering which dresses and skirts they came from.

My new quilt is stitched precisely in the right spots, but that is because it was done with a machine. It's very neat and all, but it doesn't hold the same personal value for me.

All of the stuffing inside my new quilt is evenly spread. There isn't a bump or a bulge anywhere on the entire quilt. It almost seems too perfect.

My old quilt is lumpy all over; the warm fluffy stuffing is very thick in some spots and very thin in others. It shows how much it has been used.

My old quilt is tucked up into my closet so that it won't get worn out. I want to be able to show my children one of the many things my mother has done for me. It makes me feel warm just thinking about it because I know it was put together by my mother with a lot of love and care. I really like my new quilt, but my old one will always be my favorite.

Tracy's paper is a good example of close observation and attention to detail leading to discovery. The two quilts aren't *just* different. The old quilt, because it is handmade, has become an heirloom, an object with special family meaning, to be handed on from generation to generation. Furthermore, Tracy's paper amounts almost to an argument—that the old quilt is better than the new one. Looking at two sides of an issue is indeed the structure of an argument. You can see, then, why it is important to become skilled in comparing and contrasting: this is the beginning of the process that eventually becomes *affirming* and *denying*, or arguing and counterarguing, in formal writing. Here, for example, is a writer deliberately setting out to *argue* by means of comparison and contrast:

Living in Town . . . No Thanks!

JOHN SALATINO

If I had a choice of living in town or in the country, I'd pick the country, and I think you should too. Even though some people can't choose where they want to live, others do have the choice of picking one of these two areas to settle in, a very important question for those who are spending their life savings building that "dream house," or a newly wed couple who want the best possible environment for raising their children. This decision of where to live is one that will most likely affect us all at one time or another.

Living in town does have some advantages over living in the country. Kids can usually make friends within their own block. Mother can visit the neighborhood store for groceries whenever they are needed and also visit other wives daily for coffee. Of course, Dad too finds the relaxing atmosphere of the nearest bar a good place to escape from the noise and confusion of the home. Usually lots are small, and the work on lawns, gardens, and so on, is minimal, leaving more free time available. Schools and public facilities, such as tennis courts, are quite near and can be reached easily, eliminating the need for parents to drive their children to Little League games or any type of extracurricular activities in which they may be involved.

The country has its share of advantages as well. By tradition, country life has been a simple life, and is basically that today—plenty of space, trees, and green grass. Nature is all the more present, and the change of seasons is spelled out by the surrounding countryside. The facts of life are learned more readily and naturally by children as they joyfully watch animals of forest and farm. Even though some people find the country life lonely and desolate, others find it relaxing and gain a sense of freedom from it. Even though there is more work involved with country life, it provides a good chance for a father to get his hands dirty and take pride in his house and lawn, rather than spending an hour at Joe's Bar. The children can pitch in, learning both to work and live together, rather than hanging around the malt shop all day. Mom too can use the time she might have spent having coffee at a friend's in caring for and helping her children. Then, when the time does come to visit a neighbor, this simple expression of friendship becomes a more meaningful gesture. The same is true for the kids: when a friend visits, it is a special occasion. The fact of living so far from town, and that the parents must drive their kids everywhere, only reemphasizes that the family must do more work in less time. To do this they must work as a unit, learning to get along with one another. After all, there is only one way to live, together . . . in the country.

In the following paper, the author sets out to depict the decline of one of the greatest boxers of all time. An obvious way to do this would have been to tell the story of Ali's rise and fall in chronological order, to begin with the young, powerful, lightning-fast Ali and show how he gradually deteriorated. Instead Larry Bedesky chooses to begin not at the beginning but at the end of Ali's career and to contrast the aging, beaten champion with his former self. How effective is Larry's essay? Does he win the reader's sympathy for Ali?

Ali Then—and Now

LARRY BEDESKY

"That's it. It's over," trainer Angelo Dundee screamed to referee Richard Green as Muhammad Ali slumped on his stool in the corner of the boxing ring. Ali tried to lift his head to protest but was too weak to do so. Instead, he sat motionless, with horrible welts under both his half-shut eyes, a steady trickle of blood coming from his puffy nose, and every ounce of energy drained from his thirty-eight-year-old body. Ali, who had been heavyweight champion of the world three times, had just foolishly attempted to acquire the championship an unprecedented fourth time by taking on the thirty-one-year-old, 211-pound, and superbly conditioned current champion, Larry Holmes. The fight against Holmes was the final crack in the erosion of Muhammad Ali's career. Ali had been fighting an uphill battle to retain his skills ever since his third fight with Joe Frazier, appropriately called "the thrilla' in Manila," in October of 1975. The Frazier fight seemed to sap the last bit of greatness from Ali, and he was never the same awesome fighter afterwards.

In his prime—from 1965 to 1967—and up until his third fight with Frazier, Ali needed motivation to produce greatness. When Ali seemed to be missing his punches or was less than expected, it was because of boredom and complacency. Ali claimed that he had trouble with lesser opponents like Rudi Lubbers, George Chuvalo, and Doug Jones because he had lacked the motivation, desire, and pressure to produce what he called "the real Muhammad Ali."

But since the Frazier fight, Ali had experienced a steady decline. Today it is years—not boredom—which have taken away Muhammad Ali's skills. Ali trained vigorously for the Holmes fight, losing over thirty pounds, quite possibly too much weight loss, in preparing for the fight. Just months before the fight, Ali was a blubbery 256 pounds. His flabby arms and legs, a portly gut which protruded inches out and which sagged to below his waist, and graying hair gave Ali the appearance of an unemployed, Schlitz-loving, middle-aged man.

For the Holmes fight, Ali trained to look like a Greek God. His portly gut was now trim, and his frame was sleek, thin, and muscle-toned. His gray hair was gone because Ali dyed it black prior to the fight. Ali thought that if he looked to be ten years younger, he would fight like he was ten years younger.

What Ali failed to realize was that he was still a thirty-eight-year-old man, no matter what he looked like. Ali's Greek-God frame turned out to be only a front; the thirty pounds he lost took away the strength and stamina he needed to put up a good fight against Holmes.

During the Holmes fight it was evident that Ali had lost the amazing speed, quickness, and strength which made him rank as one of the greatest heavyweights of all time. In his prime Ali fought like no heavyweight ever before. Ali circled and stalked all of his opponents, even excellent fighters like Sonny Liston, Floyd Patterson, and Frazier, deftly whipping his powerful left hand jab at unsuspecting adversaries at any time, with the quickness and accuracy of a champion lightweight. Ali used the jab to set up his vast repertoire of equally destructive punches. With the jab Ali could bring his upper cut up to the vulnerable jaw of his opponent, snapping the rival's head back to the point where he was looking straight up at the lights of the arena. Also off of the jab Ali could throw a hook or a right cross. When Ali landed these punches solidly, the result was usually the same: the opponent's mouthpiece would spiral out of the ring and into the third row of awe-struck spectators.

Ali's power was unquestioned. When he knocked out Sonny Liston for a second time to remain heavyweight champion in June of 1965, *Sports Illustrated*'s Tex Maule wrote these words (it should be noted that Muhammad Ali was known as Cassius Clay, his birthname, then. He changed his name for religious reasons): "The knockout punch itself was thrown with the amazing speed that differentiates Clay from any other heavyweight. . . . The blow had so much force it lifted Liston's left foot, upon which most of his weight was resting, well off the canvas. It also was powerful enough to drop him instantly—first to his hands and knees and then over on his back."

His jab, which sliced through the air like a machete slicing down a blade of grass, made Ali a nearly untouchable adversary. As he leaned away from opponents' punches, letting their powerful fists narrowly miss his unscathed face, Ali would taunt his opponent, "You ain't never gonna' hit this pretty face."

After the thrilla' in Manila, Ali used the jab less and less, and it became more and more ineffective. Against Holmes, the jab, when it rarely connected, didn't even make Holmes flinch. When Holmes realized that Ali's jab was weak, he knew that he could move in because Ali didn't have a searing jab to keep him away. Holmes drove Ali into the corners, forcing Ali to cover up with his eyes closed, his elbows out, and his arms in front of his face, all the while praying to Allah that he didn't get blasted. Holmes stalked his prey mercilessly, battering Ali almost at will. The only thing that kept Ali off the canvas was his unrelenting will and determination, which he had kept over the years. After the tenth round Angelo Dundee called an end to the fiasco, ridding Ali of more pain and sorrow.

When reflecting upon Ali's career and seeing the decline of Ali after his third fight with Joe Frazier, one has to wonder how correct Ali was when he said after the fight, "I'm tired of bein' the whole game. Let other guys do the fightin'. You might never see Ali in the ring again."[1]

[1] *Sports Illustrated*. October 13, 1975.

Writing the Comparison and Contrast Paper

Before you decide to sit down and write a comparison of two friends, two cars you have owned, two places you have visited, think through the subject: what are the points of comparison and contrast? What will be the outcome?

Some things are easier to work with than others. The bigger the subject is, the longer your paper must be to treat the subject adequately. Comparing Europe and America is doomed from the outset, no matter how well you know both places. You would do well to limit your first effort at comparison to physical objects: two chairs, two shoes, two hands, for example. Comparing the old with the new, as Tracy did in her paper on quilts, is a popular approach; compare your new car with your old one, your new home with the previous one, and so on.

The most important aspect of any comparison and contrast paper is *purpose:* why you are comparing and contrasting in the first place. If you chose to compare a duck and an elephant to show how different these two creature are, your readers would ask "So what?" Although there are indeed similarities and differences between these two creatures, the similarities and differences are obvious and not very interesting. The comparison would fail to enrich the readers' understanding; nothing new would have been discovered. An effective comparison and contrast paper should provide the reader with a fresh insight.

Organization   There are three possible ways to structure a comparison and contrast paper: comparison of the parts, comparison of the wholes, and a combination of parts and wholes. Although some subjects seem to lend themselves more to one method than the others, each is an acceptable method of organization.

Comparison of the parts involves dividing your subjects into discrete categories and comparing each category, as Tracy did in her paper about quilts. This method is more sophisticated than the second approach, comparison of the wholes, which involves first saying everything you intend to say about one thing and then doing the same for the other. John used this method to compare country and city life. First he described town life; then he described country life. Some readers find this an unsatisfactory plan because it requires too much effort on their part; especially in long essays, it requires them to remember too much at once. The last possibility is to combine patterns so that sometimes you compare parts and sometimes wholes, as Larry did in his paper about Ali. This is the most complex and often the most sophisticated pattern of all, demanding the most deliberate planning by the writer. And yet it is usually the most productive use of comparison and contrast because it allows you to discover insights about your subject at all levels.

What was the writer's purpose in the following paper? How did she organize the paper to achieve that purpose? Does she provide the reader with enough evidence to support her thesis? What are the strengths of Renee's paper?

Freddie

RENEE CARSON

Stuffed animals make great companions for small children. When I was a little girl, accumulating them became my most recognized pastime. By the age of five, I had acquired ownership of a ferocious orange lion, an eight-foot-long scaly snake, a bright red puppy, a furry yellow kitten, and a lime green frog with orange eyes and pink cheeks. It didn't take long for him to become my favorite. No matter where I went, I would undoubtedly take Freddie with me. During long car rides he sat on my lap, or in bed he lay at the bottom of my pillow.

On my seventh birthday, my family went to Ohio on a vacation, and I lost Freddie. We had stayed in a hotel. I thought I had packed Freddie in my suitcase before we left. When I got home to unpack him, he wasn't there. I cried over his loss, as I would have for a true friend. To me he was more than a stuffed animal, he was a companion. My mother bought me another frog thinking it would replace Freddie, but it never did.

Freddie had orange fluorescent eyes the size of Ping-Pong balls, and bright pink cheeks the size of quarters that made him look as if he were continuously smiling. His face resembled the painted face of a circus clown. There's an unending smile that gives you a warm and cheerful feeling when you look at it.

Due to frequent handling, his fur was flattened and severely spotted. His face was chocolate covered, resulting from a candy bar being ground into his nose. My girlfriend thought she'd be friendly and try to share it with Freddie. His back was stained from red pop that had been dropped onto the floor, and which consequently splattered over Freddie. You could say that, overall, his whole body was dirt covered.

My new frog was larger and fuzzier. Its thick fur was dark green, and had black patches that nicely blended in. Its large eyes sparkled when the light hit them, reflecting the colors of the rainbow. It was constructed in such a way that it appeared to be ready to leap away at any given moment.

Freddie's body had been stuffed with soft, crushable foam, where my new one was filled with hard beans the size of small pellets. But the biggest difference was the smile. When I looked at my new frog, I didn't see a happy, friendly face as I had on Freddie; I saw a sparkly eyed normal frog. There was no warmth in its face, just a sober fixed expression.

On the other hand, they both had a wide, shiny ribbon tied around the neck. Somewhere I had heard that ribbons were a sign of good luck. And even though no one else seemed to believe it, I had my mind made up and no one could change it. I also thought the bigger the ribbon was, the better the luck would be. So directly after each frog had been purchased, I had my mother tie as wide a ribbon as could be found around their necks, and they were never to be removed.

Like many small children, when I cried I liked to cuddle against something that was soft and warm. This is where both Freddie and my new frog were useful. I would bury my tear-stained face into its small body and weep.

They were both a source of security for me. Most small children have a blanket or a special doll that they like to take to bed with them. But I was attached to my frog, and I would faithfully take it along. They were the most devoted friends I had. If I had something to get off my chest, I would pour out my problem in great detail to them. I knew they couldn't hear, but just expressing my feelings always made me feel better.

It's strange how inanimate objects can have special meaning to certain people. Some people idolize money, while others idolize jewels. But to me, at the time, it was my frog.

You can see from Renee's paper the effect of a sophisticated arrangement pattern; it has so much variety that the pattern tends to fade away from the attention of the reader. As Renee moves from one thing to another, the reader simply follows along, unaware that Renee sometimes refers to the parts, sometimes to the wholes. Renee's paper demonstrates her considerable skill at observing—or at least remembering   details, but it also demonstrates her skill with sentences. She seems to be in complete control of her sentences, easily generating both long and short ones. The first sentence of her third paragraph is twenty-nine words long, full of colorful details, and it rolls along in a smooth, flowing rhythm. Notice the emphasis achieved by the shorter sentence that follows this one, expanding on the idea of Freddie's smile: "His face resembled the painted face of a circus clown."

Anything can be compared, even unrelated things, but you don't need to *strain* the comparison. (It would take a very nimble mind to make an easy comparison between dirty socks and a bottle of milk.) However, you may be surprised at what you can do with *analogy*— comparison of unlike things. An old man and an old car, for example, may produce interesting parallels. As long as two things have at least one major quality in common, you may be able to compare them meaningfully.

You might, for example, compare two points of view about the same object:

Carsickness   MARTHA GRAHAM

Until I met Dan I never appreciated the beauty of cars. To me, a car was a necessity for transportation and an unpleasant one at that, as I am extremely susceptible to car sickness. Dan, however, saw them as objects to be examined, criticized, admired, and appreciated. He looked at cars like a connoiseur looks at masterpieces in the Louvre.

Where I saw four round black tires, Dan saw wide ovals or slicks. What I called hubcaps he called mags or chrome reverses. As I would admire the color of a car, Dan would specify the paint job as being either pearled, candy appled, metal flaked, or factory. While I would cover my ears and cringe as a Corvette roared by, Dan would say, "Listen to the size of that engine!" or "It must have an over-sized cam." I detested the admiration and respect in his eyes as he watched it scream around a corner and disappear in a cloud of exhaust.

Little did I realize that there was more to an exhaust system than a muffler, until Dan bought some headers. I still don't understand their purpose, although they were patiently explained to me time and again.

I laughed when I saw a car with its rear jacked; I never saw anything look more ridiculous. I came to the conclusion that having a car tilted at a thirty-degree angle was the stylish thing to do. A lecture endowing me with the information of the purposes and functions of airlifts left me not only entirely bored but completely confused.

One thing that Dan and I both enjoyed about cars was speed. Only we both had different reasons for this enjoyment. I wanted to go fast so that the destination would be reached before I got sick. Dan drove for the pure thrill of power and control over a throbbing machine. I guess speed was our common denominator.

I dated Dan through a 1964 Chevy Supersport, a 1971 Nova, a GTO, and an MG Midget. As Dan's interest in cars increased, our relationship declined. Dan was sure he had educated me fully on the subject of cars. What can I say . . . I'm carsick.

Or you might present a shift in viewpoint while contrasting two individuals.

Dad   KEVIN STOTTS

The black pirate patch covered his left eye. But no hook extended from his sleeve, no parrot rested on his shoulder. The "pirate," my father, wore the patch to cover an eye blinded from a car accident. Another man had been killed, but Dad didn't talk about his feelings then. And for the last twenty-six years he hasn't even brought up the accident or his feelings.

Two years after the accident I watched tensely as my father flew into a rage the night he was served with a legal summons which required him to stay at least 100 feet away from my Uncle Gail after threatening to kill him. Cuss words roared out of his mouth; he kicked a can, stones, anything in his way; and his anger forced tears to roll down his face.

I never felt comfortable being his son. He fought in a war; I applied for conscientious objector status. He ended our dogs' old failing lives by shooting them himself with a .22; I'd never consider anything but a veterinarian's lethal shot. He speaks few words; I hardly ever shut up. He is content doing nothing; I am usually busy. He hated high school and especially English; I enjoy writing.

He wasn't a great athlete but he did play varsity tennis in high school and coached Little League when I was growing up. I never had the confidence or coordination to be the athlete he wanted me to be. He even made me sit on the bench most games. And until I coached a city league championship softball team, I don't think he believed I had any sports potential at all.

This same man, however, taught me how to cast for smallmouth bass and fish for northern pike on our annual two week trip to Breevort Lake in Michigan. He taught me how to whistle with my hands so that no matter where I was I could respond to his whistle, letting him know I was safe.

When I was ten Dad stopped my brother and me after getting off the bus, took us to the garage, and told us Mom had cancer. He had tears in his eyes, but controlled his emotions so carefully, correctly, manly.

Without as much control, he cried at my wedding and cried the day my wife, Sue, and I left his home after our first visit with Krysten, our new daughter and his first grandchild. It was that same day that he kissed Sue for the first time.

I've grown more like him. You should hear the swearing fly from my mouth when some idiot is in front of me when I'm driving. And Dad's changed, too. His proper male armor melts when Krysten smiles and says, "I love you, Poppie."

I hope someday I can tell him I love him, too.

Writing activity

Write a comparison and contrast paper of from three to six pages. Think about the points of comparison and/or contrast of the two things you choose for your topic. Think too about your thesis—the point of the comparison—whether or not you decide to state the thesis formally. Your paper should provide your readers with a fresh insight as a result of your comparison. Try to generate as much information as possible before you begin to organize the paper.

You may find one of the topics from the following list useful:

two short poems	two hats
two photographs	two styles of skating
two roles for an actor	two personalities
two cars	two seasons
two attitudes toward truth	two teaching styles
two paintings	two characters in a novel
two guns	two television commercials
two typewriters	two pets
two editorials	two views of yourself
two rooms	two people at a movie

CLASSIFICATION

Classification is the means by which the mind groups experiences into types. The mind cannot handle very many unrelated ideas, objects, or events. It is necessary to find some pattern, some common property in order to catalog many separate things into a smaller number of *types* of things. For example, we can discuss singers because we can classify singers as sopranos, tenors, basses, and so forth, and also as classical, rock, country, and a number of other things. Thus, classification is really a basic skill of analysis. This may seem perfectly obvious as long as you are talking about familiar subjects (like singers), but suppose you were talking about nonhuman singers. The high-pitched squeals, whistles, grunts, and clicks of the humpback whale are called songs. If you were faced with the job of analyzing whale singers you would see immediately how important it is to be able to group, sort, divide, and catalog these apparently random noises:

When you go out to listen to a humpback sing, you may hear a whale soloist, or you may hear seeming duets, trios, or even choruses of dozens of interweaving voices. Each of these whales is singing the same song, yet none is actually in unison with the others—each is marching to its own drummer, so to speak.

ROGER PAYNE, "Humpbacks: Their Mysterious Songs," *National Geographic,* January 1979

There is nothing very obvious about the number of whales making noises, and it is no simple analysis to discover that each whale is singing the same song out of synchronization with the others. And there is nothing mechanical about the act of classifying. Classification is a creative analytical procedure. Consider the English alphabět we all learn as children. We usually divide the letters into consonants and vowels but make no other classifications. Yet linguists have discovered some intriguing classifications that look like this:

GROUP I	GROUP II	GROUP III
P, B, M	T, D, N	F, V

There are several other groups (for the other letters of the alphabet) derived from the same principle of classification. Most people say, at least at first, that they cannot see what the letters in each group have in common; the classification is not immediately obvious. With a little time to study the groups, people begin to see the basis for the grouping. For example, the letters in group I represent sounds made by bringing the upper and lower lips together (bilabial). The letters in group II represent sounds made by touching the tip of the tongue to the roof of the mouth near the teeth. And as you have probably guessed by now, the letters in group III also represent sounds made a certain way.* In short, linguists have discovered an important principle: we can classify the sounds of our language (and all languages) according to the way they are produced.

Ultimately, then, classification can be a powerful tool for *invention*. Classification is related to comparison and contrast: the close analysis of separate items may produce a concept that can govern them. The principle of classification we "find" (invent) is equivalent to an *idea* about the items. Thus you should think of classification not just as a pattern for organizing a paper but as an instrument or procedure by which you may be able to invent an idea for a paper. The *power* of classification to reduce extraordinary amounts of data to manageable categories is illustrated by a space-age event in 1977:

. . . two extraordinary spacecraft called Voyager were launched to the stars. After what promises to be a detailed and thoroughly dramatic exploration of the outer solar system from Jupiter to Uranus between 1979 and 1086, those space vehicles will slowly leave the solar system—emissaries of Earth to the realm of the stars. Affixed to each Voyager craft is a gold-coated copper phonograph record as a message to possible extraterrestrial civilizations that might encounter spacecraft in some distant space and time. Each record contains 118 photographs of our planet, ourselves, and our civilization; almost 90 minutes of the world's greatest music; an evolutionary audio-essay on "The Sounds of Earth"; and greetings in almost sixty human languages (and one whale language). . . .
CARL SAGAN et al., "Preface," *Murmurs of Earth*

The extraordinary *Voyager* recording will undoubtedly outlast the earth and all its civilization. Long before any alien race is likely to find the recording, earth will have been gone for eons. The message is just a fraction of the possible messages we might send out to the stars, just a few photographs out of all the archives of the world, a few fragments of music out of all that has ever been recorded. The selection of the pieces to be included—and excluded—was a monumental job of analysis and decision-making. If the task were yours, which pictures would you send, what music? Indeed, which languages would you select from the approximately 3,000 now known to exist? To answer this question, Carl Sagan and the others on the project had to derive some principles for selection, some system for classifying the great numbers of items they had to select from. For the full story of how the project was completed, you should read the book *Murmurs of Earth;* all we can say here is that in the end, the

*The sounds are produced by placing the upper teeth on the lower lip.

Voyager record contained what was hoped would be a representative sampling of earth pictures and music and languages.

However, the *Voyager* project illustrates the primary function of classification: the analysis and sorting of large numbers of items into groups and types. It is by sorting into groups that we reduce large numbers to smaller and more readily manipulable sets. At any university, for example, there are likely to be too many students to allow us to make meaningful statements about "students." Fortunately we have a number of classifications we can take advantage of to reduce this large group to smaller subgroups: men and women students for example, or freshmen, sophomores, juniors, and seniors; or science, art, business, and education majors. The more discriminating our categories can become, the more accurate we can make our statements about them.

Which classification system we adopt depends on our purpose and, in the case of composition, on the whole purpose-audience-experience-self-code complex of factors governing writing situations. Obviously we could invent trivial classifications: students with freckles, students with younger brothers, students with expensive cars . . . but it would take an unusual writing situation to justify such classifications. If you were asked to describe the types of students who could benefit from a course in modern poetry, the writing situation would have built-in constraints that would suggest the classes or types you should use. If you found yourself in a job that involved large numbers of items, which you had to sort by some criteria, the purpose of classifying would be built into the situation. For example, two scientists were once faced with the difficult problem of determining the population of elephants in an area of Africa, because in large numbers elephants will damage whole forests. The problem was how to keep track of elephant births and deaths. The solution depended on being able to recognize elephants (who all tend to look very much alike, even to scientists):

Learning to remember an individual became like a geography lesson, in which the shape of a country's borders had to be memorized. Often an ear would be almost smooth, with only one or two small nicks, but the shape of the nick, whether it had straight or curved sides, its depth and position on the ear, provided useful material. Some nicks looked as if they had resulted from the ear catching on a thorn, others as if they had been deftly cut by a tailor's scissors in neat straight lines. Certain elephants had ears with as many holes along the edge as a Dutch coast line plastered with bomb craters along its dykes. The cause of these holes I never discovered, but I suppose it must be due to some internal physiological process, the result of which gave the ears a decaying appearance.

IAN AND ORIA DOUGLAS-HAMILTON, *Among the Elephants*

The Douglas-Hamiltons solved their problem in part by learning to classify elephants by the configuration of ears. The scientists in this instance had a ready-made problem with its built-in purpose. They needed a classification system by which they could identify elephants. However, when you are not led into situations that imply specific classification systems, you will find that analysis for classification will provide you new insight into subjects, even those you already know well. In short, classification is not simply an exercise you are asked to undertake to see whether you can do it. All the strategies of exposition are functions of the human mind, and all normal human beings can and do use them whenever the need arises.

We are not suggesting that you put together a classification paper as an exercise in orderly exposition. It is possible to write a paper in which you classify trees into two groups: those that lose their leaves annually and those that remain green all year. You could further subdivide each of these categories into several subtypes of each kind. But if we ask *why* trees should be classified in this manner, it becomes clear that the assignment is a mere exercise. What is missing here is some *purpose* for the classifying.

The actual process of analysis into types should precede the writing of the paper, even though there may be refinements and adjustments in the topic as you work on the paper. Thinking through the subject, *discovering* the principles on which to classify, should lead to new insights, new understanding of the subject. The classification paper, like any other, should make a point; the classification should lead somewhere. We all know that money can be divided into paper money and coins and that there are several varieties of each of these. So what? What is the point?

It is important to remember that *people* set up classification systems. The flowers and animals of nature exist in vast numbers and great variety because God made them so, but God did not invent the scheme by which we separate flowers from animals nor any of the other categories we use. (And just to emphasize the point, God has provided us with creatures who are ambiguously both plant and animal and not very easy to classify as one or the other.) No matter how logical or obvious our categories seem, the act of creating the categories is specifically an act of the human mind. There is no normal, natural, or necessary way to classify anything, and there should be nothing mechanical about the way you arrive at your categories of classification. A famous composer has illustrated this point:

We all listen to music according to our separate capacities. But, for the sake of analysis, the whole listening process may become clearer if we break it up into its component parts, so to speak. In a certain sense we all listen to music on three separate planes. For lack of a better terminology, one might name these: (1) the sensuous plane, (2) the expressive plane, (3) the sheerly musical plane. The only advantage to be gained from mechanically splitting up the listening process into these hypothetical planes is a clearer view to be had of the way in which we listen.

AARON COPLAND, *What to Listen for in Music*

What Copland achieves with this classification is not just a "clearer view" of listening but the conclusion, as he says later at the end of the section, that the reader should strive for "a more *active* kind of listening . . . not just listening, but . . . listening *for* something." Thus his classification has a point; it serves a purpose. It was probably not obvious to you nor to many others before Copland explained them that there *were* such planes of listening to music. They are his categories, invented to suit his purpose—to help the reader understand music better. The real question to ask is not "What classification can I make?" but "What *point* can I make that classification will help establish?"

Read the following paper. How has the author derived her categories? What purpose does her classification serve?

Who Is an
Alcoholic?

PATTI DEWITT

Alcoholism isn't a very pretty subject to talk about. It makes some people uncomfortable and others angry. College students act like alcoholism is something that happens only to old people; some students refuse to talk about it. But some people want to know what the symptoms of alcoholism are or when do you "become" an alcoholic. There doesn't seem to be just one answer to this question; alcoholism seems to be very individualistic. From my work in the Crisis Center and from what I've observed with friends and relatives, I think there are too many individual variations to give a complete list, but if people can recognize the main types, they will be more able to tell whether a roommate or friend or relative is—or probably is—an alcoholic.

The first type is simply the heavy drinker. Most people agree that two or three drinks of any kind should be the limit at a party: two or three glasses of wine, two or three mixed drinks, two or three glasses or cans of beer are the maximum for most people. And even then we are talking about occasional drinkers who drink once or twice a week. The heavy drinker usually has much more than two or three drinks and is likely to have them several times a week.

There are basically two kinds of heavy drinkers: those who get very drunk and those who don't. We all know someone who can seemingly drink all night without becoming rowdy or unsteady or falling asleep. Sometimes these heavy drinkers appear sober even after they have enough to drink everybody else "under the table." Usually people admire this kind of alcoholic; they say things like "So-and-so can really hold his liquor." But So-and-so is usually the type who looks sober enough to drive, and he will fight anyone who tries to stop him. I would say that many college students are this type. The other type of heavy drinker is easy to recognize; he (or she) is the one who gets noisy and may even fall down or pass out. People usually say, "There goes So-and-so, drunk again." While the heavy drinker obviously drinks more than the light drinker, he or she resents any suggestion of alcoholism. And since they may not drink "too much" every time, many people will say those drinkers are not alcoholics but just "heavy drinkers," people who "really like their liquor." At a college bar, these drinkers are usually the ones who make fools of themselves or start fights.

A different kind of drinker is the "binge" drinker. This is someone who does not drink at all or who seems to be just a normal (light) drinker most of the time. But every now and then the binge drinker will "fall off the wagon" and drink very heavily for a night or a weekend or several days. Since binge drinkers can sometimes go for quite a while without a drink they are frequently thought to be nondrinkers. Or they may be thought to be not alcoholics because they can "stop" drinking. Sometimes the binge drinker can go on for surprisingly long periods without a drink, but sooner or later this kind of drinker goes off on a binge and usually drinks until he passes out. Often these drinkers are not thought of as having a drinking problem; instead they are said to be people who "shouldn't" drink because liquor "affects" them so badly. Often this kind of drinker is tolerated, depending on how often and how bad the binges are. "So-and-so is on a binge again" means the binge is a laughable thing because it will soon pass and then old So-and-so will be himself again. If the binges get very bad, the drinker may find himself in a crisis center or an alcoholic hospital. But since the binges wear themselves out, this kind of drinker is quickly "cured" and released. One thing that is common among binge drinkers is unexplained bumps and bruises. Drinkers who seem to have more than their share of black eyes and split lips may be binge drinkers, who usually do not stop drinking until they pass out. Almost all binge drinkers deny they are alcoholics and become very angry at the suggestion, because they only drink "now and then" and because "having a little too much to drink," they say, is something that can happen to anyone. Many binge drinkers, to avoid the charge of alcoholism, drink "only" beer and wine because they believe beer and wine are harmless social drinks and that "everybody" drinks beer and wine.

The most common type of alcoholic is the habitual drinker, someone who drinks every day. Some of these drinkers may be heavy drinkers; if more than two or three drinks is "heavy," then most of them are heavy drinkers. But they usually don't think of themselves as heavy drinkers, and they may not be seen as heavy drinkers by their friends (who are likely to be the same type of drinker). People who have a beer or cocktail for lunch and/or a couple of before-dinner drinks and/or wine with dinner and/or one or two after-dinner drinks will usually "explain" that the alcohol is "absorbed" or "diluted" by food, and so they insist that their drinks are not the same as an equal number of drinks served without food. Or they will explain that two drinks before dinner and two drinks after dinner don't add up to four drinks because they are "separated" by food. The exact number of drinks isn't as important as the fact that drinking has become habitual. A man who has "only" two martinis for lunch and two before dinner several hours later, but *every* day, is an alcoholic, even though not very much alcohol is involved. Such drinkers will usually get upset if they have to miss one of their drinks. They will select restaurants, motels, and even their friends, based on whether or not they can get drinks. (I have a friend who won't go to a restaurant if it doesn't serve drinks.) Many drinkers of this type begin thinking about "happy hour" before it arrives, and as the drinking hour gets closer they become more and more "thirsty." Since many drinkers fall into this category, few people are concerned about this kind of alcoholic. But at the Crisis Center many alcoholics say the habit grows and gets worse. The drinking hour comes earlier and earlier, the drinking "hours" increase (morning eye-openers, mid-day pick-me-ups, after-dinner drinks, nightcaps). Potentially, the habitual drinker faces as severe a drinking problem as any other kind of alcoholic.

Finally there is the all-day drinker. There is sometimes a line between the habitual drinker who is drinking frequently during the day and the all-day drinker; at least, many habitual drinkers like to think so. If there is a line, it is crossed when there are no longer any periods between drinks. The all-day drinker is the one most people think about when you say "alcoholic." They are the ones shown in movies: housewives at home drinking all day, businessmen and laborers either secretly or openly drinking on the job, and skid-row bums drinking out of paper bags. The all-day drinker starts drinking when he or she wakes up. The same way many people need several cups of coffee to start the day, these drinkers need several drinks. After this the drinks continue in about the same way that some people drink water or coffee all day. The all-day drinker is likely to be "tipsy" or "stoned" all day. A semisober state becomes their natural condition. People who don't know such drinkers are "high" get the impression that they are "strange" or "a little off balance." Oddly enough, these all-day drinkers can become so used to their alcoholic state that they are able to live and function for years in a semistupor without being very unusual looking to others. Of course, many of them end the day passing out in bed and many others end by ruining their lives. Even many of these obvious alcoholics will deny they are alcoholics since, according to them, their drinking doesn't interfere with their lives. Most parents would be shocked to find out how many college students are all-day drinkers. Every dormitory has at least one.

These four basic types—the heavy drinker, the binge drinker, the habitual drinker, and the all-day drinker—pretty well cover the alcoholics. Surprisingly few of them end up on skid row. Some of them don't even get "drunk" in the movie and television sense. We might conclude from this that practically anybody who drinks is an alcoholic, but this is not true. Those who are defensive about their drinking like to pretend that all non-drinkers or light drinkers are little old ladies who think anyone who has "a few beers" is an alcoholic. By this they mean it's natural and even "macho" or "sexy" to drink. But this classification of alcoholics doesn't mean everyone who drinks is an alcoholic. It only means those who regularly drink are alcoholics, those whose drinking falls into a recognizable pattern. One basic difference I have observed about the way alcoholics drink is how hard it is for them to change the pattern of their drinking. Heavy drinkers can't easily become light drinkers. Binge drinkers can't stop forever or break the routine of their binges. Habitual drinkers find it very hard to become occasional drinkers. If there is anything to be concluded from this classification it is probably just that once drinking becomes a habit, the habit takes over and becomes very difficult to change.

Patti's paper is a good example of insight through classification. By grouping drinkers into different categories based on how often they drink, Patti shows that the single group called "alcoholics" is actually four groups. You may disagree with Patti; there may be more groups or fewer according to your analysis. But Patti's analysis is interesting and allows her to draw the conclusion that alcoholics are people whose drinking falls into a pattern *that they cannot easily change*. It is important to understand that Patti has *invented* this classification through analysis of her experiences (her data). Her paper is not just an exercise in organization. Instead, it is the outcome of some very purposeful thinking by Patti as a result of her attempts to classify alcoholics.

There is some overlap in Patti's categories: some habitual drinkers are also heavy drinkers. In the ideal sense, categories should not overlap. In the real world, classification may not work out so neatly, especially when the subject is human beings or human affairs. In Patti's case the overlap does not invalidate her categories and therefore is not a serious problem.

Categories don't always fall into a pattern or plan of organization, but Patti has arranged her categories more or less in order of severity—beginning with the mildest (heavy drinking) and progressing to the most severe (all-day drinking). Notice that in some cases she has additional supportive paragraphs for subcategories: under heavy drinkers there are subcategories for those who do and don't become "drunk."

We can point out one other fact about Patti's paper by contrasting it with a different paper on the same subject. Imagine a paper in which alcoholics are classified according to how much and what kind of drunken behavior they exhibit. The paper might begin with those who seem not to have any kind of abnormal behavior—people who seem not to get drunk at all—and progress all the way to those who are found raving in alcoholic wards. In between these extremes we would have all sorts of behavior, including laughter, staggering and falling, vomiting, and so on. By contrast, Patti's classifications seem much more significant. "Drunken behavior" is too individualistic for alcoholics and nonalcoholics alike. An individual in a single evening may progress from soberness through various stages of drunkenness to final collapse. Thus Patti's classification not only divides and types alcoholics, it offers *significant* classifications (even if some people might disagree with them) that help us understand something about the subject.

Patti's purpose in this paper is to convince us that alcoholics aren't only those drinkers who are entirely out of control. Although she draws on her own experience, her paper is appropriate for a general audience. Each reader must decide how effectively Patti conveys her message, but it is clear that Patti has come up with some thought-provoking insights into a very serious subject.

Writing the Classification Paper

You must keep in mind that the purpose of classification is to find (invent) an idea. A quick and obvious classification (there are three sorts of people: tall, short, and medium) merely demonstrates what we already know. You must try various groupings and classifications, looking for one that will give you a new insight. Ask yourself "So what?" about each classfication: people are fat, skinny, and medium . . . so what?

Try to invent mutually exclusive categories; avoid overlapping as much as possible. There is some overlapping in Patti's paper because she classifies alcoholics on *two* criteria: how *much* and how *often* they drink. If you classify people on how smart they are and how self-disciplined they are, you can see that there will be some crossover between categories.

It seems obvious, but it's worth saying that you should not think of the categories first and then see how well you can apply them to the subject. For example, you know you can classify people as young, old, and middle-aged; can you work this into a classification paper? This is a poor idea. For one thing it is unoriginal. For another, it *forces* the classification: the subject is being made to fit a preconceived idea. It is a much better idea to analyze the subject, and then prewrite by trying to see what categories you can find *in* the subject, versus imposing one *on* the subject.

Writing activity

For this assignment, you need a subject concerning groups of things or things that come in large numbers. You can start thinking about very elementary things or very sophisticated ones. Pursue the subject until it yields a concept suitable for a relatively short paper (three to six pages). To help you get started we have provided the following list of unrefined subjects. (By "unrefined" we mean that the subjects can be broken down further. You might do a paper about athletes, but you might also do one about ballplayers, joggers, swimmers, and so on.)

ambitions	dates	insults	police officers
animals	doctors	jobs	preachers
athletes	dreams	lies	restaurants
cars	emotions	kinds of love	roads
clothes	excuses	motives	salespeople
coaches	fads	music	sports
colors	guns	painters	students
courage	horses	parents	symbols
dancers	hunters	personalities	teachers

PROCESS

While visiting Britain, an American read in the *Daily Telegraph* the following report of a game of cricket: "Despite a slower start of 9-for-2, Davison scored a hundred before lunch. Balderstrone also batted very well, 148 until just before lunch when, against all reason, three wickets fell in six balls to Slack, who had not previously taken a first-class wicket." Obviously confused by the report, the American asked a British friend to explain cricket to him. "You have two sides, one out in the field, one in. Each man that's on the side that's in goes out. And when he's out he comes in and the next man goes in till he's out.

"When they're all out, the side that's out comes in and the side that's in goes out and tries to get those coming in out. Sometimes you get men still in and not out. When both sides have been in and out, including the not-outs, that's the end of the game."

To an American unfamiliar with the intricacies of cricket, this explanation was as confusing as the report. To someone familiar with the game, this description is accurate. But silly, too. An explanation can be both accurate and useless. If you set out to explain a process to a group of people, you must first determine what kind of information they need. The tongue-in-cheek explanation of the game of cricket was useless because it did not direct itself to solving the problem faced by people unfamiliar with cricket. Some of the group members may have wanted to know how to play cricket; others may have wanted to visit a cricket ground and watch others playing. The first group needed to know *how to do it;* the second needed to know what happens during a cricket match, *how it works*. In this section, we will examine these two different kinds of process papers.

How To Do It

The first and cardinal rule of a *how-to-do-it* paper is that it should be addressed to a specific audience—people who have never performed the task before or people who have tried it before but failed. There is no sense in explaining a process to someone who is familiar with the operation. Don't waste your time telling Jack Nicklaus how to hit a golf ball or Meryl Streep how to act. Once you have chosen readers who really need to know how to do it, don't assume that they are knowledgeable or familiar with the various terms or stages in the process. Many recipes, directions, and instruction booklets fail because they assume that readers already know most of the process and only need to be reminded of the order of the steps. But many people today would not know what is meant by "dredge chicken parts before frying" or "prime engine" or other explanations that do not really explain. As a general rule, a writer should assume that readers do not know even the most basic or routine information. Here, for example, is a rather standard description of how to change a flat tire, which relies on a considerable amount of assumed information on the reader's part.

Set brakes and block wheels so that the car will not roll. Remove jack and spare tire from trunk of car. Place jack under bumper and raise car until flat tire clears the ground. Remove hubcap and lug nuts with jack handle. Remove flat, place spare on wheel, and replace lug nuts. Tighten lug nuts securely, using alternating pattern of opposing nuts so that tire will fit evenly on wheel. Replace hubcap. Return tire and jack to trunk.

With minor variations, most people would agree that's about right—that is how to change a flat. It is basically just a matter of getting the flat off and the spare on (assuming you have a spare in working order; otherwise call the auto club). But this description is only a summary of the process; it is aimed at people who already know how to do it, or at least have a basic understanding of the problems involved. However, in the following version of how to change a flat, we get a considerably different view of the matter.

How to Change
a Flat

SYLVIA MORGAN

It makes little difference where or how the flat occurs; you may be driving or the car may be at rest, but sooner or later you will be faced with a decision to make. Changing a tire *can* be accomplished by nonmechanical mortals, and the garage mechanic *will* charge you ten dollars to come out with his wrecker and do it for you. So you have a choice to make—should you try to change it yourself or call AAA? The following explanation of what is involved may help you make up your mind.

First, you probably should "block" the wheels so that the car will not roll—it is nearly suicidal to try to change a tire on a hill or even a slight incline—but there is almost never anything available to block with, so just set the brake and hope for the best.

The first problem is getting the jack and spare out. In many big and medium-sized cars, the spare is far back in the trunk, and the only way to reach it is to climb into the trunk—which is dirty. The jack has been cleverly concealed *under* the spare, which has been bolted down by a local garage jock with a machismo problem. If you are very strong you may succeed in freeing the spare from its bolt. The spare too is dirty, it is also heavy and bulky and therefore almost impossible to wrestle out of the trunk without getting fairly covered with dirt.

The modern jack comes in four or five pieces—one of which usually manages to be somewhere else (somewhere in the garage, basement, or down under the rear seat of the car) when you need it. The jack will not work unless all the pieces are present and assembled according to the diagram that came with it. If—as is probable—you no longer have the diagram, you will just have to experiment with different arrangements until you get one that will do what a jack is supposed to do. *Warning:* when the jack is *properly* set up, you will find a very small lip of metal that just barely fits under the car, even in cars that have a little square cut out of the bumper especially for the jack to fit into, causing the jack to be set rather gingerly like a spring catapult. Jacks have a tendency to spring out at you with enough force to break bones. Never trust the jack; once you start lifting the car, proceed very slowly and carefully and be prepared to jump for safety. The idea is to lift the car, not the bumper. If the bumper starts to groan and twist upward while the car remains on the ground, you have the jack in the wrong place. Look under the car until you can see the heavy metal frame the whole car rests on; get your jack under that to lift the car.

If you do get the jack to work properly, don't lift the flat off the ground until after you have loosened the lug nuts: struggles with the nuts may spring the jack. First remove the hubcap. The procedure is to pry it off with the chiseled end of the jack handle, also called the tire wrench. Since the chiseled end is not sharp enough to really fit under the edge of the hubcap very well, it will take some effort to get the hubcap off—another reason for keeping the wheel on the ground. Once off, you can start on the nuts. The other end of the jack handle has a socket on it just shaped to fit the nuts. Theoretically this socket cannot damage the nuts (which if "chewed" up by a loose wrench must be removed by a different kind of wrench— which you haven't got), but unless you hold it firmly and flatly on the nut, it will "chew" the edges off the nut until the wrench just slides uselessly around the smoothed (chewed) nuts. And you will find that the nuts have rusted to the bolts so that it will take tremendous leverage to move them—

if they can be moved at all—which is why some of them have already been chewed somewhat. All nuts in America unscrew counterclockwise, but usually you just try it one way, and if that doesn't work you try it the other. It will usually take considerable force to loosen the nuts. You will of course not have any solvent or other helpful stuff to unfreeze a "frozen" nut.

If you get them loosened (not off yet), go back to the jack and carefully raise the car until the flat is clear of the ground. If you're lucky the nuts will give you no further trouble and you can remove them. Place the nuts inside the removed hubcap and move the cap with nuts out of the working area. Setting the nuts carefully on the ground, in your pocket, or anywhere else is a mistake. They will somehow roll under the car, where it will quite literally be worth your life to retrieve them. Inside the hubcap they will rattle and alert you if you accidentally kick them, and your chances of finding them again are infinitely greater if you remember to take this simple precaution.

Removing the flat is a little difficult. It is very dirty and heavy and *resting* on the bolts. If you are strong enough you can just squat down and lift it *up* and off the bolts; otherwise the best position is kneeling or sitting on the ground, from which you can lift and *pull* the tire toward you—you will get quite dirty this way. Be extra careful of the jack at this point, because without the wheel the car is as lethal as a guillotine and will operate like one with the slightest provocation.

With the flat off, you can now put the spare on. Make sure it has air in it first. Not only will it not work without air, but you will be very unhappy to discover it too is flat *after* you have gone through the labor of putting it on. A fully inflated tire will bounce and will solidly resist even your hardest kick—so test it first.

You will probably find that while the car is high enough to get the flat off, it is not high enough to get the spare on. Since the car is already quite high in the air and putting maximum tension on the jack, which is probably near its maximum elevation now, raising the car still higher has about the same risk as trying to defuse a bomb—extreme caution is advised.

The spare is even heavier than the flat—the air in it is not weightless—and the holes for the bolts usually refuse to line up properly so that it will take some grunting and maneuvering to get the tire on. Replace the nuts in an alternating pattern: after the twelve o'clock nut, replace the six o'clock; after the three o'clock, the nine o'clock, and so on. This is so that you won't clamp down one side of the wheel, causing it to wobble and shimmy when it turns. Most people say that you should tighten all the nuts firmly while the car is in the air but leave the final turn for when the car is on the ground. This is so the force of the last turn won't shake the jack loose and also so the wheel can "settle" on the bolts.

Lowering the car is dangerous. The jack has a trigger on it that must be released to reverse the lifting action. You do not reverse *your* actions to lower the car. With the trigger released, the jack will automatically go backwards as you continue to pump as if lifting the car.

Once the car is on the ground, you can put the final leverage on the nuts. You need a good firm twist on them, but it is not necessary to rupture yourself over it. The wheel will not come off even without the final twist. Replace the hubcap if you can. It is a size smaller than the ridge it is supposed to fit over but will stretch slightly with sufficient pressure. In a garage, the hubcap is hammered on with a rubber mallet—anything else will simply dent it. Some people can put the cap on by hitting it a karate shot with the palm of the hand. Kicking it will not work. It is the least necessary component, so if the cap gives you very much trouble, just throw it into the trunk along with the jack and the flat tire. There is no point to being neat about putting things away; the flat will have to come out again soon to be repaired. You of course need a shower and a new outfit and three fingers of Scotch by now. One last warning—never accept helpers or kibitzers. They do not help, and the presence of a critic during an already difficult job will unsettle you enough to make you unable to function—unless of course they are going to take over and do the job for you . . . accept all such offers instantly and then wander off "to look for help" while the flat gets changed.

Sylvia's explanation of the process includes everything the manufacturers's brochure does not. It includes what *not* to do, as well as what to do, and it points out problems and troubles that are likely to occur and what to do about them. Rather than make the process seem stupidly simple ("any child can do it"), Sylvia gives us a fairly realistic view of the process, explaining not only what to do but why.

Sylvia's paper is a composite of experiences—what usually happens when you change a tire. It could also have been written as a narrative of a single incident—what *happened* last Saturday. And it is possible to write a combination of both what happened and what happens: "I barked my knuckles on the lug nuts when the wrench slipped—as it usually does when you wrestle with a stubborn nut." In any case, you need the skills you have already been using in your writing. If you write in the first person, especially if you write about a specific incident, your paper will come out sounding like a personal experience. If you write in the third person about a composite of experiences, you will be "generalizing" about your experiences and will produce a less personalized paper.

The people who wrote the papers below are trying to explain how to do something. Do they succeed? Do they tell you what you need to know as well as what to avoid? What are they doing right?

Quick Amputations: How to Avoid Them

ZACH HUMMEL

Most people believe that operating a chain saw is a simple and easy task, requiring little experience or knowledge, except maybe how to start one. They assume that with one pull of the cord they will be instant lumberjacks—slicing through trees, logs, fence posts, and so on, quickly and easily. However, they seem to ignore the fact that it will cut through toes, fingers, arms, legs, and even torsos just as quickly. A chain saw must be handled knowledgeably and with a great deal of respect if one cares to keep his bodily symmetry intact. Remembering how to ready the saw for cutting, how to start it safely, what not to do with the saw, and precautions to take against accidents will give you a safer cutting spree, and lower medical expenses. Operating a chain saw is not as easy as it sounds; common sense, caution, and a little knowledge are required for safe usage.

One of the most important things in cutting with a chain saw is to have a saw that is ready to cut. If the saw is not prepared properly it will not cut well and may be damaged as a result. Obviously, it should have a full tank of gas. You should be sure to check the owner's manual for any special requirements, such as oil mixed in. This can sometimes be found on the saw itself, also. The oil in the saw itself should be checked and kept full at all times. The chain should also be tight. The blade on a chain saw consists of two parts—the bar and the chain. The chain, which is the real cutting edge, runs along the bar, the long flat piece of metal sticking out front. If the chain is too lose it will jam during the cutting, and this can cause it to break—which can be nasty if the pieces fly in your face. If the chain is too tight, it will not move and may ruin the saw. You also won't get much cutting done. Here, also, the owner's manual should be checked for how to adjust the tension on your particular saw. Now you are ready to begin cutting—if, that is, you can get it started.

On face value, starting a chain saw is easy; however, if you have used one before, you know better—much better. The first and one of the most important parts of starting the saw is addressing it properly. This does not mean remembering to include the zip code or its proper title (Mr., Mrs, Your Excellency, and so on) but the way you position yourself in relation to the saw—much as addressing a golf ball on the tee. The saw should be placed on a solid object below waist level (the ground, a stump, whatever) so that it has a sturdy base. Place one hand on the brace, flick on the starter switch, give a sharp pull on the starter cord, and give it a little gas with the throttle as it sputters to life, and your chain saw is now started.

It would be nice if the world were as bright and perfect as owners' manuals would have you believe. It is not, however, that simple. All saws have their eccentricities; some you have to use the choke on, others you can't or they will flood, and still others have to have a combination. Take my saw, for example. It has its own particular ritual that must be performed before it will start. First, it must be dropped on the ground from knee level; then I have to turn on the starter switch and pull on the starting cord a few times. It will not start, so I pull out the choke and yank on the cord some more—it still will not start. I then pause and utter a few choice words and threaten it with dirty oil next oil change. If, after a few more pulls, it refuses to start, I bang it up against my victim (a dead tree or whatever), hoping it will incur the saw's wrath so the saw will start just to cut it down. Now, after a few more pulls, it should start. If all this fails, I just tell my father I can't work because the saw won't start. He comes out, and it starts first pull. This *nev-*

er fails and can be applied to almost any situation—kids and parents, husband and wife, man and mother-in-law, whatever. As soon as you tell someone that you can't work because it won't start—it will start the next time it is pulled. Once the saw is running, the throttle will control the engine and, therefore, the blade speed. You are now ready to cut.

The actual cutting is the easiest, and therefore the most dangerous, part of using a chain saw. The minute the saw is started it is deadly. The ease with which it cuts is very deceiving. You should not be lulled into forgetting the power and destruction potential that the saw has. All that is required is to place the bottom of the blade on whatever you are cutting and apply light pressure. Always make sure your legs are not in the saw's path. Do not place any part of your body in the path of the blade. It is possible to slip off, especially when starting the cut, and to end up cutting what you had not intended to. Do not use the tip of the blade to gouge into an object. The saw will kick back hard, and if you aren't ready it could have disastrous results. Be very careful cutting with the top of the blade. It should only be done when absolutely necessary. You should position your body so that any kickback will not have a chance to throw the saw into you. If you remember these simple and obvious cautions, you will have a much safer time cutting.

I can best give a few tips on cutting down standing trees (the trickiest part of chain saw use) by telling how I found them out. Our house is heated by a wood furnace—not oil or electricity, but wood. This means that in winter we must have wood or no heat, and that means frozen water pipes, frozen feet, frozen hands—just plain frozen everything. I, being the oldest, was given the task of keeping the wood supply from running out. We live on a cherry farm and there is an old, dying orchard right out the back door. Convenient, huh? It would be except that all the dead ones are at the back of the orchard (you've heard of elephants going to their secret graveyard to die; well, it's much the same with cherry trees—they migrate to the back of the orchard to die), and in between are two hills that make the Matterhorn look puny.

So I slogged my way through the waist-high drifts of snow pulling my trusty toboggan (I pull all the wood I cut back in with it) and my chain saw. Just after I had scaled the first hill I spotted a small dead elm—considered the prime timber because it is much easier to cut and transport than cherry—and decided to cut that first. Amazingly, the saw started first try (the first such happening since the fall of 1970), and soon I was slicing into the trunk of the tree. About ten seconds later the chain jammed; I couldn't pull the saw out and it quit. The tree had leaned back toward where I was cutting from, and there I was with my saw stuck and no way to get it out. This illustrates two things: one, no matter how much the tree looks like it's leaning away from where you are cutting, it will most likely tilt back and trap your saw—so always cut a notch on the opposite side just below where you are cutting. This will cause the tree to fall in that direction. Two, always carry an axe, just in case. It will get you, and your saw, out of many a jam.

So I waded back through the drifts, got my axe, and started off once more into the frozen North.

So now you see that operating a chain saw is not as easy as it seems. You must have some knowledge as to what the saw will do, precautions to take, and even preparations that are necessary in order to operate it safely and effectively. If you follow these basic rules you can get all the wood you want yourself—and it won't cost you (either way) an arm and a leg.

Zach's paper uses a combination of what happens and what happened to show the reader how to operate a chain saw. Thus the paper differs from the preceding one in degree of personalization; Zach primarily uses third person, but he switches to first when he brings in his own experiences as examples. Note that Zach has organized the paper so that he first presents the ideal (as stated in the owner's manual) operation and then the real, thus allowing him to set up a nice contrast in the paper between the way things are "supposed" to go and the way they "really" go.

Easy Enough   BOB MCGOOGAN

"The first thing to remember is that here at Burger King, 'We Specialize in Special Fries.' Also, the more special you make your fries, the more special The King will pay you!" It was my job to show Paul how to make "Special Fries," a job at which I had become very competent. "There are four major steps to doing this, and with practice, you can become an expert fryer, like me!"

"Sounds easy enough to me," he said. I hadn't even started yet, and he was saying it was easy. The feeling of confidence he displayed almost made me mad. He seemed cocky. *I* was the experienced master, not him.

"You think?" I snapped. "Okay, which fries do you use first? What is the one-through-four method? How long before using them do you slack them? What is holding time?" Paul didn't flinch, but he did keep quiet.

We went back to the walk-in freezer, and on the left side were boxes of French fries. "This is where it all starts. Each box is dated, and you want to use the oldest fries first. Grab a bag before we freeze." Paul picked up a bag and we went back to the kitchen.

"Slacking fries is the first step. All you do in slacking is pour the fries into frying baskets to thaw. Under normal business conditions, you can slack four baskets out of one bag. We use the 'one-two-three-four-four-three-two-one' method to fill the baskets. Grab four baskets." Paul lined up four empty baskets while I stared coldly. "Some of the fries at the bottom of the bag may be broken. So, to make sure one basket doesn't get all the broken ones, we use this method. Pour a little into the first basket, some into the second, third, and fourth. Now you should still have a half bag left. Start with number four, and do the same thing, this time working backwards. That way the fries are evenly distributed. Now, if there aren't any customers, you can make six smaller baskets instead of four. But no more than six, and no less than four."

"Uh huh. So far, so good," he said as he slacked four baskets.

"So far," I said. "You have to thaw them for at least an hour before you can cook them, but you can't let them sit for more than two hours." I picked up a basket of thawed fries and walked over to the frying vats. "These are the frying vats. In there is shortening that is 340° F. Be careful around here. See these scars?" I showed him several colored spots on my hands and arms. "This is what happens when you get into the grease." (At this point, I was tempted to teach him the game of "bobbing for French fries" in that 340° grease.) "All you have to do is push the button with the fry basket picture on it and the computer will cook them." He pushed the button, and the basket was slowly lowered into the grease, which began to bubble. "About thirty seconds after you put them down, you have to lift them out and gently shake them. That's to keep them from sticking together and results in even cooking. Don't shake them too hard or they will break."

Paul lifted the basket and shook the fries. He carelessly set the basket back into the vat and was hit by splattering drops of grease. "I told you to be careful. You're lucky they were only drops." I turned and walked away, and Paul followed silently. "In two minutes and ten seconds the buzzer will go off, and the fries will automatically come up. Then you'll have to show some real skill."

While the fries cooked, I explained about the four enemies of grease: air, water, carbon, and salt. "Each of these things shortens the life of the grease. So don't put ice in there, or dump salt in, either." Those were the favorite games of employees. "And when the fryers are turned off, cover them. The covers are in the cooler."

A little while later, the buzzer went off. "Push the same button to stop the buzzer. Now watch." I picked up the basket and let the excess grease drip out. "These are nice, crisp fries, which break very easily. Carefully shake the grease out, and very, very gently set them —don't drop them— into the holding bin. Spread them out evenly. To salt them, use a front to back motion. That way, you don't get any salt in the grease. Salting is tough, because you need to cover all the fries, but you can't overdo it. Carefully mix the salt and fries with the scoop. Now comes the hard part. A regular-size order is two-and-a-half ounces, and a large order is four ounces. Scooping out the right amount takes practice. Lots of it. I can do it almost every time. You try it." Paul picked up the scoop and put a regular-size fry in a large-size carton. "You got a ways to go, kid. Finally, to make sure we sell only fresh fries, we have a holding time. Those in the holding bin are kept for seven minutes, regular-size fries can only be held for two minutes, and large orders are only bagged when called. Easy enough, eh?" Paul shook his head and looked around. "You now know everything about fries I do. All you need to do is practice. Go for it!"

That evening, Paul worked French fries for dinner. During the middle of a rush, my manager yelled, "Bob, take over on fries!" As I moved to my new station, I couldn't help but think to myself, "Sure, Paul, it's easy enough."

Bob has chosen a rather straightforward topic and made it interesting by choosing Paul, a real skeptic, and demonstrating to him the pitfalls that face a Burger King french fryer. The job is more complex than Paul thought, but Bob explains with clarity the terms he uses and divides the process into clear, recognizable stages that should be easy to follow. He consistently analyzes the process and explains why Paul should carefully follow each step. He anticipates potential problems and provides Paul with orderly solutions. Note that the writers of each of these three papers prefer the less formal "you" to "one" when referring to the reader.

How It Works

The second kind of process paper—*how it works*—is designed to describe to the reader how a particular system operates, how something works. The purpose of such a paper is to answer questions like the following: "What makes *X* happen?" "How does *Y* work?" "I've never understood why *Z* is so complicated—is such a complex solution really necessary?" As was the case with the how-to-do-it paper, the first and cardinal rule of the how-it-works paper is that it should be addressed to a specific audience—people who have no idea how the system operates or people who have tried to analyze and understand the process but failed. Once you have readers who need information about this process, don't assume that they are familiar with the various stages or terms involved. After you have carefully analyzed the process and divided it into orderly stages, try to get into your readers' shoes, to see the process from their perspective. Anticipate where they will have problems and provide them with clear solutions. Explain *why* the system works as it does, as well as how.

The people who wrote the papers below are attempting to describe how two complex mechanisms or systems work. Have they succeeded? Have they analyzed and described what happens in enough detail for their readers? How have they structured their papers? What did you find interesting and informative about their papers?

The Big Gulp   PAUL CHRISTY

The rabbit scampers nervously on the cold linoleum floor, its nose twitching, eyes searching, and ears at attention. Suddenly, the once harmless log comes alive and the rabbit realizes its fears. The rabbit is in the company of a snake, an Indian python. My pet strikes quickly, seizing the rabbit's head in its powerful jaws. The rodent hasn't a chance. The python quickly throws its thickly muscled coils around its prey; after a brief struggle, the victim suffocates. The snake may now relax its coils and begin to swallow.

The swallowing and digesting of food by a snake involves many simple but highly specialized organs. The oral cavity or mouth is comprised of the most unusual structures. The teeth of a serpent are approximately one-quarter inch long, sharp and recurved. This recurvature of the polyphyodont (replaceable) teeth prevents an organism from escaping the reptile's grasp; as the prey struggles in the snake's jaws, the teeth, like a hook in a struggling fish, sink deeper.

The jaws of a snake are unique. The mandible (lower jawbone) consists of four bones, three more than that of man. The actual mandible can be compared to that of man, except where the jaw of a man curves to form the chin, the jaw of a snake has no bone. The "chin" of a snake consists of a ligament which connects the two straight mandibles. The ligament allows the lower jawbones to separate, creating a V. This separation is one of the adaptations which allow snakes to swallow prey over three times as large as their own heads. Another swallowing adaptation of the mandible is the presence of a pair of bones called the quadrates. The mandible of a man is connected directly to the cranium; the lower jaw of snakes is connected to the quadrate bones, which are attached to the skull. The quadrate bones provide for a greater range of movement of the lower jawbones, which is very important to an animal that must feed itself without the use of limbs. The maxilla (upper jawbone) is stationary and relatively comparable to the maxilla of man.

A snake's jaws must act as hands to pull the food into the mouth. The purpose of two mandibles is to allow for unilateral movement. Unilateral movement is the movement of one mandible at a time. While one side of the jaw holds the prey, the other side releases it and, by the use of the quadrate bone, is thrust forward. This side now takes hold of the victim, while the other side of the jaw releases and thrusts forward. In this way, the snake "crawls" over its prey.

When a snake swallows an organism of any appreciable size, its nasopharynx (the tube connecting the nose to the mouth) as well as its trachea (windpipe) become blocked, thus preventing breathing. The snake gets around this otherwise fatal condition through the use of a specialized glottis. The glottis is the beginning of the trachea. Snakes, unlike any other organisms, have a convoluted glottis which can be extended from the mouth during the swallowing process. In this way, the glottis acts like a snorkel to allow the animal to breathe.

Once past the mouth, the food enters the esophagus (the tube extending from the mouth to the stomach) which has many longitudinal folds to allow for the swallowing of large prey. Muscular contractions of the tube, called peristalsis, force the food into the spindle-shaped stomach. The stomach is an extremely muscular organ which contracts forcibly to churn up the food and expose it to the digestive enzymes and hydrochloric acid.

The enzymes and acid break down the protein and bones. From the stom-ach, the food enters the elongated small intestine, where nutrients are ab-sorbed; it then enters the large intestine, where excess fluids are absorbed. The large intestine empties into the cloaca, an organ of storage for various wastes. *Cloaca* is the Latin word for *sewer*, which may give a better idea as to its function. Snakes do not possess a bladder, so all wastes are in the solid form. These wastes are expelled through the anal opening.

Two hundred million years ago a creature was formed with every think-able disadvantage: no limbs, no ears, no eyelids, no fur, no ability to regu-late body temperature, no voice, and a small brain. It began its history underground, with only the simple structures of an overdeveloped worm. When this animal shunned its subterranean world its organs adapted, and so today we may see the most remarkable creature on earth: the snake.

Paul has provided his readers with a dramatic introduction and an interesting conclusion. He has also made effective use of compari-son ("like a hook in a struggling fish"), contrast ("three more than that of man"), and analogy ("A snake's jaw must act as hands . . . the snake 'crawls' over its prey"). Paul's paper is well organized and he is careful to define and explain any technical terms that his readers might not know.

Heart Attack   NINA ELLIOTT

"Before he started to speak into the tiny, adjustable microphone hang-ing beside his head, the medical examiner cleared his throat and checked the recording volume to make sure his report on cadaver 269 would be picked up clearly. With a flick of his finger, he turned on the microphone and began his examination by first reading from the hospital report and then making his own observations.

"Cadaver number two sixty-nine," he stated matter-of-factly. "Male Caucasian of approximately twenty-eight years of age with a medium build. Cause of death: heart failure." He placed the metal clipboard hold-ing the hospital records on a small table to his right and continued his care-ful examination.

"This body exhibits superior muscular development and tone; however, a few small fatty deposits are located on the thighs."

His external observation now completed, the medical examiner pushed the microphone aside slightly and prepared for the next step: an internal probe of the chest to determine the exact cause of the heart attack.

Using the natural, vertical line on the front of the body as a guideline, the doctor, starting at the cadaver's Adam's apple, cut a perfectly straight, one-inch deep incision into the cold, chalk-white flesh.

"The skin is translucent, but springy to the touch, indicating that death occurred only a few hours ago and that circulatory collapse was not com-plete. Rigor mortis has already set in."

As he spoke, the medical examiner extended the cut down to the navel, wiping up the clear, pink fluid which slowly oozed from the wound as he went. Next, he quickly proceeded to make a horizontal incision from shoulder to shoulder, which would form a crude cross on the victim's chest. Then, by carefully pulling back and clamping the thin, opaque layer of skin to the operating table's surface, the doctor gradually exposed the massive, rust-colored pectoral muscles. As he sliced through the muscle fibers as if slicing through a stick of butter, he made another short notation into the recording machine.

"Although this male's young age probably accounts in part for the excellent color and tone of the pectoral muscles, it also seems likely that this individual exercised extensively."

He knew this to be true. Earlier, while he had been finishing up a previous case, the doctor had overheard two orderlies talking about the circumstances leading up to this man's heart attack.

Ron Eaton, the twenty-eight-year-old man lying dead on the table had jogged three miles, played four sets of tennis, and gone swimming earlier that day. At ten o'clock P.M., Ron and some friends attended a cocktail and disco party. Once there, although his friends could not remember noticing anything unusual about him, Ron began showing early signs of a heart attack. Somewhere between ten thirty and eleven o'clock, his friends reported, Ron began to complain of dizziness, nausea and stomach pain, attributing these symptoms to acute indigestion. But, an hour later, when he became short of breath and felt a tingling sensation radiating up his left arm, across his chest, and up to his neck, he asked someone to call an ambulance for him. Apparently, everyone was either too preoccupied with the party or too drunk to listen, because no one called for assistance until one-fifteen A.M. when Ron collapsed unconscious to the floor. By that time, however, it was too late. Mr. Ron Eaton was dead on arrival at Mountain View hospital at one thirty A.M.

"What a waste," the doctor stated to himself as he clamped the chest muscles back, exposing the white rib cage. Reaching to his left, he selected a miniature, bone-cutting surgical saw from the tray of instruments beside him.

The medical examiner cut swiftly through the hard sternum, not seeming to notice the sickening hum of the saw or the small white bone chips flying into the air. After finishing this task he placed the saw back onto the tray and pulled the microphone closer to his mouth, knowing he would soon have the answer.

He reached for another surgical instrument: the rib cage spreader. With one shove the doctor inserted the separating blades of the "spreader" in the opening cut into the sternum. As he cranked the handle attached to the top of the instrument, the stubborn rib cage, opening little by little, produced the grotesque sound of bones breaking. Sharp tips of shattered bone now became visible, making the ribs look like some giant mouth baring its teeth. Finally, the cadaver's still heart, or what was left of it, came into view. Where a strong, bright-red heart muscle had once pulsated with life now lay a bluish-purple glob of useless jelly.

Speaking into the microphone once again, the medical examiner continued his report.

"Entire heart muscle is now a bluish mass with no discernible form. The four chambers of the heart, the right and left atriums and the right and left ventricles, are completely ruptured from within, while the interior heart wall is badly torn. What caused such a massive destruction must still be ascertained."

Carefully probing through the destroyed muscle and its arteries, he soon found what he was looking for. A small inflamed nodule, about the size of a pea, protruded from the wall of the aorta, effectively blocking off all the oxygen blood supply to the heart.

Turning towards the microphone, the doctor prepared to make the final notation of his report.

"An aneurism, completely blocking the lower section of the aorta, caused the heart muscle to lose its fresh blood supply and thus to burst. This aneurism and a blood sample will be sent to the lab for complete analysis . . . end of autopsy report on cadaver two sixty-nine."

A few minutes after closing Ron Eaton's chest cavity, the medical examiner called two attendants to take care of the body. As he watched the two men slide the stiff form into a heavy-duty plastic body bag and zip it shut, the doctor thought to himself about the real cause of the victim's death.

"It was the aneurism that ultimately killed him," he mused, "but this man might have lived if his friends had paid attention to his complaints."

In her intricately structured process paper, Nina makes good use of the drama inherent in the postmortem process by narrating the steps in the pathologist's examination interspersed with his comments on his findings. Nina then interjects a report of the unfortunate Ron Eaton's last activities into the careful, detailed description of the autopsy. She finishes with the medical examiner's personal, philosophical musing. Note the abundant, vivid details she has generated. Nina's paper succeeds because she overwhelms her readers with information—with details and explanations that enrich and clarify.

There are many complimentary things you could say about all these papers, but one very important thing to say is that the authors know what they are talking about, and this fact allows them considerable freedom and flexibility of expression. These authors evidently enjoyed writing their papers.

Writing the Process Paper

When you describe a process, remember your audience. People who already know how a system works or how to operate that system don't need your advice. In writing for the uninformed, don't assume anything, not even names of standard tools and components, such as crescent wrench or rotor, or common scientific terms, such as mandible or aneurism.

Thoroughly analyze the process and break it into its component stages. In the how-to-do-it paper, if there are preparatory stages or a necessary order to the steps, be sure to present them in the order they are needed. Readers may not read all the directions first— even if you tell them to. It may be too late after several directions about salting and flouring the inside of a chicken to mention the fact, "You should be sure to wash out the body cavity with boiling water *first*." You must anticipate every conceivable problem and tell the reader what *not* to do *before* the reader is likely to do it. In the how-it-works paper, anticipation is also the key. Decide where your readers are likely to have problems and provide them with explanations and illustrations that will help to solve those problems.

Writing activity

Write a three- to six-page paper in which you describe a process. Keep two things in mind. First, choose a process that you understand thoroughly so that your description will be accurate and complete. Second, stay aware of your reader. A step-by-step description need not be boring, as you can tell from the process papers in this section.

You may want to choose a process to describe from the following lists. The (*a*) list gives how-to-do-it topics and the (*b*) list how-it-works topics.

(a)
How to fry, bake, roast, or otherwise cook a chicken or other food
How to clean a rifle, carburetor, typewriter, or other machine
How to make a dress, shirt, other clothing
How to tie a fly
How to clean (for cooking) a fish, rabbit, deer, other game
How to embalm a body
How to fill out the income-tax long form
How to conduct an interview
How to wax skis
How to cut down a large tree
How to use the subway
How to present yourself in traffic court
How to shop in a second-hand store
How to put on makeup
How to impress a date
How to behave at a tea party
How to bathe a dog, cat, other pet
How to conduct yourself in a job interview

(b)
How a microwave oven cooks
How a computer works

How your school's honor system works
How a river system develops
How a nitrogen-fixing bacterial system works
How your school's financial aid system works
How a bill gets passed in Congress
How your school's athlete-recruitment system works
How a volcano comes into existence
How the lungs work
How kidney dialysis works
How the heart works
How public ownership of a corporation works
How a car's brakes work
How clouds, tornadoes, thunderstorms develop
How a beehive functions
How a propeller plane gets and stays airborne
How atomic fusion occurs

DEFINITION

A considerable amount of modern knowledge is devoted simply to *identifying* reality. We are constantly defining and redefining ideas, terms, objects, situations, and so on, not out of curiosity or as an intellectual exercise but because we are aware that we react to reality according to the way we define it. Throughout the 1960s there was a great deal of discussion about the threat of communism, especially in Southeast Asia. Terms like *democracy, socialism, communism, fascism, social democracy, the domino theory,* and *national socialism* were used in ill-defined or undefined ways to mean anything . . . and came to mean nothing. *Social democracy* and *socialism* meant *communism.* A fascist state was one you disliked. People argued for the domino theory without understanding what it meant and with no knowledge of the history of Southeast Asia. No good can come from ignorance and linguistic imprecision.

Some people do not bother themselves about the definitions of things. Their concepts are unexamined; they take things for granted. They assume the world is whatever it was when they were children—when most words are learned. As a writer, you cannot afford to operate with unexamined or naive concepts. You must carefully analyze the terms you use and by doing so reexplore and redefine reality. The dictionary, unfortunately, is not very helpful. Dictionary definitions are invented by dictionary makers, who must give in the least possible space, with the fewest possible words, the most general, overall definitions. The dictionary is a good place to start if you are trying to define a word, but as a writer you then go on from this general definition to say, or try to say, what the word means specifically, in a given context.

Here, for example, is a writer's attempt to define a word:

Senioritis   CONNIE TRUJILLO

Ever since my freshman year in high school I had heard many references to people having had cases of a thing called "senioritis," but I had never seen a definition of the word. I just knew the seniors used the word to explain why they were doing things that they weren't supposed to; and when teachers used it, it provoked sighs, exasperation, and sometimes mildly indulgent smiles. Perhaps the word is relatively new? Maybe someone recently invented it? I don't know, but "senioritis" is real, as I discovered in my senior year.

Senioritis is a frame of mind particular to high-school seniors. Most seniors experience their first tinges of this feeling after the class ahead of them graduates. It is then that seniors find themselves at the top of all the other grade levels, for they represent the class with the greatest number of years of education. This advanced status and the few but well-deserved privileges that are traditionally extended to seniors lead to a feeling of superiority over the underclassmen—the proverbial "swelled head."

Senioritis's particular state of mind carries with it rather odd and sometimes whimsical actions on the part of seniors. For instance, a senior may decide to sing in the library for the sheer intention of remaining impervious to the librarian's scornful stare. I found myself caught up in the spirit of senioritis one afternoon one week, when I raced two of my best friends across the grass to the cafeteria for lunch—and our lunches were not that good! I have seen several of my fellow seniors caught up in such frenzies of whimsy that they develop "skip-school-or-die" complexes, and despite rigid penalties, many mysterious absences subsequently occur. Thus seniors' actions, while under the influence of senioritis, are not logical or subject to reason.

However, senioritis is not a mere desire to create total havoc or mischief. Although havoc and mischief frequently result, they are merely byproducts of the affected senior's mind. Also, senioritis can not be encompassed by the word "pride," for pride is only one of many elements that affect the senior's ego. However, the special treatment given seniors does lead to the formation of a class pride, which is responsible for a large portion of the senioritis symptoms. Senioritis is not quite a tradition either, for although it occurs in each subsequent class year, it is not really handed down and passed on. It seems to be more of an annually recurring phenomenon.

Thus, senioritis is a way of thinking, feeling, and acting that is not logical and is frequently impervious to social codes. It is an odd and whimsical state of being that can only be truly experienced by a high-school senior.

You can see from Connie's paper that she has set herself a difficult problem—it isn't just a *word* she wants to define, but an idea or concept. She doesn't rush to the dictionary for help; in this case there wouldn't be any help. If she had found the word in the dictionary, the definition would have been something like "The peculiar restlessness of high-school seniors." This is only a generalization and leaves the reader with a big question—"*What* peculiar restlessness?" And it is that question that Connie tries to answer by giving specific concrete examples. Connie also goes on to distinguish *senioritis* from a closely related term like *self-pride* because the reader needs to be able to see what the thing is *not* as well as what it is, especially when there are similar terms for it (like the difference between love and affection). You can try this same kind of defining with other *-itis* words: *freshmanitis, examinationitis,* and so on.

In the following paper, the writer juxtaposes two closely related terms in order to highlight the subtle distinctions between them. How successful is she?

Embarrassment and Humiliation

YOLANDA SHERWOOD

I have a friend who is forever saying that everything is so *humiliating*—it's so *humiliating* to have to live in a dorm, it's so *humiliating* to go to a lecture, it's so *humiliating* to sweat, and so on. She uses the word to cover everything from mild embarrassment to simple annoyance but almost never uses it in connection with true humiliation. I'd say the difference between embarrassment and humiliation is the difference between an accident—a *faux pas*—and an insult. The one you cause yourself, but the other has to be done to you.

For example, I was taking a survey on ecology in a men's dormitory. Being female I didn't mind at all, although I was a little uneasy at the prospect of interviewing so many men in such a short time.

Two of the things that made my rounds so hazardous were the fact that I was unannounced and that it was at about ten o'clock at night, a time when many of the men don't expect female visitors.

The first few rooms weren't very active. When I got to the sixth room, though, things really began to roll.

I knocked on the door, expecting someone to open it. Instead one of the occupants answered my knock with a gruff "Come in." Being a little apprehensive at what I might find, I knocked again, this time receiving a loud, powerful chorus of slightly irritated "Come in"s. I still didn't think that I should enter without an okay, so I knocked a third time, and what a response! I heard a thunderous, bellowing roar of "God-dammit-to-hell!" The door was suddenly flung open so hard I thought the door would rip off its hinges for sure. It was almost as if a hurricane had attacked it.

There just inside the door stood the biggest hunk of man that I had ever seen! He was a six-foot, five-inch giant with curly black hair almost completely covering his very muscular chest and legs. His huge hands were still grasping the door, making the tremendous muscles of his arms stand out. He stood there in his skivvies in absolute shock. As for myself, I was shaking so much that I thought my legs were going to buckle for sure. I could feel my face turning from white to red to darker red and then white again. All of this happened in about four devastating seconds: *this* is embarrassment.

It didn't take him long to revive. Within another second he had slammed the door in my face and retreated inside, accompanied by the laughter of his roommates. But before I could move a muscle, the door opened again and he was back, leaning smugly against the door jamb. With his arms folded across his chest and a nasty sneer on his face he said, "Well, now that you've seen it all, little girl, what can I do for you?" I could feel my face doing a slow burn, staying red this time, but I recovered my mind almost instantly. "Now that I've seen it, you haven't got it, sonny," I said and stormed out of there in a huff. We had both been embarrassed by the sudden confrontation, but when he tried to recover his poise by putting me down, that was humiliation, and I hope I gave him a little lesson in it myself.

Yolanda's paper is a good example of distinguishing between two related terms, which is similar to distinguishing between different degrees of the same term, as in the following:

EARL TORRENTO

There is drunk and then there is *drunk*. In my experience, there are at least three or four stages of drunkenness, ranging from a pleasant glow of tipsiness all the way to the roaring blind staggers. My mother immediately accuses my father of being "drunk" after the first sip of beer, and thereafter dismisses anything he says as "drunken ravings." Obviously she does not understand the term or the condition. This paper will graph the various degrees of drunkenness and its characteristic behaviors and symptoms.

One other useful technique in defining is to distinguish the real from the ideal. We have myths, stereotypes, commonly held legends, and many other variations of reality. In the following paper the writer distinguishes between the real and the ideal in an interesting way. What approach does she take?

On The Rack   MARY ELLEN TYUS

The dull pain tightens noose-like as I turn my head, crunching agonizingly on the tendons of my neck. My head is heavy and I can hardly hold it up. My temples begin to throb, and a momentary blackness passes before my eyes as dizziness washes over me.

The pain travels across my shoulders and into my arms, which quiver briefly before numbness sets in. My fingers twitch slightly as they receive the message of suffering from my brain.

My back is rigid, streaked with pain which draws its fiery fingers from hip to shoulder. My stomach searches in vain for a morsel to digest, sending out weak signals of defeat.

The agony is most intense in my legs, where I am aware of each tortured muscle. It hurts to move—it is excruciating to remain motionless. A new pain travels down the back of my right leg and explodes like fireworks in an exquisite blossom of misery in my foot—twisting it, crippling it. I long to collapse and allow that misery to spread and consume me, and in so doing, release me, but I am held and must endure more.

My body moves with a force not its own, and sometimes finds itself beyond the pain. I revel in the brief reprieve, and so find strength to continue.

A new ache slides its sly embrace around my waist like the arm of a bashful lover; tentatively, then growing bolder. I try to remain aloof. I fail, and feel the muscles of my face betray me, abandoning my impassive expression. I want to cry out, but my throat is mute.

The pain continues for an hour with only brief intervals of peace. I live for those few moments and for the time when my suffering will end, though only to be resumed tomorrow.

History has known generations of human misery, from slavery to chain gangs, through war and holocaust. Modern technology has refined the ancient instruments of torture, replacing the iron maiden and the guillotine with more advanced devices for suffering, with napalm, bombs, and even the automobile. The human mind is limitless in its capacity to create agony. Sadists and masochists design ever more awesome methods to excruciate.

But this is the height of achievement. This is carefully refined, honed to the finest, sharpest, most precise cutting edge. This is *art*. This is Ballet!

Mary Ellen both entertains us and defines the agony of ballet by *not* mentioning the idealized picture most of us have of an ethereal prima ballerina gliding over the stage in time to enchanting music. In the second from last paragraph, she compares the excruciating physical pain with the worst horrors civilization has devised and then in a mock crescendo reveals *art* . . . Ballet! as the ultimate in sadomasochism.

In all these definitions, the *concrete example* or illustration is the important element. After that, the comparison or distinction between one term and another, between different degrees of the same term, or between different interpretations of reality (the real and the ideal) helps to make the definitions precise.

Read the following paper. Is the term well defined? What method of definition does the writer use?

For Klutzes Only NANCY KROEKEL

I snitched one final fingerful of batter before reluctantly heading towards the oven. Checking the bottom of the pan to make sure it wasn't leaking, I managed to catch the cuff of my faded Levi's on the cat's water dish, and became the first mummy ever to be mummified with Betty Crocker's chocolate cake batter.

Antics such as this have led to the nickname I've been branded with: klutz. I've been called a klutz for as long as I can remember, and have resented it for just as long. I can play tennis (I even defeated Kevin Thompson once, the number one player on our high school team), pitch a softball, save a drowning victim, and run the 100-yard dash in 12.5 seconds. Who cares if I can't throw a frisbee without clobbering an innocent bystander? So why, I've often wondered, am I a klutz? I suffered from an identity crisis for a long while before I came to the realization that a klutz was not what I pictured it to be. To all of you klutzes out there, there *is* hope.

Many people confuse the words *nonathletic* and *klutzy*. A nonathletic person lacks the skills and bodily coordination needed to perform sports or games requiring physical strength, agility, or stamina. You need only to observe a high-school gym class working on gymnastics to witness all of the nonathletic students you'd ever care to see. Let's watch that kid attempting to climb the rope. (He's the one with his green-and-red striped tube socks bunched around his ankles. See him?) He's trying to heave himself off the ground, but every time he lifts his feet, he slides down the rope as though a magnet were attracting him to the matted floor. Use those arm muscles! Now he's decided to try his luck at the horse. He's taking his approach run (which resembles that of an astronaut running in a space suit) and bounces on the spring board: he's up and . . . and . . . clinging, clinging to this side of the horse, as Wiley Coyote clings to a rock cliff for those few seconds after crashing, before plunging to his fate below. Oh good! Red and green stripes is trying again. He runs, he bounces, he's up and . . . is wedged in a straddle position atop the beast. Surely cartwheels are easier. Yes, here he comes folks, over to the mat to prove he can do something. He just did his—cartwheel? It looked more like a lopsided pumpkin catapulting down a rutted country lane. Thank you, red and green, for your demonstrations.

This is a nonathletic person. There is a definite distinction between him and a klutzy person. In the world of awkward and embarrassing gestures, there are two basic types of people: those who are nonathletic and those who are klutzy. There may be a few unfortunates who are both, but these are two independent categories. It is common to be nonathletic without being klutzy; likewise, an athlete may be klutzy. We have seen nonathleticism in its raw form. Now let's view klutziness.

Klutziness exists because people continually do awkward things. These situations arise not from a lack of intelligence or coordination, but from a momentary lack of common sense. The following incident has helped to secure my nickname permanently.

Millersville State College held its orientation day in October of my senior year of high school. I, along with several classmates, attended it. After several mind-boggling hours of tours and lectures, I found myself seated in the faculty dining room. I had secured a prominent spot—the head of the biology department sat on my left while my heartthrob sat on my right. A freshly tossed salad sat staring up at me; the plump cherry tomato, which balanced right on top, invited me to attack it. I stabbed it eagerly with my fork—a juicy mistake. Its slimy insides spurted out, staining the white tablecloth, while my salad jumped, as though off of a trampoline, to the previously sparkling floor. As my face flushed to match the color of the tablecloth stains, the biology professor, in an attempt to ease the situation, said, "We don't mind if you prefer eating your salad out of your lap." To which my heartthrob responded, "Except that she wants to eat it off the floor."

Since I was not quite sure what to do with the mess, I slyly picked it up and stuffed it into my pockets. I hope it never crossed anyone's mind to wonder what happened to that leafy jumble. Later that evening, I threw away my memorable salad remains in a restroom trashcan; with them, I threw away all ideas of attending Millersville State.

Nonathletic and klutzy—two words that signify embarrassment. Most people wish there had never been a need to invent the words—life would be so much simpler (and more dignified) without the actions they imply.

To all of you klutzes who managed to read this far without ripping a page—there *is* hope. Just because we are klutzes does not mean we're nonathletic or unintelligent; we just frequently lack a bit of common sense. Look on the bright side: maybe some good has come of it—just think of all of the smiles our antics have put on other people's faces.

Writing the Definition Paper

At the heart of every attempt to define a word or concept is some kind of confusion. There is obviously no point in trying to write a definition of a term if your readers and you are in full agreement as to what it means. The best terms to define are those about which there is substantial disagreement. Then your definition becomes an act of clarification.

Approach the term you have selected from every conceivable angle. Brainstorm the term. Use the journalistic formula and Burke's pentad. Compare the word with others close in meaning. Contrast it with words that have the opposite meaning. Expand, illustrate, give examples, as many as you can think of, to demonstrate the meaning of the word. Show varying degrees of meaning. Compare the old meaning with newer meanings or contrast the ideal meaning with the real. In every case, offer the reader concrete details with which to understand the word.

Only then should you begin structuring your paper, organizing the information you have accumulated for maximum impact on your reader.

Writing activity

For your first attempt at defining, write a two- to four-page definition. Avoid large and difficult abstractions like *honor*, *philosophy*, *love*, and so on. You will have the most success with words for physical objects or physical behavior, such as the following:

dancing	mania
dating	nonathletic
freshmen	poverty
hassles	rip-off
helpful people	sarcasm
hustling	tension
insults	vitality
kleptomania	winter

CHAPTER FOUR

Evaluative and Persuasive Writing

Where there is much desire to learn,

there of necessity will be much arguing, much writing,

many opinions; for opinion in good men

is but knowledge in the making.

JOHN MILTON, *Aereopagitica*

One of the advantages of writing over speaking is the depth and precision of reasoning that writing permits. With the written word you can construct longer and more complex arguments. And since you can edit and revise the written word, you can achieve greater accuracy of thought and expression. It is no wonder, then, that people have high regard for writing that presents human thought: opinions, arguments, judgments, and persuasion.

It is not enough to collect data, sort it, and file it away. Computers are better at such work than we are. It takes a human mind to challenge the data, to argue the merits of an idea, to upset settled notions and arrive at new insights, new concepts. For the writer, the real challenge is not in recording facts, but in questioning them: ultimately, writing is *thinking*.

How we convince each other of the truth is at the heart of democracy. It is built into our legislatures and our judicial system: evidence is introduced, reasons are given, conclusions are drawn. We argue for our convictions. Learning how to create a carefully developed, reasonable argument represents a significant step in the development of a writer.

In the first part of this chapter, you will examine and practice the skills necessary for evaluative writing, writing that judges the worth of something. In order to convince your readers of the soundness of your *judgments*, you must deal with the *facts* in a fair and objective way. Your readers won't listen to your opinions if you present the facts in a biased fashion.

THE OBJECTIVE SUMMARY

A good place to begin is by practicing the objective summary, or précis. Your objective summary presents the reader with the essential *information* contained in an article, without stating, or hinting at, your opinion of the article. The specific purpose of an objective summary is to condense information into the shortest useful form for the reader.

Many readers want and need that service. In college, you may be the principal audience for your objective summaries. You will discover that a good summary is often as useful as—occasionally more useful than—a full article from a magazine or journal. (Two significant assets are portability and availability—you can take your own summary out of the library.) For example, you can tell from the following summary whether "frisbee golf" will fit into a paper on new developments in recreation:

The St. Andrews of Frisbee Golf[1]

JOAN LEONE

The Los Angeles County Department of Parks and Recreation has a new type of recreational facility—the Frisbee golf course. The course, which was opened in the summer of 1975, has become extremely popular with the public and has captured the media with enthusiasm.

Ed Headrick, founder of the International Frisbee Association, originated the proposal for developing a formal permanent Frisbee golf course. Oak Grove County Park is a fifty-three-acre natural oak grove, which is where it all began.

An eighteen-hole course was built at the park for the relatively small investment of $2,000. The sport requires no fees, scoreboard, other materials, or activities requiring personnel; there are no operating costs. In addition, it promotes casual, less competitive play and attracts many families visiting Oak Park Grove.

The course itself is relatively simple. The basic rules and diagrams of the course layout are posted at the first tee. At the start of each hole, tee-offs are ten-foot circles delineated by quartered redwood logs. Safety hazards, information on out-of-bounds, direction of the hole, and the distance involved are provided at each tee.

Target posts, presently standing four feet high, must be hit by the Frisbee. Players begin throwing one Frisbee in the tee-off area, and take their next shot with their foot on the spot where the Frisbee landed. The score is determined by the number of throws it takes to hit the target. Similar to golf, the player with the lowest score at the end of the round is the winner.

The ideal Frisbee golf course must have trees to block wind, and hilly terrain makes it all the more enjoyable. Being laid out in the hilly, densely wooded areas, the course is not confronted with other traditional activities, such as baseball.

The participation of Frisbee fans has grown, from an average of two hundred, to one thousand persons using the course on weekend days. After-school use has also become so popular that the high school located near Oak Grove Park has begun Frisbee classes! Frisbee golf has much to offer to all age groups, including men and women and the physically handicapped.

[1]Seymour Greben, "The St. Andrews of Frisbee Golf," *Parks & Recreation*, Oct. 1976, pp. 22–23.

You can see at once from Joan's summary that the article is mostly a description of how to play a new game with a Frisbee. Except for the fact that the game is popular and offers recreation to everyone, the article does not say anything about trends or developments in recreation. Joan might mention Frisbee golf in her paper, and this summary condenses the original article well enough so that she wouldn't have to seek out the original again.

It would be a mistake to think of summarizing as just a college exercise. Out of college, a supervisor might ask you to summarize a year's memos on employee productivity as one source of information for creating a new company policy on absenteeism. Or you may have to summarize a hospital patient's previous admission history or condense an article on problems of child safety for your busy day-care counselors.

Writing the Objective Summary

An objective summary should be about one third the length of the original article. The following guidelines also apply:

1 Get the main ideas by locating key sentences and words in each paragraph. How much supportive material you include depends on how important you think that material is. The main points are the heart of the article, and leaving any of them out will distort the summary.

2 Use your own words. You can condense greatly by combining ideas from the original into new sentences of your own. Avoid copying the original language as much as possible, and put quotes around any that you do borrow. Especially if you are summarizing for someone else, it is important to distinguish between words that are yours and words that are in the original. Among other things, summarizing is a good way to learn, to assimilate material, but the process doesn't work very well unless you translate the original into your own language.

3 Follow the organization of the original. Your summary should begin where the original begins and proceed in the same order as the original. Try to give a true but condensed picture of the article, including the way it is organized.

4 In an objective summary, you record only the information contained in the article, and nothing else. Keep your opinions to yourself. Do not add commentary, interpretation, or anything else not in the original. An *objective* summary means that you are conveying the information and nothing else. When you write an objective summary, you are processing information, as accurately and economically as possible, rather than evaluating, disputing, or agreeing with that information. You have an obligation to be impartial and reliable.

5 Always give the source of your material in a footnote. (Pages 204–207 cover footnote formats.) Nothing is quite as frustrating as good information without a source; the unfortunate reader must trudge back to the library to find the article again—if it can be found. Notice that Joan Leone has used a footnote number after the title of her paper. Since there is only one footnote, you do not really need to number it, but if you do use a number (superscript), put it after the title.

Summarizing is a simple but useful skill. The most frequent problems beginning writers may encounter in summarizing are either that they are too summary or that they are not summary enough. A little practice should produce summaries of the proper length, but one thing to watch out for is the article that is already too condensed or too skimpy to summarize. Select an article that *can* be summarized.

Writing activity

Write a one-page summary of a magazine article or a newspaper article. Select a recent article, one published within the past year. Assume that you are summarizing for an employer, who has asked you to condense the material. Remember, an objective summary should be about one-third the length of the original article.

THE CRITICAL SUMMARY

Every day we are all exposed to endless information on a variety of subjects, but is it all equally worthwhile? Because something has been published does not mean that it is good. One of the most important attributes of a thinking person is the ability to look at information objectively and evaluate its worth. Writing critical summaries helps you to develop that skill because it asks you to act as summarizer *and* critic. Here is an example of such a summary:

KARL WITBOLD

A sniper's shot killed Martin Luther King on April 4, 1968. *Time* magazine traces the flight from justice of convicted assassin James Earl Ray. The article covers his steps from escaping Missouri State Prison on April 23, 1967, to plastic surgery in Los Angeles and finally his arrest at Heathrow Airport in England. *Time* attempts to answer questions that still linger after eight years, using information accumulated by George McMillen, the author of a book about the crime to be published this fall. A few questions raised are, Did Ray kill King? Why did he kill him? Did he act alone? How did Ray acquire false identification and establish four credible aliases without help?

Time presents Ray as a small time, butter-fingered burglar, nazi sympathizer, and devoted racist. McMillen and *Time* seem to agree that "Ray's anti-black sentiments turned into intense hatred for King."

Circumstances around Ray's conviction are also questionable. No one saw Ray fire the shot; the bullet that killed King could not be traced. Was the one state witness against Ray reliable?

The article, though quite interesting, was not very informative, asking more questions than it could hope to answer. *Time* seemed to be more interested in plugging the McMillen book and causing controversy than seriously discussing Martin Luther King's assassination.

[1]"The King Assassination Revisited," *Time*, 26 Jan. 1976, pp. 16–17.

Karl's critique of the article in *Time* has three important parts: (1) a summary of the content of the article; (2) clues throughout that Karl is talking about a magazine article (note how often Karl refers to the magazine by name); and (3) Karl's opinion of the article. He criticizes *what* was said ("interesting" but "not very informative") as well as *how* it was said (it asked "more questions than it could hope to answer").

Writing the Critical Summary

Criticizing Content   Content is subject matter: *what* is said, as opposed to *how* it is said. In an article on alternative energy sources, for example, the content is what the author has to say about alternative energy sources, and you can discuss the author's knowledge and handling of this subject. The listed criteria can help you to evaluate content.

1 Is the author accurate? Does the author distort, exaggerate, or diminish the facts? Does the author *seem* to have the facts straight?
2 Has the author supplied the reader with new facts, new information, or new interpretation of the facts? How newsworthy is this subject?

3 Is the subject interesting? Does the material raise your curiosity about the subject? Does it hold your interest? Is it interesting only to you personally, or do you think it is likely to appeal to the general reader?

4 Is there enough information? Is this a thorough treatment or a sketchy overview? Is the author treating the subject with sufficient depth? Has the author supplied the reader with enough facts or enough details to achieve his or her overall purpose?

5 Is the material worthwhile? Does it treat a subject that most readers would agree is worth treating? If the material seems trivial or "light," did the author intend it to be that way?

6 Is the author fair? Is the overall interpretation biased, subjective, slanted, objective? Does the author present material to justify his or her stance? Does the author try to look at both sides of the issue? Do you trust this author? Can you find any errors in the author's logic?

7 Did you feel satisfied or disappointed or puzzled by the article? If the author started out to prove something, did he or she fulfill your expectation? If the author started out to analyze something, did you feel he or she lived up to the commitment? Did you come away feeling the author knew the subject and did a good job of presenting it to the reader?

Criticizing Style   Style is the author's manner of writing: how the material is written as opposed to what it says. Evaluating a piece of writing with the following criteria can help you to critize style.

1 Is the author readable? Are there unnecessary big words, too many long sentences, too many abstract concepts not explained in concrete terms? Is the writing aimed at the right audience? Can the educated general reader handle this material without difficulty?

2 Has the author chosen vocabulary that is accurate, colorful, effective? Is the author expressing a lively point of view, or does he or she sound bored? Are the language and the attitude boring? Is the author being matter of fact, disinterested, objective, ironic, or something else?

3 Is the language appropriate? Does the author treat dignified subjects with dignity and humorous subjects light-heartedly? Or is the author showing off, being sarcastic, or smart-alecky? Are there any surprises in language? An unusually good word? An especially adept phrase? A well-turned sentence? Can a careful reader find variety in the sentences? Or is there evidence that the writer was having a hard time writing: labored sentences, fuzzy language, humdrum words?

4 What is the author's attitude toward the subject? Does the author like the subject? Does the author think the subject is important? More important than you do?

5 What is the author's attitude toward the reader? Is the author friendly? Indifferent? Sarcastic? Patronizing? Too technical? Who does the author think the reader is: a little child, God, an educated adult?

6 Who does the author think he or she is? Very Important Person? Poor-little-old-me? Is the author's view of self (the author's voice) one you can relate to?

7 Did you enjoy the piece of writing? Did you feel pleased by the way it was written? Did it occur to you that the material was especially well written? Did you finish the article thinking, "This was a good piece of work"? Would you recommend the article to others?

When you talk or write about *how* something is written, you must discuss style and organization, just as you do in your composition class. Everyone's favorite comment on a piece of writing is "interesting and informative," but having said that, you should go on to explain *why* you say it. Is the reasoning acceptable? Does the author avoid imprecision, slanting, bias, exaggerations, obvious faults in reasonable writing? Do you need a Ph.D. to understand the article, or is it aimed at elementary-school children? Is the tone light, heavy, dull, and so forth? Very often some one feature of an article will stand out as the chief virtue or overriding fault—such as an overreliance on technical vocabulary. It may be a good idea to deal with that feature as the primary aspect of your critique, but then relate others to it. Why does the author use such language? Is it justified, appropriate? (It may not be.)

Read the following critical summary and explain how Joan has followed the advice above. What are the strengths of the critique?

Honk, Honk If You Love Mary Hartman, Mary Hartman[1]

JOAN LEONE

Don't be surprised if you find Mary Hartman washing lettuce with detergent. In her television parody of a soap opera, she is portrayed as being a "copeless" housewife beset by assorted calamities in Fernwood, Ohio. *Reader's Digest* brings out the reality of *Mary Hartman* by stating: "It's the news about American life—complete with issues like impotence, alienation, homosexuality and adultery, and references to Vietnam, Richard Nixon, Watergate and Howard Hughes." The article compares the show to the news by pointing out that *Mary Hartman* is the news and TV news tells us almost nothing about people's lives.

The show has been analyzed and interpreted by many viewers. Donald Freed, novelist and coordinator of an extension course at the University of California, believes that Mary's uneasy feeling that things should be different is a form of existential awareness.

The article has a relaxing and honest air to it. This casual style makes it easy to read and interpret. *Reader's Digest* justly recognizes that there are two sides to the story. "It's not all applause for *Mary Hartman*, of course. A station in Richmond, Va., cancelled the show."

Mary Hartman lives the life of a mother, a lover, rejector, and rejectee. How can she be them all? Easy, she's the star of the show. *Reader's Digest* portrays the character of Mary Hartman as a symbolic figure in today's society. Should we be laughing at her or is she capturing the true reality of our own lives?

Like a tattered housewife we search for love and understanding. What qualities make this show a success? Television critic, novelist, and teacher Peter Sourian sees the producer, Norman Lear, as a "Marxist who is chronicling the decline of a capitalist society."

The satire soap opera *Mary Hartman* is more than it is apt to project. *Reader's Digest* covers the article with humor and signifies the symbolic aspects that relate to our daily lives. Through the somewhat far-fetched half-hour episodes *Mary Hartman* reveals the real you. That is why it is a uniquely American show. It could only happen here.

Although viewers have trouble clearly defining the show, *Reader's Digest* has handled *Mary Hartman* with frankness and perspicuity.

[1]Ted Morgan, "Honk, Honk, If You Love Mary Hartman, Mary Hartman," *Reader's Digest*, Feb. 1977, pp. 57–65.

Writing activity

Write a two- or three-page critical summary of a recent article from a magazine or newspaper. Your criticism of the article is the important part of the assignment; do not devote more than one-half page to the summary.

Read and analyze the article carefully, using the guidelines on pages 133–135. It is a good idea to jot down the points you want to make and the examples you want to use. You need not make a formal outline, but some prewriting notes to yourself will be useful.

COMPARING ARTICLES

Even more enlightening than evaluating an article is comparing two articles on the same subject written by two different authors. It is not safe to rely on any one author for either the facts or the interpretation of the facts in a given case. Writers have different styles, they write for different audiences, and they write with different purposes—even when they claim to be writing objectively. It is important for you to be able to see the differences between authors and to evaluate the influence authors have on their materials. Author X says Adolf Hitler was a deranged maniac; author Y says he was a dynamic leader. What would lead two writers to draw such different conclusions about the same subject?

Here is a writer comparing two magazine articles about the boxer George Foreman. Can you tell from what the writer says that the two articles are in fact different? How does Gordon bring out the differences?

Foreman's Fight GORDON WYMORE

Far from the flag-toting days of Olympic boxing are the problems of the heavyweight boxer. George Foreman, remembered by many Americans for waving the American flag after winning the Olympic gold medal, has encountered many problems since the heavyweight title was taken from him by the flamboyant Muhammad Ali. His problems are outlined by magazine articles in *Sports Illustrated* and *Newsweek*.

Peter Bonventre is the author of the article in *Newsweek* magazine. Bonventre states, "The defeat shattered his image of himself, pulled him apart from old friends and advisors, and made him question why he had ever laced on a pair of boxing gloves."[1] Foreman fired his trainer and hired one of the best in the business—Gil Clancy. Bonventre claims Clancy has built Foreman's confidence up and changed his style of fighting. According to the author, Foreman is ready for a shot at the heavyweight championship of the world.

The *Sports Illustrated* article is written by George Foreman with Edwin Shrake assisting. This article is mainly concerned with making excuses about his loss to Muhammad Ali for the heavyweight championship. Foreman states, "First, let me tell you some truths. Let's go back to the ring at Zaire. . . ."[2] Foreman tries to lay the blame for the loss on his ex-trainer, Dick Sadler. Foreman says that Sadler trained him wrong, used the wrong strategy for the fight, and told him to stay down on the canvas, a move that lost the fight. He then goes on to defend his controversial exhibition in Toronto, where he fought and beat five challengers on the same night. Finally, Foreman concludes all his problems are behind him, and he deserves another "shot at the crown."

The two authors' approaches to Foreman's problems vary greatly. Bonventre writes his article on Foreman from a third-person point of view, while the *Sports Illustrated* article is written by Foreman himself. Foreman's facts are distorted, and he only brings out the facts that will enhance his image in the reader's mind. Meanwhile, Bonventre deals in what he considers to be the truth; however, it is enlivened by his own comments.

The grammar used by both writers also varies. Foreman's article is full of "street talk," slang, and clichés. He overuses the word "man": "Man, I really got messed over there."[3] "Man, I was back in the ring. . . ."[4] Repeated use of street talk distracts from the overall impression of the article. Bonventre's essay had more vivid details than Foreman's, but the words are such that most people can comprehend them.

> The former heavyweight champion of the world clambered into the ring, and his features froze into a glare as frightening as any of the punches that he exploded against his sparring partner. He even looked dangerously trimmer, and each blow was punctuated by a harsh grunt that echoed through the gym. . . .[5]

Bonventre's nice transitions between paragraphs make the article a pleasure to read. In contrast, Foreman's article has no pattern of arrangement. It is as if it was written down as the thoughts occurred to him. Foreman's writing could be condensed into a shorter essay, without losing the meaning, by cutting out useless material: "Maybe you didn't even read about the fight. I mean, there was no TV, and papers didn't fall all over themselves to cover it."[6] Phrases like this could be eliminated throughout the article. Bonventre's review is presented so that he puts forward the facts and draws a conclusion in one smooth-reading paper.

In conclusion, Bonventre's article is clearly superior to Foreman's if the basis for quality is grammar. Bonventre writes with a polished touch while Foreman writes at the level of his ninth-grade education. However, Foreman's article includes an inside view of boxing—a view readers rarely see. Bonventre's essay has the experienced writer's touch but lacks the "personality" of Foreman's article. Overall, the two articles are both good, but for different reasons.

[1]Peter Bonventre, "Tiger, Burning Bright," *Newsweek*, 26 Jan. 1976, p. 38.
[2]George Foreman, "Man, Big George is Back," *Sports Illustrated*, 15 Dec., 1975, p. 82.
[3]Foreman, p. 84.
[4]Foreman, p. 86.
[5]Bonventre, p. 38.
[6]Foreman, p. 86.

Gordon's analysis of the two articles is fair and insightful. He begins by summarizing the content of the two articles. After an introduction that lets the reader see that he is going to discuss two magazine articles, Gordon describes the *Newsweek* article objectively. He summarizes without evaluating. In his next paragraph, Gordon summarizes the *Sports Illustrated* article, again objectively. These two paragraphs are important for the reader; it would be difficult for us to appreciate the critical comments if we did not have some notion of what is being criticized.

In his fourth paragraph, after a transitional sentence, Gordon begins his critique of the two articles. In this paragraph Gordon presents an overview of his reactions to *what* the authors say and *how* they say it.

In the next two paragraphs, Gordon focuses on the style and organization of the two articles, because it is here that he finds the greatest differences between them.

Finally, in his concluding paragraph, Gordon gives his overall view of the two articles and concludes that whereas Bonventre's article is better written, Foreman's has a view of boxing that most people don't get to see, and therefore they are both good articles.

Gordon has managed to be both critical and fair, and the reader comes away with a good notion of what is in the two articles.

Writing the Comparison of Articles

Two articles may treat different aspects of the same subject: one article may discuss the President's foreign policy and another his relations with Congress or his family life. These different views or different aspects of the subject will work very well for your purposes. In fact, you should expect to find more differences than similarities in your sources, unless your authors have been borrowing from each other. In theory, two newspapers covering the same national or international story should come up with the same information, but *in fact* they usually do not, unless they are both relying on one or more of the news wire services for their information; and even then variations can occur.

In the first paragraph you must make clear to the reader that you are discussing two articles. Mention them by title, or refer to the magazines or the authors or all of these, so that there can be no mistake about your sources. If there is a common thread through the articles (the President's woes increase both at home and abroad), you should say so. If the two articles are very different, you need only point out this difference (two views of the President: national leader and family man).

As Gordon did in his paper on Foreman, spend two paragraphs describing what is in each of the articles. Even a one-paragraph summary can give the reader a fair notion of what is in each of the articles.

After considering the articles separately, it is a good idea, as Gordon did in his fourth paragraph, to consider them together. Analyze the overall approaches to the articles. You should be concerned with both *what* is said and *how* it is said. Do both authors have the facts? Who—or what—is the source of information? What is the point of view: objective reporter, news analyst (intepreter), human-interest reporter (entertainer), or someone else? Analyzing an author's *approach* to his or her materials can tell you a great deal about how to judge what is being said. Is the author accurate, fair, comprehensive, informed, and so on?

When considering the writers' styles, you may want to distinguish between the actual words and sentences they use as opposed to the way they have set up or organized their articles. It is important *throughout* your paper to back up what you say by quoting from the articles, but especially here, where you are talking about *how* the articles are written, it is important to quote from the sources. Not only does quoting help support what you say, it gives the reader some of the flavor and texture of the articles. Nothing is quite so revealing about a source as examples in the author's own words.

Finally, in your conclusion you must give your opinion of the articles. Are they well written? Well researched? Thorough? You need to be fair here: point out strengths as well as weaknesses. It is possible to conclude, as Gordon does, that the articles are effective on different grounds, for different purposes. You must try to avoid fence sitting and hedging too much. If one is truly superior in your eyes, say so and explain why. Try to avoid the all-purpose evaluation: "Interesting and informative." Anything well written is likely to be interesting and informative. As critic it is your job to try to explain why. On what grounds have you evaluated something as interesting and informative? You may want to review the guidelines on pages 133–135.

Footnotes Even if you have identified the articles in your paper, it is a good idea to give a full footnote for each of them at least once. Since there are only the two articles involved, it is not strictly necessary to use a new footnote reference every time you quote from one of the articles. But if you are going to footnote each of your direct quotes, it is a good idea to do it as Gordon has, with a shortened form of the first reference instead of with *ibid*. Chapter 5 covers footnote formats.

Writing activity

Find two articles on the same subject and write a three- to six-page comparison of them. It should be relatively easy to find two articles that interest you using the *Readers' Guide to Periodical Literature*, but you might also want to try two newspaper articles or one newspaper and one magazine article on the same subject: two articles on the President, two articles on the Olympics, two articles on a sensational crime, and so on.

THE CRITICAL REVIEW

Now that you have had some experience summarizing and evaluating, you should be ready to broaden your role as critic. Critical reviews permit you to examine a work—film, TV show, sports event, and so on—in detail and judge its worth. Reviews often seem negative, but a critical review can be largely positive and should always be constructive.

How does John J. O'Connor, television critic of *The New York*

Times, organize the following review? Does he give readers enough information about the new show "Matt Houston"? Too much? What is the point of the comparison with "Magnum, P.I."? What is O'Connor's attitude toward "Matt Houston"? What words and phrases show that attitude?

Old Ideas for the New Season

JOHN J. O'CONNOR, "TV View," *The New York Times*, 26 Sept. 1982

The new season is just getting under way, but it is already apparent that the television industry is up to its old tricks of cloning and recycling. One rule of thumb about programming has long been that if, say, a Western becomes a hit during one season, the next season is going to be cluttered with Westerns. More prominent among recent successes has been "Magnum, P.I.," a CBS series about a rakish private investigator living luxuriously in Hawaii. Tom Selleck, the star, has been seriously challenging Burt Reynolds for the distinction of being the nation's leading male sex symbol. Question: Will Selleck lookalikes soon be popping up on the home screen? Answer: see "Matt Houston," which begins its ABC weekly run tonight at 8 with a special two-hour premiere.

CBS's Magnum is not rich but he lives on the estate of a rich man who has hired him for security reasons. He therefore can afford to indulge his fantasies, most of which seem to have been plucked from Playboy magazine. ABC's Houston, on the other hand, is rich. He's a Texan with conglomerate holdings guaranteeing a life of endless pleasures. Private investigating is only his private hobby. At that point, differences between the two characters come to an abrupt halt.

Played by Lee Horsley, Houston is an almost perfect clone of Magnum, right down to the mustache and cool macho voice. Houston is a suave and sophisticated good ol' boy who is, needless to say, irresistible to women, especially those of the curvaciously beautiful variety. He travels to his office in Los Angeles by helicopter. He is surrounded by the latest in computer gadgets. The centerpiece of the main room is a giant hot tub, which he occasionally shares with clients, especially those of the curvaciously beautiful variety. Most of his staff, except for his finicky business accountant (George Wyner), consists of statuesque young women who spend most of their time pouting for his attention. Capping the fantasy concoction, Houston has a seemingly endless supply of gorgeous sports cars. Think of James Bond. Think of any number of girlie magazines. Think of "Magnum, P.I." Or perhaps the real clue to appreciating "Matt Houston" is not to think at all.

In this evening's debut, a vicious Italian industrialist, one Nicolo Gambaccini, is sent to his heavenly reward after a bottle of champagne he is using to christen a new supertanker turns out to be filled with nitroglycerin. His glamorous daughter seeks Houston's help in finding the murderer. "I'll give you anything," she purrs. "Anything?," asks Matt with cool suggestiveness. "Yes, anything," responds the almost panting Sirena. Eventually, the number of prime suspects is narrowed to three, one of whom is Sirena. The case widens to include porno movies made by the dead man to blackmail friends and enemies. There are the inevitable car chases, with one of Houston's prize possessions being demolished and, for a smashing finale, another vehicle tumbling, in slowed motion, from a high bridge. For good measure, there is even an overly fussy Italian woman, the mother of Houston's police detective friend. She keeps insisting that the boys finish eating huge platters of canneloni and pizza. Meanwhile, Matt Houston, in vested suit, tie, Stetson and sunglasses, never loses his sense of humor and snazzy aplomb. Can the series work? As always, it probably depends most on the competition provided by the other networks.

John O'Connor is an effective critic, at ease with his subject. His review deals not only with "Matt Houston" and "Magnum P. I." but with the important issue of "cloning and recycling" shows on television. As a critic, you too must be knowledgeable not only about the work or performance you are judging but also about the background, principles, and techniques of that discipline. If you are writing about art, music, films, sports, literature, television, and so on, you need to describe for your readers *what* happened, in a play, for example, and *how* it was performed, what techniques were used. And then you must *judge* the performance. Was it good, bad, mediocre? Were the techniques effective? Was the message worthwhile?

To make such judgments, you need a sense of quality—from your own experience, from study, from cultural tradition. To be an effective critic you must *care* about quality.

Here is a film review by a student writer:

The Deep LINDA LENAHAN

The Deep is a chilling underwater adventure based on the book of the same title by Peter Benchley. *The Deep* has mostly the same elements as *Jaws*, Benchley's first financial blockbuster: the ocean, danger, adventure, and death. It is a typical good-guys-versus-bad-guys plot.

The movie is about a young couple, played by Nick Nolte and Jacqueline Bisset, who are vacationing at a Bermuda resort. While diving one day, the two find a shipwreck which contains thousands of ampules of morphine. Under the World War II wreck, there is another old Spanish ship with royal eighteenth-century gold and jewels buried in it. A Haitian drug dealer chases the couple throughout the movie to get access to the morphine so he can sell it as heroin to dealers in New York City. The couple is more interested in the royal treasure, though. They hire a boat captain, played by Robert Shaw, who is also a courageous treasure hunter and expert diver, to help prove the authenticity of the royal treasure.

The movie is full of adventure, and parts of the show may be too violent for a young viewer to see. There are scenes of voodoo, the sound of someone's neck breaking, the sight of a turning propeller on an outboard motor held close to someone's face, a deadly moray eel attacking a man in one of the sunken ships, and an outdoor elevator falling and killing a man.

At times the movie got quite boring. This is a problem for all underwater movies, though. The basic problem is that when people swim under water, it seems like it is done in slow motion. This makes the movie seem more stretched out and boring. The writers of *The Deep* were clever enough, in some cases, to distract us from the problem of underwater slowness by piling up devices such as the moray eel, the beautiful reefs, the sunken ship, sharks, and great underwater photography.

The acting in the movie was pretty good. Of the three stars, though, Robert Shaw outdid Bisset and Nolte with his performance. Nick Nolte, who's supposed to be a prime contender for Robert Redford's spot as number one sex symbol, didn't really add too much to the role he played. Ms. Bisset just proved how nice she could look under water in her much publicized T-shirt.

It's really hard to judge acting in an underwater movie. Everyone has a mask on, and no one can talk, so it's really hard to judge a person's acting ability. It would be easier to judge their swimming ability.

My last gripe about the movie is that it makes the bad guys (who all happen to be black) look like sex fiends. In one scene they force Ms. Bisset to strip in front of them, even though they know she could not possibly hide the large medallion that they are searching for. Later, the Haitians invade her room dressed in voodoo outfits, smear her body with blood, and they seem to do something rather queer with a chicken claw that they carry around for their ritual.

Although there are many bad points to the film, there are good ones too. The photography was just terrific. Even if you don't enjoy watching underwater films, the photographs of the activities are so exceptional, you'd surely admire the photographer. Overall, it was a good movie, but it was overpublicized by the media. After seeing all of the publicity, a person would be led to believe that *The Deep* was the biggest hit next to *Gone with the Wind*, and it really can't stand up to that sort of competition.

Linda is a convincing critic. We can believe she thoroughly remembers the film. Notice the kinds of things she recalls: names of actors, key incidents of the plot, and specific details. Furthermore, she makes comparisons between this film and another based on a novel by the same author and between this film and other adventure films in general. We can believe Linda understands the work she is evaluating.

There are many elements one might judge in a film review: plot, acting, directing, dialogue, pacing, setting, photography, and so

on. The more you know about how films are made, the more confident you will feel in your critiques of them. The same is true of television shows, sports events, and any other performance or work.
The more you know about the art, the more you can analyze it critically. Linda has selected several of the key elements in film-making
to use in her critique, those that seem most relevant to *The Deep:*
the plot, pacing, acting, social commentary or point of view (which
Linda feels is racist), photography, and even the publicity campaign, which seemed to promise more than the film could deliver.

And Linda attempts to be fair. She cites problems in the film—
such as pacing—but shows that she understands this as inherent in
films of this kind. She does point out good qualities of the film.

Writing the Critical Review

One of the critic's jobs is to give the reader a reasoned evaluation
of a work. Another is to help establish or maintain standards of excellence by which to evaluate similar works. As a critic, your basic
function is to report what you observed and what you thought about
what you observed. Therefore, one good way to start a review is to
describe for the reader what the performance was like; you can't assume the reader also saw the concert or read the book or listened to
the album.

Of course, there are different criteria for evaluating such diverse
kinds of works as films, television shows, graphic arts, writing, music, and even food. As you explore any of these fields, you will learn
about both the specifics to be judged and the standards of excellence by which to judge them. But you can be a critic without being
an expert, because the general principle for criticism is to experience and judge, and then to convince the reader of the reasonableness of your judgment.

Merely describing the plot of a film, for example, isn't enough. Is
the plot believable, even if it concerns Superman or Frankenstein's
monster? (Does the audience forget about the improbable and get
caught up in the story?) Do you *care* about the story and the characters? Does the story have moral, social, psychological, or some other kind of value? In the same way, just describing the lines and
colors of a painting isn't enough. Is the idea behind the painting
clear, even if the painting is a yellow square painted on a white
background? What reaction does the painting create in you? What
causes the reaction: the idea, colors, lines, subject? Is there any value in the painting? In all cases, what do *you* think? How do *you* rate
what you've seen, heard, felt, touched, tasted?

In giving your criticisms, there are two things to remember.

First, you must be reasonable and accurate. Critics who seem to be biased or merely personal in their criticisms will appeal only to those who share their biases. Try to give a balanced criticism; state both strengths *and* weaknesses if you can. Second, back up what you say by citing examples. Note in the following papers how often the writers give examples to illustrate their criticism. Using supportive evidence goes a long way toward establishing the critic's believability. In effect it says, "Don't take my word for it; judge for yourself. Here is the evidence!"

Assume the following three papers are the winners in a contest to select the new critic for your college newspaper. Which would you select? Ask yourself these questions: Is the writer factual? Is the writer interesting? Does the review appeal to the general reader? What has the writer done to convince the reader?

An Officer and a Gentleman

JIM WARD

An Officer and a Gentleman, written by Douglas Day Stewart and directed by Taylor Hackford, exemplifies a classic story of how a sad childhood is overcome in the end. Zach Mayo, played by Richard Gere, is a long haired and out-of-luck kid who is tired of the life he's leading. In an attempt to gain personal and social acceptance, Mayo enlists in a Naval Officer Program.

The main setting of the film is a Naval Aviation Officer Candidate School on an anonymous base. The base is clean, orderly, and quickly recognizable as a place of discipline. While three soldiers stand at attention, a flag is raised overhead in front of the main gate. Troops, groomed and dressed to precision, march in perfect formation to their sergeant's calls. Several groups jog and chant quick, snappy rhymes while keeping pace with their drill instructor. Others are led through a grueling and demanding obstacle course that features drills such as tire running, wall climbing, horizontal ladder climbing, crawling through barbed-wire tunnels, fence hopping, and swinging over a mud and water hazard à la Tarzan.

The time of the setting is the late 1970s. A good clue to this is the emergence of a woman as an officer candidate. Also, the leading man, Zach Mayo, drives a motorcycle that is clearly modern. Last, the cars on the roads are 1970-plus.

A smaller, but still important side setting involves the local town just outside the base. Here, officer candidates socialize by drinking and chasing women. The local women, many of whom want to marry officer candidates, would do just about anything to get one, including getting pregnant. Marriage is their ticket out of a largely blue-collar town where most people work for a paper company. It is this setting that plays a vital role in bringing the picture and characters together.

Zach Mayo, played by Gere, is a "hard-nosed," scrappy character who gets by on guts and determination. A loner by his own admission, Mayo relies on his tough childhood upbringing to "wheel and deal" his way through officer training school. For example, he provides illegally obtained polished boots and brass buckles to fellow candidates for extra cash. If an occasion arises where he can shirk responsibility, he will. His antics, however, often cause him problems with his commanding drill instructor. Two key reasons he makes it through the training are because of fellow officer candidate Sid Worley and his "town girl friend" named Paula. These characters help Mayo to become more caring and develop a sense of what life is all about. With his companions' aid, the once directionless loner becomes "an officer and a gentleman."

Sid Worley, played by David Keith, is Zach Mayo's constant friend and drinking buddy. Worley, who came from a small town, is a people-loving man and a good complement to Zach Mayo. When Sid's girl friend claims she is pregnant, he wants to do the noble thing: get married and raise his child properly. He feels a responsibility to do the right thing. This false sense of being was his initial reason for becoming an officer candidate in the first place. He felt that because his older brother died in Vietnam, it was his duty to live up to his father's expectations and become an officer. His overall attitude leads to a number of double standards, such as wanting to marry his sweetheart at home yet killing himself after being jilted by a gold-digging town girl named Lynette Pomeroy, and not asking for help from the one person he helped, Zach. In the end, Sid goes from being the best in his class to being dead last.

Sergeant Emil Foley, played by Louis Gossett Jr., is the drill instructor for basic training. His job is to make sure that the officer candidates are trained properly and to flunk out as many as possible. His vocabulary consists of four-letter words and raunchy rhymes. Ironically, the men he is training will out-rank him in the end. Tough and unrelenting at first, he slowly mellows as graduation time nears. For example, Zach Mayo curses him out a week away from graduation. Instead of kicking Mayo out of the program, Foley fights him; the two settle their personal problems alone. On graduation day, Sergeant Foley congratulates all the candidates. But his congratulations to Zach have a special meaning, one of love and mutual respect. When Zach is leaving the base, he overhears Sergeant Foley saying to the new class of recruits what he had said to Zach's: "You people look like the worst bunch of recruits I have ever seen. Boy . . . where do you come from? Wherever you come from. . . ."

Paula, played by Debra Winger, is a local town girl with a dream to marry an officer. Her love affair and eventual marriage to Zach Mayo play an important part in the film. In the beginning, neither one wants to get personally involved in their affair; when Zach graduates, that will be the end of the relationship. But they grow closer and Paula becomes a settling force on Mayo. At one point Mayo says to her, "I don't know how I would have made it through school without your help. You gave me something to look forward to each weekend." Although important in helping Mayo, the women in the film, I thought, were portrayed as tramps. One reviewer even commented, "As for the treatment of women, it couldn't have been worse. Whereas the male heroes were endowed with honor, courage, decency, strength of character, virility, etc., the young women were one-dimensional sluts."[1]

The most convincing acting is done by Louis Gossett Jr., who plays Sergeant Emil Foley. "Fall in! Haul your ass over to the white chalk line and stand at attention." Gossett barks out orders constantly and delivers them with fear-instilling confidence. Never taking any backtalk or fooling around, he commands respect from his superiors as well as his subordinates. At approximately six-foot four and in perfect physical shape, nobody takes him lightly, including the audience.

My overall judgment rates this movie a *B*. It is an enjoyable movie with a realistic setting, but it lacks some qualities that could have made it a better movie. For instance, the beginning of the film gives the viewer Zach Mayo's background as a child, but it is dragged out too long, making me and everyone else in the audience restless. Second, it is questionable that Zach would be able to handle his academic work at school. The movie shows only his physical struggle to achieve success. With his background, wouldn't the academic test be much more difficult? After all, mathematics and aerodynamics classes are not exactly cakewalks. Even though Sid Worley *was* helping Zach with academics, I wondered if any cheating was going on. Zach did prove in the end that he was an officer and a gentleman, but his means may not have justified the end or the title of the movie.

"Conventional, but a hugely compelling drama,"[2] as described by Janet Maslin of the *New York Times*, is quite true. Even with the film's problem areas, it is worth seeing.

[1] Alexandra Mark, "Ah Romance," *The Wall Street Journal*, 31 Aug. 1982, Sec. E, p. 25, col 2.

[2] Janet Maslin, "An Officer and a Gentleman," *New York Times*, 28 July 1982, Sec. C, p. 17, col. 2.

On Golden Pond   SUE SMITH

The movie *On Golden Pond* was basically about two people growing old. It begins with Ethel and Norman Thayer (played by Katharine Hepburn and Henry Fonda) reopening their summer cottage for another season. Norman is a crotchety old man who is afraid to die, and therefore he has a bad attitude toward life. There is only one person who understands his behavior, and that person is Ethel, his wife. She is a vigorous elderly lady who is always on the go. Their daughter Chelsea (Jane Fonda) comes to stay, with her lover and his son. They have come to celebrate Norman's birthday, but he and Chelsea never got along, so the whole scene is very tense. Chelsea and Bill go to Europe and leave young Billy with Norman and Ethel for a month. The boy is resentful at first, but eventually he and

Norman become friends. Chelsea comes back later and finally she and Norman become friends also. Norman has heart trouble at the end and it looks as if he may die, but he doesn't. Norman and Ethel close up the cottage, each of them thinking this may be their last time they will be at Golden Pond.

The plot is very insightful. It shows how someone learns to cope with the fear of death. Through Ethel's love and care, Norman realizes that his life has been worthwhile and that death is peaceful, not frightening. He also learns that he has to give people a chance to be themselves before he can become friends with them. For example, he is always cutting down Chelsea, calling her "fat," and he never really takes the time to get to know her. At the end though, when he lets her show him how she can dive, this breaks the barrier between them and they begin their friendship.

The characters in this film are real people with real problems. Katharine Hepburn and Henry Fonda depict a typical elderly fear—death. Yet, Norman is afraid of it and Ethel is trying to tell him how wonderful and serene it will be. It is stated in *Newsweek* that "Hepburn is radiant and physically astonishing, whether swinging on the arms of a chair or diving from a boat to save the stranded Norman and Billy."[1] She is a bubbly lady who always says or does the right thing at the right time. Chelsea, back from Europe, is upset because she doesn't understand why Norman and Billy get along when she and Norman never did. She calls her father a son of a bitch. Ethel slaps her and tells her to give him a chance to be her friend; open up to him and he will do the same. Chelsea does this and it works.

Henry Fonda plays Norman's cold side brilliantly. He uses sarcasm to the point of being mean ("What's the point of having a dwarf if he doesn't do chores?"). Here he is complaining about Billy "but his gleeful attempt to wound reveals his own little-boy vulnerability."[2]

I empathized with all the characters in the film. They cried and I cried right along with them. I feel they were all extremely successful in playing their "real-people" roles and this is well proven by all of the awards that they won.

The setting in this film is an important part of the plot. Golden Pond is peaceful and serene, and this can be compared to Ethel's feelings of how death will be. She conveys these feelings to Norman and they both feel that if death is at all like Golden Pond, then they have nothing to fear. Another part of the setting, which is very important to Ethel, is the loons. There is a pair of loons which Ethel feeds and watches every day. They never separate and this could be a symbol of Ethel and Norman's marriage. They both have a strong bond which keeps them together. One day while Norman and Billy are fishing, Billy's line gets caught on something. They reel it in and it is one of the loons—dead. Norman gets scared by this and they head home. He realizes that he needs Ethel and wants to be with her.

There was one phrase in the film which I particularly liked. Norman and Billy are trying to get acquainted. Norman asks Billy what he does in California for fun. Billy replies, "Cruise chicks and play suck-face." Billy is trying to act cool and Norman isn't quite sure how to handle it. So he goes along with it and by the end of the movie Norman says he wants to play suck-face with Ethel. Even though Billy and Norman don't get along at first (Norman calls Billy a little son of a bitch), their age gap brings them together. Billy begins to admire Norman for all the things he has done, and Norman is, in a way, reliving his childhood through Billy.

The movie moves along very fast. You go through a variety of emotions when you are watching it; therefore it seems to move more rapidly. It is funny because of some of the expressions used. Ethel calls Norman an "old poop" all the time, and she gives someone the finger and she doesn't even know what it means. It was scary when Billy and Norman got caught in Purgatory Cove and Norman fell out of the boat. The film is also sad because at one part it looks as if Norman is going to die. You feel happy at the end because both Ethel and Norman are laughing and happy. They both realize that death will be comforting and peaceful and they have lived their lives to the fullest.

I enjoyed this film very much. The aspect which I liked the best was all the varied emotions. You walked out of the movie theater with a good feeling. Even though this is about elderly fears of death, the film is written so that all audiences will enjoy it. I strongly recommend it to every type of movie viewer.

[1] David Ansen, "A Late Autumn Sonata," *Newsweek*, 30 Nov. 1981, p. 105.

[2] Ansen, p. 105.

So Much for Rock-Jazz

SUE MACMANAWAY

Last evening was the long-awaited performance of Jean-Luc Ponty at Warriner Auditorium. Anticipation was very high among ticket buyers and in the crowd awaiting entrance before the concert. This was going to be good. Jean-Luc Ponty in person—jazz-rock would never be better.

Or so I thought. Anticipation was first replaced with thoughts of survival. When the doors opened, the crush of people for choice seats literally pushed you in ahead of them. But the ticket takers were just as quick at grabbing as people were at pushing. Next thing I knew, I lost my stub right after getting shoved into a squeeze play between two competing fans. Concert crowds are always predictably pushy and rowdy, especially for any musician who plays anything but serious music. The younger the crowd, the more pushing and grabbing there seems to be; crowd control is no control.

Back to Ponty. Promptly at 8:05 P.M. the warm-up came on. Usually, I expect the warm-up to be a bit dull and just a stall tactic so the main man won't have to play so long. Jim Amend, pianist, entered stage left and gave us all a surprise. He was good. A one-man concert that could stand on its own without leading Jean-Luc Ponty. Jim was swift to enter stage and begin playing, an unusual aspect of concerts. A late start of fifteen to twenty minutes is common, and general goofing around by the artist before he begins playing is the norm also.

Jim, with his kinky, long hair and red jump suit looked like a leftover from 1970. I awaited something brash to come out of his piano. What I got was a masterful piece of art which was a joy to hear and to watch being played. No new music experiments with finger-pluncked keys or excessively repeated strains. The style was serious, almost classical in origin. Interesting runs and chords punctuated his original melodies and themes. Between themes he would give us a sometimes humorous recital of a theme familiar to us all. Something from Looney Tunes cartoons or a horror movie. Other times he used familiar passages from the classics of Beethoven and Bach.

Two of the selections he played contained short sections of verse, mostly original, about love and loneliness. At a couple of points he borrowed verses from a popular song called "Motherless Child" and an old English song, "Wild Mountain Theme." At the conclusion of each piece, all of which were lengthy, the audience gave Jim a sound ovation. Acceptance of his music and style was complete. We were entertained thoroughly. One would almost have thought he would have been called back for an encore except that it was 9:00 P.M. and we wanted Jean-Luc Ponty.

The stage crew had it very much together and rearranged equipment quickly and with no problem. Concert crowds appreciate swiftness. The stage was set to go, but no Jean-Luc Ponty graced the stage until ten minutes later; at least he did not make it twenty minutes. Clapping was commencing and angry crowds please no one.

The band entered and then Ponty came on with violin bows in hand. We were ready. The band warmed up swiftly and they went right into "Tarantula." It was good. The sound equipment was excellent. Mixing and lighting were just as well done. Ponty's violin bow danced across the strings quickly, slowly, hopped, raced, and sent shivers down your spine. The succeeding songs, "Garden of Babylon" and "Fantastic Voyage," proved his excellence in playing violin.

One problem ruined the entire experience. The P.A. was too loud. Ponty's mix of jazz and rock is effective and beautiful, but not at 120 decibels. My ears hurt and my head ached to the point of just wanting to get up and leave. My favorite jazz violinist was driving me away. Such an excellent concert should never be ruined by such a simply corrected problem. At least the P.A. had no distortion to ruin the beauty of Ponty's music. Two encores proved that.

Writing activity

Select a recent film, television show, book, concert, athletic event, or something else to review in a three- to six-page paper. Use as your guide only that you should write about something you really do have a reaction to, and something you remember well enough to treat with detail and specificity. You will discover that with a little effort you can remember names, dialogue, and other useful details. Pick a single work—a specific performance or a specific book—to evaluate. If you try to do a composite

(what *Dallas* is usually like, instead of what last week's episode was like), you may find the job is too big to handle in a short paper and too hard to remember accurately.

REASONING AND REASONABLENESS

The foundation of much formal writing is logical thinking, or more broadly, reasoning. In informal situations, especially emotional ones (such as a fight), logic may not be very effective, because once the emotions have been aroused, most people insist on settling matters at *that* level. It is a cliché, but true, that it takes cool heads for reason to prevail. Nevertheless, it has been the hope of educated people throughout history that, at least in formal situations, especially in formal writing, the prevailing strategy would be logic, reasonableness, and an insistence on the facts.

Facts and Inferences

In writing, it is important to keep clear the difference between facts and statements *about* facts, or the difference between facts and *inferences*. Facts can be verified, usually, by physical tests you can count the number of people in a room, for example. An inference, on the other hand, is an unverified deduction or conclusion you come to in any of several ways, including guessing. If you can't see the people in the room, you might guess (infer) that some of them are male and some are female from the sounds of the voices. Or if you can see them through a window but can't hear them, you might infer that they were listening to a lecture from their seating arrangement and manner. Both these *inferences* can be verified, of course, if you enter the room. They are therefore low-level inferences—not very far removed from physical observation but inferences nevertheless. (Voices do not invariably identify sex of speakers; people sitting attentively in rows are not necessarily listening to a lecture.)

Unfortunately there is no upward limit to inferences. Suppose you happen to know the people are listening to a political speech. Can you infer (deduce, conclude, surmise, judge, gather, *guess*) that they will vote for the speaker in an upcoming election? It would be very useful to be able to make such high-level inferences; we can't verify the facts in every situation. Even direct questioning won't always provide accurate information. If it were easy to predict election results or stock-market trends or even horse-race results, ours would be a different world. Beyond physical events lie abstract philosophical and legal questions that seem (so far) entirely divorced from physical tests. How shall we conduct the affairs of the

151

nation? (Shall we have a strong President or a strong Congress?) Since these abstract questions eventually have physical consequences, it is important for us to be able to anticipate what is likely to result from any action we take—or fail to take. No one can avoid reasoning. As long as we deal with facts and inferences our choices are only between good reasoning and bad.

Induction and Deduction

If we could make logic fit our world perfectly, we would work out a list of generalizations or general "laws" to cover everything. If we could know, for example, that everyone who listens to a political speech will vote for the speaker, even if we could know just that sixty percent would and forty percent would not vote for the speaker, we would very much simplify life. And, as far as possible, that is what science and education have been attempting to do. We have two sets of principles, or two methods of handling data, to help us in this work.

Induction   The primary tool of science, induction holds that specific observations lead to general truths. (If you see enough redheads with freckles, you may conclude that, in general, readheads have freckles.) That redheads have freckles (generally) is one of our *premises*, one of the basic truths accepted by most people who have thought about the matter. Our premises are not always correct; sometimes they apply far less often than we think. But it is the business of science to keep observing and testing one incident after another, so that we become more and more confident of our premises or discard them for better ones. The term *induction* refers to the process by which specific observations "lead to" general laws or premises.

Deduction   The method of classical reasoning, deduction holds that general laws *predict* specified instances. (Once you know that redheads generally have freckles, you can predict that the next redhead you meet will probably have freckles. If your general truth is universal enough, your prediction will be true.) This is the kind of reasoning we use most often, though we usually don't realize we are doing it. When you look at the sky and conclude that it may rain, your conclusion is based on a general "truth" that a dark and cloudy sky generally means rain is coming. And you can understand why this was the preferred method of reasoning among the ancients: how much more elegant to determine truth with your mind than to trudge about observing things! Unfortunately such an attitude often led the ancients into error. Today a reasonable person would use induction to determine those things that can be observed and use deduction in those matters where induction won't help. Deduction, then, means "drawing out" specific cases from a general law.

Though the full development of a logical system can be complex, the basic machinery of logic is relatively simple. Logic is a system for making statements without error and as such has three components that any writer should learn: a method for making clear statements, a method for testing statements, and a list of typical errors to watch for in your own and in others' writing.

Clear Statements

It is sometimes said that most of our arguments would disappear if we would just define our terms. That may not be completely true, but it is a good idea to define the terms of an argument as precisely as possible. Before you test any statement, you should reduce it to its *standard form:* the simplest statement of subject and predicate.

Subject   The thing being discussed, the name of someone or some other designator of a person (usually)

Predicate   A statement about the subject, some characteristic or quality of the subject we can argue about

SUBJECT   PREDICATE

The government / is corrupt.

If you choose to argue about this statement, you will soon find yourself relying on statements about how a corrupt government differs from other governments.

SUBJECT   PREDICATE

Any government that uses tax money to support vice / is corrupt.

And this is the key to all logical statements—the distinctions made among *all*, *some*, and *none*. In order to test the truth of any specific statement, you need to know the possibility of truth in general. Before you can argue about any particular government, you must know what you believe about governments in general. *If* you believe that all governments are corrupt, you can assume that any given government is corrupt. If you believe that all philosophers are brilliant, you can assume that any specific philosopher is brilliant.

Testing Statements

The syllogism is the basic formula of deductive reasoning. It is based on the assumption that whatever is true of a group of things must be true of any member of the group. The standard form of the syllogism is as follows:

Major premise   A universal truth acknowledged by reasonable people, usually, but not necessarily, arrived at through induction.

Minor premise   A specific instance within the general statement. If you make a general statement about *all* dogs, then any specific dog is an instance within the category of dogs.

Conclusion   An "inescapable" result based on the formula that what is true for the group must be true for the members of the group; thus whatever is true for all dogs ought to be true for any given dog.

Major premise: All dogs bark.
Minor premise: Fido is a dog.
Conclusion: Fido barks.

If it is true that all dogs bark, then it *must* be true that any given dog you can find will bark. However, it so happens that some dogs do *not* bark (basenjies, for example). You can see that the syllogism would be perfectly good *if* the major premise were true. That is, the syllogism is constructed properly. You have a major premise about all dogs and a minor premise identifying a specific dog; thus the minor premise is contained in the major premise. You could introduce a different kind of error: all dogs bark, some squirrels bark; thus some squirrels are dogs. Here the syllogism isn't properly constructed. The minor premise does not identify a member in the major premise but instead introduces a new group entirely (squirrels).

To account for the different kinds of errors, you need different concepts. For *truth* we mean "coinciding with reality." (In reality some dogs do not bark.) For properly drawn conclusions in properly constructed syllogisms, we will use the concept *valid*, regardless of the "truth" of the premises. Thus a conclusion can be valid but not true. In fact, you can have these possibilities:

VALID AND TRUE
All men are mortal.
Socrates is a man.
Socrates is mortal.

VALID BUT NOT TRUE
All men have wings.
Socrates is a man.
Socrates has wings.

NOT VALID BUT TRUE
All logicians tell lies.
Socrates tells lies.
Socrates is a logician.

NOT VALID AND NOT TRUE
All women tell lies.
Socrates tells lies.
Socrates is a woman

The error in the *Not Valid* syllogisms is called "affirming the predicate." In the standard syllogism, validity is achieved by affirming the subject, not the predicate. For example, in *Not Valid but True*, the fact that logicians tell lies does not preclude the possibility that others do too; the major premise does not say that *only* logicians tell lies.

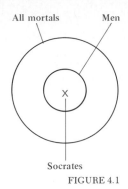

All mortals   Men

X

Socrates

FIGURE 4.1

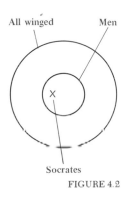

All winged   Men

X

Socrates

FIGURE 4.2

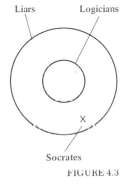

Liars   Logicians

X

Socrates

FIGURE 4.3

Diagrams can help you to understand syllogisms. Figure 4.1 illustrates the *Valid and True* syllogism. Socrates is "contained" within the inner *Men* circle, and the *Men* circle is itself contained within the outer *All mortals* circle. Thus, whatever is true of the whole group of men must also be true of Socrates. Notice, though, that the diagram leaves room for mortals who are not men.

A similar diagram (Figure 4.2) will work for *Valid but not True*. The circles show that all men are inside the *Winged* circle. You know this is not "true," but you may imagine such a thing anyway. Socrates, again one of the men, must be inside the *Winged* circle.

Not Valid but True presents a problem, as seen in Figure 4.3. It is clear enough that the logicians are all inside the *Liars* circle, and Socrates is inside the *Liars* circle too, because the minor premise puts him there. But there is nothing in the premises to tell you to put Socrates inside the *Logicians* circle; that is, there is no *necessity* for putting him there. The premises only tell us that he is inside the *Liars* circle . . . somewhere. Thus the conclusion is *not warranted*, and in fact, according to the diagram, is false—or at least not valid.

The same is true of the last syllogism (Figure 4.4). You can get all the women into the *Liars* circle, and you can get Socrates in there too, but the premises do not direct you to put Socrates into the *Women* circle, and therefore the conclusion is unwarranted.

Note the difference if you change the premise to "*Only* logicians lie" (Figure 4.5). In that case the *Logicians* circle and the *Liars* circle would be the same. If then you affirm the predicate ("Socrates is a liar"), Socrates will have to become a logician, since only they lie.

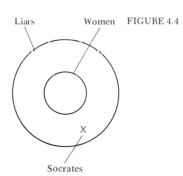

Liars   Women   FIGURE 4.4

X

Socrates

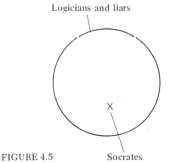

Logicians and liars

X

FIGURE 4.5   Socrates

Practice

Are the following syllogisms valid?

1 **All logicians tell the truth.**
   Plato tells the truth.
   Plato is a logician.

2 **All Greeks love beauty.**
   Socrates loves beauty.
   Socrates is a Greek.

155

3 **All logicians tell the truth.**
   Plato is a logician.
   Plato tells the truth.
5 **All rhetoricians smell bad.**
   Aristotle is a rhetorician.
   Aristotle smells bad.

4 **Descartes is a philosopher.**
   All philosophers eat meat.
   Descartes eats meat.
6 **All students love logic.**
   Professor Stout loves logic.
   Professor Stout is a student.

People seldom realize they are using syllogisms. They take short cuts and leave out one of the premises, and they don't state things in syllogistic form. For example:

Don't lend Bill money; you'll never get it back!

The implied (unspoken) syllogism is something like this:

People who don't pay me back won't pay you back.
Bill didn't pay me the $5 I loaned him.
Bill won't pay you back.

If you dig the syllogism out of its linguistic hiding place, you can determine its truth or validity. In this case, you would say that the reasoning is valid, but you'd question the major premise, which seems a hasty generalization. (Bill may very well pay you back even if he hasn't paid others.) It is this same kind of questionable logic based on debatable assumptions that causes insurance companies and credit bureaus to brand customers "risky."

Practice

Find the syllogisms in the following statements. You may be able to come up with more than one syllogism for a given statement.

1 **She reads communist books; she must be a commie.**
2 **You should take Professor Occam's course; it's got lots of logic in it.**
3 **Socrates was a fool; he killed himself to prove a point.**
4 **If you like peanut butter, you'll love Skippy.**
5 **People who live in glass houses shouldn't throw bricks.**

Universal Negatives

Negative syllogisms are slightly more complex to work with. As with affirmative syllogisms, the negatives can be valid without being "true." For example:

VALID AND TRUE
No dogs have wings.
Snoopy is a dog.
Snoopy has no wings.

VALID BUT NOT TRUE
No students like logic.
Plato is a student.
Plato doesn't like logic.

But notice:

NOT VALID

No good lawyer loses cases.
Katherine Hill doesn't lose cases.
Katherine Hill is a good lawyer.

The problem with this syllogism is that there are too many negatives in it. It would be clearer to say that good lawyers *win* cases. (So do bad ones, occasionally.) If we were to diagram this syllogism, we'd get three separate and unrelated circles: a circle for good lawyers, a separate circle for those who lose cases (containing no good lawyers), and a third circle for Katherine Hill, who also is not in the losers' circle. But there is nothing in either the major or the minor premises that allows or requires us to put Katherine Hill in the lawyers' circle. Therefore the conclusion is not warranted; it is not valid.

Practice

Are the following syllogisms valid?

1 **No rhetorician speaks ill.**
   Phaedrus speaks ill.
   Phaedrus is no rhetorician.

2 **No Greek hates logic.**
   Aristotle is a Greek.
   Aristotle hates logic.

3 **Some detectives are not smart.**
   Sam Spade is not smart.
   Sam Spade is no detective.

4 **No person is not happy.**
   Aristotle is not happy.
   Aristotle is no person.

5 **No student knows Greek.**
   Isocrates is a student.
   Isocrates does not know Greek.

6 **No angel is alive.**
   The President is not dead.
   The President is an angel.

7 **No thinking man makes errors.**
   Gorgias is a thinking man.
   Gorgias makes no errors.

8 **No clown is a philosopher.**
   Bozo is no philosopher.
   Bozo is a clown.

9 **No young woman needs makeup.**
   Athena needs makeup.
   Athena is no young woman.

10 **No girl hates what is good**
   for her.
   Andrea hates what is good
   for her.
   Andrea is not a girl.

Review

Determine the validity of the following syllogisms.

1 **All orators are speakers.**
   A rhetorician is an orator.
   A rhetorician is a speaker.

2 **Every writer is a reader.**
   Some poets are not readers.
   Some poets are not writers.

3 Every student is a scholar.
   Some students are not young.
   Some scholars are not young.

4 Every graduate is literate.
   Some graduates are musicians.
   Some musicians are literate.

5 Every book is to be read.
   Every poem is to be read.
   Every poem is a book.

6 Every rhetorician is a teacher.
   No corpse is a teacher.
   No corpse is a rhetorician.

7 No lawyer is a magician.
   Bailey is a lawyer.
   Bailey is no magician.

8 No person is a fool.
   Every philosopher is a person.
   No philosopher is a fool.

9 No animal is a stone.
   Some unicorn is animal.
   Some unicorn is not an animal.

10 No Athenian is a Roman.
   Plato is an Athenian.
   Plato is not a Roman.

11 Every gourd is a melon.
   Some squash is a gourd.
   Every squash is a melon.

12 Every human is mortal.
   Some people are human.
   Some people are mortal.

LOGICAL FALLACIES: ERRORS TO AVOID

The logical fallacies discussed in this section occur often in conversation and in writing. Watch out for them in the writing of others and avoid them when you are trying to build a reasonable case in your writing.

Logical fallacies fall into several categories: fallacies based on insufficient evidence; fallacies based on irrelevant information; fallacies based on ambiguity; and fallacies based on faulty logic. As you read the following section, it's more important to understand the flawed reasoning in insufficient evidence, irrelevancies, ambiguities, and faulty logic than to memorize the names of the logical fallacies. (But the Latin names are traditional and still used.)

Fallacies Based on Insufficient Evidence

Ad Ignorantium   Appeal to ignorance, arguing on the basis of what is not known. If you can't prove something is false, must it be true? "You can't prove there *isn't* a monster in Loch Ness, so there must be one!" Anyone who takes the Fifth Amendment [refuses to deny the charges] must be guilty!" The same fallacy is involved whether you insist on the validity of anything not proved false or on the falseness of anything not proved true.

Card Stacking   Concealing, withholding, or ignoring the evidence; *selecting* only evidence favorable to your side. "Richard Nixon was tall, good-looking, a family man, an experienced politician, a world leader. Let's get this man back into politics!"

Hasty Generalization   Drawing conclusions from too little evidence. (This is the chief error in reasoning.) "I know several jolly fat people; therefore I conclude that all fat people are jolly!" It is unlikely that we could know enough people to draw many accurate generalizations about them. *Many* generalizations turn out to be inaccurate because they are based on insufficient evidence. In argumentation, you must learn to *back up* your generalizations with specific evidence.

Post Hoc Ergo Propter Hoc   Literally, "after this; therefore because of this." Events that follow each other chronologically are falsely assumed to have a *cause* and *effect* relationship. "His grades started to fall after Harold met Cindy; she must have been a bad influence!"

Fallacies Based on Irrelevant Information

Ad Baculum   Appeal to force. "If you insult Smith's wife, you'll get a black eye!" "If you investigate Gassone Motors, they will expose your sex life!" "There are three hundred voters in my precinct; you'd better listen to me!" Force doesn't have to be physical; it can be psychological.

Ad Hominem   Literally, "to the person." *Ad hominem* attacks the person who is arguing and ignores the argument. The idea is that the person is too contemptible to have valid ideas. "What you say may be true, but aren't you a member of the Communist party?"

Ad Misericordiam   Appeal to pity. "Here's poor William's paper; the unfortunate lad's been having trouble lately. Perhaps I can cheer him with a good grade!" "There is no more pathetic sight than handicapped children; we must all give to the March of Dimes!" "Governor Wallace would have made a good President even though an assassin's bullet left him confined to a wheelchair!" Appeals to pity are not always wrong, but most readers object to them when they seem to obscure the real question.

Ad Populum   Literally, "to the people." Appeal to popular prejudices and slogans. "Down with big government!" "Down with invasion of privacy!" "Down with federal intervention!" "Vote for law and order!" "America for Americans!" A populist is someone running for office on the basis of these traditional ideas, campaigning against social change or against "newer" attitudes. Essentially populism is an appeal for a return to the good old days. (What *are* the popular ideas in America?)

Ad Verecundiam   Inappropriate authority. "O. J. Simpson says rent from Hertz, and he should know!" "What do you mean Sugar Lolly can't act? Senator Fogburn likes Sugar Lolly!" "Professor Snore has just finished his great work on Shakespeare; perhaps we should invite him to speak at the Children's Literature Festival!" When a celebrity or authority is dragged into an argument as expert witness, you have every right to challenge his or her expertise.

Bandwagon   Appeal to peer pressure, group identity. "Join the winning side!" "All the really important people smoke Torchos, you should too!" Bandwagon is sometimes called "snob appeal"; its opposite is "plain folks": "You can trust me folks, I'm just a simple, unpretentious soul like you!" "Beware of pointy-headed intellectuals!"

Common Sense   Appeal to common knowledge, practical truths. "She may be a brilliant intellectual, but she can't chew gum and walk at the same time!" "Anyone should know that it takes money to make money!" "You shouldn't insult people who control your oil supply; that's only common sense." "The world cannot be round like a ball, otherwise the people on the bottom would fall off!" Appeals to common sense are not always wrong, but often they are used to oversimplify difficult issues or to assert the virtues of the commonplace over intellectual or esoteric values. Common sense is not helpful in matters requiring *uncommon* sense.

Fallacy of Opposition   Anything the opposition approves must be bad; an attack on the ideas on the grounds that those who support them are incapable of right thinking. Fallacy of opposition is different from *ad hominem* only to the degree that the idea itself is made unacceptable because of its supporters. "Sure, you favor welfare, social security, government insurance, and all the rest. But did you know that these are socialistic ideas and communistic as well?" The attack is on the ideas *because of* those who support them.

Genetic Fallacy   The source of an idea influences its worth. Similar to fallacy of opposition, but different in that the idea is attacked, regardless of who supports it, on the grounds that where the idea came from makes the argument bad. "The new tax law is ridiculous! It was written at Montezuma State College and everyone knows that's Mickey Mouse U.!"

Guilt by Association   You are known by the company you keep. "Birds of a feather flock together!" "Don't invite Renford to the party; his roommate was caught cheating on an exam." "Why are you defending the rights of criminals; do you have a criminal record?"

Red Herring   Arguing beside the point; *switching* to some side issue or entirely new issue to distract from the main argument, a favorite device of politicians when asked hard questions: "Perhaps you're right about integration and busing, but has anyone considered the *safety* of those buses?" Also favored by some students on exams: "In order to understand the causes of the Civil War, we must look at the warlike nature of human beings. The history of Europe is full of wars. . . ."

Tu Quoque   You did it too; the accusation is invalid because the accuser is guilty of the same "sin." "Anyone in prison obviously cannot pass judgment on criminal matters!" "The senator accuses his opponent of campaign irregularities, but has anyone examined the senator's campaign practices?" "So what if I cheat on my taxes? So do you!"

Fallacies Based on Ambiguity

Amphiboly   Language ambiguity, deliberately misusing *implications*. "Three out of four doctors recommend this type of pain relief!" The implied assertion here is that three out of four means seventy-five percent of *all* doctors and also that what is true of a *type* of pain reliever is true of *this* one.

Begging the Question   Tautology, circular reasoning; the conclusion is merely a restatement of one of the premises. "The President is such a good man . . . because he is so moral!" "Murderers should be executed . . . because they are killers!" "You can see that God exists . . . because of all the things He made!"

Equivocation   Arguing over the meaning of a word; using the connotations of a word to disprove or distort an argument. Equivocation always involves the *meaning* of words—deliberate or accidental misuse that confuses argumentation. "Senator Gonzo claims to be a *conservative*, yet he lives lavishly!" (Two meanings for *conservative* are involved here.) "How can you claim to be *pious*? You never go to church!" "No, we are not retreating; we have moved into the Vietnamization phase of the war!"

False Metaphor or False Analogy   The metaphor or analogy used
has more dissimilarities than similarities. "The President has seen
us through a crisis of state; he has kept late hours in lonely vigil; he
has brought us soothing relief; he has wasted his strength to revive
our faltering nation. Let us reward him now with our gratitude!"
The metaphor or analogy of the President as doctor tending a sick
nation is false, however poetic it may be.

Fallacies Based on Faulty Logic

Complex Question   Loaded questions that are not safe to answer.
"When did you stop beating your wife?" "Do you favor our current
policies of fiscal irresponsibility?" "If elected will you put an end to
frivolous welfare programs?" The complex question need not be put
in the form of a question; it can be worded as a complex issue: "Let
us examine whether the President's aggressive foreign posture is
weakening our bargaining power!" It is necessary to determine first
whether the President's "posture" is aggressive before we can examine its influence on our bargaining power.

False Dilemma   Either/or thinking; presents only two options,
both (usually) unattractive. "Either we must support private chari-
ties or we must increase welfare taxation!" "If you don't quit smoking, you'll die of lung cancer!" In almost all situations there are more
than two options.

Non Sequitur   Literally, "it does not follow"; this general term is
often applied to any fallacy in which the argument cannot be followed. A non sequitur argument is one in which the conclusion does
not follow from the major premise. "Inflation has made our money
worth less, so we might as well spend it and enjoy life."

Rationalization   Making excuses; choosing the least threatening
(or most self-serving) explanations. "I'm flunking calculus; that instructor hates me!" "Of course I hit the mailbox; you've got the stupid thing where it's impossible to miss."

Reductio ad Absurdum   Literally, "reduce to an absurdity"; dis-
proof of an argument by showing some absurdity to which it leads if
carried to its logical end. This is not always an error. It is an error if
the user is merely being sarcastic, ridiculing the opposition, or erro-
neously leading (via hasty generalization, either/or, and so on) to an
absurdity that doesn't necessarily follow. "So you would give the

government the power to tax, would you? The next thing you know they'll use that power to take away your home and property, and finally your life. We will then have the amusing consequence of the government taxing its citizens out of existence—and finally the government itself must fall with no citizens and no new taxes to support it!"

Slippery Slope   One thing leads to another. "If you eat desserts you'll end up weighing three hundred pounds!" Of course it is possible that one thing *may* lead to another, but it is obviously not true that one thing *must* lead to another.

Practice

Identify the fallacy in the following; in some cases you may feel that more than one fallacy is involved.

1 Did you see the way those Indians made it rain? Just as soon as they stopped dancing it really poured!

2 All Germans are warlike and belligerent!

3 Everybody's going to the rally to listen to protest songs; you better come along too!

4 God never lies. The Bible is the word of God, and the Bible clearly teaches that God exists. Therefore, God must exist, because of course He never lies!

5 Pay your taxes or go to jail; it's just that simple!

6 The great capitalist free-enterprise system must struggle against the godless, enslaving communist conspiracy!

7 Consider joining the American Nazi Party. It is a small, fraternal group permitting individual participation. It is active, vibrant, alive. Its objectives are clear and comprehensible!

8 Ustislav Keldysh's ideas and designs for space flight cannot be considered here: the man is a communist.

9 About a month ago, Stultus failed to sacrifice to Vulcan; later he was killed when Vesuvius erupted. Impiety is always avenged by the gods!

10 Are nuclear plants safe? There are so many complex aspects of this issue; consider for example what abundant cheap energy will mean to our economy!

11 What do you mean, my clothes look terrible? You've got the same thing on!

12 Either you are a liar or you aren't; there are no degrees of honesty.

13 It is a good thing that it is so cold out in the winter; otherwise, the heat in our homes would serve little purpose!

14 Find out why Drivel is the number one ice cream; twenty million Americans can't be wrong!

15 Historically, the leaders in every field—art, science, business, medicine, and so on—have been predominantly *men*, and therefore it is difficult to understand why women should now be treated as *equal* to men.

16 You can say what you want about the good work of unions, but I think the whole idea is communistic.

17 All politicians are crooks.

18 Despite endless efforts, no one has been able to prove that God exists; we may as well stop trying and accept the truth: there is no God.

19 Alicia started gaining more weight than ever when she started taking Slimdown; the stuff must be fattening.

20 Sure, Arbuckle argues for conservatism; he's a paid establishment flunky!

21 My worthy opponent accuses me of owning shares in Devilish Corporation; yet he himself is a major stockholder in Awful Products Incorporated!

22 It isn't fair to ruin students' lives with poor grades; let us give only good grades!

23 A day's work for a day's wages; no more gold-bricking!

24 For that chic, *au courant* look, wear Slick, the elegant skin cream of celebrities and beautiful people everywhere.

25 If you don't study, you won't pass.

26 The rattlesnake is a beautiful creature, attractively colored, clean, and has an intriguing rattle with which to catch your attention; excellent mouser and house pet!

27 Men don't make passes at girls who wear glasses.

28 Dr. Hessel, well-known physicist, has taken a stand against our policy toward African nations on the grounds that our racial policies are hypocritical.

29 Clearly the Democrats are the true defenders of democracy, else why would they be called "democrats"?

30 This critic would suggest that the new treatise in philosophy before her is a new adventure in confusion, were its author not the head of the philosophy department at one of our greatest schools, Maxima Ivy League University!

The twentieth century has become so science oriented that we are all unconsciously skeptical. We are accustomed to thinking in terms of evidence, counterevidence, proofs. Even advertising today has taken to pseudoscience: nine out of ten doctors approve Mopex; three out of four people prefer Schnitz; Ammeloy works twenty percent faster. . . . Yet there is very little in life that we can solve with this approach. In most human affairs—politics, religion, romance, and so on—science can offer information, but usually not answers to our questions. Who should be our next President? Should everyone go to college? Is television harmful? Is the press too powerful? Should teenagers get married?

The time-honored solution to these problems is to discuss them and perhaps eventually take a vote on them. Without using force, it is very difficult to *make* people do anything. You can *prove* that cigarette smoking causes cancer, but that fact won't make people quit smoking. In fact "proving" things in human affairs seems almost irrelevant. The discussion goes on, sometimes for decades.

If facts and figures and sometimes even aggression won't move people, what will? Obviously something *does* operate on people or we would never get anything done. Advertisers try to get us to buy products—and succeed, by and large—teachers try to get students to learn, politicians try to get other politicians to pass bills. People are often successful at getting others to do what they want. Even in the home, family members "work their wiles" on each other. How does a teenager get the family car, avoid chores, and so on?

Persuasion is the high art of getting others to agree with you. In almost any human activity we rely on our ability to persuade each other: something is or isn't good, should or shouldn't be done. Guns, bombs, armies, and other means of force may make people do certain things temporarily, but they do not persuade people. Force begets force and resistance, and though you may beat up and tie up your opponents and temporarily triumph over them, as soon as they get loose they will come after you again, this time with friends. To persuade means more than just winning an argument; it means changing the opponents' minds so that they agree with your position. Persuasion means to urge, to coax, to influence, to encourage—it is much more related to psychology than to debate. In a debate, you can present facts and figures, brilliant reasoning, counterarguments, and so forth, and make your opponent look foolish, and this will win the debate; but after the debate your opponent may blacken your eye.

The point to remember is that if you want to *persuade*, you must avoid starting a *fight*. And there is no quicker way to start a fight than to accuse someone of being emotional or irrational. The heavy reliance on rationality has always been our means of warding off superstition and ignorance. Thus, to be irrational carries a very negative connotation. To accuse opponents of being irrational or emotional amounts to accusing them of being superstitious, ignorant, primitive. It is the verbal equivalent of a slap in the face:

An Incredibly Short Lesson . . . in Persuasion?

HE: Which sweater should I wear, the red one or the yellow one?
SHE: Oh, I don't know . . . the yellow one looks okay.
HE: What's the matter with the red one?
SHE: Nothing. Wear the red one.
HE: My mother gave me that red sweater.
SHE: The red one is fine.
HE: You hate my mother.
SHE: Wait a minute. I didn't say that.
HE: Why do you hate my mother?
SHE: Hey . . . you're getting emotional! Let's be rational about this.
HE: Rational! I'll show you rational. You can just go to the show alone!

Persuasion relies on some very basic human interactions, all of which can be summarized by the word *reasonableness*. If you wish to persuade other people, it is not enough to use reasonable arguments. You must also present *yourself* to them as a reasonable individual, someone worth listening to. Three general principles should govern your efforts to persuade: respect worthy opponents, be fair, and accept compromise.

Respect Worthy Opponents

No one knows everything, and no one knows nothing. You cannot be entirely right, nor can your opponents be entirely wrong. Each of you has *part* of the truth. Thus you must show that you respect your opponents. There is no point in trying to persuade those who do not respect you, and there is no point in trying to persuade those you do not respect. Any word or tone or hint that your opponents are less intelligent, less well informed, less honorable, or even less *right* than you are will alienate them, thus preventing them from even hearing, let alone considering, your point of view. You should approach the issue with the idea that both you and your opponents have misunderstood something. You are reasonable; they are reasonable. Working together, you will both come to see the matter more clearly and understand each other better.

Be Fair

Most people enter an argument spoiling for a fight. The chances for reason to prevail, then, are slim at best, and they will immediately disappear if you act unfairly toward your opponents. Sarcasm, name calling, insults, and other attacks on an opponent violate the worthy-opponent rule. Even something as hard to define as an air of superiority will set off hostile vibrations. Lying, distorting, falsifying evidence, using unsupported generalizations—all put the opponent on the defensive and have no place in *reasoning* between reasonable people. You must be sure that your evidence is honest, your arguments fair.

Unfairness is a fatal mistake in persuasive writing. The heart of law and morality is *justice*—another word for fairness. The concept of fair play is so powerful that it *alone* can carry more weight than all your evidence. Thus it is a mistake to manufacture or distort the evidence.

Why is it that most reasonable people have such a bad reaction to unfairness? Unfairness is a form of dishonesty (distortion of or outright violation of the truth), and those who would use it to convince us that they have the *correct* view of the argument are caught in a contradiction: you cannot convince us that you have the correct opinion when your evidence is dishonest (unfair). Most reasonable people know that there are two sides (at least) to any question—two good sides, not one good one and one bad.

To be fair means to *weigh* the evidence; that is why the statue of *Justice* is represented as blindfolded and carrying a set of scales. If you wish to convince the reader that you are fairly presenting your opinion, it will be necessary to weigh both sides of the case. Then, if you have presented both sides well, the reader will be able to see which side has the better evidence. Thus to convince the reader it is not necessary—nor advisable—to *force* the reader to agree with you (by biasing the evidence). Instead, you only have to show the reader which of two sides to a question is better; if you have been fair, your readers will convince themselves that you are right.

Accept Compromise

Democracy requires compromise. Our culture is highly competitive and most of us are conditioned to *win*, but you must be willing to accept less than total victory if persuasion is your goal. If your opponents are partially right and you are partially right, then both of you must accept *partial* victory. Some issues seem so loaded with emotion, so obviously one sided, that only one solution is possible. Rape of a child is so horrible that nothing but the death penalty will do; bigotry and prejudice are so repugnant that there can be no good in a racist, and so on. Yet when you investigate these one-sided questions, they often turn out to be complex, many sided, and confusing. To enter an argument at all is to acknowledge that the issue is arguable, that there are at least two sides to the question—two valid sides. Moral outrage accomplishes little and violates the fairness rule. Democracy is slow; we argue back and forth and eventually come up with answers that may not satisfy anyone completely. Yet no one has found a better way. A *considered* opinion is precisely one that has been analyzed and argued and has finally been evaluated as the best answer that can be had at the moment . . . all things considered.

You should not go into a persuasive argument to prove the opponent wrong or to prove yourself right. Through an exchange of ideas you *advance the argument*, not your own exclusive idea of the truth. If, after all, you succeed in getting a watered-down gun law passed, you are closer to your objective than you were. The gun-law argument has moved off dead center. Your opponents who wanted no gun law whatsoever must accept partial change, and so must you, who wanted the strongest possible law. It is a maddeningly slow way to proceed—you may die before the issue is resolved—but the only other alternative so far is violence. In a nuclear world, violence is too dangerous, no matter what good we imagine it might produce.

In the following paper, the writer tries to convince us that hunting is a worthwhile sport, an emotional issue with some people who feel that hunters are senseless killers destroying wildlife. Should hunting be outlawed? Is the writer being reasonable? Is he also being persuasive?

The False Hunters

KEN FROMER

As a hunter, I have probably heard all of the arguments against hunting and hunters; and although most can be countered effectively, there is one that I agree with wholeheartedly: there are too many dangerous, thoughtless, and inconsiderate hunters. While these kinds of people go hunting for different types of game, and in all seasons, deer season is the biggest attraction for most hunters, therefore the time when the greatest number of these pseudohunters is in the woods. I call them pseudohunters because any true hunter and sportsman sees them as a sham, a mockery of the real thing. I will give some examples to illustrate exactly the types to which I am referring.

On the second Saturday of deer season this year, I went back in the woods for some morning hunting on my dad's enclosed land. I walked quietly back to a spot that I had chosen, hoping that I could be quiet enough to catch one by surprise, but no such luck. After I had stood in my spot for perhaps two hours, I decided to go back to the house to warm up, and maybe go back out in the afternoon. It was while walking back to the house that I discovered it—an abandoned deer. It was a small doe lying on its side, bloated and misshapen, its eyes open and glazed. It looked as if it might have been dead for several days, and one hindquarter was partially torn away, probably by some kind of wild animal. The doe was shot through the neck and abdomen. Several questions arise in a situation like this—questions of who, where, and why. Who was the person who shot it? Did he shoot it right there where it was, or had it wandered onto our property after it was wounded? Last, why did he shoot it? Did he think it was a buck?

When all factors are considered, just about any set of answers one could give to these questions would be damning. For instance, even if the hunter was one who had permission to hunt wherever he was when he shot the deer, even if he wasn't trespassing on private property, the question of why he shot the deer is still unanswered. Does he have poor eyesight? Is he the excitable kind who shoots first and looks for antlers after he has made his kill? Did his gun go off by accident? Was he shooting at a nearby buck and hit the doe instead? Not likely with two bullet holes in the body. Did he realize all along that it was a doe, and intend to take the meat, or did he just shoot it to be shooting something? If he had taken the meat, it wouldn't have been nearly so bad, because, even though it was killed illegally it wouldn't have been wasted. Of course, he might have been afraid of being caught and punished. He should have thought of that first. If it ran after he shot it, was he too lazy to track it? Any of these alternatives raises serious doubts about his competency as a hunter.

Later that same day I went over to hunt with my girlfriend's father, who lives in Flint, but has a trailer and a lot bordering on state land near Beaverton. Joe wasn't there when I arrived, so I was going to go out in the woods anyway, thinking I'd probably find him. When I started out along the trail, I saw three "hunters" walking ahead of me. One of them I knew as Joe's acquaintance who owned a lot near Joe's and had a camper set up on it. The other two I didn't know, but one thing became very clear to me, walking along behind them—all three were staggering drunk. They passed a pint bottle of liquor around two or three times, and I saw one of them stumble and fall. The other two weren't walking much better. Watching them staggering along, their gun barrels swinging crazily, I suddenly felt very sick, and not at all certain that I wanted to be in the woods with those fools. If there is anything more stupid than carrying a gun, hunting, while drunk, I can't think of it. No wonder people are killed in accidents.

I think there are some measures which should be taken to reduce the number of pseudohunters in the woods. These would include vision and marksmanship tests administered when the individual applies for a license, and stricter fines and punishments for trespassers. This would mean that the only licensing agencies would be Department of Natural Resources headquarters, since most of the sporting-goods stores, and so on, that now distribute hunting licenses wouldn't have the facilities for such tests. This may help to cut down the number of people hunting. Also I think it might be a good idea to require prospective hunters to pass a complete physical examination before receiving their permits. This would help assure that they are at least physically able to undergo the rigors of tracking a wounded deer, and also cut down the number of hunters who die of heart attacks in the woods. All these things considered, there would probably need to be an increase in the cost of a hunting license, but this too might be advantageous, in cutting down the number of hunters.

The problem of drunken hunters can't really be solved on this level, but I believe that if such measures were taken, as I have suggested, there would probably be fewer people inclined to be drunk while hunting. I think that we would have mainly true sportsmen and hunters in the woods. We would certainly have fewer hunters, a fact which would in effect make the drunks less dangerous.

Ken starts his paper by agreeing with the opposition; there *are* some hunters who are dangerous and thoughtless. And this isn't just an agreement for effect; Ken wholeheartedly agrees and goes on to *illustrate* the point. He thoroughly condemns the thoughtless hunter and the drunken hunter. It isn't necessary for him to point out where he disagrees with the opponent or where the opponents (those who condemn all hunters) are in error. By concentrating on the positive, on those aspects where he and the opponents *agree*, Ken has turned an argument into a problem, for which he has a solution. Antihunters may not like Ken's solution, but they must be impressed with his reasonableness. He acknowledges there *is* a problem; and therefore he invites the opposition to acknowledge that he may have a solution.

Writing the Persuasion Paper

Audience and Purpose　The art of persuasion involves getting people to change their behavior, to see the world differently, to feel differently about an issue, to act differently. In persuasion, you are not trying to win a fight, debate, or even an argument; you are trying to get people to change their minds. To accomplish this difficult task, you must establish a bridge of mutual respect and understanding between you and your audience.

Think about the people whose view of the issue differs from yours. You can assume that they are at least willing to hear you out, even if they disagree with your point of view. Ask yourself these questions about the audience:

1 What do they *know* about this issue?
2 What do they *feel* about it?

3 Why don't they already agree with your position?

4 What ideas or feelings do you share with them that will help to build a bridge of understanding between you?

5 What arguments and evidence might they use if they were to try to persuade you to change your position on this issue?

6 How might they respond to the arguments and evidence you are planning to use?

If you have trouble answering these questions for yourself, find people in your college or community who are opposed to your position. Ask them why they think as they do. What do they think of your point of view? What aspects of the issue make them angry? What aspects of your position can they accept? Do they have solutions? How do they react to solutions you suggest? Try to find aspects of the issue both you and your opponents can agree on.

Evidence The bigger the subject, the more evidence you will need. If you are trying to show that capital punishment does or does not deter violent crime, you will need a great deal of evidence; the subject is so big and controversial now that there may not *be* enough evidence to convince people one way or the other. For a short composition (two or three pages), you need to limit your subject so that you can be persuasive without having to bring in a great deal of evidence. (For a three-page paper, two or three examples are the minimum.) If your evidence is high quality—reliable, authoritative, and fair—you will be persuasive.

As a general rule, the more evidence you have, the more convincing you will be. It is not enough to say that the vegetables are overcooked to show that the cafeteria food is not good. If the vegetables are overcooked, the meat is tasteless and tough, and the potatoes are either lumpy or runny, the evidence is convincing. If you eat most of your meals in the cafeteria (versus just Wednesday night) the case is better yet. If your friends have the same opinion and you also observe that others return their trays with half-eaten meals, the case is highly convincing.

The quality of the evidence can also be convincing. Showing that the food is tasteless and inedible is only one kind of evidence, no matter how many examples you have. Suppose however that the food also *looks* bad (shapeless, mud-colored blobs of apple pie; beef slices covered with congealed white ooze). Suppose too it *smells* bad (rank asparagus emitting fumes of decay). If the food actually makes people ill too, you then have different kinds of evidence—all supporting the same argument—that the cafeteria food is bad.

It's important to be aware, however, that there is a point of diminishing returns with evidence. At some point most people feel they have heard enough; to go on piling up evidence after this point can turn the tables so that *you* become the villain and your opponents become unfortunate underdogs. It can seem that the case is so heavily loaded against the opposing view that your reader begins to suspect you of bias, of unfairness.

Organization   In persuasion, remember, you are *not* trying to *win* an argument. Instead you are trying to get your audience to change their own minds. (In fact, your realistic objective may be not so much convincing them to abandon their position as persuading them to agree to the coexistence of the two positions.) It is important, therefore, to organize the arguments you plan to use in the most "psychologically" effective order.

It is sensible to describe the issue briefly in the introduction and to suggest that there are reasonable ideas on both sides. Begin with any aspect of the issue that you and your opponents can agree on. If you can start from a position of accord, your opponents won't feel they have to respond as antagonists. Then deal with your opponents' arguments, explaining why you cannot accept these views. Finally, present your own case to appeal to your audience's logic and emotions. Remember, you are trying to *persuade*. In the ideal world, logical arguments—arguments based on reason—should convince your audience. But audiences are made up of people, and in our daily lives emotions are often more powerful than logic. A paper that appeals to your audience's reason *and* emotions is likely to be more memorable and persuasive than one that depends exclusively on cold facts and statistics.

A simple plan of organization is often the best. For example:

Gun Control
  I. **Introduction: There are too many deaths by guns in the United States.**
  II. **The opposing side: There are strong historical, sociological, and political arguments against gun control.**
  III. **Your side: Although there are important problems associated with gun control, our legislatures must stop unnecessary carnage caused especially by "Saturday night specials."**
  IV. **Conclusion: Gun control is a complex issue and an effective law must be carefully drafted, but "Saturday night specials," easily concealed and with no legitimate uses, should be outlawed.**

Some people favor the classical plan of organization, which reverses the second and third steps. When you organize that way, you run some risk of having the opposing view remembered better than your own. Then too, people who hold the opposing view will tend to respect you and listen to your position if you deal with their arguments first, especially if you make it clear that you see the merits in their position.

Read the following papers. What are the authors trying to do? Do they have enough evidence? Are they fair? Do they convince you? Do they use logical arguments, emotional arguments, or a combination?

Mandatory Seat Belts

JENNY LEVY

Cars, trucks, jeeps, and vans have been a major part of transportation for many decades. Collectively, these vehicles—along with mass transportation—have set the country into motion. They get people to work, school, appointments, home, vacation spots, and numerous other places with speed, comfort, and ease. These vehicles are the most accessible, motorized, high-speed modes of travel available today. Almost anyone can own these signs of prestige and property. Yet these fantastic, convenient machines can almost be *too* powerful; they can easily kill (and quite often do). So, in order to protect the drivers and passengers, automobile manufacturers designed and installed safety equipment to help restrain persons from injury. One of these safety devices is the seat belt. Seat belts are technically known as active or passive restraint safety systems. Most people know what a seat belt is and how to use one, yet all too often they do not use them. Therefore, passive restraint systems should be required by law to be installed in every motor vehicle as a standard feature for all 1983 models and on.

Seat belts have been a standard part of all new cars since the late 1960s. However, the majority of safety restraints installed are the active type—called this because a person must take action (buckle up) in order for the system to work. The minority, then, is the passive restraint system. A few cars have them in the front seats only. Passive seat belts are intended to protect the person behind the belt without that person having to do anything. A shoulder belt attaches to the door frame and extends when the door is open. Then the person can simply sit down in the seat as if there were no belt there at all. Once settled, the person can pull the door shut and the belt automatically retracts to the proper fit across the left shoulder, chest, and right hip. (Some systems also come with a separate lap belt that must be manually buckled.)

Seat belts save lives. Not enough drivers are fastening their belts, though. While some people would not think of leaving their driveway without buckling up, far too many others do so only for high-speed freeway driving. Yet, according to the National Highway Traffic Safety Administration (NHTSA), seventy-four percent of all motor vehicle accidents happen less than twenty-five miles from home.[1] Over a driving lifetime, which averages about forty thousand trips, a motorist has a one-in-three chance of getting into a fatal accident or of being critically injured.[2] Wearing a seat belt more than doubles the chance to come out of a serious accident alive.[3]

These reasons alone should convince any driver or passenger to buckle up. As a nation, the general atmosphere and principal philosophy is peace and longevity. Therefore, not wearing a safety restraint is a major contradiction to this cause. The NHTSA estimates twelve thousand or more deaths from traffic crashes that occur each year might have been prevented if the victims had been wearing seat belts.[4] A number of other injuries may have been reduced in severity or avoided altogether. Yet only fourteen percent of drivers and a small percent of passengers wear safety restraints.[5] However, they are not unaware of seat belts, because forty-five to fifty percent wear them for special conditions and occasions.[6]

So, why do people not wear seat belts more often? Drivers and passengers alike cite numerous reasons and justifications for not buckling up regularly. The most popular excuse: forgetting. Forgetting to use a seat belt is fairly common. The habit of buckling up simply has not been acquired yet. Most cars have warning buzzers and lights to remind people to buckle up before starting the car. Another paranoia is entrapment in a burning or submerged car. The NHTSA reports that fire is the cause of death in only .01 percent of accidents.[7] A third excuse is that the driver is not going very far or very fast. However, injuries are not related to how fast the vehicle was going. Fatal accidents can occur at the speed of fifteen miles per hour. It is not the speed, but the momentum that injures or kills a person when striking an object. Finally, people complain that seat belts are uncomfortable and restrict movement. They do not have to be. Seat belts can be adjusted to a person's height and weight. Safety restraints are designed for maximum movement while buckled up. A person should be able to bend over far enough to reach the radio, heater, lighter, or even touch the floor. Only a quick snap on the belt will restrict it from moving any further—such as in the case of an accident when a person is jerked forward very quickly. All these excuses are flimsy and can easily be rebutted with common sense.

Passive restraint systems are not more effective than active systems, but they do make more people wear belts. A survey of owners of passive-system-equipped Volkswagens found that seventy-nine percent used the system, an impressive figure compared to the national average of fourteen percent.[8] All the Volkswagen owners could have disassembled the automatic belts, but only twenty-one in every one hundred did. With the passive restraint system, far more people will be "buckled up." There would be no excuses: no forgetting; no fear of not being able to unbuckle; no restriction on movement because the passive restraint works the same way as the active restraint in that sense; and no reason for not wearing one for short trips because the belt is automatic.

To "drive the message home," the NHTSA is undertaking a two-year, five million dollar campaign to urge motorists to use safety restraints. Whoever is involved in affecting the public opinion—teachers, police, scouts, doctors, judges, and even the P.T.A.—will get into the act. The Administration is also working on insurance companies and auto rental firms to have them lower their rates to seat belt wearers. This effort could result—especially with passive restraint systems—in the saving of up to fifteen thousand lives a year. I firmly believe that the United States Court of Appeals for the District of Columbia was correct in making automobile manufacturers buckle up for America. The Court reversed a Reagan Administration decision and ruled that all cars sold in the United States after September 1, 1983, must have passive restraint safety systems. This would raise the cost of each car about one hundred to one hundred and fifty dollars a car;[9] that does not even come close to the pricelessness of a human life.

[1] Anna Rush, "Do You Buckle Up?" *McCall's*, November 1981, p. V-1.
[2] Rush, p. v-1.
[3] Rush, p. v-1.
[4] Government Study by the National Highway Traffic Safety Administration, "Study of Methods For Increasing Seat Belt Use," Doc. Y4, P96/11:96–40.
[5] Government Study, 96.
[6] Government Study, 96.
[7] Kim Garretson, "Seat Belt Savvy," *Better Homes and Gardens*, October 1982, p. 81.
[8] Garretson, p. 81.
[9] "The Courts Buckle Down," *Newsweek*, 16 Aug. 1982, p. 48.

My Opinion on
Tallahassee
Policemen

ELLEN SLATER

Maybe if my brother had never gotten a beach buggy in the first place, I wouldn't feel so hostile towards Tallahassee policemen, but he did, and the one year he had it was long enough to prove to me that our local police force is indeed prejudiced against unconventional cars.

At first glance, any policeman might think that the buggy was a hazard. It was homemade, unpainted, and appeared to be held together by baling wire. The fact that it lacked doors, a roof, a trunk, and fenders would tempt any officer to reach for his ticket pad. In addition to this, the appearance of my brother was enough to make anyone stop and stare. Dressed in a bright red sweater, green gardening gloves, and a pair of welder's goggles, he could easily blow any cop's mind from two blocks away. Policemen just seemed forced to believe that this car and driver had to be illegal.

As a matter of fact, the buggy had passed inspection for highway driving. All equipment required was in working order—brakes, headlights, taillights, and so forth. But this fact did not stop policemen in their search for violations. On one occasion, the officer began to lecture us on the penalties and other consequences of not having a car inspected, and even when my brother pointed out the safety sticker on the dashboard, the officer would not concede. He proceeded to write out a ticket for not having a windshield. Later, in court, this charge was dismissed. Another incident that supported my observation of such malicious attitudes in our policemen was the night we were stopped by an off-duty cop in a silver Corvette. The Corvette had pulled up to us at two red lights. My brother raced his engine only to a small level (mainly because it would probably have stalled out if he really raced it), and then the other guy raced his. The light turned green and away we sped at the amazing speed of twenty-five or thirty miles per hour. At the next red light he pulled up and flashed a very challenging grin. At this, we chuckled and repeated our performance of such speed. As we rounded a corner and began to slow up for the next light, the Corvette rumbled up and the policeman let us see his badge, which he had beside him. He pulled us over and charged my brother with reckless driving. This charge was later dismissed in court when my brother explained it all to the judge.

It is true that policemen do have the responsibility of checking suspicious-looking cars. Many beach buggies are not even licensed to be driven on the roads—only beaches. Also many teen-age boys are very risky drivers and have conditioned the police to be extra watchful of them. Therefore, it is understandable that officers would pay this special attention to my brother and his car. But the extent of this search for culprits must also be considered. In our case, the officers went "beyond the call of duty" in enforcing the law. They not only were extra bitter in their language, but actually gave illegal citations. It is because of this that I believe that many policemen prejudge beach buggies and are unfair to their young drivers.

Writing activity

Write a persuasion paper three to six pages long. Keep your subject simple. You need a subject you have first-hand evidence on, something you have personally experienced or can easily research with an article or two. The length of the paper rules out most of the big, controversial subjects like inflation control and energy problems.

CHAPTER FIVE

Writing with Sources

The folly of mistaking a paradox for a discovery,

a metaphor for a proof,

a torrent of verbiage for a spring of capital truths,

and oneself for an oracle,

is inborn in us.

PAUL VALÉRY, *The Method of Leonardo da Vinci*

Research writing is probably the most challenging and demanding writing you'll undertake in college. It requires the greatest attention to formal procedures and the "rules" of writing. Because formal writing is orderly and predictable, there is a danger of its becoming stuffy and boring. You have to control both style and content; the challenge is to remain lively and interesting while writing with sources. For an example of effective research writing, read the following paragraph from a respected scientific journal, reporting an experiment in which students pretended to be insane:

The pseudopatient, very much as a true psychiatric patient, entered a hospital with no foreknowledge of when he would be discharged. Each was told that he would have to get out by his own devices, essentially by convincing the staff that he was sane. The psychological stresses associated with hospitalization were considerable, and all but one of the pseudopatients desired to be discharged almost immediately after being admitted. They were, therefore, motivated not only to behave sanely but to be paragons of cooperation. That their behavior was in no way disruptive is confirmed by nursing reports, which have been obtained on most of the patients. These reports uniformly indicate that the patients were "friendly," "cooperative," and "exhibited no abnormal indications."
D. L. ROSENHAN, "On Being Sane in Insane Places," *Science*, 19 Jan. 1973

The author of "On Being Sane in Insane Places" is a professor of psychology and law, and he is writing for psychologists and lawyers.

In the experiment, no doctor ever discovered that the "pseudopatients" were only faking insanity, and this fact has serious implications for both psychology and law! The article represents very formal writing. It deals with academic subject matter, and there is little or no attempt on the author's part to "express self." The writing is clear and informative and objective. Later in the article, Rosenhan writes in the first person: "I do not, even now, understand the problem well enough to perceive solutions." He does this to avoid what many think is an awkward research point of view: "This researcher does not now understand the problem. . . ." Even with an occasional first person reference, Rosenhan's article remains objective research writing aimed at a very special audience, and it is therefore quite formal in tone and language.

For most research writing in college, something less than extreme formality is desired. You should aim for language suitable for educated audiences; that is, you should write on the formal side but not at the extreme end of the writing continuum, where only the most specialized audiences will be able to read your work. For example, here is the beginning of a research paper written with about the right degree of formality:

The Navy's
Doomsday
Machine: Project
Seafarer

MARK STARBUCK

The discovery of power from the atom had once accompanied a dream of a world moving on to bigger and better achievements. Atomic energy could be harnessed to do a number of things. It was soon to be discovered, however, that the power from the atom was capable of great destruction. With nations growing and becoming more powerful, with science and technology at their fingertips, the threat of a nuclear attack by an aggressive nation has been a major concern of the government's defense planners for as long as such a threat existed. The navy came up with what it believed to be the answer—a communications system capable of communicating with submerged American submarines armed with nuclear-tipped missiles.

"The logic on which the U.S. retaliatory nuclear weapons system is based rests on strategies of mutual deterrence in a world where the superpowers depend upon weapons of extreme technological sophistication in order to keep their fears of each other manageable."[1] Consider a hypothetical day in 19—. Scores of nuclear missiles advancing toward the United States suddenly show up on radar screens, early warning systems, and nearly all detection devices. The nightmares we have lived with since Hiroshima and Nagasaki begin to take place as nuclear warheads explode on their targets. There can be no doubt, our country is under a massive attack by an aggressor nation with first-strike capability.[2] To prevent such a disaster, one need possess such a strong retaliatory force to make any aggressor think twice before launching such an attack. The United States Navy has spent over seventeen years researching and developing a communications system with a proposed potential for retaliation called Project Seafarer (originally known as Project Sanguine). So far, the system has cost over $100 million.[3]

The construction and development of Seafarer in Michigan, has, to date, been stopped. Political and social forces have brought the controversial communications system to a halt. Nevertheless, it is still believed by the navy that Seafarer is essential to the nation's security in the event of a nuclear war, but obviously this belief is in doubt. Is Seafarer truly what the navy has envisaged or has it been an expensive miscalculation?

Mark's paper has about the right tone. The language is formal, but not too formal. We are aware of the writer's personality, though his voice is submerged under the technical talk about Seafarer. If we had to identify the writer's self, we might say, "This sounds like an intelligent, well-educated, easygoing person. He knows what he is talking about, but he isn't being stuffy or showing off." Mark offers the reader a hypothetical attack on the United States to dramatize the importance of the Seafarer question. Mark knows he has an audience, an audience that will listen to him as long as he doesn't get too technical or dull. Other than that, Mark's writing here is not drastically changed from his other writing. The subject itself has forced him to be a little technical, but that is unavoidable. Note that Mark's semiformal writing is very readable.

SELECTING AND REFINING
A RESEARCH QUESTION

Naturally we would all like to discover some important new fact; we would all like to write a significant research paper. But should researchers start out with enormous questions of great significance: Is there a God? What will the future be like? How can the political structure of the world be changed? It might be rewarding to be able to answer questions like these, but they are just *too* big for any researcher. A skillful researcher with endless energy, time, and financial backing must still settle for quite a small research question. For example, medical science has been trying to cure cancer for decades, but each researcher has a much smaller problem to work on, which may or may not lead to the answer to the overall question. Some researchers are in chemotherapy, others are in radiology, and still others are in immunology (the study of the body's own defense mechanisms against disease). Researching is patient, painstaking, detailed work, and it often takes years of such patient work from many researchers before the right answers are found. Generally speaking, the bigger the question, the longer the research will take.

In a classroom, then, with no more than a semester or quarter to work in, you cannot tackle a big question. You must find the smallest possible question to work on. Sexism was a popular subject throughout the 1960s and the early 1970s. Many students attempted to write research papers about it (Are men and women equal? Are girls and boys taught stereotyped sex roles?). Such questions could not be researched very well in a short time. They involved areas of research that had not been examined in depth by science or law. To answer such questions (Are girls and boys taught stereotyped sex roles?) requires *primary* research—experiments, laboratory investigations, field work. Few beginning researchers are ready for such work. For your first research paper, you should rely on research you can do in the library.

Mostly, the library contains what other researchers have *said* about various subjects, and it is well suited, then, to *secondary* research. Suppose we change some of those sexism questions so that they could be answered with secondary research, in the library: Do scientists believe that men and women are physically equal? Does the public believe that women and men should be paid the same wages for doing the same work? Have there been any court cases about the denial of opportunity based on sex? Questions like these could be answered through library research. The basic question for secondary research is, *Who said what?* The *words* that have been written on nearly anything are in the library. Any question involving who said what or how many people said what or what kind of people said what starts research off in the right direction: looking for things in the library. In short, the answer to the question, Does sexism exist in America? probably cannot be found in the library. What can be found is what people have said about this question, what judges, lawyers, doctors, and others have said. And this leaves the *conclusion*, the answer to the question, up to you, as it should in worthwhile research.

For example, there is growing concern in this country over euthanasia (mercy killing) and the right to die. One day you may have to vote on this issue. After reading everything you can find about this issue, how could you as a researcher reach your conclusion? The question involves morality, law, medicine. Imagine being the judge listening to all the evidence on both sides of the case. Research usually does not *prove* anything, in the sense of providing a single, indisputable answer; you will not discover a Dead Sea scroll that says at what point life-support measures should be discontinued. Instead, you will find evidence, pieces of information. You must weigh the evidence. Finally you must *decide* what the answer is. It is not surprising, then, that many researchers decide that the evidence is inconclusive, that there is not enough evidence or that the evidence is not good enough to allow a single, final conclusion to be drawn. Such research is perfectly valid; far better to know that the question is still open than to draw an incorrect conclusion.

Coming up with a good topic for research is usually the hardest job. Even after preliminary reading and thinking, you may still start off with a subject that is too big or that has some other built-in problem. You must keep reminding yourself that no matter how small the subject is, you are likely to find large amounts of research materials you will have to read, so the smaller the better. Three guidelines—specific, limited, worthwhile—can help you develop, evaluate, and refine your research question.

Specific   Is the wording of your research question specific enough? Is the object of investigation clear? A researcher who sets out to investigate "morality" will quickly discover that there is no single interpretation of that term, and even what people do with regard to that concept differs widely. To investigate today's morality might involve things like numbers of robberies, incidents of cheating, church attendance, any number of *subtopics* within morality. One of the subtopics may be what you should investigate.

Limited   "Trucks," "labor unions," "World War II" all seem specific enough; at least most people will know what you are talking about. But even "trucks" is a large subject. To test the size of any subject, see how many questions you can ask about it. The more questions, the bigger the subject. (How did the truck develop? How many kinds of trucks are there? How are they made? How does a truck work? What are the political issues involving trucks? And so on.)

The *smallest* question you can ask about anything may be one that can be answered *yes* or *no*, and that is what you need for a controllable thesis. Do trucks pay sufficient taxes to pay for the damage they do to highways? (Yes or no?) Do trucks cause more pollution than cars? (Yes or no?) Are truck drivers the safest drivers on the road? (Yes or no?) You may discover through your research that these questions really cannot be answered with a yes or no; the issues may be far more complex than they seemed at the outset (they almost always are). But if you frame your question in this highly limited yes-no formula, your chances of having a workable research thesis will be much improved. If the answer then comes out to be "maybe" or "sometimes yes and sometimes no," so much the better; your conclusion will show the reader how to make sense out of the question. Making sense of a question is the point of research in the first place. Furthermore, stating your question in a *two-sided* manner like this avoids the problem of what to do with contrary evidence. If you start out determined to prove that trucks cause more pollution than cars, you may have to ignore evidence that contradicts your thesis.

Worthwhile   Is the question worthwhile? Does it provide information that most people would care to hear about? What seems relevant and important to the researcher may not strike the public or the funding agency as worthwhile. A researcher who wants to study a rare sea creature off the shores of California will have to show why the research is worthwhile. Since almost anything will interest someone, it shouldn't be too hard to show that even very rare and unusual subjects have their value. But you should follow the formula that the more specialized and limited in interest your subject is, the fewer readers you will have. As a general rule, you should not select subjects that appeal only to a very specialized audience. Still, this is no easy decision to make. If the subject is worthwhile, even to a limited audience, perhaps it should be pursued. If you are truly interested in and excited about a subject, you should be able to show your audience why it is interesting, why it is worthwhile, why it should be researched. In college, you can assume that you have an educated audience, but your classmates all have different interests and areas of specialization. Even your professor is likely to have interests different from yours, so you cannot assume an elite audience of enthusiasts.

Thesis exercise

Using the criteria *specific*, *limited*, and *worthwhile*, try to decide which, if any, of these suggested topics could be turned into a workable research thesis. Which ones seem to you the most promising for research? Why would you vote against the others? The topics are given here just as they were proposed by students; some of them could be worked into good research questions; others we decided were not so good. What do you think?

Honor   Is there any honor left in America? What is honor today? I plan to show how honor has declined in many aspects of America.

Hobbies   Many people have fascinating hobbies. Some surprising people have hobbies that you wouldn't think of. My paper will discuss the different kinds of hobbies different people have.

Arabian horses   Why are these horses so much loved by everyone? What makes them wanted by kings and movie stars? I want to tell why I think the Arabian is the most beautiful horse in the world.

Campus sex   Who is doing what on campus? I want to do a survey by interviewing students. I'll ask them about their sex lives and write up the results as a research paper.

Republicans   What does it mean to be a Republican? I want to tell about my work as a Young Republican, what we stand for, what we are trying to do.

Witchcraft   Are there any witches today? There have been lots of books and magazines about modern witches. I want to write about modern witchcraft.

Lincoln   I think he was our greatest President, and I think more people should know about his real life. I want to tell about Lincoln's life.

Euthanasia   Do we have a right to end a life? I'd like to show both sides of this issue.

Motorcycles   The motorcycle is a fantastic device. There is more to it than most people think.

Childless marriage   Children are no longer thought of as necessary to modern marriages. The attitude about having children has changed.

Ecology   We have got to stop polluting our atmosphere. We will all die of suffocation if the factories don't stop.

Horror movies   What is it about horror movies that fascinates people? Why are people drawn to terror and horrible stuff?

USING THE LIBRARY

Most research begins in the library. You will discover that a college library can provide you with information on nearly any subject. Unfortunately, many students avoid the library or are confused and overwhelmed by it.

Good libraries are information systems, parts of which you can use on your own. Other parts of these systems you can approach through the librarians. Your librarians may set up library orientation programs; many libraries use computerized systems for storing and retrieving information and an increasing number have computerized their catalogs. Learning how and why to use the library is one of the most useful steps you can take in the first months of school.

The next section of this chapter shows you a strategy for library research. The search strategy gives you a plan for moving from general to specific information on any subject. Keep in mind that once you get beyond the stage of gathering background information, your librarians—especially reference librarians—can help you. They know the value of different sources on a given subject. Librarians may be able to guide you to material too recent to be included in indexes, material in special collections, even local people knowledgeable about your topic.

When you are ready to begin investigating a research subject, how can you find the information you need in the most efficient way? You need a *search strategy*, a step-by-step procedure for finding and evaluating information. A search strategy enables you to approach your topic systematically, beginning with general information and going to specific material.

You should research the smallest possible aspect of an issue, one that can be phrased as a yes-no question. The general-to-specific direction of the search strategy helps you to discover that sort of thesis question. You may know you want to (or have to) write about legislation or social planning. But more often than not, you won't know at the outset the exact "limited, specific, worthwhile" thesis question. The search strategy helps you to move in an efficient way from legislation to "The Freedom of Information Act: Genuine Threat to National Security?" or from social planning to "Arcosanti: Workable Model for the Future?" Through a continuous process of evaluation, you define the question *and* select the most useful materials for your needs.

The search strategy has nine steps:

Step 1: Refer to *encyclopedias*.
Step 2: Refer to *dictionaries*.
Step 3: Examine the *card catalog*.
Step 4: Refer to indexes for *journal and newspaper articles*.
Step 5: Refer to *essays*.
Step 6: Consult *biographical sources*.
Step 7: Consult *book reviews*.
Step 8: Consider *statistical sources*.
Step 9: Consider *government documents*.

These nine steps are meant to be flexible. You may find yourself going back to earlier steps—to check an index for additional information, for example, or to look for more specific journal articles—as you refine your thesis and evaluate the evidence.

Step 1: Refer to Encyclopedias

To get an overview of your subject and any relevant background material, begin your search with encyclopedias. For example:

GENERAL ENCYCLOPEDIAS

The Encyclopedia Americana: Excellent for American history, science, and technology
Encyclopedia Britannica: Emphasis on arts, literature, and the humanities; excellent bibliographies

Encyclopedia of Education: Covers educational interests, practices, philosophies, and institutions and educators

The Encyclopedia of Philosophy: Encompasses Eastern, Western, ancient, medieval, and modern philosophies and people important in those fields

International Encyclopedia of the Social Sciences: Covers economics, history, political science, psychology, sociology, and law

McGraw-Hill Encyclopedia of Science and Technology: Encompasses physical, natural, and applied sciences

Quoting from an encyclopedia or listing one as a source may raise questions about your research, because information in encyclopedias tends to be general and cannot be completely up to date. Then why consult encyclopedias at all? First, for an overview: articles in good encyclopedias are written by authorities in given subjects, and their coverage is broad and accurate, but not always deep. A second reason to consult encyclopedias is that many encyclopedia articles contain *bibliographies* and cite source materials that you might use in your research.

Look for bibliographies in *all* the sources you examine: books, handbooks, journals, biographies, and essays. Finding a bibliography in a reputable source can be invaluable. *Annotated bibliographies*—those that briefly evaluate specific works—are more useful than general bibliographies in that they give you some clues about the content of the works cited and the compiler's estimate of their value.

Bibliographies can also be published as separate volumes. Sheehy's *Guide to Reference Books* is a good example of a single-volume general bibliography of reference titles in all disciplines. Other bibliographies can be located by searching in the card catalog by subject; for example, English literature—Bibliography. A very useful index to bibliographies is *Bibliographic Index: A Cumulative Bibliography of Bibliographies* (1937 to present). As you scan the bibliographies, copy the information on sources that look promising.

Step Two: Refer to Dictionaries

Dictionaries offer definitions for any unfamiliar words or terms you come across in your research and also provide information on the pronunciation, spelling, syllabication (division), usage, and etymology (origin and development) of those words. You may refer to dictionaries throughout your search.

There are two kinds of dictionaries: general and special. General dictionaries are broad in their coverage; special dictionaries concentrate on a single subject or specific function.

Dictionaries also vary in the *depth* of their coverage. An unabridged dictionary is comprehensive, containing no omissions or reductions. An abridged dictionary gives less complete information and is narrower in scope than an unabridged dictionary.

Webster's Third New International Dictionary of the English Language, Unabridged, and *Webster's New International Dictionary of the English Language,* 2nd edition, are the accepted general unabridged dictionaries of the English language.

The Oxford English Dictionary (12 volumes), commonly called *OED,* is the most authoritative, scholarly, and complete English dictionary. It traces and explains the historical development and meaning of all English words in use between 1150 and 1933.

Abridged general dictionaries, also known as desk dictionaries, include only commonly used words. Since they are much smaller, abridged dictionaries are revised frequently, and they are, therefore, a good source for information on new words. Listed below are some of the better known desk dictionaries:

The American Heritage Dictionary of the English Language
Random House College Dictionary
Webster's New Collegiate Dictionary
Webster's New World Dictionary of the American Language

Special dictionaries are selective by subject or function. Subject dictionaries cover words associated with a particular subject, as you can see from the following examples:

The American Political Dictionary
Black's Law Dictionary
Harvard Dictionary of Music
McGraw-Hill Dictionary of Scientific and Technical terms
Webster's Sports Dictionary

Other specialized dictionaries are known by the function they perform. They cover a particular aspect of a word or group of words, such as usage, etymology, synonyms or related words, pronunciation, slang, and abbreviations. Below are some examples:

Acronyms and Initialism Dictionary: Abbreviations
Partridge, *A Dictionary of Slang and Unconventional English:* Slang
Roget's International Thesaurus: Synonyms

Step Three: Examine the Card Catalog

The card catalog in your library contains a systematic list of the books on its shelves. Many card catalogs also list magazines and other periodicals, newspapers, and, sometimes, maps, pictures, and other "nonbook" items.

Libraries use either the Library of Congress or the Dewey Decimal system of classification. If you know which system your library uses, you can quickly learn the overall scheme by which its materials have been organized and shelved.

LIBRARY OF CONGRESS

A	General Works	L	Education
B	Philosophy-Religion	M	Music
C	History	N	Fine Arts
D	World History	P	Languages and Literature
E	U.S. History	Q	Science
F	Local History	R	Medicine
G	Geography, Anthropology	S	Agriculture
H	Social Sciences	T	Technology
J	Political Science	U	Military Science
K	Law	V	Naval Science
		Z	Library Science, Bibliography

DEWEY DECIMAL

000–099 General Works (bibliographies, encyclopedias, periodicals)
100–199 Philosophy, Psychology, Ethics
200–299 Religion and Mythology
300–399 Sociology (civics, economics, education, vocations)
400–499 Philology (dictionaries, grammar, language)
500–599 Science (biology, botany, chemistry, mathematics, physics, zoology)
600–699 Useful Arts (agriculture, aviation, engineering, medicine, radio)
700–799 Fine Arts (music, painting, photography, recreation)
800–899 Literature (criticism, novels, plays, poetry)
900–999 History, Geography, Biography, Travel

Most of the items in the card catalog are listed in three different ways: by author, by title, and by subject. The first two are straightforward: you locate the material alphabetically by using the author's last name or the first word of the title. If the title begins with *A*, *An*, or *The*, use the second word.

Locating material by subject is a little trickier. The *Library of Congress Subject Headings* (*LCSH*) books, usually shelved near the card catalog, are the key to searching by subject in libraries that use the LC classification system. These books help you to identify both the correct subject heading and related headings for your topic. Suppose your topic is communication among animals. The card catalog has nothing under that subject heading, but when you consult *LCSH*, you discover that the subject heading used in the card catalog is *Animal communication* (see Figure 5.1).

Animal coloration
    See Color of animals
Animal communication
    sa Animal sounds
        Human-animal communication
        Sound production by animals
    x Animal language
        Communication among animals
        Language learning by animals
Animal communication with humans
    See Human-animal communication
Animal courtship
    See Courtship of animals
Animal culture (Indirect) (SF)
    sa Deer culture
        Domestic animals
        Fish-culture
        Fur farming
        Game bird culture
        Laboratory animals
        Livestock
        Pets
        Poultry
        Radioactive tracers in animal culture
        Small animal culture
    x Animal husbandry
    xx Animals

The first section of the *LCSH* books explains how to use them.

How to Read the Information on a Catalog Card Each catalog card tells a good deal about a work and its contents. Perhaps the most important information for you is the call number. Think of the call number as an address that will help you to locate material in the library. *Be sure to copy the complete call number of each item you find on your topic.*

If you were to look up in the card catalog the subject heading *Animal communication,* you would find cards like the subject-heading card in Figure 5.2.

Figure 5.3 shows the author card for the book in Figure 5.2.

Tracings Figure 5.3 shows an important feature of catalog cards: they list related subject headings—tracings—in the catalog. Trac-

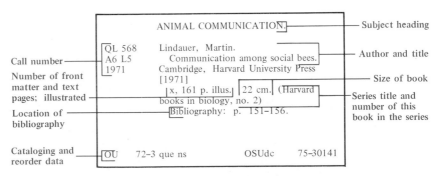

189

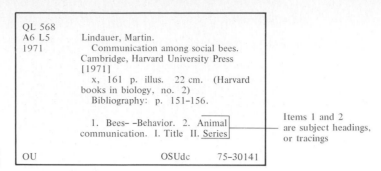

FIGURE 5.3
AUTHOR LISTING

ings are usually given on the main entry card, which is almost always the author card.

Always make a note of the author, title, publisher, and place and date of publication for any source you consult in your research.

Step Four: Refer to Journals and Newspapers

To find specific articles on your topic, examine journal and newspaper indexes. Journals (also called periodicals and magazines) and newspapers usually provide the most current information on a topic. Newspapers are especially valuable for public reactions or attitudes toward an issue or event at the time of its occurrence and are, therefore, primary sources for historical research.

Indexes are comprehensive catalogs of articles, essays, reports, and other information not published as books. Like encyclopedias and dictionaries, indexes can be categorized as general or special. A general index helps you find popular or general information on almost any topic. A special index provides information in a particular subject area, such as education, business, science, and so on. You will be able to find a specialized index for every academic discipline. In addition, many of the world's major newspapers, such as *The New York Times, The Wall Street Journal*, and *The Christian Science Monitor*, have their own indexes. Listed below are examples of general and specialized journal indexes:

GENERAL JOURNAL AND NEWSPAPER INDEXES

Reader's Guide to Periodical Literature: Indexes of general and popular journals; author, subject and fiction title index; 1915 to present

The New York Times Index: National and international news, critical commentaries, primary source materials such as reports and speeches, critical commentaries; 1851 to present

SPECIALIZED JOURNAL INDEXES

Art Index: Covers art and allied fields; subject index; 1929 to present

The Education Index: Elementary, secondary, and higher education; subject and author index; 1929 to present

Humanities Index: Covers language and literature, philosophy; author and subject index; 1974 to present (part of *Social Sciences and Humanities Index,* 1907–74)

Social Sciences Index: Covers history, psychology, political science; author and subject index; 1974 to present (part of *Social Sciences and Humanities Index,* 1907–74)

Public Affairs Information Service Bulletin: Indexes journals, books, reports and pamphlets in economics, social conditions, government; subject index; 1915 to present

When you begin your search for current information, you may want to ask a reference librarian which index best covers the subject you're gathering information on. Most indexes list articles alphabetically by subject, but a few also index by author and by title.

Many of the entries are abbreviated in order to save space, and most indexes contain keys to their abbreviations in the front of the book. Here are a few hints that will help save time when searching indexes.

HOW TO SEARCH INDEXES

1. Use the most precise language or terms you can think of for your topic. Unlike the card catalog, where the *LCSH* provides standardization, each index has its own subject headings and key terms, which make up the "language" of the index. Try to determine each index's language as you look through it.
2. If you don't find your topic under a specific heading, use a *broader* or *similar* term.
3. Follow the *see* and *see also* references to the correct heading or to similar headings.

You can determine the content of an article or essay (and thus its usefulness) by reading the introduction (usually the first two or three paragraphs), skimming the body of the article, and reading its conclusion. In using journal articles, it is important to determine the authority, credibility, and possible biases of the journals. Two books, Farber's *Classified List of Periodicals for the College Library* and Katz' *Magazines for Libraries,* evaluate a wide range of journals in these respects.

Step Five: Refer to Essays

Your next step is to look for essays, articles, and symposiums that are published in collections and are, therefore, more difficult to find. *The Essay and General Literature Index* (1900 to present) is a valuable source for locating these materials and is especially useful for criticism and biographical information.

Step Six: Consult Biographical Sources

The next step is to search biographical sources for information on the education, accomplishments, and professional activities of individuals involved in your topic. These sources also help you to evaluate the credentials and reputations of the authors whose works you are examining.

To select the most appropriate biographical source, ask yourself the following specific questions and then select the index that seems appropriate.

1. Is the person living (current source) or dead (retrospective source)?
2. What is the person's nationality or place of birth?
3. What is the person's occupation or profession?

Some of the most useful indexes are listed below. Note that most of them refer to citations in books; in addition to books, *Biography Index* indexes other kinds of materials and is therefore an especially useful source.

Biography Index: International, retrospective and current, all occupations; indexes sources of biographical materials in books, periodicals, letters, diaries, genealogies, obituaries; 1947 to present

Biographical Dictionaries Master Index: Emphasis on living Americans; all occupations; indexes more than 725,000 listings in over 50 current *Who's Who* and other indexes

Dictionary of American Biography: Notable Americans; retrospective, all occupations; scholarly; bibliographies

Dictionary of National Biography: British; spans earliest historical period to the present; all occupations; scholarly; bibliographies

Author Biographies Master Index: Index to biographical dictionaries; international; retrospective and current

European Authors, 1000–1900: Brief bibliographies

British Authors before 1800: A Biographical Dictionary: Bibliographies of works by and about the authors; portraits

American Authors 1600–1900: A Biographical Dictionary of American Literature: Brief bibliographies of writings by and about the authors

Contemporary Authors: Long bibliographies; current and retrospective; 1962 to present

World Authors, 1950–1970: Long biographies; current and retrospective

Directory of American Scholars: U.S. and Canadian college professors and researchers; current

American Men and Women of Science: International; current

Step Seven: Consult Book Reviews

Book review indexes are a vital step in your search strategy. Book reviews help you to evaluate and criticize a book and to summarize its contents. Some of the most useful book review indexes are listed below.

Book Review Digest: Covers reviews in popular magazines; excerpts of three or four reviews for each title; 1905 to present

Book Review Index: Covers humanities, social sciences, fiction, literature, and general nonfiction; citations only; 1965 to present

Current Book Review Citations: Fiction and nonfiction; foreign language, new editions, etc.; indexes large number of periodicals; 1976 to present

Index to Book Reviews in the Humanities: Covers art, drama, literature, adventure, etc.; 1960 to present

Assume that your search strategy to date has yielded several book titles that might provide useful information for your paper. Since you may not have time to read each book in its entirety, read the reviews for some idea of each book's content and quality. This process will allow you to eliminate some of the books and focus on those that seem most promising.

HOW TO EVALUATE A BOOK

1. Turn to the front matter (introduction, foreword, preface) and read the author's or editor's description of the book.
2. Turn to the table of contents and see how the author has organized the information into chapters, subsections, or other content categories.
3. Write down three questions on topics you have become curious about as a result of this preliminary examination of the book.
4. Review the first question and find in it a key word or phrase that you think might be in the book's index.
5. Turn to the index and look up that key word or phrase. If the word or phrase is not there, think of a synonym and see if the synonym is there. If it isn't, then see if the table of contents can lead you to the page of the book where the question can be answered.
6. Now turn to the part of the book that deals with your question and find the answer. If the author refers to material in other parts of the book, pursue these leads until you have all the information relevant to your question.
7. Follow the same procedure with your second and third questions.

Step Eight: Consider Statistical Sources

Facts and statistics can often provide credibility for your research. They reinforce the ideas you are developing. When intelligently used, they help you formulate convincing arguments.

Almanacs are published *annually* and record many kinds of facts and statistics. For this reason, almanacs are usually referred to as *books of facts*. They contain not only current and historic statistics, but all kinds of facts about government, the economy, business, sports, the arts, current events, and many institutions in our society. Listed below are two of the most important general almanacs:

World Almanac and Book of Facts: American; 1968 to present
Whitaker's Almanac: British and European; 1869 to present

Specialized statistical sources, usually published by government organizations, such as the U.S. Bureau of the Census, limit themselves to publishing statistics alone. Below are two of the most useful specialized statistical sources:

Statistical Abstracts of the United States: Covers politics, society, economics, industry, education, law, geography, and science; 1879 to present
Statistical Yearbook: Annuaire Statistique: Presents statistical tables about every country in the world; covers such topics as population, agriculture, mining, manufacturing, finance, trade, education, culture, housing, and social statistics; published by the United Nations

Step Nine: Consider Government Documents

Finally, always consider examining government documents in your search. The United States government is the largest publisher in the world and is constantly pouring out detailed census materials, vital statistics, Congressional papers and reports, Presidential documents, military reports, and "impact statements" on energy, the environment, and pollution. Government publications are valuable sources of information on almost any topic in science, business, the social sciences, arts, and humanities. These materials are indexed in the *Monthly Catalog of United States Government Publications:* Published monthly; lists books, pamphlets, maps, and serials; 1895 to present.

A SAMPLE SEARCH

Imagine a student, Bill, interested in the general subject of animal communication, who hasn't formulated a thesis question yet.

Step One: Encyclopedias

Bill examines the *Encyclopedia Americana*, which reveals that bees communicate by dancing and bats through sound waves. *The McGraw-Hill Encyclopedia of Science and Technology* describes four channels of communication: acoustic, visual, chemical, and electrical. Finding the visual aspect of communication interesting, Bill begins to wonder whether animals can communicate visually with humans. The bibliography at the end of the article has one promising, although not very recent, title—*Animal Communication: Technique of Study and Results of Research*, edited by T.A. Sebeok, 1968. *Grzimek's Animal Life Encyclopedia* states that animals have the ability to speak and that "anthropoid apes are able to use words which they have learned appropriately." In the same article, B. Rensch, who raised a female chimpanzee, states that anthropoid apes "can form abstract concepts, can generalize, can recognize causal relationships and symbolic representations. . . ." The information on apes is interesting, and Bill's intuition tells him that if animals and humans *do* communicate in any complex way, apes are the most likely candidates. He decides for now to concentrate on apes—keeping his eyes open for *ape, gorilla, chimpanzee* as key words. But if another kind of animal-human communication sounds interesting, he is willing to change his focus.

Step Two: Dictionaries

Few words so far have given Bill any problem. He looks up *anthropoid* and *sign language* in *Webster's New Collegiate Dictionary, McGraw-Hill Dictionary of Scientific Terms*, and *Oxford English Dictionary*.

Step Three: Card Catalog

Bill goes now to the card catalog to do a subject and author search. Using the *Library of Congress Subject Headings*, he finds that *Animal communication* is a correct subject heading; listed under the heading are three *see also* headings, one of which is *Human-animal communication*. Under "Animal communication" in the card catalog are three books that seem relevant: *Sign Language and Language Acquisition in Man and Ape*, 1978, edited by Fred C.C. Peng; *Speaking of Apes: A Critical Anthology of Two-Way Communication with Man*, 1980, edited by Thomas Sebeok and Jean Umiker-Sebeok; and *Nim* 1979, by Herbert Terrace. The catalog cards also show that the first two books have bibliographies. Under the subject heading *Human-animal communication congresses* is a collection of conference papers, *The Clever Hans Phenomenon: Communication with Horses, Whales, Apes, and People*, 1981. The title sounds provocative, and it mentions apes, so Bill decides to include it.

At the card catalog, he also looks for information on Sebeok's book *Animal Communication*, which was listed in the encyclopedia article. For all these sources Bill copies complete call numbers, titles, and authors from the catalog cards.

Step Four: Journal Articles

Now Bill goes to the *General Science Index* and *Reader's Guide to Periodical Literature*, looking up the headings *Animal communication* and *Human-animal communication*. Two articles are listed in *Science:* "Can an Ape Create a Sentence?" November 23, 1979, and "Ape-language Controversy Flares Up," March 21, 1980. *American Scientist* has "Do Apes Use Language?" January 1980. *Science News* has two: an untitled October, 1978, article about Koko, a talking gorilla, and "Ape-talk Two Ways to Skinner Bird," February 9, 1980. There are three in the November 1979 issue of *Psychology Today:* "The Trouble with Ape-language Studies: An Introduction," "How Nim Chimpsky Changed My Mind," and "Performing Animals: Secrets of the Trade."

Are these articles worthwhile? As one clue, Bill checks Farber, *Classified List of Periodicals for the College Library*, and Katz, *Magazines for Libraries*, for evaluations of the journals. Farber states that *Science* is the official journal of the American Association for the Advancement of Science and that its articles are excellent, and that *American Scientist* and *Science News* are reliable journals. *Psychology Today*, according to Farber, is a "scientifically accurate" journal. Bill puts an asterisk beside the titles of the *Science* articles, because Farber seems to suggest that it is the most authoritative of the journals.

Step Five: Essays

Bill's next step is to look for essays written on the topic. He looks in the *Essay and General Literature Index* and discovers that all the essays in the *Speaking of Apes* book are indexed there. He decides to evaluate the entire book later by looking up book reviews, but he wants to examine one specific essay that sounds especially relevant: "Language, Name, and Concept" by Bronowski and Bellugi.

Step Six: Biography

Bill is gathering many potential sources, and there seems to be a legitimate yes-no question about whether apes have language. With at least a tentative thesis question in mind, he wants to find out about the credentials and accomplishments of some of the researchers in the ape-language controversy. Looking up Herbert Terrace, Thomas Sebeok, and Beatrice Gardner in *American Men and Women of Science*, Bill discovers that all three researchers seem to have solid reputations. Terrace has a Ph.D. in psychology from Harvard and has received numerous grants at Columbia University, where he is a professor of psychology. Sebeok has a Ph.D. from Princeton, has an impressive list of publications, and is a professor of anthropology at Indiana University. Gardner has a Ph.D. from Oxford, is an expert in physiological psychology and verbal behavior, and has received various research awards.

Step Seven: Book Reviews

Realizing that book reviews of the four books he is considering should help him choose the most valuable ones, Bill begins with the *New York Review of Books*, which has long, analytical reviews of *Nim* and *Speaking of Apes*. He also reads another review of *Nim* in the *Times Literary Supplement*. *Nim* sounds worth examining because it deals with a single case of the ape-language issue, and Bill is beginning to suspect that the only yes-no question he will be able to answer adequately is whether *one* ape acquired language. He then reads a review of *Sign Language and Language Acquisition* in *American Anthropologist* and decides to take all three books out of the library. The review of *Animal Communication* in *Science*, on the other hand, suggests that this book is too general for his needs.

Step eight (statistical sources) and step nine (government documents) seem unlikely to yield relevant information about this particular topic, so Bill decides that his search is over, at least for now. It is time to examine and evaluate the evidence he has accumulated.

SUMMARY AND EVALUATION OF THE EVIDENCE

Having accumulated a substantial body of evidence for and against the question as to whether primates can use language to communicate, it is time for Bill to take stock of that evidence, to both summarize and evaluate it. Eventually, he must decide whether primates can or cannot talk; or he may decide that, given the state of scientific and linguistic thought at this time, the question cannot be answered with any certainty.

EVIDENCE FOR

Using American Sign Language (ASL), Beatrice and Allen Gardner of the University of Nevada taught a chimpanzee named Washoe a vocabulary of 160 signs. The Gardners reported that Washoe was able to create novel combinations, such as "water bird" for swan and "you me go out there hurry," and that her performance compared favorably with that of two-year-old children.

Roger Fouts, a student of the Gardners, taught ASL to six chimpanzees at the University of Oklahoma. Using the same handmolding methods, Penny Patterson of the Gorilla Foundation near Stanford,

California, taught a gorilla named Koko 375 hand signals. Patterson also reported that Koko was able to improvise and rhyme words (*blue, do; squash, wash*). According to Patterson, Koko even had a tendency to accept bribes and to lie—responses that are not a mimicry of humans but the normal workings of a mind that can predict future events.

Using plastic tiles of different shapes and colors to symbolize words, David Premack taught a chimpanzee named Sarah 130 words.

E. Sue Savage-Rumbaugh of the Yerkes Primate Research Center reported that chimpanzees Sherman and Austin were the first nonhuman primates to communicate symbolically with each other.

The Gardners, Roger Fouts, Penny Patterson, E. Sue Savage-Rumbaugh, David Premack, and others assert that, like humans, chimpanzees and gorillas can use symbols to convey information and that, since they can be taught fairly large vocabularies of symbols, nonhuman primates are capable of true language.

EVIDENCE AGAINST

Herbert Terrace, a Columbia University psychologist, taught a chimpanzee named Nim to sign by a method similar to that of the Gardners and Fouts. Like them, he raised Nim as a human child, hoping to prove that the chimpanzee would be able to form sentences. At first Terrace believed that Nim was indeed using a grammar. However, careful analysis of video tapes of Nim's training forced Terrace to conclude that Nim's sequences of words, although they looked like sentences, were in reality merely imitations of the teacher's promptings.

When Terrace examined Nim's hand signals, he discovered that they differed from the phrases spoken by children in two highly significant ways: spontaneity and length. The average length of Nim's signs was 1.5 during the last two years of his training. Children's utterances show a dramatic increase in both length and complexity over the same period. Nim's signs were essentially imitative; they lacked spontaneity and creativity, the hallmark of human language. Terrace concluded that although Nim appeared to be producing sentences, he was simply responding to his trainers' signs.

Since Terrace's conclusions were opposed to those of the Gardners, Fouts, and others, he then examined two films depicting aspects of the training of Washoe and Koko, the animals taught by the Gardners and Patterson. Viewing these films, Terrace reached the same conclusions about Washoe and Koko that he had about Nim. Washoe, Koko, and Nim's "language" production was for the most part imitative; they were merely mimicking their trainers' cues.

T.A. Pettito, R.J. Sanders, T.G. Bever, Thomas and Jean Sebeok, and Terrace grant that projects like those of the Gardners, Fouts, Patterson, and Terrace indicate that primates can learn vocabularies of visual symbols. Extending the issue beyond that of primates, Harvard behaviorist

B.F. Skinner asked whether pigeons are capable of symbolic communication and discovered that they indeed are. He trained two Carneaux pigeons, Jack and Jill, to communicate symbolically. Skinner speculated that the "language" produced by primates should be viewed as nothing more than responses to conditioning.

Pettito, Sanders, Bever, the Sebeoks, Skinner, and Terrace argue that although primates appear to be able to learn words, to use language symbolically, there is no evidence that they have grammatical competence. Primates cannot use symbols to create new meanings; they cannot combine words to produce original sentences. They are incapable of language as human beings know it.

Now that Bill has finished reviewing the evidence for and against the question as to whether primates can use language to communicate, he is aware that the issue is fairly complex. To answer this question intelligently, he'll have to decide whether sign language is a legitimate language; he'll have to think carefully about the nature of language itself. Further complicating the issue is the fact that not all linguists agree as to what constitutes human language. An additional problem is that there is no way to know what a primate, or any animal for that matter, is thinking whenever it appears to use signs symbolically. Last, and perhaps most important of all, is it reasonable to measure primate language against that of a human being?

Although the researchers who take the position that primates are capable of language have presented interesting, thought-provoking evidence, the most persuasive evidence has been presented by those who deny primates the ability to use language. Apes can use language symbolically, but so can pigeons. But neither pigeons nor apes can approach the linguistic spontaneity, dexterity, and creativity of a normal three-year-old human child. In this paper, then, Bill will present both sides as objectively and persuasively as he can. His conclusion, however, will be that although there is evidence that primates can use signs to communicate symbolically, there is no evidence that they are capable of language as human beings know and use it.

DOCUMENTATION: BACKING UP
WHAT YOU SAY

The purpose of documentation is to back up what you say. It is not enough to say that current research shows that nuclear waste can be safely disposed of in deep-shaft mines; you must show the reader *who* says so and *where*. Other researchers will wish to check and verify your findings; the more thorough and accurate documentation you offer your readers, the more reliable your research becomes. Faulty documentation violates the basic concept of research.

Stylesheets

There are several different stylesheets used by modern researchers in different fields. The chief "rule" about documentation is to be logical and consistent in the way you write your notes; therefore, it might be a good idea to buy one or another of the available stylesheets and then follow it carefully. The style in this chapter is based on the *MLA Handbook for Writers of Research Papers, Theses, and Dissertations* (New York: Modern Language Association, 1977), a standard stylesheet for work in English and the humanities. On page 208 there is an example from another widely used stylesheet, the *Publication Manual* of the American Psychological Association (the APA).

Documentation Notes

Documentation notes were, by convention, placed at the foot of the page (hence, "footnotes"), but modern practice increasingly moves them to the back of the research paper, preceding the bibliography, on a page or pages marked "References," or "Footnotes" or "Endnotes." For most college writing, notes numbered consecutively throughout and listed at the end of the paper will be the most efficient procedure.

Note that if you use APA or another name-date style, there are no notes. Instead, there are short references in the text to sources fully identified in the bibliography:

```
The long-term effects of dumping nuclear waste in the ocean "are
impossible to predict but horrifying to speculate about" (Trent, 1983,
p. 89).
```

Substantive Notes

Most of your notes will be references to books and articles. But occasionally you may wish to give a *substantive* note, an actual note from you to the reader in which you give additional information relevant to your research but not entirely necessary to what you are saying at that point in the paper. There are mixed feelings about these substantive notes; many researchers feel that any *relevant* information ought to be included in the main text and that irrelevant information should be omitted entirely. But because other researchers do use substantive notes, the best advice is to use substantive notes only when you cannot get the information into your text otherwise.

WHAT TO DOCUMENT

Direct Quotations

Any words you copy from a source should be placed in quotes, followed by a note number. The note number is a superscript, a number raised a half space above the line of text. No period follows the superscript:

Even Holden's brutal encounters with reality are quickly transformed into fantasy: "About halfway to the bathroom, I sort of started pretending I had a bullet in my guts. Old Maurice had plugged me."[1]

Ideas and Words from a Source

Words and concepts that you take from a source and incorporate into your own sentences should be documented.

Never at a loss for words, Holden manufactures adjectives from nouns and verbs to describe "vomity" taxicabs and "hoodlumy-looking" street people.[2]

Be especially aware of the obligation to acknowledge ideas, interpretations, analyses, and concepts that represent someone else's thinking on your topic. It can sometimes be easy to incorporate ideas from your sources into your paper as though they are your own. To do so is dishonest scholarship, and it is to be avoided rigorously. You may have been warned about *plagiarism* before now; people often describe plagiarism as copying words from a source and passing them off as your own in a composition. But you are plagiarizing too if you pass off someone else's ideas as your own in a composition. You can document someone else's thinking the same way you do his or her words:

Holden can be thought of as a model of lost and confused adolescence,[3] but he is a prototype for a very small, privileged class of modern youth.

[3] See Sarah Birkfeld, "A Jungian Look at Catcher in the Rye," Psychology Today, May 1979, pp. 72-77, for the interpretation of Holden Caulfield as an archetype.

Paraphrases and Restatements

When you change a source's phrases or ideas into your own words, document them:

Jefferson's notion in the Declaration of Independence that everyone is born with the same rights and privileges as everyone else[4] simply ignores the privileges of wealth.

Allusions and Incomplete References to Sources

Regardless of whether you quote or paraphrase from them, document all allusions and incomplete references:

For a full discussion of footnote style, the reader is referred to the MLA Handbook.[5]

References in the Text

Unless you give *full* documentation in the text itself, containing all the information normally found in a note (and in many cases it is cumbersome to do so), use a note in addition to the text reference:

S. I. Hayakawa in Language in Thought and Action[6] warns that we confuse both language and thought when we forget that words are not the same as the things they stand for.

[6] Harcourt (1964), p. 211.

Major Source

If you make many references to the same source—for example, if you are writing *about* a book, poem, play, or other source—you need not keep documenting it:

[7] Leo Tolstoy, Anna Karenina, trans. David Magarshack (New York: Signet Classics, 1961), p. 98. All further references to this work appear in the text.

Later references in the text need only the page number:

Kitty's love affair with Christianity began with her acquaintance with Madame Stahl (p. 233).

Source Within a Source

You may discover one author quoting another in such a way that you will want to quote the second author yourself. If it is at all possible, you should find the *original* source and quote from that, instead of quoting from the second-hand source (for accuracy's sake, if nothing else). Suppose you were doing a paper on the relevance of grammar to composition, and you were reading Virginia Allen's article "Teaching Standard English as a Second Dialect." In it you would find the following:

Martin Joos, who has made a special study of people's attitudes toward language, says:

> **Long before any teacher began to correct his English, the child has learned all he needs to know, at his age, about people and their places; he has developed considerable skill in judging adults by their speech . . .[8]**

The note number refers to Martin Joos's article "Language and the School Child." If you want to use the Joos quote, you should find the article it comes from and quote that, instead of quoting from Virginia Allen's article:

[1] Martin Joos, "Language and the School Child," Word Study, 11, No. 2 (1964), 95.

However, sometimes the original source is not available, or for some other reason the researcher must rely on the second-hand source (and you must be very certain that there *is* a good reason for so doing). In that case, you need a rather complicated note:

[1] Martin Joos, "Language and the School Child," Word Study, 11, No. 2 (1964), 95, as quoted in Virginia F. Allen, "Teaching Standard English as a Second Dialect," Teachers College Record, 68 (Feb. 1967), 358.

You can see that the business of quoting second-hand sources can easily get out of hand. Your job is to tell the reader where you found your information; if, for example, you found the Allen article not in its original journal but in an anthology of journal articles, to be perfectly accurate you would need the following:

[1] Martin Joos, "Language and the School Child," Word Study, 11, No. 2 (1964), 95, as quoted in Virginia F. Allen, "Teaching Standard English as a Second Dialect," Teachers College Record, 68 (Feb. 1967), 358, in Teaching High School Composition, eds. Gary Tate and Edward P. J. Corbett (New York: Oxford Univ. Press, 1970), pp. 359-60.

Not only is such a note ungainly, but you rely upon Tate and Corbett to quote Allen accurately, not to mention the additional reliance on Allen to quote Joos accurately. Because these are all respected scholars there is reason to assume the quotes are accurate, but there is always the possibility of error. There is the further danger that in quoting Joos out of context (without reading the rest of his article) you may distort his intention or misapply his meaning.

WHAT NOT TO QUOTE

Common knowledge need not be documented. There is no certain test for common knowledge, but in general you can consider knowledge to be "common" if it is widely known by educated people, if it is readily available in most general reference works such as encyclopedias or almanacs, or if it is available through the popular communications media—television, newspapers, and popular magazines. There is no need to document, for example, who the President is or where the White House is or that Shakespeare is the author of *Hamlet*.

Uncontested knowledge need not be documented, even if it is not common knowledge. Dates of historical events, for example, may or may not be considered common knowledge; but unless the precise date is relevant to the case you are arguing or unless the date is a matter of dispute in the research, it can be considered uncontested information. A handy rule to follow is this: anything that would damage your case if it were removed from your paper or proved to be wrong should be documented.

To a degree, documenting is part of a researcher's style, part of his or her view of self. Some researchers are very careful to document everything in their work. Others take a more relaxed attitude. To avoid the suspicion of plagiarism, beginning researchers should be very careful to document everything taken from sources.

HOW TO DOCUMENT: NOTES

The following examples give note entries for a variety of sources. Bibliographic entries for the same sources are given in the section How to Document: Bibliographies.

BOOK, ONE AUTHOR

[1] K. M. Elisabeth Murray, <u>Caught in the Web of Words</u> (New Haven: Yale Univ. Press, 1977), pp. 87-100.

BOOK, TWO AUTHORS

[2] Eugene Burdick and Harvey Wheeler, Fail Safe (New York: McGraw-Hill, 1962), p. 159.

BOOK, MORE THAN TWO AUTHORS

[3] Richard Braddock et al., Research in Written Composition (Champaign, Ill.: NCTE, 1963), pp. 52-53.

BOOK WITH AN EDITOR

[4] Gary Tate, ed., Teaching Composition: 10 Bibliographic Essays (Fort Worth: Texas Christian Univ. Press, 1976), p. vii.

CHAPTER IN AN EDITED WORK

[5] Richard Young, "Invention: A Topographical Survey," in Teaching Composition: 10 Bibliographic Essays, ed. Gary Tate (Fort Worth: Texas Christian Univ. Press, 1976), pp. 1-43.

BOOK, COMMITTEE OR GROUP AUTHOR

[6] Commission on Obscenity and Pornography, The Report of the Commission on Obscenity and Pornography (Toronto: Bantam Books, 1970), p. 228.

BOOK, TRANSLATION

[7] Fyodor Dostoyevsky, Crime and Punishment, trans. Constance Garnett (New York: The Modern Library, 1950), p. 224.

MAGAZINE ARTICLE, AUTHOR NAMED

[8] Robert Hughes, "Night and Silence, Who Is There?" Time, 12 Dec. 1977, p. 59.

MAGAZINE ARTICLE, NO AUTHOR GIVEN

[9] "Byrd of West Virginia: Fiddler in the Senate," Time, 23 Jan. 1978, p. 13.

NEWSPAPER ARTICLE

[10] Bob Talbert, "Why Are We in Such a Downer?" Detroit Free Press, 10 Jan. 1978, Sec. A, p. 9, col. 3.

PROFESSIONAL JOURNAL, EACH ISSUE STARTS WITH PAGE 1

[11] David M. Rubin, "Remember Swine Flu?" Columbia Journalism Review, 16, No. 2 (1977), 45.

PROFESSIONAL JOURNAL, PAGES NUMBERED BY VOLUME

[12] Richard H. Haswell, "Eight Concepts of Poetry for College Freshmen," College English, 39 (1977), 299.

DISSERTATION (UNPUBLISHED)

[13] William Earl Blank, "The Effectiveness of Creative Dramatics in Developing Voice, Vocabulary, and Personality in the Primary Grades," Diss. Univ. of Denver, 1953, p. 12.

HANDOUT, MIMEOGRAPH, AND SO ON

[14] John L. Olson, "Chronology of Renaissance Events," Handout, Central Michigan University, 1979.

LECTURE OR SPEECH

[15] Lorna H. Haworth, "Figuratively Speaking," Annual Meeting, National Council of Teachers of English, New York, 25 Nov. 1977.

FILM

[16] Hal Ashby, dir., Coming Home, with Jane Fonda, Jon Voigt, and Bruce Dern, United Artists, 1978.

PLAY

[17] Michael Lindsay-Hoagg, dir., Whose Life Is It Anyway? by Brian Clark, with Tom Conti and Jean Marsh, Trafalgar Theater, New York, 19 April 1979.

MUSICAL PERFORMANCE

[18] James Levine, cond., Parsifal, with Jon Vickers and Christa Ludwig, The Metropolitan Opera Company of New York, Metropolitan Opera House, New York, 16 April 1979.

RADIO OR TELEVISION PROGRAM

[19] "TV or Not TV," comment. Bill Moyers, Bill Moyers' Journal, PBS, 23 April 1979.

RECORD ALBUM OR TAPE

[20] Kate Taylor, Sister Kate, Cotillion Records, SD 9045, 1971.

PERSONAL LETTER

[21] Letter received from K. T. Easterly, 6 Dec. 1979.

PERSONAL INTERVIEW

[22] Personal interview with Jane Fonda, 10 Oct. 1978.

HOW TO DOCUMENT:
BIBLIOGRAPHIES

  The following examples give bibliographic entries for the items in the preceding section. A bibliography should always include all works you quote from; some users of bibliographies want you to include all works you consult. In college, your instructors will tell you which type of bibliography to submit.

BOOK, ONE AUTHOR

Murray, K. M. Elisabeth. Caught in the Web of Words: James A. H.

  Murray & the Oxford English Dictionary. New Haven: Yale Univ.

  Press, 1977.

BOOK, TWO AUTHORS

Burdick, Eugene, and Harvey Wheeler. Fail Safe. New York: McGraw-

  Hill, 1962.

BOOK, MORE THAN TWO AUTHORS

Braddock, Richard, et al. Research in Written Composition. Champaign,

  Ill.: NCTE, 1963.

BOOK WITH AN EDITOR

Tate, Gary, ed. Teaching Composition: 10 Bibliographic Essays. Fort

  Worth: Texas Christian Univ. Press, 1976.

CHAPTER IN AN EDITED WORK

Young, Richard. "Invention: A Topographical Survey." In Teaching

  Composition: 10 Bibliographic Essays. Ed. Gary Tate. Fort Worth:

  Texas Christian Univ. Press, 1976, pp. 1-43.

BOOK, COMMITTEE OR GROUP AUTHOR

Commission on Obscenity and Pornography. The Report of the Commission
on Obscenity and Pornography. Toronto: Bantam Books, 1970.

BOOK, TRANSLATION

Garnett, Constance, trans. Crime and Punishment. By Fyodor Dostoyevsky.
New York: The Modern Library, 1950.

MAGAZINE ARTICLE, AUTHOR NAMED

Hughes, Robert. "Night and Silence, Who Is There?" Time, 12 Dec.
1977, pp. 59-60.

MAGAZINE ARTICLE, NO AUTHOR GIVEN

"Byrd of West Virginia: Fiddler in the Senate." Time, 23 Jan. 1978,
pp. 12-16.

NEWSPAPER ARTICLE

Talbert, Bob. "Why Are We in Such a Downer?" Detroit Free Press,
10 Jan. 1978, Sec. A, p. 9, cols. 3-4.

PROFESSIONAL JOURNAL, EACH ISSUE STARTS WITH PAGE 1

Rubin, David M. "Remember Swine Flu?" Columbia Journalism Review,
16, No. 2 (1977), 42-46.

PROFESSIONAL JOURNAL, PAGES NUMBERED BY VOLUME

Haswell, Richard H. "Eight Concepts of Poetry for College Freshmen."
College English, 39 (1977), 294-306.

DISSERTATION (UNPUBLISHED)

Blank, William Earl. "The Effectiveness of Creative Dramatics in
Developing Voice, Vocabulary, and Personality in the Primary
Grades." Diss. Univ. of Denver 1953.

HANDOUT, MIMEOGRAPH, AND SO ON

Olson, John L. "Chronology of Renaissance Events." Handout for Class
in European History. Central Michigan University, 1979.

LECTURE OR SPEECH

Haworth, Lorna H. "Figuratively Speaking." Annual Meeting, National
Council of Teachers of English, New York. 25 Nov. 1977.

FILM

Ashby, Hal, dir. Coming Home. With Jane Fonda, Jon Voigt, and Bruce
Dern. United Artists, 1978.

PLAY

Lindsay-Hoagg, Michael, dir. Whose Life Is It Anyway? By Brian Clark.
With Tom Conti and Jean Marsh. Trafalgar Theater, New York
19 April 1979.

MUSICAL PERFORMANCE

Levine, James, cond. Parsifal. With Jon Vickers and Christa Ludwig.
The Metropolitan Opera Company of New York. Metropolitan Opera
House, New York. 16 April 1979.

RADIO OR TELEVISION PROGRAM

"TV or Not TV." Comment. Bill Moyers. Bill Moyers' Journal. PBS, 23
April 1979.

RECORD ALBUM OR TAPE

Taylor, Kate. Sister Kate. Cotillion Records, SD 9045, 1971.

PERSONAL LETTER

Easterly, K. T. Letter to author. 6 Dec. 1979.

PERSONAL INTERVIEW

Fonda, Jane. Personal interview. 10 Oct. 1978.

See page 200 for a brief explanation of APA reference style.

Murray, K. M. Elisabeth. Caught in the web of words: James A. H.

Murray & the Oxford English dictionary. New Haven: Yale University

Press, 1977.

Sekuler, R., & Levinson, E. The perception of moving targets.

Scientific American, 1977, 236 (1), 60-73.

ABBREVIATIONS AND BIBLIOGRAPHIC TERMS

In general, we recommend that you avoid using abbreviations. The space they save can cost much in terms of possible misreading. However, as a researcher you will encounter some common abbreviations and bibliographic terms used in writing and publishing and in college reading in general. You should become familiar with the following:

A.D.	*Anno Domini,* **in the year of our Lord**
anon.	**anonymous; the author's name is unknown (never appropriate for an article which is merely *unsigned* as in a magazine or newspaper.)**
ante	**before**
attrib.	**attributed; authorship is not positive**
B.C.	**before Christ**
b.	**born**
bib.	**biblical**
bibliog.	**bibliography**
©	**copyright; date of publication**
ca. or c.	*circa,* **about; date is approximate**
cap.	**capital; capitalized**
cf.	*confer,* **compare**
ch. (chs., *plural*)	**chapter (s)**
col. (cols. *plural*)	**column(s)**
d.	**died**
diss.	**dissertation**
ed. (eds., *plural*)	**editor; edited by; edition; editors**
e.g.	*exempli gratia,* **for example**
esp.	**especially**
est.	**estimated, estimation**
et al.	*et alii,* **and others**
etc.	*et cetera,* **and so forth**
f. (ff.,*plural*)	**and the following page(s)**

fn.	footnote
fr.	from
ibid.	*ibidem*, in the same place; cited immediately above
id.	*idem*, the same person
i.e.	*id est*, that is
l. (ll., *plural*)	line(s)
loc.cit.	*loco citato*, in the place cited; in the same place mentioned earlier
MS (MSS, *plural*)	manuscript(s)
n.	note
N.B.	*nota bene*, note well; take notice
n.d.	no date of publication
n.n.	no name of publisher
no. (nos., *plural*)	number(s)
n.p.	no place of publication
obs.	obsolete
op.cit.	*opere citato*, in the work cited recently
p. (pp., *plural*)	page(s)
passim	here and there; at intervals
pl. (pls., *plural*)	plate, plural plates
pseud.	pseudonym
pt. (pts., *plural*)	part(s)
q.v.	*quod vide*, which see
rev.	revised, revision; review; reviewer;
rpt.	reprint; reprinted
sec. (secs., *plural*)	section(s)
ser.	series
sic	thus it is; mistake in the original
var.	variant
v.	*vide*, see
viz.	*vidalicet*, namely
vol. (vols., *plural*)	volume(s)
vs., v.	*versus*, against

WRITING THE RESEARCH PAPER

After you have read all your evidence, have come to *know* the subject thoroughly, and have given yourself time to assimilate the information, you are ready to begin structuring your paper. Since the research paper is usually longer and more formal than most of your other writing, it is almost impossible to write one without making some kind of outline. You may keep refining the outline as you work on the paper, but you will avoid headaches for yourself if you work from at least a simple version of your outline. The outline need not be very elaborate, just detailed enough to give you (and anyone else) a clear picture of the points you are going to try to cover.

The overall plan of your paper, and thus of your outline, should follow these principles:

I Introduction

Research usually needs an introduction for the same reason everything else does—to catch reader interest, to help the reader "get into" the paper. Somewhere in the introduction you must ask your thesis question. The thesis *question* is preferable to the thesis statement, because it does not give away at the outset what position you intend to take. Some instructors prefer to see the thesis question as the first sentence of the introduction, but it also makes very good sense to have it as the *last* sentence of the introduction, to finish the introduction and make an effective transition to the rest of the paper. An introduction is ordinarily a single paragraph, but you may write an introduction of more than one paragraph if doing so doesn't give the impression that the introduction is holding up the paper unnecessarily.

II The Opposing View

When you start to research an issue, you strive to be unbiased; as we've said, you do not approach a research issue "knowing the answer." If you have isolated a legitimate yes-no issue, the question obviously has two sides.

Your research, however, will help you to answer the question, even if a definitive answer isn't possible yet. In organizing your paper, it is wise to present the "opposing" view first, if there is one. If your research has convinced you that cigarette smoking causes cancer, first present the other side, the side of those who feel that cigarette smoking does not cause cancer. Presenting the other side first, and presenting it well, will help to convince the reader that you thoroughly understand the issues, that you are a fair and unbiased researcher. It also has the advantage of providing you with something to argue *against*.

Present the case for the other side fairly and completely with the reasons and evidence that an intelligent opponent would use. Do not offer any counterevidence or argue against the opposing view here. In this section you are trying to present the opposing side's case as well as possible. Instead of finding fault, you should end this section by showing which of the opposing arguments are the strongest. Point out to the reader what a reasonable person should concede in the opposing argument. (It is necessary to concede, for example, that some people have smoked all their lives without contracting cancer.) The more positively you can treat the opposing side, the stronger you can make the opposing side look, the fairer you will seem—and of course the more imposing your own side will seem. Anyone can win an argument against a weak opponent; but it takes a skillful debater to win against a *strong opponent*. It is conceivable that you could concede *all* of the opposing view (the opponent is not "wrong") and still demonstrate the superiority of the other side—which may simply have newer information to offer in the argument. Keep in mind that you do not have to *prove* anything in a limited research paper; your job is only to examine both sides of the question for the reader's benefit. In the *conclusion* you can tell the reader what a reasonable person should conclude from the data in your paper.

III Your View

Usually, a research writer will decide that one side of the case is in fact better than the other side. If your research leads you to conclude that both sides are equally strong or equally weak (for lack of data, for example), then you must arbitrarily pick one side or the other to present first; but in such a case you must also take extra precautions not to bias the arguments in favor of one side or the other.

However, if there is a "better view," this section can be started with counterarguments, if you have some to offer. If you have discovered, for example, errors in data or reasoning in the opposing view, this is the place to point them out. You must still try to remain the objective, dispassionate researcher; it would be well to offer contradictory evidence if you are going to find fault with the opposition. But you need not go looking for flaws in the opposing view. If you have a good research question, solidly two-sided, you will probably find that both sides have plausible data and authorities to back them up. You yourself may find abortion, euthanasia, or capital punishment abhorrent, but there is quite likely to be a valid point of view on the other side of the question. In a good research paper, it is to your advantage to present the opposing view in a fair and interesting way; otherwise, you will not have a worthy opponent to argue against. The better view will seem obvious and unimpressive.

In a counterargument, an effective strategy is to concede the more reasonable points of the opposing view, especially if they have some basis in fact or are founded on believable assumptions. The challenge is then to show that the stronger side is more powerful, more persuasive, a more reasonable *interpretation* of the evidence.

With or without counterarguments, make the case for the better view—present examples, data, arguments. Especially if you have new arguments to offer—new, meaningful ideas that apparently have not occurred to the opposition—this is the place to present them.

IV Conclusion

The conclusion of a research paper should be the *climax* of the paper. There is still important work to do in the conclusion; so far, your paper has shown that there is a research question, that there are two opposing sides to the question. Now, you must *answer the thesis question*. It may be helpful to the reader if you start the conclusion with a brief summary of the arguments. But you must, finally, conclude with one of three positions: the first view is correct, your view is correct, or there is not enough evidence available for any intelligent conclusion to be drawn. If you decide after all that your view is indeed the correct one, you must help the reader understand why it is better: more substantive data, better authorities, more convincing and logical arguments, and so on. Perhaps the whole argument will hinge on some key point: "If the Heidegger study done three years ago is correct, as several authorities have indicated, the evidence is conclusive—five million case histories are difficult to dispute."

You should save something good for the conclusion. The conclusion isn't just the end of the paper—it is the *point* of the paper. If you use up your best material in the body of the paper, the conclusion will look weak by comparison. In addition to showing the reader the outcome of the argument, you must bring the paper to completion, give the reader a sense of "ending." An apt quote, some striking fact or statistic, a relevant personal note, or even an especially well-worded final sentence will round off the ending and help the reader to "get out" of the paper (similar to the problem in the introduction of getting the reader into the paper). But you must avoid raising any new or irrelevant questions in the conclusion. If you have demonstrated to your satisfaction that cigarettes have been shown to cause lung cancer and heart attacks, you must resist the temptation to increase the charge ("and perhaps they will one day be linked to arthritis and insanity as well") or to extend the argument by easy analogy ("and if cigarettes are so bad, we must suppose that cigars and pipes and even chewing tobacco must be as bad or worse").

V References

Different publishers require different formats for documentation notes and other references; some professors also have different requirements. Before handing in or submitting documented papers, ask first which format is preferred. In general, footnotes (at the bottom of the page) are going out of style. Preferred modern practice is to list endnotes, numbered in sequence, on a separate page (or pages) immediately preceding the bibliography. These endnotes are usually titled "References." Follow your stylesheet exactly.

VI Bibliography

There are many different kinds of bibliographies; they serve different purposes. For example, an annotated bibliography gives the author's evaluations of the sources cited. However, a bibliography that is nothing more than a list of the same books and articles in your references is not the best idea. A bibliography should be a useful part of your paper by itself—a list of significant books and articles on the issue, not just those you have actually cited in your paper. The bibliography lets the reader see how recent your research is and also whether you are aware of important publications. It would seem strange for a researcher to miss a very important book, for example. Thus, the bibliography is indeed an aid to other researchers who may come after you.

A selected bibliography is a list of resources available, not just those you actually cite in your paper. You will undoubtedly *read* more than the works you cite. Ideally, you should read and assimilate everything available on a research question, but practically, there is likely to be too much available for such thoroughness in anything shorter than a doctoral dissertation. You can at least *skim* through a great deal of material to determine whether it would be useful for researchers on your topic. The idea is that research is cumulative, and as each new researcher adds to the existing bibliographies, an increasingly complete list of the works available will be compiled. You will soon get to know from a little reading which are the important works, which things you *must* read. You read as much of the available material as you have time for—aiming to have read and understood as much as possible in the time you have. Never put anything into your bibliography that you haven't actually seen. You will find many things listed in the indexes, for example, but you must not simply build your bibliography from the indexes without at least skimming through each item, to see that it is, in fact, related to the issue and likely to be useful to other researchers.

A STUDENT RESEARCH PAPER

Read the following research paper. Does the topic seem to you to be specific, limited, worthwhile? Does this writer do a good job of research? That is, do you understand the evidence he presents? Is the evidence believable?

Gentrification: Pros and Cons

Bob Burlingham, the author of the outline, research paper, notes, and bibliography reproduced in the following pages, submitted these materials with a separate title page. Your instructor will probably tell you how to submit your papers. If not, a heading format is suggested inside the back cover of this text.

I. What Is Gentrification?

A. Definition of Gentrification

B. Description of Effects of Gentrification on Poor and on City Economies

C. Thesis Question: Can gentrification be justified when the poor are forced out of their homes, their neighborhoods, and the dissolution of their political power as a group is a consequence?

II. A Negative View of Gentrification

A. The Arguments

1. Relocating the Poor

2. Weakening of Political Power among Certain Groups

3. The Taxation System

B. Evaluation of the Arguments

III. The Case for Gentrification

A. The Arguments

1. The Increased Tax Base

2. Development of a New Industry: Renovation

3. "Radiation" Effects

4. Historic Preservation

5. The Environment and Conservation

B. Evaluation of the Arguments

IV. Conclusion: The Necessity of Gentrification

V. References

VI. Bibliography

What Is Gentrification?

The term "gentrification" is derived from ". . . the
British word 'gentry' which refers to the upper or ruling
class, or land proprietors who--through superior buying
power--squeeze the poor out of desirable locations."[1] In the
sixties, a trend began in which housing in older city neighborhoods in the United States increased in demand and now, in
the eighties, these neighborhoods are becoming gentrified.
Problems are also coming of age in the eighties. Residents
of inner-city homes, the poor for the most part, are being
displaced.

Notes are numbered
consecutively throughout
the paper. The numbers
refer to the documentation
entries on the Notes page
at the end of the paper.

Note that the block-style
quote is indented from the
left. Indenting takes the
place of opening and closing
quotation marks. (Format
guidelines for typed papers
are given inside the back
cover of *The Writer's
Work*.)

> For the poor, the displacement cycle is a devastating
> combination of politics and economics: it is good for
> entire cities, good for most politicians, and certainly
> good for the developers and speculators who are harvest-
> ing hefty profits from the change. The poor are, in
> effect, subsidizing the long-overdue revitalization of
> their cities. They are being outrageously shortchanged.[2]

As is evident, those with financial and political power
favor the return of middle-class residents to inner-city
areas. For the first time in decades, growth is occurring
without government backing in urban areas. The revitalization
of many neighborhoods, while admittedly isolated, is entirely
market oriented.

An increase in the need for existing housing has made
prices soar. The effect on the poor, critics argue, is
devastating. Others disagree:

217

This term (gentrification) has opened up a new can of
worms that has elicited concern and even protests from
public agencies and a few organized resistance groups.
However, preliminary government studies seem to show
that the so-called displacement problem caused by
gentrification has been overstated.[3]

The thesis question

Can gentrification be justified when the poor are forced
out of their homes and neighborhoods and when the dissolution
of their political power as a group is a consequence?

A Negative View of Gentrification

As an objective researcher, the writer presents the case for the opposition in the best light, without limiting or diminishing the facts.

Minorities, the elderly, and other poor are being forced
out of their homes as the neighborhoods they live in are
gentrified and tax assessments go up. "The neighborhoods
please everyone except those who are pushed out."[4] James
David Besser, a critic of gentrification, describes the problem the poor face when their homes become more valuable and
they are displaced; he explains that displaced persons must
move to neighborhoods that are poorly located. Important
social services and access to public transit--qualities
middle-class residents now seek in a neighborhood--are often
not available in neighborhoods the poor are moving into.
Ironically, they require access to these types of services
more than those who are well off. The poor lose cultural
ties that were present in their close-knit ghetto neighborhoods.

Displaced residents tend to develop a pattern of geo-

graphic instability. People who live in the same house
or apartments for many years move frequently after displacement. Typically, their first moves are made in
haste, with few options open to them. Dissatisfied
with worsened conditions, they move again. The pattern
repeats itself as they become trapped in a downward
spiral.[5]

In the sixties, there were programs that provided new
housing for the poor in high-rise-type apartment complexes--
Model Cities, Community Renewal, Neighborhood Development,
and so forth--crime and vandalism became a problem in this
type of public housing, and still is. Recently in Detroit,
a heroin ring called Young Boys Incorporated was uncovered
near a public-housing development. Even without crime, the
apartments were sometimes worse than the slum neighborhoods
that the residents were imported from. Old abandoned housing
became the victim of urban renewal: "The neighborhood is
transformed--much of it in fact eliminated outright by construction. . . ."[6] Demolished housing, or worse yet, plans
for demolition never got off the ground after residents were
told to leave--vandalism destroyed any remaining hope of
saving the homes. Residents of public housing became disil-
lusioned with government-funded housing projects.

Political power is weakened when neighborhoods are
broken up. The poor have few organized groups through which
they can be heard. "Dispersal to distant suburbs diffuses
their political power and perpetuates a system in which the

needs of the poor are conveniently ignored."[7]

In a Grand Rapids development, one board member of the Greater Grand Rapids Housing Corporation commented: "Neighborhood kids are having an opportunity to see black craftsmen at work on a very exciting project, giving them some very positive role models that they haven't seen before."[8] There is a relatively low rate of vandalism at the site.

Unfortunately, the neighborhood where these kids live is one that is being gentrified--Heritage Hill Historic District. The "exciting project" the board member speaks of is Heritage Commons Townhouses, a unit priced for young married professionals. The Housing Corporation hopes to influence the removal of nearby blighted housing with the project--the homes of those neighborhood kids.

Private money is necessary to rehabilitate housing. Business, neighborhood associations, and churches and other charity groups are willing to invest money in their cities. Tax laws and restrictions are also needed to protect the poor in gentrified neighborhoods. The handling of transfer payments and availability of loans are problems that need government reform.

> . . . according to a militant young staffer in a state
> regulatory agency, the banks [are responsible for
> decline] . . . By strangling the flow of mortgage money,
> they've made it impossible for a healthy replacement
> process to continue . . . [they] deposit capital in
> more profitable, lower risk suburban developments.

. . . It is the city [say the banks] , not the banks,
which is responsible for dirty streets, inequitable
assessments, venal building inspectors, indifferent
police.

The city now suggests the Department of Housing
and Urban Development is responsible. HUD did it with
its ill-conceived, mismanaged FHA low-downpayment ownership program.[9]

In Grand Rapids there is a program that distributes
money to the poor for rent, improvement of living quarters,
and other related purposes. Qualification requirements include private ownership of property. In the Heartside Dis-
trict--the city's poorest--the average resident is an older
male, white, below poverty levels, and usually a former
mental patient or person with other problems (alcoholism
and police records are predominant traits). Of the 800 known
residents, not one is a property owner.[10] If the money is
intended to help pay rent, why do applicants have to own
property in the first place?

In the National Coalition Study of 1977, researchers
reported that there is a "consistent inability of the poor
to successfully resist displacement in a rehabilitated
area."[11] If this is true, it is because taxes, programs,
and rehabilitation plans have not been made that include the
poor. They are being "conveniently ignored."

The Grand Rapids case is an instance in which funds
intended to help rehabilitate housing of the poor are caught

up in regulations that prohibit any aid to be given to those who need it. Property taxes also are directed to those who have, rather than to the have-nots.

Consider the case of two houses of equal size and age located in a central city residential area. One of the houses is well maintained, and the other is run-down. The one in good repair is assessed and taxed much more heavily than the other. In effect, the tax system penalizes development and rewards decay.[12]

Transition from presentation of data to evaluation of arguments. Note that the writer concedes there is some validity to all the arguments. He estimates the relative strength of each argument.

Morally, the arguments about the poor have the greatest weight. An injustice is being done against these people. They are being forced out of their homes, scattered around the suburbs, doomed to cheaper and cheaper housing until they end up in ghettoes. When this happens during a war, such people are called refugees. Gentrification is another example of the inequality between the rich and the poor. These arguments show that the poor are exploited by the rich.

Legally, the economic issue raises a serious question-- the key to the gentrification problem. Landlords have a right to do whatever they want with their property. Slum buildings are good investments. They are bought cheaply, and the purchaser gets to depreciate the entire cost of the building as a tax deduction, no matter how many previous owners also depreciated it. The "slumlord" makes more pro- fit and pays lower taxes if he or she doesn't repair or improve the property, and this is strictly legal. But this means there is a built-in incentive in the housing business that encourages the decay of old buildings. On top of that, to reverse this decay by improving the buildings results in driving out the poor residents. Economic facts of life favor the rich and penalize the poor in this situation. Gentrification thus looks very unfair, and the arguments against gentrification appear to be very strong and convincing.

The Case for Gentrification

There are three major reasons for an increasing interest in urban homes in the past decade. The first and foremost is construction costs. The prices of lumber, labor, and land have skyrocketed. Existing homes, larger and better constructed, sell for prices comparable to small suburban homes. "Older homes may show wear and tear and require more maintenance and renovation expenditures, but the quality of construction of an older home is often much higher than the standard in new construction."[13] Related to high costs for new homes, another reason for gentrified neighborhoods is a shortage of new homes. The housing market is highly influenced by economic trends--the recessions of the seventies have caused a subsequent housing slump.

A third, and perhaps more important, long-term cause of renewed interest in urban locations is the high price of fuel. Both gasoline for transit between suburban areas and work, and fuel oil for heating homes in remote locations is expensive. Hence, home buyers today are turning to existing homes close to work, schools, and other important urban areas.

Until quite recently it was fashionable to debate whether cities were worth saving. Housing experts seemed to be on an endless quest to cure blight, and the focus was on efforts to arrest decline and to restore the tax base for struggling urban areas . . . suddenly urban neighborhoods are being rediscovered, urban chic is becoming "in," and the cultural excitement and vitality of cities is receiving increasing attention.[14]

This may seem to be a little exaggerated to the Michigan reader; in many areas however--even in Detroit--the above statement is true.

The number one advantage to urban revitalization is that cities are now becoming more powerful with the badly needed tax dollars from property owners in urban neighborhoods. Since prior assessments were so low and crime and vandalism so high, cities were running deficits. While it cannot resolve changes in demographics, the gentrification process does help ease the strain somewhat.

Some buyers are rehabilitating homes for investment purposes. "Some people become so interested in renovating and preserving older homes that they make a business of purchasing, renovating, and reselling their houses and contracting for other homeowners."[15] This new business is likely to boost the economy of cities and possibly even the nation. "All research points to remodeling as the number one growth area in the construction industry," says David M. Sauer. "In 1981," he predicted, "professional home remodeling will be up nearly 27 percent [over 1980] , to almost $30

billion, and commercial remodeling will increase 10 percent,
to $44 billion."[16] Sauer is president of Qualified Remodeler
Inc., of Chicago, and publisher of Commercial Remodeler, a
trade magazine. Renovation of homes could put the housing
industry back on its feet--a signal of economic recovery
when prospering.

In a recent interview with Ron Hoort, a Grand Rapids
realtor, in the Grand Rapids Press, the effect of a new
development of the Heritage Commons Townhouses was discussed:

> Hoort noted many "radiation" effects of the large invest-
> ment in the area, most importantly a new willingness by
> financial institutions to loan money for home financing
> and rehabilitation. Just across the street from Heri-
> tage Commons, for example, a sound but elderly house
> recently was okayed for an FHA mortgage, something that
> was unheard of in the area a year or so ago.[17]

As mentioned earlier, the Heritage Commons townhouses
are forcing poor people out of their homes. Here is the positive side to this particular development it's a matter of
what goals people are seeking that determine a project's
strong and weak points.

There are other advantages to gentrification that have
less impact. Historic preservation is one.

> . . . the Bicentennial fostered a reappraisal of our
> American heritage. Many now place a greater value on
> older things. And experience has taught us that new-

ness sometimes means shoddiness, advertisers' claims
notwithstanding.[18]

Historic districts have sprouted throughout the nation
in an effort to preserve the America that was. Georgetown,
Washington, D.C.; Chicago's Gold Coast; Oak Park, Illinois;
Pittsburgh; Boston; Denver; San Francisco; Seattle; Atlanta;
Salem; and Alexandria predominate among cities undergoing
extensive rehabilitation. Old homes will not become victims
of the bulldozer any longer; the trend is increasing in
intensity.

One of the reasons for gentrification is to save on
fuel costs. As the trend increases, there should be an
effect on overall fuel consumption in the nation.

> Sprawl is a profligate waster of land, energy, and
> other resources. Urban sprawl may take the form of
> single-family dwellings stretching in ever-widening
> circles around the city. It may extend even farther,
> voraciously eating into mountainsides, seashores, and
> farming areas.[19]

An increase in the number of urban inhabitants will reduce
the growth of fringe areas slightly. The baby boom, however,
will continue to create a greater than normal need for housing until the end of this century. Sprawl will not cease in
the near future: ". . . most demographers believe rural
areas and small cities will continue to claim more than their
share of the country's population growth."[20]

Says Calvin Beale, a population expert with the Department of Agriculture: "There's now a much better chance to make a living in the country at things other than mining and farming. More people have a negative attitude toward big cities, and the growing retiree population is searching for places where living costs are cheaper."[21]

Of these arguments, the strongest is the decay of our cities. Urban blight is a creeping disease that is destroying many of our cities. As neighborhoods become low-rent areas and slums, the cities lose tax money for services, maintenance, police, and so on, in those areas. Wealthy and middle-income people move away from the surrounding areas, and the blight spreads. Something must be done, and gentrification seems like a positive approach. In this view of the case, gentrification becomes almost a necessity to stop the decay. Private investors who can profit from their investments can stop the decay better than the cities themselves could with urban renewal projects, because the city-sponsored projects just take more tax money away from municipal services, including education and police.

Furthermore, the housing industry is one of the major industries that the recession has badly damaged. The price of building suburban homes and the cost of borrowing mortgage money make renovated city housing much more attractive, not to mention the added benefits of living close to your work and enjoying the many features of city life. Young people today need housing but can't afford it; so again gentrification looks like a positive step--for the salvation of the housing industry and for the needs of millions of people who otherwise could not find homes.

The research on this side of the question is very strong. The data I have been able to find for gentrification seem to suggest that it may be the only sensible way to deal with the problems of city housing.

The Necessity for Gentrification

Gentrification in itself is not the cause for displacement among the poor; there are other factors that contribute to the problem. Revitalization of our cities and urban areas will, in the long run, benefit all, the poor as well as those better off financially. Problems must be realized for what they are, and gentrification must be encouraged. But even though it effects displacement only indirectly, it does have an important bearing on the problem.

Gentrification causes housing values to rise. When one home on a street is improved, others soon follow suit. Dollars run through the neighborhoods of broken-down homes like antibiotics fighting disease. Rehabilitation spreads to other areas and then associations are formed to help maintain those neighborhoods. Assessments increase as the quality of the housing does--taxes go up. Minorities, the largest segment in these neighborhoods who are poor, are forced out. This isn't a side effect of gentrification, it is a side effect of that well-known villain of the sixties' demonstra-

tors--"The System." There are few naysayers of gentrification that are willing to give up capitalism and the free-
market system. The handling of transfer payments (a socialistic aspect of our government) can be used to benefit
neighborhoods and reduce displacement problems, though they
haven't been doing so yet. "Gradually, the system is being
adjusted so that the poor have less responsibility for support of public services than they did in previous years."[22]
In short, what this means is that the rich are going to be
paying for the expenses of the poor. The status quo is
maintained, or grows wider. While it may be true that the
poor have less responsibility, they are also receiving less
in government aid under the Reagan Administration's policies. It will be up to the states, the cities, and poor
people themselves to insure "a chicken for every pot," a
car in every garage, a home for every family--the American
dream of the fifties and sixties is still not reality.

Changes in tax laws will benefit the general public if
they are handled correctly. Past reforms, such as Proposition 13 in California and Nevada's reforms, are becoming
popular in other states as well. Homestead exemptions, which
place less burden on poor property owners, was one attempt:
"The weakness of the homestead exemption is that it does
not help the renter."[23] Circuit-breaker reforms are also
used, which give rebates to poor people--in this case, landlords are reluctant to pass on the savings to renters in the
form of lower rent. President Reagan "has told . . . cities
that we have to make it on our own."[24] Urban homesteading

is one such attempt that may become popular. This renewal policy leaves the work to the citizen, who buys inner-city homes at nominal costs (usually $1.00) and fixes them him- or herself--much in the same way that the West was settled.

City neighborhoods can be restored and homes revitalized without totally displacing those already living there. One possible way to protect residents of neighborhoods undergoing gentrification is to create both single-family dwellings and homes subdivided into apartments, the latter for those who cannot afford to own homes. The increasing costs of living in a single-family dwelling may make the apartment alternative more appealing than it has been up to now.

The problems of displacement are not going to be solved easily, but the cost--not just in the monetary sense but in terms of overall benefits versus drawbacks--of preventing (or not encouraging) gentrification is far greater than any side effects the trend may have.

Housing "injustice" is just one of many results of poverty; poverty itself is the greater "injustice." The evidence on hand suggests that gentrification is a positive step in reversing the decay of cities, increasing the tax base of cities, reviving the housing industry, and providing housing for many people who otherwise couldn't afford it.

Endnotes

[1] Dorothy Weddell, "Gentrification: A New Trend for Older Areas," Detroit Free Press, 26 Apr. 1980, Sec. B, p. 1, cols. 1-4.

[2] James David Besser, "'Gentrifying' the Ghetto," Progressive, Jan. 1979, p. 30.

[3] Weddell, p. 1.

[4] Besser, p. 30.

[5] Besser, p. 30.

[6] Tom LaBelle, "Down Where Lights Are Gay," Grand Rapids Press, 12 Mar. 1979, Sec. B, p. 1, col. 6.

[7] Besser, p. 32.

[8] Jan Blaich, "Heritage Townhouses Are Visionary," Grand Rapids Press, 12 Sept. 1977, Sec. C, p. 4, col. 2.

[9] Rolf Goetze and Kent W. Colton, "The Dynamics of Neighborhoods," Journal of the American Planning Association, 5 (1977), 185-186.

[10] Personal interview with Arlene Burlingham, member of Heartside Association, Grand Rapids, 26 Mar. 1982.

[11] Bill Dalton, "Task Force Urges Rent-Subsidized Housing Program," 24 Nov. 1980, Sec. C, p. 4, col. 3, as quoted from the National Urban Coalition Study of 1977 in the Grand Rapids Press.

[12] Henry S. Reuss, "Land Use Planning: A Need for New Approaches," in Land Use Planning Abstracts (New York: Environment Information Center Publishers, July 1979, Vol. 5), p. 14.

[13] Richard J. Roddewig, "The Three R's: Renovation, Restoration, and Re-Use," Real Estate Today, Oct. 1980, p. 22.

[14] Goetze and Colton, p. 185.

[15] Roddewig, p. 26.

[16] "Fixing Up Is Moving Up," Detroit Free Press, 1 Nov. 1980, Sec. B, p. 2, cols. 1-2.

[17] LaBelle, p. 1.

[18] Goetze and Colton, p. 185.

[19] Reuss, p. 13.

[20] "Where Supercities Are Growing Fastest," U.S. News and World Report, 30 June 1980, p. 52.

[21] "Where Supercities Are Growing Fastest," p. 52.

[22] William O. Winter, State and Local Government in a Decentralized Republic (New York: Macmillan Publishing Co., 1980), p. 100.

[23] Winter, p. 100.

[24] Richard Cassell, "Say 'Yes' to Detroit Businesses," Detroit News, 20 Apr. 1982, Sec. A, p. 12, col. 3.

Bibliography

"Access: Eastown Community Association." Neighborhood newsletter. Grand Rapids, Mich. Mar. 1980.

Banta, David. "Last Stronghold of a Threatened Species."
Eastkent Photo Reporter, 18 Sept. 1979, p. 1, cols. 1-3.

Besser, James David. "'Gentrifying' the Ghetto." Progressive,
30 Jan. 1979, pp. 30-32.

Blaich, Jan. "Heritage Townhouses Are Visionary." Grand
Rapids Press, 12 Sept. 1977, Sec. C, p. 4, cols. 1-3.

Burlingham, Arlene. Personal interview. 26 Mar. 1982.

"Buy an Old House, Fix It Up." Changing Times, Mar. 1982,
p. 28.

Dalton, Bill. "Heartside Renewal Cost Put at $4.5 Million."
Grand Rapids Press, 20 May 1976, Sec. D, p. 1, cols. 1-4.

----------. "Task Force Urges Rent-Subsidized Housing
Program." Grand Rapids Press, 24 Nov. 1980, Sec. C,
p. 1, cols. 1-2.

DeMaagd, Pete. "GR's Reputation Is Well Known." Grand
Rapids Press, 23 Nov. 1980, Sec. C, p. 1, cols. 1-2.

English, Carey. "U.S. to Pump $25 Million into Public
Housing." Grand Rapids Press, 16 Sept. 1980, Sec. A,
p. 1, cols. 5-6.

"Fixing Up Is Moving Up." Detroit Free Press, 1 Nov. 1980,
Sec. B, p. 2, cols. 1-2.

"For the Joy of Homeowning, Some Spend 42% of Their Pay."
Wall Street Journal, 1 Feb. 1982, Sec. 2, p. 2, cols. 2-3.

Goetze, Paul, and Kent W. Colton. "The Dynamics of Neighborhoods." Journal of the American Planning Association,

Apr. 1980, pp. 184-189.

"In the Inner City . . . 10 Years After the Riots." Grand
    Rapids Press, 24 July 1977, Sec. B, p. 1, cols. 1-5.

LaBelle, Tom. "Touring the World that Was." Grand Rapids
    Press, 15 Mar. 1979, Sec. B, p. 1, col. 6.

"Realtors Among the Ruins--Recycling Old Buildings."
    Realtors Review, Aug. 1978, pp. 6-11.

Reuss, Henry S. "Land Use Planning: A Need for New Ap-
    proaches." Land Use Planning Abstracts. New York:
    Environment Information Center, July 1979.

Rowe, Stephen, and Phyliss Thompson. "Equitable Access:
    Employment and Housing in the Grand Rapids Area."
    Class Project, William James College, Winter 1973.

Thompson, Phyliss T. "Equitable Access: Public Service and
    Facilities." Class Project, William James College,
    Fall 1972.

Weddell, Dorothy. "Gentrification: A New Trend for Older
    Areas." Detroit Free Press, 26 Apr. 1980, Sec. B,
    cols. 1-4.

----------. "Senior Citizen Renters Receive the Gift of
    Time." Detroit Free Press, 4 Oct. 1980, Sec. B, p. 1.

"Where Supercities Are Growing Fastest." U.S. News and
    World Report, 30 June 1980, pp. 52-55.

Winter, William O. State and Local Government in a Decen-
    tralized Republic. New York: Macmillan, 1980.

"Young People Are Pessimistic About Ever Affording a Home."
    Wall Street Journal, 17 Feb. 1982, Sec. 2, p. 27, col 1.

Bob's thesis concerns a very significant problem: the benefits of gentrification versus the losses poor people suffer from it. As he shows, there are two sides to this problem, two significant sides. It is important to remember here that Bob is investigating an argument. As an objective researcher, it is his job to find the data on both sides of the question and to evaluate the arguments on both sides. Even though gentrification is a complex issue, Bob has done a fine job of isolating and explaining the arguments.

Is Bob convincing? Can we trust his analysis of the question? He reasons logically, and his data seem compelling. He has been able to investigate gentrification as a local issue (he is a Michigan resident) rather than as a more abstract problem, and that too helps us to believe that he thoroughly understands the two sides. Perhaps some readers would have more confidence in the analysis if there were more data—it is true that research gains in validity in relation to the amount and quality of the data—but each reader must decide this question for him- or herself. It is clear that Bob understands the subject and has done some solid research. His conclusions seem reasonable given the data he presents.

After discussing and documenting the arguments against gentrification, Bob begins his evaluation of these arguments: "Morally, the arguments about the poor have the greatest weight." This is a key component of his research. The presentation of the data amounts to an objective summary, but the *evaluation* is a critique of the facts, of the quality of the evidence. It is here that the researcher has the opportunity to analyze and validate, and it is here that the researcher has the greatest opportunity for objective insight into the problem. Note that the opportunity arises again after presentation of the arguments for gentrification. In both places, Bob has given us his interpretation, his view of the data. In short, his research is more than a mere compilation of the facts. He tells us the facts, and he shows us what they mean.

Finally, Bob's paper ends with a reasonable conclusion, in which he answers his research question. This answer is a data-related conclusion; that is, it is not simply Bob's "feelings" but a conclusion that he feels is justified by the data. If he has done a good job of presenting his research, the reader too should feel persuaded by the data.

Popular research topics

You may find the following list helpful in determining a research issue for yourself if you are assigned a research paper for your composition course. These topics are some of the research questions our students have asked in recent years:

1 Should Marijuana Be Legalized?
2 Capital Punishment: Yes or No?
3 Abortion versus Right to Life: Who Is Right?
4 Euthanasia: Do We Have a Right to Death?
5 Is There Too Much Sex in Advertising?
6 Gun Laws: Good or Bad?
7 Hunting: Sport or Massacre?
8 The Resurrection: Hoax or History?
9 Nuclear Waste: Safe?
10 Bermuda Triangle: Natural or Supernatural?
11 Freedom of the Press versus Gag Rule
12 Modern Witches: Neurotics or Mystics?
13 TV Violence: Harmful or Harmless?
14 Legalized Prostitution: Pro and Con
15 Pornography: Harmful or Helpful?
16 Legalized Homosexuality: Pro and Con
17 School Athletics: Good or Bad?
18 Genetic Engineering: Pro and Con
19 Imprisonment versus Rehabilitation
20 ERA: Necessary or Unnecessary?
21 Vegetarianism: Healthful or Harmful?
22 Reincarnation: Fact or Fiction?
23 Malpractice: Patients' Rights versus Doctors'
24 Transcendental Meditation: Real or Gimmick?
25 Biofeedback: Science or Fiction?
26 Nudity: Good or Bad?
27 UFOs: Science or Fiction?
28 John F. Kennedy's Assasination: Lone Assassin or Conspiracy?
29 Snowmobiles: Sport or Mayhem?
30 The Army: Volunteer or Conscriptive?
31 Shroud of Turin: Real or Fake?
32 National Health Insurance: Pro and Con
33 American Nazis: A Threat?
34 Women in West Point: Yes or No?
35 Are Fat People Discriminated Against?
36 Hockey Violence: Necessary?
37 Drinking Age: Raise to 21?
38 ESP: Fact or Fiction?
39 Advertising: Pro and Con
40 Cigarettes and Cancer: Proved or Not?
41 Fear of Snakes: Justified or Not?
42 American Funerals: Tragedy or Travesty?
43 Transsexuals: Should They Compete in Sports?

If you keep in mind that a research paper is not a "report," not a mere collection of facts, you will avoid topics like "The History of the Tank," "The Advantages of Dentistry," "The Development of Feminism."

Such one-sided topics are usually well researched in encyclopedias, history books, and elsewhere. They require you only to compile the known facts. To create a topic you can think about, one that will allow you to weigh the evidence and reach conclusions, change such topics into two-sided questions (see pages 182–183). For example: "Are Tanks Essential to Modern Warfare?" "What Are the Advantages and Disadvantages of Dentistry?" "Do Women Still Face Job Discrimination Today?"

PART TWO

SKILLS

CHAPTER SIX

Effective Paragraphs

You write with ease to show your breeding.

But easy writing's curst hard reading.

Richard Sheridan, *Clio's Protest*

WHAT IS A PARAGRAPH?

A paragraph is a group of sentences developing a single point or idea. It is possible, occasionally, to write a paragraph consisting of a single sentence, but in general, paragraphs contain more than one sentence. In formal writing, most paragraphs contain three or more sentences, and this is a good guideline for you to follow in college.

A paragraph can be used as a division of a composition, or it can be a complete composition itself. In either case the paragraph begins with an indented sentence: half an inch for handwritten paragraphs, five spaces for typewritten. The indentation indicates the beginning of a new idea, a subdivision of a preceding idea, an additional example, or any other new development of thought.

Indenting for paragraphs is a tradition in writing, like punctuating or starting a new sentence with a capital letter. Hundreds of years ago, writers did not indent to signal paragraph divisions. Instead, they used a signal (¶) in the left-hand margin: the word *paragraph*, meaning "write beside," is derived from that practice. In modern writing, however, indenting has become a custom or "convention," meaning it is an agreed-upon way to indicate units of thoughts. Readers expect paragraphs to show the development of an idea, the organization of the writer's purpose. Therefore there are two common paragraph problems to avoid:

1. *Paragraphs that are too long* It is true that the more formal writing becomes, the longer paragraphs become. But you must not allow yourself to ramble on and on. Paragraphs a page long are rare in college writing (though not unheard of). If some of your paragraphs are over half a typewritten page long, you should read them critically to be sure you haven't skipped a necessary indentation.

Revise for length

The following passage comes from a student's process paper. We have removed any paragraph indentations, producing a rather long paragraph. If you were revising the paper, where would you suggest paragraph breaks?

"What a pickle!" That was the motto which I remember so well from my pickle packing days. Working with pickles is a unique experience, and thus many times I have been asked, "How do you 'pack pickles'?" After spending one chaotic, depressing summer at Aunt Jane's Pickle factory, a division of Comstock Foods, Inc., I am proud to say I'm still alive to tell you about it. The first day I reported for work, I was handed a hair net, which had a "nursey"-looking crown on it, and a name tag. With these necessities, I was rushed off to the pickle-packing line. "You work here," the forewoman said with an authoritarian voice. There she left me standing at an empty steel table next to a row of jars that were noisily riding on a conveyor belt. The jars had garlic in the bottom of them, which contributed to the intolerable smell of the factory. As I stood in my assigned place waiting for someone to show me what to do, I recalled the awful comments my friends had made about working at Aunt Jane's and wondered if I would feel the same way.

RENAYE GEIGER, "How to Pack Pickles Aunt Jane's Way"

2. *Paragraphs that are too short* If you read a newspaper you will discover that nearly every sentence is indented. While this choppy paragraph style meets the needs of newspaper writing, it is not standard in more formal writing situations. A short paragraph now and then is acceptable; sometimes a short one makes a good change of emphasis from longer paragraphs. That is, sometimes you can emphasize a point by writing a short paragraph after a long one. Professional writers do use short paragraphs, but sparingly. In college, short paragraphs usually should be combined, more fully developed, or removed.

As reader-editor of your own paragraphs, you must ask yourself why your paragraphs are short. In rough-draft paragraphs, shortness often means you have not fully thought out your subject.

Sometimes short paragraphs are the result of rushing, not taking time to develop ideas fully. You must prewrite until you have enough material.

Revise for shortness

Assume the following paragraph is a description of your room: add words, ideas, phrases, and whole sentences; change the paragraph in any way that will help to make it a more fully developed paragraph.

My room is where I have all my stuff. It has a bed in it. The walls are painted. It looks good to me.

The long, rambling paragraph causes the reader to lose the thread of your ideas; short, choppy ones quickly become distracting to educated readers.

GUIDELINES FOR PARAGRAPHS

Nonfiction writing comes in many forms; there is almost as much variety in writing techniques as there are different writers. For that reason it is not possible to say that a paragraph must absolutely look this way or that. However, there are some guidelines and general principles for paragraph writing.

Paragraphs are not written by formula. If you are writing a composition of several paragraphs, the overall purpose of your composition will suggest how you should write your paragraphs. If you are writing a one-paragraph composition, you must prewrite, just as you would for a longer paper (See Ch. 1). Who is your audience? What is your purpose? What voice will you use? What will you write about? What kind of language will you use?

Coherence

The most important quality of a paragraph is *coherence*. Beginning writers sometimes produce incoherent paragraphs because they forget that the audience doesn't share the writer's own thorough grasp of the subject. You yourself may have a clear sense of the relationships among the details in your paragraph: "It's perfectly clear to me," you may think. The question is, of course, is it perfectly clear to the *reader*? The writer is responsible for making clear to the reader the relationships between and among sentences in a paragraph. The reader needs clues in order to follow what the writer has to say.

The word *coherence* literally means "sticking together," and your paragraphs should "stick together" too. That is, the reader must be able to follow along from sentence to sentence within the paragraph—and from paragraph to paragraph within the whole composition. Within the paragraph, all the sentences must develop your purpose. The reader must see how each sentence logically follows the other; if the reader becomes lost or confused, the paragraph is incoherent.

Coherence Through Unity One way to create a coherent paragraph is to make sure your paragraph is unified; a paragraph is unified if it develops only one idea. In your rought draft, paragraphs may contain irrelevant sentences or words and phrases not clearly related to the central idea. Your central idea itself may not be clear, so that the whole paragraph seems like a loose collection of ideas not clearly related to each other. Revise such paragraphs by removing unrelated ideas and clarifying the main point.

In the following paragraph by a professional writer, we have inserted an extra sentence that breaks the unity.

At dawn, after several hours of listening, Arkady walked outside the hotel to revive himself. Around the empty taxi stand, hedges crackled in the wind. Taxis were too expensive in Moscow. As he gulped air he heard another sound, a rhythmic thud from overhead. Workmen were tapping the parapets of the Ukraina's roof for the false notes of bricks loosened by the winter.
MARTIN CRUZ SMITH, *Gorky Park*

This paragraph is about sounds, about things that Arkady heard. Each sentence contains some reference to this fact except the sentence about the cost of taxis in Moscow (which we inserted). Although this sentence seems at first to add an interesting note about the taxis, closer analysis will reveal that the taxis are not present at all—it is the empty taxi stand that is mentioned, because of the sound of the hedges near the stand. Thus the cost of taxis does not belong here and should be edited out.

Question for Coherence You could say that each paragraph is the answer to a question. When you brainstorm anything—the full composition, any paragraph in a composition, even individual sentences and words—you must ask yourself, "What am I trying to say? What do I want the reader to hear?" Obviously, the clearer the question is to you, the clearer you can make it for the reader. Finding the right question to ask, then, is an important step in writing coherent paragraphs.

Revise for coherence

The following paragraph is a rough draft of a one paragraph composition in which a student writes about her high school teacher. Read the paragraph to see if you can understand why each sentence is in the paragraph: how does each one contribute to the overall development of the paragraph?

Miss Andrews was one of the best teachers I ever had. She was very pretty and very young for a teacher. Most of the boys were in love with her. She was very businesslike in class, always well prepared. And each day's lesson was related to the previous day's, so you always felt like the class was well organized. But she was not stiff or formal; she was very friendly and pleasant in class and seemed to be interested in each student. She was one of the few teachers who cared whether anyone really learned anything. She got married after her first year and left teaching.

Clarifying the Question For a rough draft, the paragraph above is not bad, but it could be better. It is all pretty general: there are no examples or concrete details that would help the reader see Miss Andrews. Still, as a one-paragraph composition it has promise. If you ask, "What question does this paragraph answer?" you might say it answers the question "What was Miss Andrews like?" However, this is a rather broad and general question for a paragraph; it sounds like the kind of question that might take several paragraphs to answer. Perhaps this is why the paragraph ended up sounding so general. A paragraph is not a good form for big, general questions. You need to prewrite until you can find a specific, limited question for your paragraph. Perhaps the paragraph is not ready because the writer is not ready—the writer hasn't found what he or she wants to say about Miss Andrews. The writer's purpose is not clear.

On the other hand, perhaps the first sentence implies the question the writer really meant to answer: "Why was Miss Andrews one of the best teachers I ever had?" This is a much more specific, limited question—one that might conceivably be answered in a paragraph. As the editor of your own paragraphs, you will have to decide whether what you need is more prewriting to find out what you are trying to say or revision to make your paragraphs say what you intend.

Testing for Coherence If you assume that the student wanted to write about things that made Miss Andrews the "best" teacher, you can see that some of the sentences are clearly not about teaching. The second and third sentences and the last one seem to be about

Miss Andrews personally; it is not clear how they relate to the specific question of her teaching. The writer might know how these sentences relate, and you as reader-editor might guess how they relate, but that is not the point. There is a simple test for coherence: change the paragraph question into a proposition and see if the suspect sentences can logically support the proposition. For example: Miss Andrews was one of the best teachers because she was very young and pretty(?) Miss Andrews was one of the best teachers because most of the boys were in love with her(?) Miss Andrews was one of the best teachers because she got married and left teaching(?)

Clarifying Relationships   Perhaps there is a relationship that the writer has not clearly expressed. For example, perhaps, the idea in the second and third sentences could be expressed differently:

Because she was very pretty and young, she did not look like she had the authority or the experience to run a classroom. However, despite her appearance, which caused most of the boys to fall in love with her, she was very businesslike in class.

With this revision, it can be seen that the two ideas are meant to contrast Miss Andrews' appearance with her behavior. And with these changes the paragraph becomes more coherent—it is easier for the reader to see how the ideas are related.

Deleting Unrelated Ideas   However, the last sentence in the paragraph is harder to understand. If this paragraph is about why Miss Andrews was a good teacher, it is not clear how her getting married and leaving teaching are related to the topic. If the writer keeps this sentence, it will seem *ironic* (a sudden reversal). If that really is the point, it might be better to revise the whole paragraph with this idea in mind instead of tacking it on at the end. Ultimately, of course, only the writer can decide what point the paragraph is supposed to make.

Revise for coherence

Explain orally or in writing what is wrong with the coherence of the following paragraph: has the student found the question he or she wants to answer? Is it a suitable question for a paragraph? If some of the sentences seem not clearly related, would it be better to remove them or to try to revise them? Revise the paragraph for coherence.

College is a lot of fun, but the professors are too demanding. For one thing, they assign too much to read. I read a lot in high school. Furthermore, they assign too many papers to write. Writers make very little money. Professors also give too many quizzes and tests. You don't take quizzes in real life. And on top of it all, the professors seem to think that all this is only a minimal amount of work.

Coherence Through Common Transitional Signals   Part of a paragraph's coherence derives from the overall strategy: if you are telling a story, the reader anticipates the chronological order of a story. In addition, writers sometimes use transitional signals to tell the reader how one sentence relates to another.

FOR ADDITION

again, also, and, and then, besides, finally, first, further, furthermore, in addition, lastly, moreover, next, second, secondly, too

FOR COMPARISON

also, as, by the same token, in comparison, likewise, similarly, then too

FOR CONCESSION

after all, although it is true, at the same time, granted, I admit, I concede, naturally, of course, while it is true

FOR CONTRAST

after all, although, and yet, but, by contrast, however, nevertheless, on the contrary, on the other hand, otherwise, still, whereas, yet

FOR EXAMPLES AND ILLUSTRATIONS

by way of illustration, for example, for instance, incidentally, indeed, in fact, in other words, in particular, specifically, that is

FOR RESULT

accordingly, as a result, consequently, hence, in short, then, thereafter, therefore, thus, truly

FOR SUMMARY

as I have said, in brief, in conclusion, in other words, in short, on the whole, to conclude, to summarize, to sum up

FOR TIME

afterwards, at last, at length, hence, immediately, in the meantime, lately, meanwhile, of late, presently, shortly, since, soon, temporarily, thereafter, thereupon, while

Coherence Through Association Chains   In addition to these transitional signals, skilled writers make use of association chains—repetitions of key words and concepts and synonyms or pronouns that substitute for these key terms. Note the several techniques used in the following paragraph.

Two rangy shepherd dogs trotted up pleasantly, **until** they caught the scent of strangers, **and then** they backed cautiously away, watchful, their tails moving slowly and tentatively in the air, but their eyes and noses quick for animosity or danger. *One of them*, scratching his neck, edged forward, ready to run, and little by little he approached Tom's legs and sniffed loudly at them. **Then** he backed away and watched Pa for some kind of signal. *The other pup* was not so brave. He looked about for something that could honorably divert his attention, saw a red chicken go mincing by, and ran at it. There was the squawk of an outraged hen, a burst of red feathers, and the hen ran off, flapping stubby wings for speed. *The pup* looked proudly back at the men, **and then** flopped down in the dust and beat its tail contentedly on the ground.

JOHN STEINBECK, *The Grapes of Wrath*

The italicized words indicate the subjects of the paragraph, the dogs; the black words show specific transitional devices signaling chronological sequence; and the chain of pronouns referring to the dogs is marked in light print.

Analyze for coherence

Discuss orally or write out your analysis of the coherence techniques of the following paragraph. How has this author achieved coherence?

Several days later, Father Cieslik started hunting for the children's family. First, he learned through the police that an uncle had been to the authorities in Kure, a city not far away, to inquire for the children. After that, he heard that an older brother had been trying to trace them through the post office in Ujina, a suburb of Hiroshima. Still later, he heard that the mother was alive and was on Goto Island, off Nagasaki. And at last, by keeping a check on the Ujina post office, he got in touch with the brother and returned the children to their mother.

JOHN HERSEY, *Hiroshima*

Practice coherence

Write a paragraph of your own using as many different coherence techniques as you can. Write about a short incident, a visual memory such as the one in Steinbeck's paragraph above. Mark the coherence devices in your paragraph with underlining, parentheses, circles, and so on.

Coherence Through Topic Sentence   You have one simple option to help your reader understand what your paragraph is about: state its topic clearly in a topic sentence. The topic sentence is a good device to use anytime you think the reader may have difficulty following you. Some paragraphs may not need topic sentences, and some topic sentences may not come first in their paragraphs, but as a general rule, a topic sentence per paragraph helps to make your compositions coherent. The topic sentence states what the paragraph is about; it is the italicized sentence in the following example:

Civil War antiques are popular, and chances for appreciation are excellent. Tintype photos, for example, says Saddle River (N.J.) auctioneer Howard Wikoff, are in the $25-to-$600 range now and seem to be "heading way up." He notes that village scenes, showing generals of the war, are most coveted. "Guns and rifles that sold for $50 a short time ago are now going for $200," Wikoff adds.

"A Summer's Hunt for Country Antiques," *BusinessWeek*, 10 May 1982

Analyze for topic sentence

Where is the topic sentence in the following paragraph? How can you tell? Explain the relationship of the sentences in this paragraph.

The Argentine reaction to the *Belgrano*'s sinking was heated. At first, Buenos Aires said that Britain's announcement was "a lie" and part of a campaign of "psychological warfare." The next day, however, Argentina conceded the ship's loss and denounced the attack as a "treacherous act of armed aggression."

GEORGE RUSSELL, et al., "Two Hollow Victories at Sea," *Time*, 17 May 1982

Practice topic sentence

Starting it with a topic sentence, write a paragraph of your own about some subject you know well. Refer to the examples above for guides.

Plan of Development

The plan of development of your whole composition is likely to become the plan for your paragraphs too. If you are writing a story, you are likely to use chronological development (time order) throughout. But paragraphs shouldn't just "happen." Plan each paragraph as carefully as you plan an entire composition. The wandering, rambling, confused paragraph may appear in an early draft of your work, but the finished paragraph should be carefully shaped according to a logic the reader can see. For example:

Development by Time Order   In narrative paragraphs, begin at the beginning and continue to the end—from the past to the present to the future. Or you may begin at the present and "flash back" to the past, as long as you give the reader clear signals.

Development by Spatial Order   In descriptive paragraphs, begin where the observer (writer) is and move toward the horizon, or begin at a distant point and move toward the observer. Or select any point and move clockwise or vertically or in any other orderly fashion as long as the reader can follow the development.

Development by Order of Importance When presenting examples, explanations, arguments, begin with the least important and end with the most important. This plan fulfills your readers' expectations. Random order or diminishing order (ending with the weakest point) rarely works.

Development by Order of Specificity Many paragraphs present specific details leading up to some generalization about them (observations of specific college students, for example, may lead to some idea about college students in general). The most common plan presents the general idea first and then supplies specific examples or details to illustrate the generalization: for example, some generalization about novels is illustrated by citing several specific novels.

Development by Supportive Details Details are the heart of all good writing. A list of unsupported generalizations and unexplained abstractions soon becomes tedious to read. To develop an idea or explain a concept requires supportive details that expand and illustrate the idea. A paragraph must do more than make an interesting assertion—a paragraph must *show* as well as *tell*.

There are degrees of specificity, even among details, depending on your purpose. If you are trying to *explain* in a paper discussing heart attacks why your grandfather had a heart attack, a general description of what he was doing when he had the attack may be enough. But if you want the reader to *visualize,* to *participate* in the event, a much more detailed description is necessary. The general rule for college is the more details the better. Read the following general description and compare it with the fully detailed paragraph that follows. What does the writer achieve with the details?

A GENERAL DESCRIPTION

As I was walking along, suddenly I noticed that there were a lot of grasshoppers all over the place. There really were quite a lot of them, so many that I thought I was under attack. There were all different kinds, and they were all over everything.

Without details, and understanding only that there were many grasshoppers, the reader is inclined to ask "So what?" This very general paragraph leaves too much unstated. As a single-paragraph composition, it is unsatisfactory; it doesn't seem to say anything or mean anything. If there were many paragraphs like this, in a multi-paragraph composition, the reader would likely find the composition boring and tiresome.

A DETAILED DESCRIPTION

I had stepped into the meadow to feel the heat and catch a glimpse of the sky, but these grasshoppers demanded my attention, and became an event in themselves. Every step I took detonated the grass. A blast of bodies like shrapnel exploded around me; the air burst and whirred. There were grasshoppers of all sizes, grasshoppers yellow, green and black, short-horned, long-horned, slant-faced, band-winged, spur-throated, cone-headed, pygmy, spotted, striped and barred. They sprang in salvos, dropped in the air, and clung unevenly to stems and blades with their legs spread for balance, as redwings ride cattail reeds. They clattered around my ears; they richocheted off my calves with an instant clutch and release of tiny legs.

ANNIE DILLARD, *Pilgrim at Tinker Creek*

By contrast with the undeveloped paragraph, the highly detailed paragraph by Dillard makes a vivid experience for the reader. Participation in that experience becomes the point of the paragraph, and this paragraph might almost be a little composition—though it was taken from her book, *Pilgrim at Tinker Creek*.

Revise for Details

Suggest added details for the following paragraph. Type the paragraph and then mark it with a pen as if someone else were going to retype it for you. That is, don't just start over, writing your own paragraph about a "creepy place"—revise this one. Add extra words and sentences to help the reader feel and see and hear. Revise it so that the experience itself becomes the point of the paragraph. Then prepare a clean copy from your revised copy.

I'd been in creepy places before, but not like this. The old place was very dark, but there was a little light. It made things look strange—furniture and stuff. Some sort of weird noise was coming from upstairs. As I started up, something went past me. I was so scared I could hardly get out of there fast enough.

In addition to these organizational strategies, paragraphs may be developed by the traditional patterns for full compositions: *narration, description, illustration, comparison-contrast, classification, process, definition, analysis,* and so on.

Analyze for traditional pattern

Look back to page 249 for Spatial Order: describe the pattern of development in the following student's paragraph. Explain orally or in writing why this is an effective paragraph.

I spent the first summer of my life there, so I'm led to believe. It is a place that I have always enjoyed visiting. As one approaches this place, he sees a sturdy, snow-white, block-frame cottage. It may be close to 40 years old but it never seems to age. To the rear I can see two somewhat-faded silver rainbarrels connected to a rigid rain trough. Also in the back I see five giant cement slabs underneath an outdoor shower, where my uncle used to tease us by squirting us with water. Attached to the cottage, a flat porch made of gray baseboard rests on a rectangular concrete slab, where I can see how the sand has left its imprints over the years. If I follow a narrow cement sidewalk out toward the lake, I notice, jutting out from the rest of the building, six heavy wooden shutters about five feet by four feet in dimension, hanging at right angles and supported by six strong wooden planks. These always had to be put up and down with great effort before and after a storm. Surrounding all this is ivory-like sand as far as I can see, dotted with various rocks, shells, and weather-beaten driftwood.

MIKE SCHAIBERGER, "Yesterday"

Paragraph Structure

The structure of a paragraph is the relation of the sentences to each other. That is, one useful method for looking at a paragraph is to describe it as a sequence of structurally related sentences. Ordinarily, the topic of a paragraph is a *generalization*, and the development of a paragraph is usually made up of one or more *specific instances* of the generalization. In other words, a paragraph makes a general statement that is illustrated with more specific statements as the paragraph develops.

Topic plus Development   The *topic plus development* structure is generated by addition. Notice in the following example how many specifics (illustrations) have been added to the topic sentence:

TOPIC (GENERALIZATION)

Dr. Steele points to a number of characteristics most abusive parents have in common.

DEVELOPMENT (SPECIFIC INSTANCES)

They are immature.

They lack self-esteem; they feel incompetent.

They have trouble finding pleasure and satisfaction in the outside world.

They possess a strong fear of spoiling their children and hold an equally strong belief in the efficacy of corporal punishment.

Finally, they are markedly deficient in the ability to empathize with, and respond to, their children's needs.

MYRON BRENTON, "What Can Be Done about Child Abuse?" *Today's Education*, Sept./Oct. 1977

This paragraph illustrates the basic *topic plus development* structure of many paragraphs, in which the topic sentence expresses a generalization and the development is made up of specifics (illustrations) within the generalization. We have listed five sentences, but there are six illustrations (the second sentence contains two closely related illustrations punctuated with a semicolon).

The topic sentence and the developmental sentences have a general-to-specific relationship to each other. All the sentences in the Brenton paragraph may look like generalizations in the logical sense, but with reference to each other, the topic sentence is the generalization that contains all the others. It names a category (parental characteristics). The details in the developmental sentences are included in this category. They are in fact specific instances (immaturity, incompetence, dissatisfaction, and so on) or specific causes of child abuse.

The Brenton paragraph also illustrates a paragraph moving from generalization to specification, but the possibilities for movement within paragraphs can be complex. Another movement is from specific to general, in which the topic sentence comes last:

DEVELOPMENT (SPECIFIC INSTANCES)

We had old, temperamental amplifiers, with their dented and tarnished casings.

We had either used or home-made speaker boxes in various sizes and shapes and a small, hardly adequate P. A.

Dick's drums were the only matching equipment.

TOPIC (GENERALIZATION)

We were constantly improving, but we looked rather comical with all our misfit equipment.

CRAIG EYCHANER, "Gigs"

Coordinate Structure　In these examples, the developmental sentences have all been added to the topic sentence. Each developmental sentence looks like the one above it; that is, each merely gives another example. All the developmental sentences, therefore, have the same relationship to the topic sentence—removing any of the developmental sentences will not make the paragraph incoherent (though it might sound a little underdeveloped).

This kind of relationship is called *coordinate*. It means that all the developmental sentences have the same kind of relationship to the topic sentence. You can number the sentences to illustrate coordinate structure:

COORDINATE STRUCTURE

TOPIC (GENERALIZATION)

1 **You can buy practically anything in a supermarket today.**

DEVELOPMENT (SPECIFIC INSTANCES)

2 **Naturally there is food: meat, fruits and vegetables, dairy products and anything else you can think of to eat or drink.**

2 **But you can also buy pots and pans and mops and flyswatters, and other household goods.**

2 **You can also buy books and magazines and records.**

2 **And any large market will have a drug and medicine section where you can get your Dristan and nasal spray.**

2 **Some stores even have a clothing section, or at least a rack full of panty hose.**

IRENE SMALL, "This Little Piggy Went to Market"

Practice coordinate structure

Imagine writing a letter in which you describe a party, an athletic event, a musical performance, or some other group activity. Make the focus of your paragraph what two or three people—either performers or members of the audience—did that made the event enjoyable or pleasant for you. Write your paragraph so that it has a topic plus development structure, moving either from general to specific or specific to general. Label your paragraph like the one above.

Subordinate Structure   In the *subordinate structure* pattern, each developmental sentence adds only to the sentence immediately above it. If you remove any sentence but the last one in a subordinate pattern, the paragraph will immediately become incoherent. To show descending order of subordinate sentences, you can give each one a different number:

SUBORDINATE STRUCTURE

TOPIC (GENERALIZATION)

1 *The garlic bulb*, often rejected by picky eaters as bad smelling and common, is one of nature's greatest gifts.

DEVELOPMENT (SPECIFIC INSTANCES)

2 *The bulb* breaks into a dozen or more cloves, each shaped somewhat like a tear and covered with a paper shell.

3 *Each clove* releases a powerful *aroma and taste,* a warm, friendly
taste of home and familiar things.

4 This wonderful garlic *flavor* is used by most of the people of the
world to spice up the *taste* of bland food.

LOUISE GLEIMAN, "Garlic"

In the Gleiman paragraph, development sentence 2 comments on the topic sentence, providing a detail of the garlic bulb mentioned in the topic sentence. But sentence 3 adds to sentence 2, giving a detail about the garlic cloves mentioned in sentence 2; and sentence 4 adds a detail about the taste of garlic mentioned in sentence 3.

Analyze subordinate structure

Explain orally or in writing the subordinate structure of the following paragraph. How should its sentences be numbered? Why?

The common table lamp is composed of a shade and some kind of base. The shade diffuses the light; the base contains the electrical components. The electrical components are composed of a socket and a cord running through the lamp and ending in a plug. The socket has an opening for the bulb and a switch for opening and closing contacts with the cord.

LON GWAINER, "Repairing a Table Lamp"

Practice subordinate structure

Write a paragraph explaining some simple mechanism like a can opener, hair blower, pruning shears; or some simple activity such as filling a salt shaker, sharpening a pencil, changing a cartridge in a pen, and so on. Keep the subject simple, something you can deal with reasonably in one paragraph. Write your paragraph so that each sentence adds to the sentence immediately above it. Label your paragraph like the example above.

These examples represent two basic paragraph patterns: the sentences added directly to the topic sentence form a *coordinate* pattern; those added to each other from a *subordinate* pattern. The sentences in a coordinate pattern all have the same relationships to each other; they are all of the same order and bear the relationship of addition to the topic sentence. The sentences in a subordinate pattern are not parallel to each other, and each makes a comment on only the sentence immediately preceding it. Coordinate structure is good for *listing* examples, details, and so on. Subordinate structure is good for *analyzing* objects, events, and so on.

These examples illustrate what is meant by unity and coherence in a paragraph. Because the sentences are held together in one or the other pattern of relationship, the paragraph becomes a unit (or unified); because the sentences are related to each other, the reader is able to follow a coherent flow of information from one sentence to the next. Thus, any sentence that breaks the pattern or seems not to be clearly related to either a sentence above or the topic sentence breaks the unity of the paragraph and may cause the reader to lose the thread.

The most common type of paragraph mixes coordinate and subordinate patterns, as in the following example:

MIXED COORDINATE-SUBORDINATE STRUCTURE

TOPIC (GENERALIZATION)

1 Despite this need for public approval, football does not demand—or particularly welcome—a discriminating public.

DEVELOPMENT (SPECIFIC INSTANCES)

  2 The football fan, compared to the baseball fan or the tennis fan—is an absolute oaf.

  3 The baseball fan, particularly, is a man of high perceptivity and learning.

    4 He can recognize each player; he knows what each batted last year, when and where each broke which clavicle and why, and how good the prospects are for each rookie who comes along.

  2 The football fan knows nothing.

    3 He can't recognize one player from another, except by the number on the uniform.

    3 He can't tell a right guard from a left kidney.

    3 It is all he can do to follow the ball, and often he can't even do that.

WADE THOMPSON, "My Crusade Against Football," *The Nation*, April 1959

This paragraph by Wade Thompson has several levels of generalization and several descending degrees of specification. (There is no specific limit to the number or complexity of the levels possible in a subordinate structure or mixed coordinate-subordinate structure paragraph.) All the development sentences illustrate the topic sentence, supporting the statement that the game of football does not demand a discriminating public. But as you can see from the numbering system, there are several coordinate-pattern sentences, sentences that are at the same level of specification (for example, those listing the the limitations of the football fan); and the whole paragraph is built on a pattern of subordination.

Thus we have the basic paragraph patterns: *coordinate, subordinate*, and *mixed*. You can see that by relating your sentences to each other in these ways, you can generate very complex paragraphs.

Describe the pattern of development in each of the following paragraphs. How are the sentences related to each other? It may be helpful to write out the paragraphs, showing the coordinate or subordinate relationships and numbering the levels of generality.

1 In general, armadillos are pretty well liked. They amuse people. Homely, ungainly, and not too bright, they epitomize the underdog and elicit our sympathy. Armadillo festivals, races, comic books, T-shirts, and posters have swept the South during the past decade. Texas jewelers have recently advertised gold armadillo rings, pendants, and pins.

ELEANOR E. STORRS, "The Astonishing Armadillo," *National Geographic*, June, 1982

2 A woman teacher ate the flesh of her own dead beloved sister. For this she was taken by the Khmer Rouge guards and beaten in front of the entire village. They beat her without mercy from the morning until the evening, when, thank God, she died. And all this time her own child sat weeping, helpless and baffled, beside her.

PIN YATHAY, "Escape from Cambodia," *National Review*, 22 Dec. 1978

3 Giraffes are well adapted for reaching up, awkwardly built for reaching down. To feed on a bush, drink from a pool, or lick the salt in the dirt, they have to spread their front legs wide apart. Water holes are notorious hideouts for predators, and in their spraddled drinking position, giraffes are vulnerable. When a three-hundred-pound lion affixes itself to the end of a giraffe's six-foot neck, the victim is more than likely doomed to die by strangulation.

BRISTOL FOSTER, "Africa's Gentle Giants," *National Geographic*, Sept. 1977

4 No country can touch us when it comes to heartburn and upset stomachs. This nation under God, with liberty and justice for all, neutralizes more stomach acid in one day than the Soviet Union does in a year. We give more relief from discomfort of the intestinal tract than China and Japan combined.

ART BUCHWALD, "Acid Indigestion," *Esquire*, Dec. 1975

5 On this circle the old man could see the fish's eye and the two gray sucking fish that swam around him. Sometimes they attached themselves to him. Sometimes they darted off. Sometimes they would swim easily in his shadow. They were over three feet long and when they swam fast they lashed their whole bodies like eels.

ERNEST HEMINGWAY, *The Old Man and the Sea*

6 Automobile aerodynamics is the science of managing the flow of air over, around, and through vehicles in order to reduce the drag exerted by air. The amount of air drag is expressed in a mathematical shorthand called the CD—coefficient of drag. The lower the coefficient, the lower the drag.

MOTOR VEHICLE MANUFACTURERS ASSOCIATION, AD, "Autorama USA," in *Time*, 10 May 1982

7 Yale psychologist Phoebe Ellsworth conducted a telephone survey of 120 adults in the New Haven area. She began by asking the people if they were generally in favor of capital punishment. Fifty-five percent said yes, feeling it deterred potential criminals. She then proceeded to read the adults in her test group the facts of a crime committed by a real-life murderer. She described cases involving killing a policeman, beating a woman to death, and shooting a friend who had stolen money. Only 15 percent said they would consider the death penalty for these cases.

RANDY DYKSTRA, "Capital Punishment"

8 Once upon a time, most families earning more than $25,000 could not get a government-subsidized student loan. A kindly congress quashed that rule in 1978, and we've been paying for it ever since. Loan volume quintupled as well-to-do parents invested their own money and borrowed the government's cheap money instead.

JANE BRYANT QUINN, "The Student-Loan Scare," *Newsweek*, 24 May 1982

9 Inside the store the year seems temporarily lost. The worn wooden floor fits like a comfortable old pair of jeans, and the calendars on the walls show faded pictures of painted young women wearing dresses from the twenties. A big blue box on the shelf brags of "Zud Suds: the newest type of soap for modern wringing washers." In front of the old post office boxes stand an iron, woodburning stove and a big, square, marble-topped table to sit around and pass the time of day.

JOANNE GIBBONI, "A Village by the River," *Penn Statements*, Winter 1979

10 All extraterrestrial beings are "bug-eyed monsters," or BEMs to science-fiction buffs. And, sure enough, the eyes of the alien creature in Steven Spielberg's *E.T.* are very large and prominent. At first startled glance—and he takes some getting used to—you could call him a BEM.

"Creating a Creature," *Time*, 31 May 1982

Practice coordinate-subordinate paragraphs

Practice writing coordinate and subordinate sequences. Write paragraphs of your own in which the subsequent sentences are specific instances of the topic sentence; and paragraphs in which each sentence comments on the one above it.

VARIATIONS ON PARAGRAPH BEGINNINGS

We have been using the term *topic sentence* to mean the sentence that states what the paragraph is about and also to mean the sentence in the paragraph to which the others are related. But we said earlier that some paragraphs don't have topic sentences. In fact, there are three variations on the way paragraphs begin.

The Transitional Sentence

Experienced writers sometimes start a paragraph with a sentence that relates back to the preceding paragraph. The transitional sentence does for the paragraph what the transitional signal does for the sentence: it establishes coherence. Note the following example:

TRANSITIONAL SENTENCE

(TR) At Moreton Drive peace was pouring in a bland golden flood out of the park opposite.

TOPIC SENTENCE

1 There were birds in mother's garden.

DEVELOPMENT SENTENCES

  2 Somebody had put out seed for them, in a little terra cotta dish suspended from the branch of a tree.

    3 Sparrows and finches were fluttering, flirting; a rain of seed scattered from the swaying dish.

    3 From the lawn at the foot of the tree, a flight of blue pigeons took off clattering, and away.

PATRICK WHITE, *The Eye of the Storm*

In this paragraph by Patrick White, the first sentence is not the topic of the paragraph. It is a transitional sentence relating this paragraph to the preceding one. The topic sentence is the one numbered 1. Notice that if you remove this sentence, the rest of the sentences have nothing to attach to.

Topic plus Restriction

Sometimes the topic of a paragraph is first stated in a general way and then restricted immediately by a more specific sentence. Often the decision to write a topic-plus-restriction beginning is simply a decision in favor of readability—the topic may be easier to read if written as two or more sentences instead of one long one.

TOPIC SENTENCE

1 The LSD state varies greatly according to the dosage, the personality of the user and the condition under which the drug is taken.

TOPIC RESTRICTION SENTENCE

1R Basically, it causes changes in sensation.

DEVELOPMENT SENTENCES

  2 Vision is markedly altered.

    3 Changes in depth perception and the meaning of the perceived object are most frequently described.

    3 Illusions and hallucinations can occur.

2 Thinking may become pictorial and reverie states are common.

    3 Delusions are expressed.

3 The sense of time and of self are strangely altered.

2 Strong emotions may range from bliss to horror, sometimes within a single experience.

2 Sensations may "cross over," that is, music may be seen or color heard.

2 The individual is suggestible and, especially under high doses, loses his ability to discriminate and evaluate his experience.

National Clearing House for Drug Abuse Information, A Federal Source Book: Answers to the Most Frequently Asked Questions about Drug Abuse

The topic sentence, number 1, identifies the subject of the paragraph, the LSD state, which differs from person to person. The next sentence, number 1R, restricts the topic of the paragraph to the basic changes in sensation caused by LSD. All the level 2 sentences, then, refer to the topic and restriction in 1 and 1R.

Implied Topic Sentence

Although some paragraphs have no topic sentence, they must have a topic idea that is clearly implied.

2 The amounts and concentrations of fertilizer to be applied to your lawn depend on your lawn area.

2 The same is true for the herbicides, fungicides, and insecticides; your bill is calculated on the basis of lawn area.

2 If you should die suddenly, the executor of your estate may want to know your lawn area.

TIMOTHY F. BANNON, "Lawn Order," *Harper's*, June 1982

We have labeled these sentences 2 because they are all second-level examples of an implied topic sentence (lawn area is important). Since the examples themselves clearly make the point, there is no need for a topic sentence here.

Practice revision

Revise the following excerpt from a student's paper. As a reader-editor, help the writer express what he or she wants to say. You may delete words, add words, change words, move words around, add or delete sentences, add paragraph indentations. But do not change the intention of the original. Copy the excerpt as it is and then mark it carefully to show how you are changing it—assume a typist will follow your marks to type a clean copy. Try to reduce it to approximately 100 words or less of effective writing. Then write out the revised version.

There is this high school by the name of Horace Greeley High School which is located in New York in the city called Chappaqua. This is a school for secondary education. But at this school they had a serious kind of problem, namely it was concerned with drinking by the students. This is a serious problem. The problem was attempted to be fought by the school two years ago when the problem was serious in the students' drinking. And now the control of the situation is being brought in. How bad this problem was can be seen by the name of the school which was a nickname that said "Hangover High." The reason why it was named this was because of its reputation that was bad. Students shouldn't drink so much. The principal of the school was Edward J. Hart. The principal is the one who is head of the school. He was very much concerned about what he was hearing. He heard many reports of students. They had hangovers. They were being drunk at dances. His concern was great. When people have worries like this so much it is called that they have great concern. Mr. Hart decided things had went too far. Because of the empty bottles and beer cans. These were found numerously on the school ground when there had been dances at the school. So the principal met with those who were the leaders of the school. He said to them a declaration. There couldn't be any events of socializing again at the school place because of this problem unless it went away, meaning the students wouldn't do it or they could drink with control. So then he told them that.

INTRODUCTORY PARAGRAPHS

The first paragraph is often the most important. You may win or lose your reader right at the beginning of your composition; therefore, the extra time it takes to write an effective beginning is well spent. The beginning is usually the hardest part in writing, so we recommend that you postpone serious work on the introductory paragraph until you have completed a rough draft of the entire paper. With a clear sense of the overall scope of your paper—its details, its methods of development, its conclusion—you will be in a better position to shape an effective introduction.

Your introduction should convince the reader that you offer an original approach to an interesting topic in a lively style. A well-crafted introduction must be accurate; the reader becomes confused when the subject of a composition is not what you promised in the introduction. Finally, your introduction should lead the reader smoothly into the body of the paper.

Problems to Avoid

The One-sentence Introduction   Formal writing seldom uses the one-sentence introduction. Usually, these one-sentence paragraphs ("Fishing is a very interesting sport") are empty statements, and they must be edited out. The true introduction is likely to be found in your next paragraph. Either remove these one-liners entirely, connect them to the next paragraph, or build them into more substantive introductions.

The Empty Introduction　　Papers sometimes begin with several sentences that wander around without really saying anything. Often these sentences are simply variations on the title of the paper: "Fishing can be a very interesting sport. There are many people who take it up as a hobby. The rewards of fishing are great. There is no doubt that fishing can be a fulfilling and meaningful experience for all concerned." In this introduction, the writer is displaying little concern for the reader; instead, the writer is wandering around trying to find a subject. Most readers, anticipating that the body of the paper is likely to be as empty as the introduction, will simply stop reading.

The Assumption-of-Knowledge Introduction　　The writer assumes the reader knows the subject and, as a consequence, the writer fails to include important information. Your introduction must stand on its own, informing, as well as interesting and leading the reader. Avoid references to the assignment: "*This* is a very difficult *subject.*" "I am not really an expert on *this topic.*" Avoid starting off with pronouns whose antecedents are assumed: "*It* is a very sad play" (reference to *Hamlet*). Avoid references to the title of your paper: "Yes, *he* certainly was!" (title: Was Hamlet Crazy?). Though every paper should have a title, the title is not part of the introduction.

Examples of Introductory Paragraphs

The following introductory paragraphs come from fiction and nonfiction works of writers with widely different styles. As you read them, decide what is effective about these introductions, using the following criteria:

1 Who is the likely audience? The general reader? Young people? Sports enthusiasts? The academic community? Do you think the introduction will appeal to its audience?
2 What personality does the writer project? Does the author sound intelligent, bland, humorous, superior, knowledgeable, sarcastic? Is the author's tone suitable for subject and audience?
3 Is the introduction interesting? Informative? Does it lead smoothly into the paper?

START WITH A DRAMATIC INCIDENT

It looked as ridiculous as a dead shark on horseback—a snub-nosed, thick-bodied, powerless rocket ship called *Enterprise* perched on three struts atop a Boeing 747, five miles up in the bright California sky. Suddenly the 747 dipped and gunned its engines. Inside the *Enterprise*, Cmdr. Fred Haise punched the disconnect button, and the stocky craft popped free of its ferry. "She's flying good," Haise yelled jubilantly. He pushed the ship through two ninety-degree turns, then pointed its nose downward toward the salt-and-clay flatbed of Edwards Air Force Base, where he glided into a landing five minutes later.

RICHARD BOOTH, "Free Enterprise," *Newsweek,* 22 Aug. 1977

START WITH A CONTRAST

Some people inherit beauty and grace, others have the intelligence of their learned ancestors, still others are born into a family of famous athletes. I, on the other hand, have inherited absent-mindedness and a flair for the ridiculous. I stumble in the footsteps of my father, laughing all the way.

EILEEN COUGHLIN, ". . . And for Some People They Sing"

START BY TELLING A STORY

I have seldom had the chance to meet the scientists who work a few buildings away from my own or live just doors away in this small college town, but I remember a neighbor physicist who came to the door once and asked if I would look at his refrigerator, which had gone off while his wife was making toast. While I was still making uncomfortable apologies for my ignorance when snapping his circuit breaker off and on, I heard the refrigerator begin to purr.

STERLING EISEMINGER, "On Parblind Scholars," *Phi Kappa Phi Journal,* 1977

START BY SETTING THE SCENE

The dawn over the South Atlantic was gray with drizzle. Before sunup on Saturday morning, a Vulcan bomber roared down on the Falklands. While Argentine troops scrambled for their anti-aircraft batteries, the British avenger dropped 1,000 pound bombs on the asphalt airstrip outside Stanley. Before the defenders could fully assess the damage, Sea Harrier jump jets delivered a new barrage on the makeshift runway near the little settlement of Goose Green and hit Stanley again. The skies clouded up; the hours wore on. As dark drew near, British ships steamed toward the jagged coast. Their guns suddenly flashed, pounding targets near Stanley while Sea King helicopters rained rockets and missiles on Port Darwin. The besieged Argentines were left to sweat through night fears that British marines might soon hit the shore.

STEVEN STRASSER ET AL., "The War Is On," *Newsweek,* 10 May 1982

START WITH A QUESTION OR PROBLEM

What is it like to die? That is a question which humanity has been asking itself ever since there have been humans. I have had the opportunity to raise this question before a sizable number of audiences. These groups have ranged from classes in psychology, philosophy and sociology through church organizations, television audiences and civic clubs to professional societies of medicine. On the basis of this exposure, I can safely say that this topic excites the most powerful of feelings.

RAYMOND A. MOODY, "Is There Life after Death?" *Saturday Evening Post*, May/June 1977

START WITH A DESCRIPTION

Mr. Frost came into the front room of his house in Cambridge, Massachusetts, casually dressed, wearing plaid slippers, offering greetings with a quiet, even diffident friendliness. But there was no mistaking the evidence of the enormous power of his personality. It makes you at once aware of the thick, compacted strength of his body, even now at eighty-six; it is apparent in his face, actually too alive and spontaneously expressive to be as ruggedly heroic as in his photographs.

"ROBERT FROST," *Writers at Work*, George Plimpton, ed.

START BY EXPLAINING THE THESIS

Critics of the Equal Rights Amendment contend that ratification of the ERA will result in women being subject to the military draft and having to fight in the front lines in any future war. With or without ERA, it is very difficult to postulate in this era that women should not be drafted into a peacetime Army.

YVONNE BRAITHEWAITE, "Let's Play Taps for an All Male Army!" *Saturday Evening Post*, Oct., 1977

START WITH A BRIEF HISTORICAL BACKGROUND

The Constitution of the United States of America was drafted between May 14 and September 17, 1787, by fifty-five men in the city of Philadelphia. It was made effective on June 21, 1788, by the vote of nine state ratifying conventions. Under the governmental system set up by this document, a group of thirteen sparsely populated states strung out along the Atlantic Ocean from Massachusetts to Georgia has developed into one of the greatest powers of world history. Appropriately, the parchment sheets on which the Constitution was written are preserved as a national shrine in the National Archives at Washington, and the document has come to be regarded with the awe and reverence reserved for religious objects.

C. HERMAN PRITCHETT, "The American Constitution," *The American Constitutional System*

START WITH UNUSUAL FACTS AND FIGURES

Steve Brinkley is a sandy-haired lawyer with the amiably innocent look of a Teddy bear; his wife Jane is a teacher's aide at a nearby school. Together they earn $40,000 a year. They live with their eight-year-old son Peter in a handsomely renovated Victorian house in a wealthy suburb of Chicago. They have a new car and a new kitchen, and their lawn has no crab grass. Peter has just learned to do handstands. They look like the All-American Family living the All-American Dream. They are also broke. They are not only broke, but $18,000 in debt. "The question is," says Jane, a pug-nosed brunette in preppy red wrap-around skirt, "shall we eat this week or shall we pay the electric bill?"

OTTO FRIDRICH, "The American Way of Debt," *Time*, 31 May 1982

START WITH A QUOTATION

"The world isn't used to your open diplomacy. It stiffens the back of Israel and raises the expectations of the Arabs, which, once frustrated, will retard rather than bring peace." During a week of buffeting over US-Soviet relations, Jimmy Carter needed that sober assessment of his Middle East Policy. But it came last Wednesday from Rabbi Alexander Schindler, one of the 53 Jewish leaders invited to a dialogue with the President at the White House.

"Jimmy Woos the Jewish Leaders," *Time*, July 1977

START WITH A DEFINITION

First of all for the sake of clarity, I must say that the term "oriental medicine" is in fact too broad to be strictly meaningful, but I use it in a special—and today generally accepted—sense to mean medicine that originated in China and travelled to Japan by way of Korea. Chinese medicine—or Kampo—may be divided into two major streams of development. Therapeutical systems arising in the area of the Yellow River include acupuncture, mox, and amma massage, all of which are widely practiced in Japan.

KATSUSKE SERIZAWA, "The Philosophy of Chinese Medicine," *Massage: The Oriental Method*

START WITH AN IDEA TO BE REFUTED

"One of the most common errors of modern folklore is that because of our advanced technology, people in America today have more leisure time than anybody anywhere before," said Struever. "That's baloney. The hardest workers the world has ever seen could be today's Americans. People think primitive peoples like those at Koster struggled from dawn to dusk simply to survive. Not true. How hard a man works depends a lot on what he considers necessary goals in life, and at that time there was no environmental imperative in the valley requiring man to work hard. The large valleys of the Midwest probably had the heaviest plant and animal population in North America, and therefore could support large human populations, and did. In 4200 B.C. man lived in a land of milk and honey, with tremendous food resources all around him in this valley, and the taking was easy."

FELICIA HOLTON, "Seven Thousand Years of Prehistoric Man in Illinois," *Vista*, Spring 1975

CONCLUDING PARAGRAPHS

It is important to keep in mind that the function of the conclusion is to bring the paper to an end. Papers should not arbitrarily and abruptly stop. Especially in nonfiction, the reader expects the writer to round off, to give a clear signal that the final point has been made.

A summary is the most common, but not always the most effective, technique beginning writers use to conclude their essays. Everything depends on your purpose. In a simple report ("Russia's Economic Problems," for example), the summary may be a good ending. In other writing situations, the summary ending may insult your readers' intelligence, thus alienating them at a crucial stage in the writer-reader transaction. Since the conclusion is the last thing your readers encounter, it tends to have a disproportionate impact on them. A weak conclusion can too often spoil an otherwise competent paper.

The conclusion is your last chance to establish the significance of what you have to say; therefore, it should be one of the high points of your essay. End on a strong note, leaving the reader something to remember, satisfied that you have delivered what you promised in the introduction.

Problems to Avoid

The One-Sentence Ending   "I never dreamed Look-out Point could be so breathtaking on a moonlit night in October." Like the one-sentence introduction, this kind of ending is weak. It suggests that you couldn't think of a good conclusion. Sometimes these one-liners can be edited out; sometimes you have to spend more time rethinking your ending.

The Tacked-on Moral or Lesson   Especially in personal-experience stories, readers should know what the moral is from what has been said. An ending like "I'll never again take Dead Man's Curve at ninety miles an hour in my father's station wagon" can ruin the impact of a strongly written paper. Trust your readers to get the point of your paper for themselves.

Contrived or "Hokey" Endings   "I woke suddenly; it had all been a dream!" The inexperienced writer may have been impressed with "surprise" endings from reading O. Henry stories. Then too, sometimes the writer cannot think of a strong ending and therefore resorts to inventing a fictitious one. In nonfiction, such artificial endings are rarely appropriate or effective.

Trite Concluding Phrases   "In conclusion," "To sum up," and so on. Much depends on your reader; it is better to be trite than misunderstood. But trite, obvious concluding phrases can seem condescending or boring.

Self-Conscious Endings   Drawing attention to yourself is usually not a good idea, even in personal-experience writing. It is one thing to write about an event that happened to you some time ago, even if you write it in the present tense. It is another thing entirely to draw attention to yourself as a writer at work on your composition. Phrases like these call the reader's attention away from what you are saying and toward yourself as the writer: "I will now conclude by . . . ," "Now that I have come to the end of this paper . . . ," "I think it is time to end this . . . ," and so on.

Introducing New Problems or Subjects   "Yes, there are many joys to fishing, but our fishing areas are in danger!" The conclusion is meant to end the subject, not to introduce new ones. If you suddenly discover in the last paragraph that what you really want to write about is the "dangers to our fishing areas" instead of "the joys of fishing," you should start over and write about the new subject you found in your conclusion.

The Weak Ending   Don't use up all your material in the body of the paper; save something interesting for the conclusion: a final example, a relevant quotation, a well-worded analysis of the point of the paper. The conclusion must have some substance; it cannot be a mere ornament. In most papers the conclusion is not just the end of the composition: it is the *point* of the composition.

Examples of Concluding Paragraphs

The following passages are concluding paragraphs from articles, essays, books, and chapters in books, written by a variety of authors. First, note the specific techniques used to develop each paragraph; then decide what is effective about each paragraph.

END WITH A CALL FOR ACTION

So call us soon. Metropolitan representatives understand the problems of being a single parent. We'll make sure that an insecure future won't be one of them.

Metropolitan Life Insurance advertisement, *Time*, 21 June 1982

END WITH A PREDICTION

But I do not think the young themselves will fall asleep. They have been through remarkable experiences and have found one another. There is the potentiality of a kind of youth international. Most important, the present power-systems of the world are indeed unfit for modern conditions, and this will become increasingly apparent. If the young continue to be in conflict, to try out innovations, and to study professionally what ought to be done with our technology and ecology, mores and authority-structure, and the fact of one world, they will gradually shape for themselves a good inheritance to come into. Considering the tremendous power and complexity of the systems they want to displace, twenty years is a short time to devise something better.

PAUL GOODMAN, *Like a Conquered Province*

END BY DRAWING A DEDUCTION FROM THE FACTS

The real lesson of the week of October 22, 1962, was that the cause of life on earth is too important to be left to the national aggregations. That lesson will make its mark only when a genuine world order comes into being that is able to resolve disputes on the basis of justice and codified law and that is responsible not just to national governments but to the society of humans on earth.

NORMAN COUSINS, "The Cuban Missile Crisis: An Anniversary," *Saturday Review*, 1 Oct. 1977

END WITH A QUESTION

In asking whether the equal protection clause really requires all this, I have found myself rereading two of the most famous of all judicial comments on the Constitution—what it is and what it permits. They both came from the pen of John Marshall in 1891.

> in considering this question, then, we must never forget, that it is a *constitution* we are expounding.

And later in the same opinion:

> Let the end be legitimate, let it be within the scope of the constitution, and all means which are appropriate, which are plainly adapted to that end, but consistent with the letter and the spirit of the constitution, are constitutional.

If the Constitution is read in this grand manner, can it truly be *unconstitutional* to make room for qualified members of racial minorities on the staircase to the professions?

McGEORGE BUNDY, "The Issue before the Court: Who Gets Ahead in America?" *Atlantic Monthly*, Nov. 1977

END WITH A QUOTATION THAT ESPECIALLY ILLUSTRATES YOUR POINT

Farber's dream will not be easy to realize. But it may not be impossible, either. *Fortune* magazine, in a recent article documenting the many problems in using solar energy, concluded that "if . . . costs could be brought down, the move to solar energy just might grow into the biggest economic development since the automobile revolution." Outright enthusiasts have no such reservations. "There are no ifs involved with solar energy anymore," says Professor Y. B. Sofdari, of Bradley University. "It's merely a question of when."

C. P. GILMORE, "Sunpower!" *Saturday Review*, 30 Oct. 1976

END ON A STRONG CONTRAST

The United States Supreme Court has always been a political institution. There is ample precedent and high-minded language to support both sides in this case. I am not overly sanguine about the outcome of the Bakke case. The public mood is against affirmative action, and the Burger Court has not always been sensitive to minority interests. Still, there is reason to hope that the court will have the foresight to understand that no one's interest will be served if we continue to exist as two nations divided by color and opportunity.

CHARLES LAWRENCE III, "The Bakke Case: Are Racial Quotas Defensible?" *Saturday Review*, 15 Oct. 1977

END BY DISMISSING AN OPPOSING IDEA

Cloning of animals, particularly livestock, may, on balance, be a worthwhile idea deserving thorough investigation. But for humans, cloning would be, on balance, unjustifiable. The hazards, the ethics, the meager chances for any significant gain for mankind, should impel us to reject it as anything but a challenging stunt.

VANCE PACKARD, *The People Shapers*

END WITH A FINAL ILLUSTRATION

But Lebanon's agony was far from over. The country was still a tinderbox. Syria has more than doubled the number of its troops in Lebanon since the fight began, and Sharon estimated that the Palestinians could still count on 15,000 to 20,000 combatants. The "peace in Galilee" that Prime Minister Begin had proclaimed as his goal when the shooting started was still far out of the Israelis' reach—and may have been moved even farther away by the assault.

ED MAGNUSON, et al., "Israel Strikes at the P.L.O.," *Time*, 21 June 1982

Writing Activities

Before starting the paragraph writing activities here, reread Chapter 1. The considerations that inform effective paragraph writing are the same as those that govern the whole composition: purpose, audience, experience, self, code.

1 Prepare a piece for the school newspaper about some aspect of college that annoys students: application and registration procedures, cafeteria food, parking fees, class hours, dorm regulations, and so on.

2 A television survey requests your view of television programs' and advertisements' insult to the viewer's intelligence. Write a paragraph illustrating the "insult" of just one program or ad.

3 Your political science exam asks for a summary of a current political event. Write a one-paragraph summary based on a newspaper or magazine article about some domestic or international happening.

4 Write a letter for a future generation, an unborn grandchild who will never know the energy-rich world of the twentieth century. Try to explain what ordinary life was like, when there was ample energy, to a child who must live without fossil fuel.

5 Write a paragraph to be put up on the public memo board, advertising a room for rent. Describe the room for prospective renters.

6 You have been asked to contribute a paragraph to your church newsletter. Select some passage of your religion's principal text (Bible, Torah, Koran, and so on) to explain or interpret.

7 An application form for a job asks you to describe either the one aspect of your previous work (including chores at home) you liked best or the one aspect you liked least. Illustrate in detail for an employer who wants to see how you handle the language.

8 The school yearbook invites you to compose a piece on "someplace special." Write a description of a place special to you.

9 You must return to your high school to deliver a short speech on the question, "Do Americans admire conformity and obedience more than individuality and creativity?" Illustrate one incident of conformity and/or obedience you have observed or experienced.

10 Your animal husbandry exam asks you to speculate about why Americans spend so much money on the care and feeding of their pets. Illustrate one aspect of the appeal pets have for people.

11 Write a paragraph to be added to your lawyer's directions, in case of accident or illness, concerning euthanasia for yourself. From a personal point of view, describe any situation in which you would or would not want the doctors to "pull the plug."

12 You are a caseworker for the Office of Student Affairs. You must write a paragraph for the files, reporting the facts in an incident in which a student was disorderly at a party you attended. Write a second paragraph describing the same incident to a friend back home.

13 You have failed your earth sciences final exam; write a paragraph to the Dean of Students explaining why that happened. (Do you, for example, need a tutor, or a reduced work load?) Write another letter explaining the failure to a friend at a distant school.

14 A future employer asks for a biographical sketch that will show your personality. Describe just one event from your life that might be part of the biography.

15 Write a letter to your representative or senators urging them to support or speak against some issue currently before Congress.

16 Assume you have lost something: write a paragraph for the "Lost and Found" section of your local newspaper, describing your lost item, any reward, and so on.

17 A national newspaper is offering space to students who need a job and would like to advertise in the "Positions Wanted" section of the paper. Write a paragraph in which you try to sell yourself: limit 100 words.

18 You have been hired by an advertising firm; your job will be to write copy for a new product—a hair dryer, a lawn mower, a desk lamp, a kitchen appliance, or some other product. Write the introductory paragraph for an ad that will appear in several national magazines.

19 Your testimony is needed for a trial in a distant state concerning a traffic accident you witnessed. Since it would be a hardship for you to travel a great distance, you are asked to submit a written deposition. Write a paragraph describing in detail what you witnessed.

20 Your history professor has asked you to speculate about what the world would be like if any event in history had been different: if you could change anything in the world now to alter future history, what would you change? Write a paragraph in which you explain in detail what you would change and why.

CHAPTER SEVEN

Sentence Combining for Effective Sentences

By being so long in the lowest form (at Harrow)

I gained an immense advantage over the cleverer boys . . .

I got into my bones the essential structure

of the ordinary British sentence—

which is a noble thing.

Sir Winston Churchill, *Roving Commission: My Early Life*

The aim of this chapter is to help you write sentences that say what you mean and affect your reader as you intend. No matter how interesting your ideas are or how well you organize your essay, your writing appears on the page one sentence at a time.

The traditional method for helping students to produce more mature sentences was to teach parts of speech and rules of grammar, and then to have students analyze and label and diagram sentences. However, after as much as twelve years of this kind of language study, many students entering college still wrote in short, choppy, immature-sounding sentences.

Furthermore, experienced writers frequently say that they learned to write, not by studying grammar books, but by *practicing* the craft of writing. But any language with as many words as ours—over 500,000—will permit an almost infinite number of combinations of words; no human could practice every possible combination.

Practice improves sentence skills, to be sure. With practice your sentences will sound more mature, better crafted, more expressive. But *what* needs to be practiced? It is the *connective devices* of language that let experienced writers generate good sentences. Though there are thousands upon thousands of words in English, there are surprisingly few ways to connect them to each other. It is this connecting, or *sentence-combining* skill that experienced writers have mastered and beginning writers need to practice. Research shows that if you practice these sentence-combining skills, you can quickly learn to write more mature sentences.

You can see this for yourself. Read the following two passages. Passage *B* was written by a professional writer, Sinclair Lewis. How does it differ from passage *A*?

A He dipped his hands in the bichloride solution. He shook them. The shake was quick. His fingers were down. His fingers were like the fingers of a pianist. The fingers of the pianist were above the keys.

B He dipped his hands in the bichloride solution and shook them, a quick shake—fingers down, like the fingers of a pianist above the keys.

Sinclair Lewis's sentence sounds "smoother"; he uses fewer words, is less repetitive, and builds a more consistent image. Passage *A*, on the other hand, sounds choppy, wordy, repetitious; it lacks flow. The immature sentences are harder to read, and in fact, reading very many such sentences could become an unpleasant chore.

However, both passages contain the same information; the chief difference between them is in the way Lewis has combined that information. Here's how the first passage can be revised:

He dipped his hands in the bichloride solution. He shook them. The shake was quick. His fingers were down. His fingers were like the fingers of a pianist. The fingers of the pianist were above the keys.

Lewis has gained rhythm, emphasis, and power by deleting redundant expressions (*he, his, his fingers were*) and by using simple connecting devices (*and* plus commas). With practice, you can learn to use these sentence-combining devices to revise your own sentences.

Suppose you were asked to revise the following three sentences into one, more mature sentence:

The officer took out his pistol.
The officer calmly pointed it at the prisoner's head.
He then pulled the trigger.

You might come up with the following revision:

The officer took out his pistol, calmly pointed it at the prisoner's head, and then pulled the trigger.

Revising these three sentences involves three easy operations: first, you delete redundant phrases, *The officer* and *he;* then you add a comma between *pistol* and *calmly;* and last you put , *and* between *head* and *then*.

Different writers would probably combine the three sentences in different ways. For example:

The officer took out his pistol, calmly pointed it at the prisoner's head, and pulled the trigger.

The officer took out his pistol and calmly pointed it at the prisoner's head before pulling the trigger.

The officer took out his pistol and calmly pointed it at the prisoner's head, then pulled the trigger.

After taking out his pistol and calmly pointing it at the prisoner's head, the officer pulled the trigger.

And there are still other possible combinations. It is obvious, then, that three short sentences can be revised into a number of different sentences, each with its own emphasis and rhythm. A writer can, with relative ease, convey essentially the same information in a variety of ways.

In this chapter you will work with many of the combining devices experienced writers use, and you will exploit the language ability you already have. As you practice revising sentences, you will begin to produce better-sounding sentences in your compositions. Remember, though, that because writing is a physical as well as a mental act, you must go beyond merely solving the sentence problems in your head. You must practice putting each sentence on paper, one word at a time.

WORKING THE PROBLEMS

In order to help you with sentence combining, we will begin by using a series of *signals*. These signals show you how you can combine several sentences into one. Generally, signals to the right of a sentence direct you to move whatever is inside the parentheses to the beginning of the line.

EXAMPLE
The armies of Alexander the Great swept through Baktria and Scythia.
The armies invaded India.   (,)
Then they returned to Persia.   (, AND)

The *slash* signal (/), a diagonal line through a word, means to delete that word. In the example, the slash signals direct you to delete *the*, *armies*, and *they*.

The *comma* signal (,) means to add a comma at the beginning of the line on which the comma signal appears. Since you have deleted

The and *armies* in the example, you would be left with , *invaded India* after inserting the comma signal.

The *comma-and* signal (, AND) means to put a comma and *and* at the beginning of the line on which the signal appears. In the example, put , *and* in front of *Then* to complete the solution. You must of course change the capital letters and remove periods to fit the new sentence.

In general, work the problems in your head and then write out the one-sentence answer. In particular:

STEP 1: READ THE WHOLE PROBLEM

The students read everything their professors assigned.
They spent long hours studying their notes.   (,)
Then they took their final exams.   (, AND)

STEP 2: SOLVE EACH LINE OF THE PROBLEM BEFORE YOU TRY TO SOLVE THE WHOLE PROBLEM.

The students read everything their professors assigned.
They spent long hours studying their notes   (!)
Then they took their final exams.   (, AND)

It's usually possible to do step 2 in your head, but write it out if you feel it will help.

STEP 3: WRITE OUT THE NEW SENTENCE

The students read everything their professors assigned, spent long hours studying their notes, and then took their final exams.

Practice

Write out each of the following sentence-combining problems as a single sentence. You have been given all the necessary signals in the first two and limited assistance with the third. In the last two, combine the sentences in any way you choose.

1 The snowmobile roared through the trees.
   The snowmobile plowed through the brush.   (,)
   The snowmobile disappeared into the wilderness.   (, AND)

2 Set your government's affairs in order.
   The opposing party will do it for you.   (, OR)

3 The drought hung over Oklahoma.
   The drought was drying up rivers.   (,)
   It was emptying ponds and lakes.
   It was parching the land.
   It was threatening the region with another Dust Bowl.

4 Genghis Khan spent his nights in revelry.
   Genghis Khan spent his days in butchery.

5 The alien creature was lost.
It was alone on earth.
It was afraid of humans.
It was lonely.
It was looking for its companions.

What is gained by revising these ideas into one sentence? Think of someone learning to skate. At first the movements are short, jerky, and uncertain. With practice, these separate, disconnected movements will blend together into the smooth and gracefully flowing motions of the mature skater. So too with sentence combining. With practice, you will develop the ability to make the disconnected elements of your thoughts flow together. As you work the sentence problems, concentrate on creating a better sentence and not merely on getting the problem "right." Soon, when you can see several possibilities for a sentence, you will be well on your way to writing mature sentences. Eventually, mastery over your sentences will help you to achieve the effects you desire in your writing.

CLARITY

All things in writing are relative of course. Sometimes graceful and elegant sentences will have the desired effect on your audience. But at other times the short, forceful sentence may be the most appropriate for your purpose. No language rule says that good sentences are always long- or short- or medium-length.

The point is not length but effect on the reader. No sentence is good if it is not *clear* to the reader. In writing, everything is governed by purpose: what effect do you want to have on the reader? What do you want the reader to hear? When sentences sound choppy and immature, they should be revised. But if this idea is applied carelessly, inexperienced writers may make the opposite mistake. The fact that you *can* connect ideas to each other does not necessarily mean that you *always* should. Arbitrarily running sentences together is not the idea; such a practice will often produce baby talk: "I have a dog, and his name is Spot, and he is white, and he follows me, and I play with him." You need not limit yourself to simple concepts that can be expressed in the language of children. On the other hand, inexperienced writers need to be especially alert against getting carried away with sentences. Sentences that ramble on and on, especially when they cause the reader to lose the main idea, should be revised into shorter units. One goal of sentence combining, then, is to help you achieve greater *clarity* in your sentences.

RAMBLING SENTENCE

His last stop was his doctor's office, where complaining of chest pains, Daley, who had suffered from angina for several years, dropped by for a check-up—and collapsed, so that even ninety minutes of efforts by medical teams could not revive him, and therefore after twenty-two years as mayor, at the head of a political machine without parallel in America, Daley was dead at seventy-four.

REVISED FOR CLARITY

His last stop was his doctor's office. Complaining of chest pains, Daley, who had suffered from angina for several years, dropped by for a check-up—and collapsed. Ninety minutes of effort by medical teams could not revive him. After twenty-two years as mayor, at the head of a political machine without parallel in America, Daley was dead at seventy-four.
"The Man Who Made Chicago," *Time*, 3 Jan. 1977

Sometimes beginning writers will write one sentence while thinking of another, combining parts of both of them on the paper. The result usually doesn't quite make sense. For example, imagine a writer thinking, "The story contains many good details. I admire the outcome of the story." But instead of writing two sentences, the author writes, "The details of the story admire the outcome." This is an illogical sentence (*details*, inanimate, can't *admire*), the result of faulty combining of ideas. Often such sentences can be revised by changing one or more words; but sometimes you must rethink to clarify first your ideas and then your sentences.

ILLOGICAL SENTENCE

From seventy throats, ugly howls and infernal laughter examine the darkness of an African night.

REVISED FOR CLARITY

From seventy throats, ugly howls and infernal laughter break the darkness of an African night.
VITUS B. DROSCHER, *The Friendly Beast*

In the example by Droscher, the illogical sentence was revised by substituting a more appropriate verb ("break") in place of a verb that doesn't quite make sense in this context ("examine"). But notice in the Ramirez example below it is necessary to rethink, to figure out what the writer is trying to say, before revising the sentence.

ILLOGICAL SENTENCE

After turning the engine off in which I am sitting behind the wheel for five minutes by trying to get my head together, I slowly open and step out the door in the thirty-degree cold.

REVISED FOR CLARITY

After turning the engine off and sitting behind the wheel for five minutes trying to get my head together, I slowly open the car door and step out into the thirty-degree cold.

VICTOR RAMIREZ

ECONOMY

Clarity relates to economy in writing; both are effects on the reader. Often sentences become unclear, illogical, or rambling because of the *extra* words in them. However, economical or "concise" writing is not necessarily related to sentence length. A sentence may sound "wordy" even if it is relatively short. And a long sentence may be very concise. It all depends on your purpose, the effect you intend on your reader. Senators may "filibuster" to prevent the passage of a bill, deliberately rambling on and on, killing time with as many words as possible. On the other hand, Abraham Lincoln's Gettysburg Address is composed of relatively long, yet concise, sentences.

A good rule of thumb for any writer is *don't waste words*. The idea is not simply to use as few words as possible, but to use only as many words as necessary to express what you mean. Like unclear sentences, wordy sentences cause negative reactions in most readers; such sentences seem unedited, as if the writer had been rushing or writing carelessly or filibustering to fill up the page. If any words *can* be removed without changing the intent of your sentences, they usually should be.

Revise for redundancy

The deletion (slash) signal means to remove redundant expressions; the other signals tell you to blend ideas into a more unified sentence. Remember that signals at the end of a line are to be moved to the front of that line.

1 He was prone to superstition.
   He was not prone to credulity.   (, BUT)

JAMES BOSWELL, *Life of Samuel Johnson*

2 Darling trotted back.
   He was smiling.   (,)
   He was breathing deeply.   (,)
   He was breathing easily.   (BUT)
   He was feeling wonderful.   (,)
   He was not tired.   (,)
   This was the tail end of practice.   (, THOUGH)
   He'd run eighty yards.   (AND)

IRWIN SHAW, "The Eighty Yard Run"

279

3 **A lawyer without history or literature is a mechanic.**
   The lawyer is a mere working mason.   (,)
   He possesses some knowledge of these.   (; IF)
   He may venture to call himself an architect.   (,)
SIR WALTER SCOTT, *Guy Mannering*

Note   Writers sometimes combine their ideas by deleting a repetitious word or phrase and substituting such words as *who*, *which*, *that*, *whom*, or *whose* for the repeated element. In the following sentence the (WHO) signal directs you to delete the repeated phrase, *The witnesses*, and substitute *who*. The (WHICH) signal directs you to delete the repeated element, *the facts*, and substitute *WHICH*. You would then move the phrase *upon which* to the front of its line.

4 **In court cases, considerable trouble is sometimes caused by witnesses.**
   The witnesses cannot distinguish
   their judgments from the facts.   (WHO)
   Those judgments are based upon the facts.   (UPON WHICH)
S. I. HAYAKAWA, "Reports, Inferences, Judgments"

5 **Slow performance may indicate**
   momentary attention gaps.   (WHILE)
   Extremely rapid performance may be indicative of a person.   (,)
   The person sacrifices accuracy to speed.   (WHO)
   The person's personality demands a challenge.   (, AND WHOSE)
J. R. BLOCK, "A Test That Tells Who Is Accident Prone," *Psychology Today*, June 1975

Note the position of (WHILE) in sentence problems: it goes to the front of its sentence.

Not all "wordiness" is caused by redundancy; sometimes the writer just has too many words. Some writers use the *who*, *which*, or *that* options carelessly instead of taking the time to write the most concise sentences. In other cases writers use the most roundabout ways to say things.

Revise for wordiness

1 **The civilization of Egypt was remarkably homogeneous.**
   It reached its fullness in the first few
   dynasties of the Old Kingdom.   (, WHICH . . . ,)
J. KELLY SOWARDS, *Western Civilization to 1660*

Note   The signal (, WHICH . . . ,) directs you to *insert* the clause into the sentence instead of just adding it on at the end of the sentence.

2 The voice of science is itself impeccably rational.   (BECAUSE)
The voice of science is insistently reasonable.   (,)
The voice of science is forever self-correcting.   (, AND)
It is such a thing as cannot be deduced out of existence.   (,)

KENNETH MACCORQUODALE, "Behaviorism Is a Humanism" *The Humanist*, Mar./Apr. 1961

3 The life of Man is a long march through the night.
It is surrounded by invisible foes.   (,)
It is tortured by weariness and pain.   (,)
It is towards a goal.   (,)
Few can hope to reach the goal.   (THAT)
None may tarry long.   (, AND WHERE)

BERTRAND RUSSELL, *Mysticism and Logic*

4 Picture poor old Alfy coming home from football practice every day.
He is bruised.   (,)
His body is aching.   (AND)
The game has made him agonizingly tired.   (,)
He's scarcely able to shovel the mashed potatoes into his mouth.   (,)

PAUL ROBERTS, "How to Say Nothing in Five Hundred Words," *Understanding English*

5 Paley was not a mere corporate figure.
Paley was a total individual.   (BUT)
He was a man.   (,)
This man lived a life which was rich in its texture.   (WHO)
He knew and enjoyed quality.   (, WHO)
The man demanded it in every aspect of his own life.   (, AND WHO)

DAVID HALBERSTAM, "CBS: The Power and the Profits," *Atlantic Monthly*, Jan. 1976

REVISING BY EMBEDDING

In order to achieve economy and clarity in their writing, experienced writers often revise their ideas by embedding all or part of one sentence *into* another sentence. Embedding allows you to show that the two ideas are not merely related to each other, but that one is actually part of the other. When you work on the embedding problems, think of one sentence as having a slot (which we will label SOMETHING) in it. The SOMETHING signal tells you to insert a clause or phrase into the SOMETHING slot. For example:

A She knew SOMETHING.
He was going to leave her.   (THAT)
She knew that he was going to leave her.

JAMES BALDWIN, "Come Out of the Wilderness"

In example *A*, *that* moved to the beginning of its line, and then *that he was going to leave her* was inserted into the SOMETHING slot.

B This is due largely to SOMETHING.
Many writers think, not before,
but as they write.   (THE FACT THAT)
This is due largely to the fact that many writers think, not before, but as they write.
W. SOMERSET MAUGHAM, *The Summing Up*

C She wants me to believe SOMETHING.
The body is a spiritual fact.   (T~~H~~AT)
T~~he body is~~ the instrument of the soul.   (,)
She wants me to believe the body is a spiritual fact, the instrument of the soul.
SAUL BELLOW, *Herzog*

The word *that* is often optional in English. In example *C*, Saul Bellow chose to delete *that* and simply embed *The body is a spiritual fact* in the SOMETHING slot in the first sentence. We have signaled the deleted *that* by putting a slash mark through the signal: (T~~H~~AT)

Revise for clarity and economy through embedding

1 **The transactional analyst believes SOMETHING.**
Psychiatric symptoms result from
some form of self-deception.   (THAT)
ERIC BERNE, *What Do You Say After You Say Hello?*

2 **We can make useful observations from photographs.**
We err.   (, BUT)
We forget SOMETHING.   (IF)
The camera is not a complete reproduction
of the objects photographed.   (THAT)
DAVID K. BERLO, *The Process of Communication*

3 **Some thought SOMETHING.**
They were the only person to hear the cries.   (T~~H~~AT)
The rest believed SOMETHING.   (;)
Others heard them, too.   (THAT)
DARLEY AND LATANE, "Why People Don't Help in a Crisis," *Reader's Digest,* May 1969

4 **SOMETHING is belts of Flexten cord, instead of steel.**
It makes the Goodyear American Eagle
Radial the tire for today.   (WHAT)
Advertisement, *People Weekly,* 14 Mar. 1977

5 I know SOMETHING
   You think SOMETHING.   (THAT)
   I'm wasting my time.   (THAT)
DONALD BARTHELME, "See the Moon?"

More Revising by Embedding

For the IT . . . THAT signal, remember the following rule: *it* substitues for the SOMETHING slot; *that* goes to the beginning of its own line. For example:

A SOMETHING is incomprehensible.
   Such drugs could be dispensed without
   competent medical advice.   (IT . . . THAT)
   It is incomprehensible that such drugs could be dispensed without
   competent medical advice.
NORMAN COUSINS, "The Toxified Society"

B SOMETHING was lucky.
   We were both of us only fourteen.   (IT . . . THAT)
   It was lucky we were both of us only fourteen.
WILLIAM GOLDING, "Thinking as a Hobby"

Revise by embedding

1 SOMETHING seems to be generally taken for granted.
   Wife-beaters are not gentlemen
   in twentieth century terms.   (IT . . . THAT)
   Self-control is expected of a gentleman, under even the most trying cir-
   cumstances.   (AND THAT)
RUSSELL LYNES, "Is There a Gentleman in the House?" *Look*, 9 June 1959

2 SOMETHING is hard to believe.
   She is the only girl Riley knows.   (IT . . . THAT)

3 Throughout this book, SOMETHING is important to remember.
   We are not considering language
   as an isolated phenomenon.   (IT . . . THAT)
S. I. HAYAKAWA, "The Language of Reports"

4 SOMETHING would put him in an awful spot.
   Lois Farrow somehow found out SOMETHING.   (IT . . . IF)
   He had let her daughter go to sleep
   with her legs across Duane's.   (THAT)
LARRY MCMURTRY, *The Last Picture Show*

5 Stimulating the brains of lightly anesthetized patients in the operating
   room became a most important way to localize functions.

SOMETHING was found.   (SINCE)
**Physical landmarks were not sufficiently uniform
to be completely reliable.**   (IT . . . THAT)
ELIOT S. VALENSTEIN, *Brain Control*

EMPHASIS

As you begin to write longer, more sophisticated sentences, you must craft them consciously to give the appropriate emphasis to your ideas. Even in short sentences a writer must make clear for the reader which ideas are to be emphasized.

Emphasis Through Effective Repetition

Deliberate repetition of words or phrases is one way to achieve emphasis within a sentence, as long as you don't create the impression of redundancy.

WITHOUT EMPHASIS

In every time, tongue, lonely, troubled corner on earth, this bewilderment has been uttered.

REVISED FOR EFFECTIVE REPETITION

In every time, in every tongue, in every lonely, troubled corner of the earth, this bewilderment has been uttered.
BENJAMIN KOGAN, *Health*

WITHOUT EMPHASIS

Society is sustained by communication, which makes human life possible.

REVISED FOR EFFECTIVE REPETITION

Society is sustained by communication: communication makes life possible.
PETERSON, GOLDHABER, PACE, *Communication Probes*

Revise for emphasis through effective repetition

1 You should hit hard.
  You should hit fast.   (,)
  You should hit often.   (,)
ADMIRAL W. F. HALSEY, "Formula for Waging War"

2 **SOMEHOW the lorries sway.**   (MONOTONOUSLY)
  SOMEHOW come the calls.   (, MONOTONOUSLY)
  SOMEHOW falls the rain.   (, MONOTONOUSLY)
ERICH MARIA REMARQUE, *All Quiet on the Western Front*

3 It is time for a new generation of leadership.
It is time to cope with new problems.   (,)
It is time for new opportunities.   (AND)

JOHN F. KENNEDY, Television Address, 1960

4 The importance of events mounted.   (AS)
More points on the map needed coverage.   (, AS)
More reporters were hired.   (AND)
The *CBS World News Roundup* was born.   (,)

DAVID HALBERSTAM, "CBS: the Power and the Profits," *Atlantic Monthly*, Jan. 1976

5 They were sick.
They were tired.   (,)
They felt chills.   (,)
They would not be in today.   (:)

Emphasis Through Parallelism

Parallelism is a basic concept in writing, much like consistency, to which it is related. It is a convention that similar concepts should be written in similar forms; that is, they should be parallel. Parallelism is a form of repetition. Thus, "I like *fishing* and *skiing*," not "I like fishing and to ski."

WITHOUT EMPHASIS

But perhaps more important, the future home will provide room and equipment for drying, things used to clean food with, and canned foods and other processed food chores.

REVISED FOR EMPHASIS THROUGH PARALLELISM

But perhaps more important, the future home will provide room and equipment for drying, cleaning, canning, and other food processing chores.

ROBERT RODALE, "Gardens of the Future," *Organic Gardening and Farming*, Jan. 1977

We were heading out for an afternoon of SOMETHING.
It would be to fish.   (ING)
It would be to swim.   (ING)
It would be to boat.   (, AND + ING)
We were heading out for an afternoon of fishing, swimming, and boating.

Note that the (ING) signal adds *ing* to *fish*, *swim*, and *boat*, and deletes the redundant words *It would be to*.

Revise for emphasis through parallelism

1 The trackers scuttled along.
They stopped.   (, ING)

They looked.   (, ING)
They hurried on.   (, AND + ING)
JOHN STEINBECK, *The Pearl*

2 **Monterey sits on the slope of a hill.**
It has a blue bay below it.   (, WITH)
It has a forest of tall dark pine trees at its back.   (AND WITH)
JOHN STEINBECK, *Tortilla Flat*

3 **Our boys were headed for basketball fame.**
They were filled with myths of the good life.   (,)
They were determined to win at any cost.   (, AND)

4 **FOR SOME REASON they added oversized racing slicks to the old Buick.**
It was in order to give it extra traction.   (,)
It was in order to add a touch of mystique.   (,)
It was in order to give Mr. Valeni
something to worry about.   (, AND)

We have left some of the slashes out, but you can see that the redundant expressions *It was in order* should be deleted.

More Revising for Clarity, Economy, and Emphasis

A SOMETHING enchanted the audience.
Baryshnikov danced.   ('s + ING)
Baryshnikov's dancing enchanted the audience.

The sentence is derived like this:

Baryshnikov + ('S) **= Baryshnikov's**
danced + (ING) **= dancing**

You then insert "Baryshnikov's dancing" into the SOMETHING slot.

B Alfred Lord Tennyson recalled SOMETHING.
The innumerable bees murmured
in immemorial elms.   (ING + OF)
Alfred Lord Tennyson recalled the mumuring of immumerable bees in immemorial elms.

C The television audience was delighted by SOMETHING.
Nadia Comanechi won a gold medal
at the 1976 Olympics.   ('S + ING + OF)
The television audience was delighted by Nadia Comanechi's winning of a gold medal at the 1976 Olympics.

D SOMETHING put the class to sleep.
The professor lectured endlessly.   (LY + ING + OF)
The endless lecturing of the professor put the class to sleep.

The signals (L~~Y~~ + ING + OF) tell you not only what to do (delete *ly*, add *ing*, insert *of*) but how to change the order of the words: the deleted *-ly* word comes first (*endless*), then the *-ing* word (*lecturing*), and finally the *of* insertion (*of the professor*).

E SOMETHING was morally outrageous.
He butchered political
opponents mercilessly.   ('S + L~~Y~~ + ING + OF)
His merciless butchering of political opponents was morally outrageous.

In example *E*,

He + ('s) = His

Similarly, when you add *'s*, *I* should be changed to *my*, *we* to *our*, *she* to *her*, *they* to *their*, and *it* to *its*. (Note the spelling of *its*.)

Emphasis in Inverted Sentences

One way of achieving emphasis is to invert your sentences. (Inverting your sentences is one way to achieve emphasis.) However, one kind of inversion is not much admired. the *backward* sentence, a sentence whose inverted structure sounds unnatural or obscures meaning (Learning English are the students). It is this kind of unnatural backwardness that Wolcott Gibbs had in mind in *More in Sorrow* when he wrote: "Backward ran sentences until reeled the mind." For example:

BACKWARD SENTENCE

Engulfing thousands of families is excessive debt.

REVISED FOR BETTER EMPHASIS

Excessive debt is engulfing thousands of families.

U.S. News and World Report, 20 June 1970

BACKWARD SENTENCE

In his drawings and more clearly and variously than in his painting or his notes appears Leonardo the man.

REVISED FOR BETTER EMPHASIS

Leonardo the man appears more clearly and variously in his drawings than in his paintings or his notes.

WILL DURANT, *The Renaissance*

Emphasis in Passive Sentences

A passive sentence is one in which the actor is invisible (*The bear was chained*), or the actor is hidden behind the word *by* (*The bear was chained by the trainer*). In terms of actions, you can describe the "normal" order for most sentences this way:

ACTOR	ACTION	TARGET
The trainer	chained	the bear.

These sentence elements correspond to the grammatical concepts of *subject*, *verb*, and *object*. This is called normal order because most English sentences start with the subject (the actor), followed by the verb (the action), and end with the object (target or recipient of the action) if there is one.

However, in the passive sentence, the actor and the target (subject and object) have become inverted so that the target now appears in the actor's slot and the actor in the target's slot, as you can see in Figure 7.1.

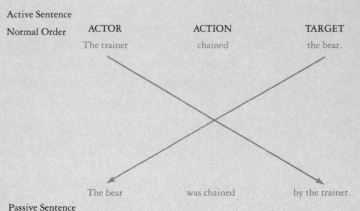

Active Sentence
Normal Order

ACTOR	ACTION	TARGET
The trainer	chained	the bear.
The bear	was chained	by the trainer.

Passive Sentence

FIGURE 7.1   Inverted Order

The two sentences mean the same, but the emphasis is different. Some readers and writers dislike the passive because of its confusion of the logical subject and the grammatical subject. That is, in both sentences the logical subject is *the trainer;* but in the passive sentence the grammatical subject is *the bear* (because it is in the subject position, before the verb, *was chained*), even though logically it is still the trainer who is doing the chaining.

Whether there is any real need for the passive depends on whether the actor or the target is being emphasized. Writers must not hide behind the passive, but obviously there are occasions when the passive would be appropriate. The most direct statement is, of course, "The trainer chained the bear"; but if we ask, "What happened to that bear?" the best answer may be, "The bear was chained by the trainer." Even so, some passives are more awkward than others, and many sound pointlessly indirect by comparison with the active version of the same idea: "The paper was received by him" (passive) as opposed to "He received the paper" (active). As a general rule, write active sentences rather than passive ones.

AWKWARD PASSIVE

The pit that held her grandfather's bones was leaped into by Miranda.

REVISED TO ACTIVE

Miranda leaped into the pit that held her grandfather's bones.

KATHERINE ANNE PORTER, "The Grave"

AWKWARD PASSIVE

Little things were fumbled at by the boy's mind.

REVISED TO ACTIVE

The boy's mind fumbled at little things.

THOMAS WOLFE, *Look Homeward Angel*

Revise for passive

*The signal (***pass***) means to turn the sentence into a passive sentence by reversing the actor and target (if there is one). The signal (***pass + BY***) means to turn the sentence into a passive sentence using the word* by *at the end, before the logical subject. The signal (***act***) means to turn the sentence into an active sentence by reversing the actor and the target. For example:*

A Our latest test plane has flown at near-orbital heights.   **(pass)**
   Our latest test plane has been flown at near-orbital heights.

B The President himself had issued
   the order for a new tax cut.   **(pass + BY)**
   The order for a new tax cut had been issued by the President himself.

C In plain white envelopes were carefully sealed their
   secret love letters by the two girls.   **(act)**
   The two girls carefully sealed their secret love letters in plain white envelopes.

1 The whistle of the shells was heard
   by all of us as they went by.   (act)

2 These wild-eyed, killer horses should try to be ridden
   only by desperate men who will do anything for money.   (act)

3 They took the final vote at a late hour.   (pass)

4 In all the confusion, no one realized that the students
   had captured the president of the university.   (pass + BY)

5 The great crown of the emperor was necessary to be
   sealed in its glass display case.   (act)

More Revising by Embedding

*The (***FOR . . . TO***), (***IT . . . TO***), and (***IT . . . FOR . . . TO***) signals*   The (FOR . . . TO) signal directs you to change a sentence like

"John runs" to "For John to run. . . ." The (IT . . . TO) and (IT . . . FOR . . . TO) signals function like the (IT . . . THAT) signal on page 283. The *it* replaces the appropriate SOMETHING signal and *to* or *for . . . to* operate on their own lines. For example:

A SOMETHING is easier than SOMETHING.
A camel goes through the eye of a needle.   (IT . . . FOR . . . TO)
A rich man enters the kingdom of God.   (FOR . . . TO)
It is easier for a camel to go through the eye of a needle than for a rich man to enter the kingdom of God.

B SOMETHING won't be easy.
We send him into any of the three phases.   (IT . . . TO)
It won't be easy to send him into any of the three phases.
THOMAS PYNCHON, *Gravity's Rainbow*

The (DISCOVER ⟶ DISCOVERY) signal   Certain transformations involve changing the form of a word; thus "discover" can be changed to "discovery," "fail" to "failure," "investigate" to "investigation," and so on. Rather than supply a signal for these changes, we will simply give you the word you need. For example:

A Winston Churchill denounced SOMETHING.
Hitler seized Czechoslovakia.   ('S + SEIZURE + OF)
Winston Churchill denounced Hitler's seizure of Czechoslovakia.

B The nation finally insisted on SOMETHING.
Richard Nixon immediately resigned
as President.   ('S + L̸Y̸ + RESIGNATION)
The nation finally insisted on Richard Nixon's immediate resignation as President.

Revise for Clarity, Economy, Emphasis

1 The only thing necessary for the triumph of evil is SOMETHING.
Good men do nothing.   (FOR . . . TO)
EDMUND BURKE, "Letter to William Smith"

1 An aspect of the political change was SOMETHING.
The political change was revolutionizing Europe.   (WHICH)
They encouraged foreign adventure
and exploration.   (THE ENCOURAGEMENT + OF)
ROBERT L. HEILBRONER, *The Worldly Philosophers*

3 Even she seemed cheered by SOMETHING.
The manager came.   ('S + ING)
She sensed SOMETHING.   (;)

Her husband had an irrationally light spirit.   ('S + LY + LIGHT-NESS + OF)

DORIS LESSING, "The Second Hut," *African Short Stories*

4 **The rocking horse bounded forward on its springs.**
It startled the child into SOMETHING.   (, + ING)
The child scampered noiselessly back to bed.   (A + LY + SCAMPER)

DYLAN THOMAS, "The Tree," *Ten Modern Masters*

5 **Essentially, SOMETHING means SOMETHING.**
I love my neighbor.   (ING)
I recognize SOMETHING.   (ING)
SOMETHING is as real as mine.   (THAT)
He exists.   ('S + EXISTENCE)

W. H. AUDEN, *Hiroshima Plus 20*

Emphasis Through Sentence Rhythm

Just as you have learned to recognize the flat intonation of a recorded telephone message, and just as you know when someone is reading "without expression," you can learn to tell when there is something wrong with the rhythm of a sentence. It is very difficult to describe poor sentence rhythm; teachers usually mark such sentences "awkward." But you can probably already tell when a sentence doesn't sound right. Something halting, unnatural, or awkward announces that the rhythm is off beat. The rhythm may be too obvious, singsong. The sentence may lack variety or emphasis; its rhythm may be so homogenized that it is a robot sentence—flat, dead. For example:

FAULTY RHYTHM

On his heels Stormgren spun, and into the shadowy corridor stared.

REVISED FOR BETTER RHYTHM

Stormgren spun on his heels and stared into the shadowy corridor.

ARTHUR C. CLARKE, *Childhood's End*

FAULTY RHYTHM

Where there was dew they were feeding where the long shadows were above the fields below which already had twilight on them.

REVISED FOR BETTER RHYTHM

They were feeding among the dew and the long shadows, with twilight already in the fields below.

RICHARD ADAMS, *Watership Down*

Emphasis Through Structure

Sometimes you can gain more importance for an idea by expressing it in more words, at least in theory. This theory, however, is always tempered by context. As you have already seen, sometimes a *short* expression gains greater power by following a longer one. Certainly no one recommends that you pad your sentences with words to make your ideas seem more important. But note the following:

LEAST EMPHASIS: SINGLE WORD
She reacted *sarcastically* to his proposal.

REVISED FOR MORE EMPHASIS: PHRASE
She reacted *with sarcasm* to his proposal.

REVISED FOR MAXIMUM EMPHASIS (IN THIS CONTEXT): CLAUSE
As she reacted to his proposal, *her sarcasm was evident.*

Emphasis Through Position

Moving things around usually causes a change in emphasis. There is no hard rule about position except that ideas often gain emphasis when they show up in unexpected places. Modifiers tend to be most emphatic at the beginning of the sentence; independent clauses tend to be most emphatic at the end.

LEAST EMPHASIS: MODIFIER AT END
She reacted to his proposal *sarcastically.*

REVISED FOR MORE EMPHASIS: INSIDE MODIFIER
She reacted *sarcastically* to his proposal.
She *sarcastically* reacted to his proposal.

REVISED FOR MAXIMUM EMPHASIS: INITIAL MODIFIER
Sarcastically she reacted to his proposal.

Emphasis Through Contrast

It is not always enough to say what a thing is; it is sometimes necessary to say what a thing is *not*. Contrast is an excellent way of achieving emphasis.

CONTRAST LOST
She had been painting for a short time and had little acquaintance with her brushes, which she handled with a certain ease and freedom from a natural aptitude.

REVISED FOR EMPHASIS THROUGH CONTRAST
She handled her brushes with a certain ease and freedom which came, not from long and close acquaintance with them, but from a natural aptitude.
KATE CHOPIN, *The Awakening*

CONTRAST LOST
And so we smile our way through the day, and in fact we may feel angry and annoyed beneath the smile.

And so we smile our way through the day, though in fact we may feel angry and annoyed beneath the smile.

JULIUS FAST, *Body Language*

EMBEDDING WITH PUNCTUATION

You have already had extensive practice with the comma, semi-colon, and period. Two other marks favored by many modern writers are the colon and the dash; they allow writers greater flexibility to achieve economy, clarity, and emphasis.

A We have only one thing to say about Uncle Buster.
He's a terrific cook.   (:)
We have only one thing to say about Uncle Buster: he's a terrific cook.

B In sum, there are at least two types of faith.
There are possibly many more.   (, THOUGH)
There is the faith of the true believer.   (:)
There is the faith of a heretic.   (AND)
In sum, there are at least two types of faith, though possibly many more: the faith of the true believer and the faith of a heretic.

WALTER KAUFMAN, *The Faith of a Heretic*

C Fifty years have expired since this adventure.
The fear of punishment is no more   (—)
Fifty years have expired since this adventure—the fear of punishment is no more.

JEAN JACQUES ROUSSEAU, *Confessions*

D The hour of Yellow Sky was approaching.   (BUT)
It was the hour of daylight.   (— . . . —)
But the hour of Yellow Sky—the hour of daylight—was approaching.

STEPHEN CRANE, "The Bride Comes to Yellow Sky"

The double-dash (— . . . —) in example *D* indicates an interrupter set off on both sides by dashes. The interrupter *the hour of daylight* was inserted into the sentence above, not just attached to the end of it.

E There is, after all, another side to the human spirit, too.
It is a dark side.   (— . . . —)
There is, after all, another side—a dark side—to the human spirit, too.

ERIC SEVAREID, "The Dark of the Moon"

F Nevertheless, character is the source.
Character is the willingness to accept responsibility for one's own life.   (— . . . —)
Self-respect springs from the source.   (FROM WHICH)

Nevertheless, character—the willingness to accept responsibility for one's own life—is the source from which self-respect springs.

JOAN DIDION, "On Self-Respect," *Slouching Towards Bethlehem*

G The crimes have changed in rapid succession.
The Jews have been charged with the crimes
in the course of history.   (WITH WHICH)
They were crimes.   (—)
The crimes were to justify the atrocities.   (WHICH)
The atrocities were perpetrated against them.   (. . .—)
The crimes with which the Jews have been charged in the course of history—crimes which were to justify the atrocities perpetrated against them—have changed in rapid succession.

ALBERT EINSTEIN, "Why Do They Hate the Jews?"

The signal (. . .—) instructed you to put a dash at the *end* of its sentence, immediately after "perpetrated against them" and, of course, immediately in front of "have changed in rapid succession."

Practice

1 Down drifts the calf.
The calf is dead.   (—)
GUNTER GRASS, *Dog Years*

2 So I would say to the organizations and groups SOMETHING.
They would force integration on the South by legal process.
(WHICH)
"Stop now for a moment."   (:)
WILLIAM FAULKNER, "A Letter to the North"

3 The phone was downstairs.   (SINCE)
I didn't see SOMETHING.
We were going to call the police.   (HOW)
Nor did I want the police.   (—. . .—)
Mother made one of her decisions.   (BUT)
Her decisions were quick.
JAMES THURBER, "The Night the Ghost Got In"

4 To understand the physical world, and ultimately man himself, one must eliminate the living soul.
Man exists in this world as merely a product
of mass and motion.   (—WHO . . .—)
LEWIS MUMFORD, "The Pentagon Power"

5 This revolution has resulted in a growing understanding of the forces.
This revolution is as profound as the revolution
in astronomy 500 years ago.   (—)

**Copernicus displaced the Earth from its position
at the center of the universe.**   (WHEN + . . .—)
The forces shape the continents.   (WHICH)
The forces set them drifting about the world.   (AND)
JOHN R. GRIBBIN AND STEPHEN H. PLAGEMANN, *The Jupiter Effect*

VARIED TYPES OF SENTENCES

Variety Through the Cumulative Sentence

The cumulative sentence is built by addition; it adds details after
the main idea has been established. For example:

A He showed up in a new car.
It was a brand new Italian sports car.
It was a roaring red sex symbol.
He showed up in a new car, a brand new Italian sports car, a roaring
red sex symbol.
MERRIAM COLLINS

The two modifying sentences are reduced to descriptive phrases
and added to the main clause. Since these cumulative modifiers are
nonrestrictive (they can be removed without changing the main
idea of the sentence), they must be set off with commas. Notice too
that the modifiers add not only descriptive details, but specificity.
The main clause here tells you only that there was a new car; the
added modifier specifies that it was an Italian sports car; the last
modifier adds details of color and sex appeal.

B SOMETHING brought her to her feet and across the front porch.
It was the confused shouts.   (ING)
The shouts rose so suddenly.   (THAT)
She was without her slippers.
Her hair was half braided.   (,)
The confused shouting that rose so suddenly brought her to her feet
and across the front porch without her slippers, her hair half braided.
KATHERINE ANNE PORTER, *Noon Wine*

In this sentence by Katherine Anne Porter you have an ordinary
sentence until you get to the added detail about the woman's hair.
This detail is nonrestrictive—it could be removed without changing
the main idea—and thus it is set off with a comma.

The cumulative sentence permits you to add more and more specific details, building highly descriptive pictures for the reader. The
more specific details you add, the more highly "textured" your sentence will become, as in the following.

295

C He watched them.
They were holding themselves.
Their noses were into the current.   (WITH)
They were many trout deep.   (,)
Fast moved the water.   (, + ING)
There was a slight distortion.   (, + LY + DISTORTED)
He watched them far down through the surface of the pool.   (AS)
The surface was glassy and convex.
Its surface pushed and swelled smoothly.   (, + ING + ING + LY)
It pushed against the resistance of the log-driven piles of the bridge.
He watched them holding themselves with their noses into the current, many trout deep, fast moving water, slightly distorted as he watched them far down through the glassy convex surface of the pool, its surface pushing and swelling smooth against the resistance of the log-driven piles of the bridge.

ERNEST HEMINGWAY, "Big Two-Hearted River"

Practice

1 They looked like toy soldiers.
They stood at attention.   (, + ING)
Their eyes were straight ahead.   (,)
They did not move a muscle.   (, + ING)

2 They were faded.
They were torn.
They were dirty.
Her once-elegant clothes had become SOMETHING.
They were the very rags.
She had so despised the rags.   (THAT)
The rags were on the poor people of the villages.

3 One gray-haired man nearby stood erect.
His hands were jammed into his pockets.   (,)
His mind was adrift.   (,)
He was ignoring the bustle around him.

4 SOME THINGS were long, long gone.
They were the hurried dashes in the early morning fog.
The dashes were to cheat the late bell once again.
They were the long hours into the night.   (,)
I spend the nights to sweat out another
yearbook deadline.   (SPENT + ING)
They were the happy times spent in the
smelly confines of the locker room.   (, + AND)
I snapped towels.   (, + ING)
I cracked stupid jokes.   (AND + ING)

MIKE POORMAN, "A Run Through My Past," *Penn Statements*, Winter 1979

5 It is the sound of the megalopolis.
It is the final distillate of all the blaring radios and tinny TV sets.   (:)
It is the ear-splitting traffic and whispered phone conversations.   (,)

~~It is~~ the relentless sounds of the machinery
that sustains modern civilization.   (,)
~~The~~ sounds hum.   (, + ING)
~~The~~ sounds buzz.   (, + ING)
~~The~~ sounds whir.   (, + ING)
~~The~~ sounds drone.   (, + ING)

ALBERT GOLDMAN, "The Delirium of Disco," *Life*, Nov. 1978

Variety Through the Balanced Sentence

Often used in oratory, the balanced sentence is very formal and
elegant. It is crafted by balancing two similar ideas in similar words
and structures.

WEAK

And so my fellow Americans when you want to know what your country
can do for you, just ask yourself that question the other way around.

REVISED AS BALANCED SENTENCE

And so my fellow Americans, ask not what your country can do for you;
ask what you can do for your country.

JOHN F. KENNEDY, Inaugural Address

WEAK

It is no vice to be extreme in defending liberty; and . . . to pursue justice
only moderately lacks virtue.

REVISED AS BALANCED SENTENCE

Extremism in the defense of liberty is no vice; and . . . moderation in the
pursuit of justice is no virtue.

BARRY GOLDWATER, Acceptance Speech

WEAK

The only way to win is through perseverance; however, if you quit, obviously winning will not be yours.

REVISED AS BALANCED SENTENCE

Winners never quit; quitters never win.

WEAK

Those who are successful are at their best when they are faced with ad-
versity.

REVISED AS BALANCED SENTENCE

When the going gets tough, the tough get going.

Variety Through the Periodic Sentence

The periodic sentence builds to a climax: your readers must wait
for the end of the sentence before they can get the meaning. The periodic sentence is created by placing all modifiers and subordinate
elements first in the sentence so that the main clause comes last, in
the most emphatic position. Technically, even a short sentence

could be called "periodic" if it were so constructed, but the term usually applies to longer sentences in which there is a clear sense of waiting for the end. For example:

STANDARD ORDER

She liked to watch soap operas on TV in the early afternoon once the clothes were done and the children were off to school.

REVISED AS PERIODIC SENTENCE

In the early afternoon, once the clothes were done and the children were off to school, she liked to watch soap operas on TV.

STANDARD ORDER

Beethoven might have remained a talented and serious musician but not much more if he had been restricted to a less enlightened court circle and had not known the Breunings or had not been exposed to the repercussions of the French Revolution.

REVISED AS PERIODIC SENTENCE

If Beethoven had been restricted to a less enlightened court circle, had not known the Breunings, had not been exposed to the repercussions of the French Revolution, he might have remained a talented and serious musician but not much more.
FRIDA KNIGHT, *Beethoven and the Age of Revolution*

STANDARD ORDER

A mysterious and terrible change had come over the elephant in an instant that one would have thought was too short a time even for a bullet to get there.

REVISED AS PERIODIC SENTENCE

In that instant, in too short a time, one would have thought, even for a bullet to get there, a mysterious, terrible change had come over the elephant.
GEORGE ORWELL, "Shooting an Elephant"

STANDARD ORDER

Some remarkable conclusions are derived from this dream and its associations with a number of rather ordinary childhood memories and several fairy tales familiar to the patient during his early years.

REVISED AS PERIODIC SENTENCE

From this dream and its associations with a number of rather ordinary childhood memories and several fairy tales familiar to the patient during his early years, some remarkable conclusions are derived.
C. H. THIGPEN AND HERVEY CLECKLY, *The Three Faces of Eve*

VARIED BEGINNINGS

One easy way to avoid monotonous sentences is to vary their beginnings. Not every sentence needs to have a novel beginning, but then neither should every sentence begin alike. As a writer you must read your own sentences with a critical eye and listen to them with a critical ear. If you think too many of your sentences start not only with the same words but also with the same structures (too often starting with the subject, for example), add a little variety now and then with some of the following options:

BEGIN WITH A PREPOSITIONAL PHRASE (See Glossary for list of prepositions.)

In the tumultuous business of cutting-in and attending to a whale, there is much running backwards and forwards among the crew.
HERMAN MELVILLE, *Moby Dick*

In the exciting business of registering for classes, there is much running backwards and forwards among the freshmen.
YVETTE WILLIAMS

BEGIN WITH MORE THAN ONE PREPOSITIONAL PHRASE

On this public holiday, as on all other occasions, for seven years past, Hester was clad in a garment of coarse gray cloth.
NATHANIEL HAWTHORNE, *The Scarlet Letter*

On this exam day, as on all other exam days, for the whole semester, I was half asleep from studying all night.
FOSTER RANDOLPH

BEGIN WITH A SIMILE

Like a razor also, it seemed massy and heavy, tapering from the edge into a solid and broad structure.
EDGAR ALLAN POE, "The Pit and the Pendulum"

Like a steam hammer, Professor Haroldson kept pounding away at Aristotle and the Sophists.
DAN LING

BEGIN WITH AN ADJECTIVE OR SEVERAL ADJECTIVES

Silent, grim, colossal—the big city has ever stood against its revilers.
O. HENRY, "Between Rounds," *The Four Million*

Wet, tired, hungry—I stood in the rain in front of the Union waiting for Felicia.
LUANA JOHNSON

BEGIN WITH AN APPOSITIVE

The elephant, the slowest breeder of all known animals, would in a few thousand years stock the whole world.
CHARLES DARWIN, *The Descent of Man*

Bubba Revere, the fastest talker on campus, would in a few minutes wear out any listener.
RON SEVEILLE

BEGIN WITH AN INFINITIVE

To see her, and to be himself unseen and unknown, was enough for him at present.

THOMAS HARDY, *Jude the Obscure*

To know Bentley, and to be in his company for very long, was one of life's least rewarding experiences.

LARRY TATE

BEGIN WITH A MODIFYING CLAUSE

Start with a subordinator (*after, although, as, as if, because, before, if, since, though, unless, until, when, whenever, wherever, while*):

When little boys have learned a new bad word, they are never happy till they have chalked it up on a door.

RUDYARD KIPLING, "The Phantom Rickshaw"

When teachers make a point, they are never happy till they see you scribble it in your notes.

BEGIN WITH A NOUN CLAUSE

Start with a relative pronoun or certain subordinators (*that, what, whatever, when, where, wherever, which, who, whoever, whom, whomever, whose, why*):

What was meant by this ceremony the reader may imagine, who has already gathered some idea of the reckless irreverence of Roaring Camp.

BRET HARTE, "The Luck of Roaring Camp"

What was meant by chug-a-lug the reader may imagine, who has already gathered some idea of the rowdy uproar of a kegger.

RON LIEBERMANN

BEGIN WITH A PARTICIPLE

Crawling on all fours, I made steadily but slowly toward them; till at last, raising my head to an aperture among the leaves I could see clear down into a little dell beside the marsh, and closely set about with trees, where Long John Silver and another of his crowd stood face to face in conversation.

ROBERT LOUIS STEVENSON, *Treasure Island*

Creeping up to the door, I made steadily but slowly toward them; till at last, peeking through the glass in the door I could see clear into the foyer of the dorm, where Big Mother Maisy and her Little Snitch were blabbing away at each other.

SALLY NEWTON

BEGIN WITH A SUSPENDED TRANSITION

Scientists, furthermore, had succeeded in creating life, so that human evolution need no longer be left to chance.

ALVIN C. EURICH, "Higher Education in the Twenty-First Century," in *The Campus in the Modern World*, John D. Margolis, ed.

Heinie, furthermore, had succeeded in getting his boot stuck in the latrine, so that there was no possibility of getting it out without falling over backwards.

JACK STOWKOWSKI

IMITATING SENTENCE STRUCTURES

Try some sentences of your own in which you combine ideas with connecting words and punctuation. Model your sentences on those in the exercises or invent your own sentences.

MODEL

When her date dropped her off, Agnes slipped into her room after the dorm supervisor had gone to bed.

CLOSE IMITATION

When the police left the scene, the burglar climbed in through a downstairs window after the unsuspecting couple had retired for the night.

LOOSE IMITATION

When the police car had left and the residents had retired for the night, the burglar was free to climb through a downstairs window and rob the wall safe.

CREATIVE APPLICATION

Whenever I think of Laura, I always remember the night we stayed out in the rain after the dance, until dawn, watching the sunrise together.

Write two or three sentences for each model you select or each combining device you want to practice. You will find that the more you practice with these structures, the more familiar they'll become to you and the more easily you'll be able to incorporate them into your own writing.

REVISING WITHOUT SIGNALS

Revise these ideas any way that seems to you to produce a good sentence. Avoid choppy, immature sentences; revise for clarity, economy, emphasis, and variety. You are free to add words and concepts to these sentences, and you are also free to delete words and concepts. You may or may not want to make many changes; remember that you can sometimes join sentences just the way they are—with punctuation. The aim here is for you to practice the revision techniques you have been learning in this chapter. There are no right answers here, only the opportunity for you to be creative with your sentences. The only requirement is to produce a single good sentence from those in each problem.

1 **Here man attains the ultimate in fear. He fears himself.**

NORMAN COUSINS, "Where Hell Begins," *Present Tense: An American Odyssey*

2 **You walk into a room full of people. You communicate with everyone in the room. You do it without ever saying a word.**

ELIZABETH MCGOUGH, "Body Language—It Tells on You," *American Youth Magazine*, Mar./Apr. 1979

3 **This poem can help explain Keats' life. His life cannot explain the poem.**

HAROLD BLOOM, *The Visionary Company*

4 **An honest man has hardly need to count more than his ten fingers. In extreme cases he may add his ten toes. And then he can lump the rest.**

HENRY DAVID THOREAU, *Walden*

5 **The noise in the cell quieted. The door clanked open. The silence deepened. It was as if a quilt had been thrown over the prisoners. It was just when they watched Yakov enter.**

BERNARD MALAMUD, *The Fixer*

6 **A single-celled animal moves as a whole. It has neither cells nor muscles. It takes account of its environment. It has no brain.**

CHARLES HARTSHORNE, *Reality as Social Process*

7 **In California, farmers were well equipped to expand their production quickly. They had already developed one of the most highly mechanized types of agriculture in the nation.**

GERALD D. NASH, *The American West in the Twentieth Century*

8 **There is some ambiguity about the knowledge an educated man should have. There is none at all about the skills.**

BERTRAND RUSSELL, *The Art of Philosophizing and Other Essays*

9 **In the end we shall make thoughtcrime literally impossible. There will be no words in which to express it.**

GEORGE ORWELL, *1984*

10 **This emulsion has many valuable properties. It penetrates the skin. It does not become rancid. It is mildly antiseptic, and so forth.**

ALDOUS HUXLEY, *Brave New World Revisited*

11 **A good novel phrases the reader's imagination.**

12 **The astronomer's job emits long hours of lonely work in mathematics and analysis of photographs.**

13 **His glance was quizzical. His glance was curious. His glance was imperative.**

THEODORE DREISER, *An American Tragedy*

14 **The tragedy at Kent was partially the result of the current clash between two different life styles. The life styles are contending for the spirit of America.**

JAMES A. MICHENER, *Kent State*

15 At 9 A.M. he assembles his own staff, and each in turn concerns about where difficulties may lie for the President.

16 More particularly, they rediscovered Panini's magnificent grammar of Sanskrit. Sanskrit is the ancient literary dialect of India. The grammar was probably written late in the fourth century, B.C.

OWEN THOMAS, *Transformational Grammar and the Teacher of English*

17 On top of the craft's triangular surface, a 30-inch antenna dish unfolds. The antenna dish searches the star-sprinkled sky for homing signals from earth. It finds them. It locks on.

K. E. KRISTOFFERSON, "Message from the Surface of Mars," *Reader's Digest*, Feb. 1976

18 The bull charges. The banderillo rises on his toes. He bends in a curve forward. He drops the darts. It is just as the bull is about to hit him. The darts go into the bull's hump. The hump is just back of his horns.

ERNEST HEMINGWAY, "Killing a Bull," *By-Line Ernest Hemingway*

19 In slow pulses the thick plume (that is, it looked sort of like a plume) of fountain rose, fell upon itself, and slapped the pool in lazy rhythms.

THOMAS WOLFE, *Look Homeward Angel*

20 Adding weights in ten-pounds of barbells by increments, I slowly increased up to two hundred and fifty pounds of lifting my total bench-press weight.

21 He had one mistress. He was faithful to the mistress to the day of his death. It was Music.

DEEMS TAYLOR, "The Monster," *Of Men and Music*

22 You're going to repair a motorcycle. To do this a supply of gumption is necessary to be the first tool. It is the most important of the tools. Such a supply of gumption needs to be an adequate supply.

ROBERT M. PIRSIG, *Zen and the Art of Motorcycle Maintenance*

23 The garbage had been burned. And then the residue is dumped onto barges. From this then the residue is cooled. So then the barges are towed off by means of ships which are tugboats. The place where they take the barges is one of five landfill sites which are around the city.

KATIE KELLY, *Garbage: The History and Future of Garbage in America*

24 The Yankelovich poll is certainly not wrong. It tells us something. Eighty-two percent of Americans *think* of themselves as "middle class."

ROBERT HEILBRONER, "Middle-Class Myths, Middle-Class Realities," *Atlantic Monthly*, Sept. 1976

25 They were not only able to say something. They were close to dying. Many were able to predict the time of their death. The time was approximate.

ELISABETH KÜBLER-ROSS, "Facing Up to Death," *Today's Education*, Jan. 1972.

26 No doubt anyone would agree to the notion that there are in effect really just three parts to all interviews—the first of course being the

opening, and then there would come the second, being the substantive, and finally at the end would come the third and last, the closing.

PETERSON, GOLDHABER, PACE, *Communication Probes*

27 Futurism is also an attitude. It is a perspective toward change.

ALVIN TOFFLER, "What Futurists Can Do," *The Futurist*, Apr. 1976

28 Starting in 1965, a number of cable-tray fires in plants alerted the AEC to something. The cable-tray fires were serious. The plants were nuclear. To save space and money, the plant builders were squeezing the trays so close together. A fire in one could quickly spread to others.

JAMES NATHAN MILLER, "The Burning Question of Brown's Ferry," *Reader's Digest*, Apr. 1976

29 Once, I had been taken to one of our old marsh churches to see a thing that was a skeleton. The skeleton was in the ashes of a rich dress. The skeleton had been dug out of a vault. The vault was under the church pavement.

CHARLES DICKENS, *Great Expectations*

30 He was addressed by other slaves as Toby. It was the master's name for him. The African said angrily something. His name was Kin-tay.

ALEX HALEY, "My Furthest-Back Person—'The African' "

31 They were maddened. They were angry. They leaped and howled round the trunks. They cursed the dwarves in their horrible language. Their tongues hung out. Their eyes shone as red and fierce as flames.

J. R. R. TOLKIEN, *The Hobbitt*

32 He whirled back to Yossarian. He sneezed thunderously six times, before he could speak. He staggered sideways on rubbery legs in the intervals. He raised his elbows ineffectively to fend each seizure off.

JOSEPH HELLER, *Catch–22*

33 Writers often read aloud at this stage of the editing process. They mutter. They whisper to themselves. They call on the ear's experience with language.

DONALD M. MURRAY, "The Maker's Eye: Revising Your Own Manuscript," *The Writer*, Oct. 1973

34 I was so embarrassed on my first date which I was so shy and nervous that at first I could hardly at all articulate and then later I couldn't stop talking, so then I had this idea that I would just keep on asking questions so much that my date would have to do most of the talking all of the time, and so then I just kept on doing it and rambling on all the time with these questions, so what an interrogation!

35 There are two types of connotation. One is personal. The other is general.

RICHARD D. ALTICK, *Preface to Critical Reading*

BEYOND THE SENTENCE

Revising sentences is good practice—in each of the problems so far your goal was to produce a single sentence. However, few compositions are made of one sentence alone; furthermore, the revision of any sentence frequently depends on relations with sentences preceding or following. Effective writing depends on a series of sentences working together smoothly.

Sentence Chunks

The following exercises are composed of multisentence structures we have named *chunks*. They are groups of two or more sentences from a paragraph; that is, a chunk can be any group of coherent sentences lifted out of a paragraph. You can think of a chunk as a unit between the sentence and paragraph—longer than one sentence, but shorter than a whole paragraph. This is of course a theoretical distinction, because sometimes a paragraph might be a single sentence—see Chapter 6. But for the purposes of practice here, you can say that a chunk is any group of sentences less than a full paragraph.

Sentences can surprise you. Looked at in isolation, a single sentence may be uninteresting, even boring. Used with other sentences, that same sentence can come alive. It can gain much of its meaning and effect from the surrounding sentences. For example, a short sentence can have a strong impact if you place it either after or between longer sentences. A long sentence can attract and hold the reader's attention if you contrast it with a short sentence. Rhythm, variety, meaning, and structure all contribute to cohesive discourse, not merely within a single sentence, but within longer units of writing.

Look, for example, at the following sentence:

It happens in an instant.

If you were asked whether you find that sentence interesting or well written, you might reply that the sentence isn't especially interesting and you have no idea what *It* refers to. But if you were provided with a limited context for the sentence—if you were given the sentence immediately preceding "It happens in an instant"—and then asked to comment, your reaction would probably be very different:

Most people tend to think of going to sleep as a slow slippage into oblivion, but the onset of sleep is not gradual at all. It happens in an instant.

In this context, "It happens in an instant" is a very effective piece of writing because it plays off the first, longer sentence. It is short, sharp, and to the point in this context. The first sentence provides "going to sleep' and "the onset of sleep" as referents for "It" in the second sentence. The first sentence (25 words) sets up a sharp contrast with the second sentence (5 words). "It happens in an instant" gains most of its meaning and effect *from the other sentence*.

A third sentence locks into the unit:

Most people tend to think of going to sleep as a slow slippage into oblivion, but the onset of sleep is not gradual at all. It happens in an instant. One moment the individual is awake, the next moment not.

The last sentence clearly relates to the second sentence by emphasizing how fast "happens in an instant" is. You can find less obvious examples of the interplay between this sentence and the two that precede it. (Look at "moment" and "instant," for example.)

You may wonder why this set of sentences is not a paragraph. Indeed, if a short paragraph suited the writer's purpose in a specific composition, these three sentences might make an effective one. But, in this case, the writer uses the paragraph to say more about the onset of sleep. Notice how smoothly the chunk coheres with the rest of the paragraph:

A number of curious experiences occur at the onset of sleep. A person just about to go to sleep may experience an electric shock, a flash of light, or a crash of thunder—but the most common sensation is that of floating or falling, which is why "falling asleep" is a scientifically valid description. A nearly universal occurrence at the beginning of sleep (although not everyone recalls it) is a sudden uncoordinated jerk of the head, the limbs, or even the entire body. Most people tend to think of going to sleep as a slow slippage into oblivion, but the onset of sleep is not gradual at all. It happens in an instant. One moment the individual is awake, the next moment not.

PETER FARB, "The Levels of Sleep," *Humankind*

Working with chunks can help you to extend your writing proficiency beyond the sentence. As sentence-combing practice improves the maturity of your own sentences, practice with sentence chunks will translate into a noticeable improvement in longer stretches of your writing. Revising groups of concepts and strings of words into more than one sentence will give you useful practice in playing one sentence off another, as you would in a composition.

Revising Sentence Chunks

The groups of sentences you will be working with in this section have been taken from the paragraphs of experienced writers. When revised, these strings of ideas will form chunks—groups of two, three, or more sentences that go together in some way; they form a subset within a paragraph. Think of these strings of information as a hurriedly written first draft of a composition, an invitation to revise. For example:

There are no books. There are no newspapers. There are no magazines. There are no pictures on the wall. There is a television set. He watches the television set all day long. He drinks beer. He smokes cigarettes. I am sufficiently familiar with the literature. It is on schizophrenia. I realize something. This room is a statement. He is making a statement about himself.

There are any number of ways this information might be revised, depending on the writing situation (See Chapter 1).

THE ORIGINAL AUTHOR'S VERSION

There are no books, no newspapers, no magazines, no pictures on the wall. There is a television set, which he watches all day long while drinking beer and smoking cigarettes. I am sufficiently familiar with the literature on schizophrenia to realize that this room is a statement he is making about himself.

JOHN LEONARD, "An Only Child," *New York Times*, 27 July 1977

ANOTHER VERSION

There are no pictures on the walls. There is a television set, and he spends his whole day watching it, drinking beer and smoking cigarettes. There are no newspapers; no magazines; not even a book. I am familiar enough with the literature on schizophrenia to perceive that the room is a reflection of what he thinks of himself.

Practice

Revise these strings of information into more effective sentences. You are free to add or delete words and information, to revise in any way that seems effective to you. In some cases you may feel the information could be expressed in a single sentence; feel free to do so. However, the original authors of each of these chunks used more than a single sentence.

1 The dog backed up. It did not yield. A rumbling began to rise in his chest. The rumbling was low. The rumbling was steady. It was something out of a midnight. The midnight was long gone. There was nothing in that bone to taste. Shapes were moving in his mind. The shapes were ancient. They were determining his utterance.
LOREN EISELEY, *The Unexpected Universe*

2 Students complete a first draft. They consider something. The job of writing is done. Their teachers too often agree. Professional writers complete a first draft. They usually feel something. They are at the start of the writing process. A draft is completed. The job of writing can begin.
DONALD M. MURRAY, "The Maker's Eye: Revising Your Own Manuscripts," *The Writer*, Oct. 1973

3 I can think back over more than a hundred nights. I've slept a hundred nights in the truck. I sat in it. A lamp burned. I was bundled up in a parka. I was reading a book. It was always comfortable. It was a good place to wait out a storm. It was like sleeping inside a buffalo.

BARRY LOPEZ, "My Horse," *North American Review*

4 A commencement orator advises students. They are to enrich themselves culturally. Chances are something. He is more interested in money than he is in poetry. A university president says something. His institution turned out 1,432 B.A.'s last year. He tells us something. He thinks something. He is running General Motors. The style is the man.

DONALD HALL, "An Ethic of Clarity," *Modern Stylists*

5 Mental retardation occurs in some parts of your city. It occurs at a rate. The rate is five times higher than it is in the remainder of your city. Twenty-five percent of some prison populations are mentally retarded. Mental retardation does not just happen. It is caused.

RAMSEY CLARK, *Crime in America*

6 It is on Ellis Island. They pile into the hall. The hall is massive. It occupies the entire width of the building. They break into dozens of lines. The lines are divided by railings. The railings are metal. There they file past the first doctor.

IRVING HOWE, *World of Our Fathers*

7 Once I entered a mansion. I blew the safe. I removed six thousand dollars. A couple slept in the same room. The husband woke up. The dynamite went off. I assured him something. The entire proceeds would go to the Boys' Clubs of America. He went back to sleep. Cleverly I left behind some fingerprints of Franklin D. Roosevelt. He was President then.

WOODY ALLEN, "Confessions of a Burglar," *The New Yorker*, 18 Oct. 1976

8 Velva has no organized charity. A farmer falls ill. His neighbors get in his crop. A townsman has a catastrophe. The catastrophe is financial. His personal friends raise a fund. It is to help him out. Bill's wife, Ethel, lay dying. She lay so long in the Minot hospital. Nurses were not available. Helen and others took their turns. They drove up there just to sit with her. She would know in her gathering dark something. Friends were at hand.

ERIC SEVAREID, "Velva, North Dakota," *This Is Eric Sevareid*

9 Many recounted their own experiences. The experiences were bitter. They were at the hands of funeral directors. Hundreds asked for advice on something. It was to establish a consumer organization in communities. None exists in the communities. Others sought information about pre-need plans. The membership of the funeral societies skyrocketed.

JESSICA MITFORD, *The American Way of Death*

10 He [Richard Wagner] had the emotional stability of a six-year-old child. He felt out of sorts. He would rave. He would stamp. He would sink into gloom. The gloom was suicidal. He would talk darkly of going to the East. It was to end his days as a Buddhist monk. It was ten min-

utes later. Something pleased him. He would rush out of doors. He would run around the garden. IIe would jump up and down on the sofa. He would stand on his head.

DEEMS TAYLOR, "The Monster," *Of Men and Music*

Sentence evaluation practice

In each of the following pairs, one sentence is better than the other in one or more aspects of sentence effectiveness. Which is the better sentence in clarity, economy, emphasis, or variety? Why?

1[1] A My wife was overwhelmed by the number of things she had to do that seemed to have nothing to do with teaching when she first taught.
  B When my wife first taught, she was overwhelmed by the number of things she had to do that seemed to have nothing to do with teaching.

2[2] A I believe the President, who is elected every four years, has an obligation to lay before the American people and its Congress the basic premises of his policy and to report fully on the issues, developments, and prospects confronting the nation.
  B I believe the President has an obligation to lay before the American people and its Congress the basic premises of his policy and to report fully on the issues, developments, and prospects confronting the nation.

3[3] A ORU exists to serve the whole body of Christ, worldwide.
  B To serve the whole body of Christ, worldwide, exists ORU.

4[4] A The boys were a more rowdy lot, and no teacher in her right mind would have turned her class over to them.
  B They were boys who were such a rowdy lot that no teacher who was in her right mind would have turned her class over to them.

5[5] A Leroy was the best athlete, the best whistler, the best horse-shoe player, the best marble shooter, the best mumblety-pegger, and the best shoplifter in our neighborhood.
  B Leroy was the best athlete, whistler, horse-shoe player, marble shooter, mumblety-pegger, and shoplifter in our neighborhood.

6[6] A The medulla is laid just inside the skull, just above the large hole at the bottom of it.
  B The medulla lies just inside the skull, just above the large hole at the bottom of it.

7[7] A Edison developed a 100-watt carbon-filament lamp having an efficiency of 1.61 p. w. and a life of 600 hours.
  B A 100-watt carbon-filament lamp having an efficiency of 1.61 p. w. and a life of 600 hours was developed by Edison.

8[8] A Presidents Roosevelt and Johnson were good examples of articulate speech and using plain language to get their ideas across to the American public.

B Presidents Roosevelt and Johnson were articulate speakers who used plain language to get their ideas across to the American public.

9[9] *A* A curious choice for a starring role in Disney's bright, upbeat world Mickey Mouse may have seemed at first glance.

B At first glance, Mickey Mouse may have seemed a curious choice for a starring role in Disney's bright, upbeat world.

10[10] *A* Teachers accept the concept of the whole child; this concept includes the child's immaturities, his feelings of inadequacy, his anger, his joy and his exuberance, which must be dealt with.

B Teachers accept the concept of the whole child; but they are not ready to deal with the child's social immaturities, his feelings of inadequacy, his anger, his joy and his exuberance.

11[11] *A* When Father Cassidy drew back the shutter of the confessional, he surprised the appearance of the girl at the other side of the grille.

B When Father Cassidy drew back the shutter of the confessional, he was surprised at the appearance of the girl on the other side of the grille.

12[12] *A* Before the rich man there was a fish casserole baked in a cream sauce and garnished with parsley.

B There was a casserole in front of the man who was rich; it was a fish casserole, baked in a sauce of cream, and garnished with parsley.

13[13] *A* A star crept out from among the overhanging grasses as the time passed.

B As the time passed, a star crept out from among the overhanging grasses.

14[14] *A* He had come to avoid a scandal, make plain the danger, and offer the truth, and others thought he had come to make a scandal, raise a danger, and oppose a truth.

B He had come not to make a scandal but to avoid it; not to raise a danger but to make one plain; not to oppose a truth but to offer it.

15[15] *A* Sex can be an exaggeration to a point where it becomes dull.

B Sex can be exaggerated to a point where it becomes dull.

16[16] *A* You should report any lost keys at once to the head resident.

B Any lost keys should be reported by you at once to the head resident.

17[17] *A* Of the four, Peanuts, who was the quiet one, was living in a land of silence.

B Of the four, Peanuts was the quiet one, living in a land of silence.

18[18] *A* All week long I lived for the blessed sound which was the dismissal gong at three o'clock on Friday afternoons.

   B All week long I lived for the blessed sound of the dismissal gong at three o'clock on Friday afternoons.

19[19] **A** Denied political freedom and economic capability, a man can accomplish little in his home or his community.

   B A man can accomplish little in his home or his community denied political freedom and economic capability.

20[20] **A** She demanded from those who surrounded her a rigid precision in details and being preternaturally quick in detecting the slightest deviation from the rules she laid down.

   B She demanded from those who surrounded her a rigid precision in details, and she was preternaturally quick in detecting the slightest deviation from the rules which she laid down.

21[21] **A** Through more than the traditionally enumerated five senses is the way man knows his world.

   B Man knows his world through more senses than the five that are traditionally enumerated.

22[22] **A** A dog is an animal of much greater intelligence than a chick, and in Pavlov's laboratory, dogs require long series of repeated experiences for learning to relate certain perceptual signs to the imminence of food.

   B A dog is an animal of much greater intelligence than a chick, and yet in Pavlov's laboratory, dogs require long series of repeated experiences for learning to relate certain perceptual signals to the imminence of food.

23[23] **A** With her marriage, Tehani seemed to take on a new dignity and seriousness, though in the privacy of our home, which had a thatched roof, she showed at times that she was still the same wild tomboy who had beaten me at swimming at Matavai.

   B With her marriage, Tehani seemed to take on a new dignity and seriousness, though in the privacy of our home she showed me at times that she was still the same wild tomboy who had beaten me at swimming in Matavai.

24[24] **A** Let us never negotiate out of fear, but let us never fear to negotiate.

   B Fear should never be the motivation behind our negotiations and so we should always be brave enough to negotiate.

25[25] **A** The course of the *Mayflower* was now in mid-Atlantic and making steady headway.

   B The *Mayflower* was now in mid-Atlantic and making steady headway.

[1] HERBERT R. KOHL, *The Open Classroom*

[2] RICHARD NIXON, *U. S. Foreign Policy for the 1970's, Building for Peace*

[3] ORAL ROBERTS, *ORU Catalogue, 1973–1974*

[4] JAMES MICHENER, *Hawaii*

[5] ED LUDWIG AND JAMES SONTIBANE, *The Chicanos*

[6] GUSTAV ECKSTEIN, *The Body Has a Head*

[7] "Lighting," *Encyclopaedia Britannica*

[8] GEORGE A. HOUGH, *News Writing*

[9] ANTHONY LUCAS, "The Alternative Life-Style of Playboys and Playmates," *New York Times Magazine*, 11 June 1972

[10] DON DINKMEYER, *Understanding Self and Others*

[11] FRANK O'CONNOR, "News for the Church"

[12] CARSON MCCULLERS, "The Jockey"

[13] RICHARD ADAMS, *Watership Down*

[14] GIORGIO DE SANTILLANA, *The Crime of Galileo*

[15] EDWARD FORD, *Why Marriage?*

[16] *CMU Residence Hall Handbook, 1975*

[17] THOMAS THOMPSON, *Richie*

[18] ALFRED KAZIN, *A Walker in the City*

[19] JOSEPH R. BRANDT, *Why Black Power?*

[20] LYTTON STRACHEY, *Queen Victoria*

[21] ROBERT WHITMAN, *Understanding the Behavior of Organisms*

[22] ARTHUR KOESTLER, *The Act of Creation*

[23] CHARLES NORDHOFF AND JAMES NORMAN HALL, *Mutiny on the Bounty*

[24] JOHN F. KENNEDY, Inaugural Address, 20 Jan. 1961

[25] GEORGE F. WILLISON, *Saints and Strangers*

CHAPTER EIGHT

Effective Diction

The difference between the almost right word

and the right word,

is really a large matter—

'tis the difference between the lightning bug—

and the lightning.

MARK TWAIN, *The Art of Authorship*

No two words in English have exactly the same meaning, nor do they carry exactly the same attitudes or values. For the writer this means choosing exactly the right word for any situation; and choosing words means considering your audience, knowing the effect you want to make, understanding the words you might use. In short, word choice is directly related to your purpose. In this chapter, you will learn to consider all the shades of meaning and subtleties of context our language has to offer.

CONNOTATION AND DENOTATION

Words do not automatically "mean" what the dictionary says. There are two kinds of meaning: connotation and denotation. When people ask for the "definition" of a word, they are usually asking for the denotation of the word, its generally accepted meaning. The dictionary maker must do what you and I would do upon encountering a new word—see how people use it and then *deduce* its meaning. Thus the denotation of a word becomes the general definition of the word. The denotation of sear, for example, is "to cause to wither or dry," or in some cases "to burn or scorch," as when we sear meat to trap the juices inside. It is this general definition that we all more or less agree to when we say that the word *sear* denotes (means) to dry, parch, or burn.

However, words change over the course of time. They pick up "extra" meanings or they acquire particular associations. Very often words acquire emotional or attitudinal labels (some words are "bad" and some are "good"). These additional associations, connotations, can cause problems for writers. For example, we can accept "sear the meat," "sear the cloth with the iron," "the sun will sear the flowers," and even "her kisses will sear his lips!" But most native speakers of English will not accept "sear the wood in the fireplace," "sear the garbage," nor "fell and seared my knee," though in every case the meaning "to burn" is intended. Historically, the word has come to be used in some contexts but not in others, so we say that the word *denotes* burning and scorching perhaps, but it *connotes* the effect of heat on moisture. (When we speak of a "searing pain," we have in mind the kind of pain caused by touching a hot stove: scorched flesh.)

Thus, knowing the denotation of a word is usually not enough; you need to be aware of its connotations too in order to avoid the kind of language error involved in an old story about the first translating computer, which when translating the English "Out of sight, out of mind" into Chinese, came up with "Absent idiot." When revising for effective diction, a good place to being is in your dictionary.

USING THE DICTIONARY

In order to make effective word choices, you need a thorough understanding of at least one good dictionary. Since dictionaries vary considerably, it may be worth your while to become familiar with several. A little investigation will reveal that the dictionary can provide an astonishing amount of information if you know how to use it. For example, *Webster's New Collegiate Dictionary*, in addition to the definitions of words, contains a detailed explanatory chart to show what all the parts of the definitions mean; additional notes that explain each element of the entries (pronunciation, spelling, usage, and so on); a brief essay on the English language and its history by W. Nelson Francis; a list of abbreviations and pronunciation symbols used in the dictionary; a long list of famous and important people; an equally long list of geographical names; an exhaustive list of the names and addresses of colleges and universities in English-speaking North America; a list of signs and symbols; and even a handbook of style. Thus the writer can have a small encyclopedia of useful information in a good dictionary

Reading the Entries

The entry for *choreography* shows a number of features of the dictionary:

cho·re·og·ra·phy \\ˌkȯr-ē-ˈäg-rə-fē, ˌkȯr-\\ *n. pl* **-phies** [F *chorégra-phie*, fr. Gk *choreia* + F *-graphie* -graphy] **1** : the art of symboli-cally representing dancing **2** : stage dancing as distinguished from social or ballroom dancing **3 a** : the composition and arrangement of dances esp. for ballet **b** : a composition created by this art — **cho·reo·graph·ic** \\ˌkȯr-ē-ə-ˈgraf-ik, ˌkȯr-\\ *adj* — **cho·reo·graph·i·cal·ly** \\-i-k(ə-)lē\\ *adv*

Note that the word is given with dots between the syllables (for the purpose of word division). It is followed by a guide to pronunciation with a secondary accent on the first syllable and a primary accent on the third. The vowel chart at the bottom of the dictionary page (not shown here) explains the pronunciations indicated by the umlaut (ä) and the schwa (ə). Note that the first syllable is pronounced with ei-ther a long *o* (kōr) or an *aw* sound (kȯr). In this dictionary, variant pronunciations are equally valid unless specifically marked other-wise. Note that the syllabication, marked with dots, does not exactly correspond to the divisions of pronunciation, marked with hyphens (see Word Division in Chapter 10).

Following the pronunciation guide is the part of speech *n* (noun) and the spelling of the plural. In this dictionary, plural forms are not usually given unless the plural requires some change in the root word: in *choreography*, *y* changes to *i*, as **-phies** shows.

The etymology of the word (history of its development) is given in reverse order. The immediate ancestor of *choreography* is the French word *chorégraphie*, which is itself formed from the Greek word *choreia* (dance) and the French *-graphie* (write). The word has its origin, then, in the two concepts, dancing and writing.

The dictionary shows three meanings for this word. They are giv-en in order of development; that is, the oldest meaning is given first. And you can see from this that *choreography* originally re-ferred to pictures or diagrams of dances. The third meaning has two submeanings, marked *a* and *b*, relating to either the art of compos-ing or the composition of a dance.

Last, the dictionary gives an adjective and an adverb form for this word, and the pronunciations of each of them.

Other entries show various other kinds of information about words. For example:

civ·il \'siv-əl\ *adj* [ME, fr. MF, fr. L *civilis*, fr. *civis*] **1 a** : of or relating to citizens ⟨~ liberties⟩ **b** : of or relating to the state or its citizenry **2 a** : CIVILIZED ⟨~ society⟩ **b** : adequate in courtesy and politeness : MANNERLY **3 a** : of, relating to, or based on civil law **b** : relating to private rights and to remedies sought by action or suit distinct from criminal proceedings **c** : established by law **4** *of time* : based on the mean sun and legally recognized for use in ordinary affairs **5** : of, relating to, or involving the general public, their activities, needs, or ways, or civic affairs as distinguished from special (as military or religious) affairs
syn CIVIL, POLITE, COURTEOUS, GALLANT, CHIVALROUS *shared meaning element* : observant of the forms required by good breeding. CIVIL is feeble in force, often suggesting little more than avoidance of overt rudeness. POLITE is more positive and commonly implies polish of manners and address more than warmth and cordiality ⟨the cultured, precise tone, *polite* but faintly superior —William Styron⟩ COURTEOUS implies an actively considerate and sometimes rather stately politeness ⟨listened with *courteous* attention⟩ *Gallant* and *chivalrous* imply courteous attentiveness esp. to women but GALLANT is likely to suggest dashing behavior and ornate expression ⟨ever ready with *gallant* remarks of admiration⟩ while CHIVALROUS tends to suggest high-minded and disinterested attentions ⟨felt at once *chivalrous* and paternal to the lost girl⟩ **ant** uncivil, rude

Note the context aids for this word ⟨~liberties⟩ and ⟨~society⟩. Note too the presentation and discussion of synonyms. Here all the synonyms more or less "denote" the shared meaning element: "observant of the forms required by good breeding." But notice too the connotative explanations provided for each of them. The context aid ⟨ the cultured, precise tone, *polite* but faintly superior—William Styron ⟩ indicates a quote from the author Styron. Note the antonyms at the end of the entry.

If you have a good college dictionary and understand how to use it, you can improve the quality of your diction. This does not mean finding "fancier" words but rather the words best suited to what you are trying to say. As a general rule, it is a mistake to ransack the dictionary for new words; a writer needs to be thoroughly familiar with a word before using it in a composition.

USING WORDS

Most readers agree that clear, concise, and accurate language is the preferred style for formal or semiformal writing, but even these simple guidelines must be interpreted in the light of an author's purpose. A letter to the President of the United States should not be written in street slang. On the other hand, there may be times when street slang is the most effective language to use. The best language is whatever is most appropriate and effective for an author's purpose.

In the following sections, we discuss some stylistic problems good writers avoid and some options you may wish to incorporate into your writing. By comparing sentences revised for effective diction with less effective ones, you will begin to develop a sense of the kinds of choices skilled writers make.

ABSTRACTIONS

Abstract means removed from physical reality; it refers to qualities and ideas. Abstractions are necessary and worthwhile aspects of language; they carry our intellectual concepts. Few writers can do without them entirely; but too many abstractions, without tying ideas to concrete reality now and then, may bore and frustrate your readers. Abstractions can also contribute to blurring reality, as for example when a salesperson claims to want to discuss your "insurance needs" but actually wants to sell you a policy.

ABSTRACT SENTENCE

That a governmental agency should exercise regulatory influence over private transportation is analogous to the same extension of power over private possession of weaponry.

REVISED FOR CONCRETE DICTION

People are licensed to drive cars, and should be licensed to possess firearms.
Towne Courier, 24 Sept. 1975

ABSTRACT SENTENCE

There need be no more effective demonstration of financial competency than successful self-maintenance on government benefits and compensation.

REVISED FOR CONCRETE DICTION

Anyone who can live on welfare should be courted by Wall Street.
JOANNA CLARK, "Motherhood," in Judith Carnoy and Marc Weiss, *A House Divided*

CLICHÉ

A cliché is a worn-out word or phrase, some expression so familiar that it no longer has any force: "She's as pretty as a picture, as smart as a whip, as cute as a button," and so on. These tired old expressions are poor substitutes for more forceful, direct ways of saying things.

CLICHÉ

It's not whether you win or lose, it's how you play the game that matters.

REVISED FOR EFFECTIVE DICTION

It's tiresome as hell to lose, but I still enjoy the game.
"Limping for Life," *Time* 11 Nov. 1975

CLICHÉ

Her answer was short but hit the nail on the head.

REVISED FOR EFFECTIVE DICTION

Her answer was short but accurate.
LEN BRAVELL

CONFUSING NEGATIVES

Avoid the double negative ("I don't have none.") Any time a sentence contains more than one negative, there is likely to be confusion: "It is by no means not shameful not to stand up to a bully!" "They didn't realize that they were not the ones who wouldn't be going!" For clarity, these should be revised into positive statements, if possible.

CONFUSING NEGATIVES
There is no reason not to suppose that we cannot directly observe what happened in the past.

REVISED FOR CLARITY
We cannot directly observe what happened in the past.
THOMAS C. PATTERSON, *America's Past: A New World Archeology*

CONFUSING NEGATIVES
Initially, I never fail to assume that any physician I go to will not refrain from teaching me any less about my health than my garage mechanic teaches me about my car.

REVISED FOR CLARITY
Initially, I assume that any physician I go to will teach me as much about my health as my garage mechanic teaches me about my car.
MANUEL J. SMITH, *When I Say No, I Feel Guilty*

EFFECTIVE MODIFIERS

Not every sentence requires modifiers, but when you do use modifiers, you will gain clarity and accuracy by choosing carefully. It is not just more "interesting," it is more accurate to use specific modifiers in your descriptions.

IMPRECISE
The fish turned in an even movement and followed the sound that was growing dim.

REVISED WITH SPECIFIC MODIFIERS
The fish turned, banking as smoothly as an airplane, and followed the receding sound.
PETER BENCHLEY, *Jaws*

IMPRECISE
A watchman adopted a small parti-colored kitten he had found lying tired and hungry on a vegetable bag.

REVISED WITH SPECIFIC MODIFIERS
A night watchman adopted a tiny orange-and-white kitten he had found lying exhausted and half starved on an onion bag.
JEAN BURDEN, *Woman's Day*, 1975

319

EFFECTIVE NOUNS

Nouns can powerfully influence your writing. Searching for the right word, the one that is most specific for your meaning, is one mark of a skilled writer. Given the context of why you are writing, who you are writing to, and what you are writing about, any word ought to be selected because it is the clearest, most concise, most accurate word. Students sometimes hunt through dictionaries to come up with a *new* word for a familiar concept, but this can be dangerous if the word has subtle connotations.

IMPRECISE

It was like a stove outside, with the light splintering into shiny places on the ground and water.

REVISED WITH SPECIFIC NOUNS

It was like a furnace outside, with the sunlight splintering into flakes of fire on the sand and sea.

ALBERT CAMUS, *The Stranger*

IMPRECISE

To emphasize his notion, Dr. Straith even included a picture of the interior of his vehicle, showing the stuff that he had installed.

REVISED WITH SPECIFIC NOUNS

To emphasize his point, Dr. Straith even included a photograph of his own automobile, showing the padding he had installed.

ROBERT CIRINO, *Don't Blame the People*

IMPRECISE

The Russians were on the verge of Hungary.

REVISED WITH SPECIFIC NOUNS

The Russians were on the edge of Hungary.

WINSTON CHURCHILL, *Triumph and Tragedy*

EFFECTIVE VERBS

While some textbooks advise beginning writers to select "colorful" or "vivid" verbs, keep in mind that *accuracy* is the best guideline. "She passed out" may be more vivid than "she fainted," but the difference between the verbs in those phrases isn't just a matter of degree. The danger of overstatement often accompanies efforts to be colorful. Thus a paper on hunting may speak of "blasting to bits" when, in fact, the less vivid "shooting" may be more accurate.

IMPRECISE

Inside the plane, the handful of boys who were able took a shot at getting up the seats which held so many of the wounded.

REVISED WITH SPECIFIC VERBS

Inside the plane, the handful of boys who were able tried to prize away the seats which trapped so many of the wounded.

PIERS PAUL READ, *Alive*

IMPRECISE

Horses moved along, lifting up dust.

REVISED WITH SPECIFIC VERBS

Horses clopped along, shuffling up dust.

RAY BRADBURY, *The Martian Chronicles*

IMPRECISE

William now gave it to be known that his archers should make their arrows go high into the air, so that the arrows would be right behind the shield wall, and one of these went into Harold's right eye and gave him a mortal wound.

REVISED WITH SPECIFIC VERBS

William now directed his archers to shoot high into the air, so that the arrows would fall behind the shield wall, and one of these pierced Harold in the right eye, inflicting a mortal wound.

WINSTON CHURCHILL, *A History of the English Speaking Peoples: The Birth of Britain*

Note The forms of *to be* (*am, is, are, was, were, be, being, been*) are often the weakest verbs of all.

EMOTIONAL LANGUAGE

Emotional language means that instead of calm and objective reporting, the reader finds name calling, exaggeration, and unfair and unreasonable language abuse: "loaded language." Such emotionalism may be intentional in humorous writing, but for most nonfiction writing more objective language is preferred.

EMOTIONAL LANGUAGE

The market place will tend to pay women less than men as long as wives kowtow to their lord-and-masters' jobs.

REVISED WITH MORE OBJECTIVE DICTION

The market place will tend to pay women less than men as long as wives give priority to their husbands' jobs.

GEORGE E. GILDER, *Sexual Suicide*

EMOTIONAL LANGUAGE

This sort of financial flim-flammery clearly showed that evil and vicious minds were at work on this project in order to tie the legislature in red tape and bamboozle the public.

REVISED WITH MORE OBJECTIVE LANGUAGE

This sort of financial legerdemain clearly showed that tricky minds were at work on this project in order to avoid legislative consideration of it at all, and public review and understanding.

FERDINAND LUNDBERG, *The Rockefeller Syndrome*

EUPHEMISM

Using pleasant words, or inoffensive ones, to cover hard truths is generally considered evasive writing. There are legitimate uses for euphemisms (when trying to spare someone's feelings perhaps), but in general, authors avoid them. Common euphemisms, such as "pass on" for "die," are easy to spot because they have obvious plain English equivalents.

EUPHEMISM
You see, sir, we spent those two hours telling ribald stories.

REVISED WITH PLAIN ENGLISH
You see, sir, we spent those two hours telling dirty jokes.

MURRAY LEINSTER, "First Contact," *Science Fiction Hall of Fame*

EUPHEMISM
Many men decided that laws forbidding introduction of African labor were unjust to newly settled areas; a few, believing the laws were lacking in the force of law, determined to test them.

REVISED WITH PLAIN ENGLISH
Many men decided that laws forbidding introduction of African slaves were unjust to newly settled areas; a few, believing the laws unconstitutional or not legally enforceable, determined to violate them.

TOM HENDERSON WELL, *The Slave Ship Wanderer*

FIGURES OF SPEECH

A figure of speech should be fresh, clear, and should make an image for the reader. The purpose of the figure of speech is to create a picture, to make an idea clear and forceful through comparison. An effective figure pleases the reader, brings the "well said" reaction. Writers must judge whether their images will work for the reader. "She's as graceful as a squirrel," for example, would probably fail. The squirrel may be graceful to some, but to most people it is a symbol of quickness; using it to evoke gracefulness may not work very well. Does the following figure work for you? "The sun came up in the morning like a huge grapefruit."

Metaphor

A metaphor makes an implied comparison, as in this description of tuna:

Powerful torpedoes of shining silver and steel, with perfect proportions and streamlined shape, they had only to move one or two fins slightly to set their 150 to 200 pounds gliding about in the water with consummate grace.
THOR HEYERDAHL, *Kon-Tiki*

Simile

An expressed comparison, a simile uses the words "like" or "as."

The train was curving the mountain, the engine loping like a great black hound, parallel with its last careening cars, panting forth its pale white vapor as it hurled us ever higher.
RALPH ELLISON, *The Invisible Man*

Personification

In this form of comparison, some object or animal is given human qualities.

An occasional timid horn squeaked off in the distance.
JACQUELINE SUSANN, *Once Is Not Enough*

Mixed Metaphors

These metaphoric comparisons are illogical or inconsistent; the writer mixes more than one idea into an image.

The lightning stabbed at the ground with long tentacles of light.
JOHN TUTTLE

Dead Metaphors

These metaphors have become part of the language and are no longer considered figures of speech. Too many of them make your writing trite. They can sometimes create accidental humor.

You have to wear heavy shoes on the foot of the mountain.
Mr. Blaine dropped his false teeth into the mouth of the river.

MIXED METAPHOR
Then the lids opened, revealing pale pools of blue vagueness that finally cleared into horizons that hung over the vet, who looked down unsmilingly.

REVISED FOR CONSISTENT IMAGE
Then the lids opened, revealing pale pools of blue vagueness that finally solidified into points that froze upon the vet, who looked down unsmilingly.
RALPH ELLISON, *The Invisible Man*

LITERAL LANGUAGE

She would analyze his character for any evidence of weakness and finding any, would exploit them without regard for his discomfort.

REVISED WITH METAPHOR

She would look for dark spots in his character and drill away at them as relentlessly as a dentist at a cavity.

MARY McCARTHY, *Cruel and Barbarous Treatment*

INEFFECTIVE FIGURE

She wore her hair in two braids wound tight around her head like pale silk strings.

REVISED FOR MORE EFFECTIVE IMAGE

She wore her hair in two braids wound tight around her head like pale silk ropes.

PAUL DARCY BOLES, "The House Guest," *Seventeen*, Oct. 1975

INEFFECTIVE FIGURE

The rising moon was beginning to light up the eastern sky with a pale, ermine glow.

REVISED FOR MORE EFFECTIVE IMAGE

The rising moon was beginning to light up the eastern sky with a pale, milky glow.

ARTHUR C. CLARKE, *Childhood's End*

JARGON

Jargon covers all specialized vocabulary and terminology, but it often means unnecessarily technical language. Most readers would call the following *necessary* jargon; it is very difficult to express this idea in simpler words.

NECESSARY TECHNICAL LANGUAGE

The photons which strike a crystal on the stage of a light microscope do not alter the crystal's position.

A. TRUMAN SCHWARTZ, *Chemistry: Imagination and Implication*

UNNECESSARY JARGON

By two months of age, the child at the developmental median will smile at his maternal parent's face.

REVISED FOR PLAIN ENGLISH

By two months of age, the average child will smile at the sight of his mother's face.

ATKINSON AND HILGARD, *Introduction to Psychology*

UNNECESSARY JARGON

The development of my educational innovation was founded on the simple expedient of inverting the prevailing curricular design and pedagogy of the public schools and teachers.

REVISED FOR PLAIN ENGLISH

I followed a simple plan. I studied what the public schools and teachers do and did the opposite.

LESTER VELIE, "Give Us This Day Our ABC's," *Reader's Digest*, Aug. 1975

NEOLOGISMS

Inventing new words is one of the privileges of writers, but there is no point to creating new words when old ones will serve as well. In general, readers expect a new word to achieve something that old words do not. In this example—"The team's attackage strength was low"—*attackage* isn't an improvement over existing words such as *attack* or *offensive*.

NEOLOGISM

The great smooth trunks stood motionless in their green shade, the branches spreading flat, one above the other in crisp, light-besquinched tiers.

REVISED FOR PLAIN ENGLISH

The great smooth trunks stood motionless in their green shade, the branches spreading flat, one above the other in crisp, light-dappled tiers.

RICHARD ADAMS, *Watership Down*

NEOLOGISM

She held out her hands to him and he lipped her.

REVISED FOR PLAIN ENGLISH

She held out her hands to him and he kissed her.

PAT FRANK, *Alas Babylon*

NEOLOGISM

Although skier injuries have been on the decline in recent years, one statistic hasn't changed: the incidence of death on the hill heart-failurewise.

REVISED FOR PLAIN ENGLISH

Although skier injuries have been on the decline in recent years, one statistic hasn't changed: the incidence of heart failure on the hill.

Ski, Sept. 1975

OVERSTATEMENT

Using unnecessary intensifiers, exaggerating, or overdramatizing with language strikes most readers as amateurish. For example: "The *worst* day of my life was the day Buffy Allen discovered I had been using her tennis shoes! I was just *devastated* when she found out!" This writer is trying to make a relatively insignificant event sound more important than it could possibly be.

SOME INTENSIFERS TO USE WITH RESTRAINT

absolutely, basically, certainly, completely, definitely, incredibly, intensely, passionately, perfectly, positively, quite, really, simply, totally, unbearably, very

SOME DRAMATIC MODIFIERS TO USE WITH CAUTION

awful, fabulous, fantastic, gigantic, horrible, horrid, incredible, sensational, stupendous, terrible, terrific, unbearable, unbelievable

OVERSTATEMENT

The darling little plane zoomed back and forth over the ever so neatly square fields, all of them terribly flooded—it had actually been raining here quite recently.

REVISED FOR SIMPLICITY

The small plane flew over square fields, all of them flooded—it had been raining here recently.
SVETLANA ALLILUYEVA, *Only One Year*

OVERSTATEMENT

When we look at the stars, we definitely see them arranged in the form of perfect geometrical figures—lines, semicircles, triangles, squares.

REVISED FOR SIMPLICITY

When we look at the stars, we see them arranged in the form of geometrical figures—lines, semicircles, triangles, squares.
ROBERT S. RICHARDSON, *The Fascinating World of Astronomy*

SWITCHING TENSE

You may write in any tense that fits your purpose; the rule is to be consistent. Write in the present tense or in the past, but not both. Present tense is very difficult to manage (you must somehow account for the fact that words appear on the page while, for example, "I am running for my life"). For formal and semiformal writing, the past tense is usually easiest to use as well as most logical.

TENSE SWITCH

He lived then in a home which, though cheap and unfashionable, possesses its picturesque distinction.

REVISED FOR CONSISTENT TENSE

He lived then in a home, which, though cheap and unfashionable, possessed its picturesque distinction.
REBECCA WEST, *The New Meaning of Treason*

TENSE SWITCH

She'd attached herself to Fred the moment he arrives at the party and sees to it that his glass is filled with punch whenever it is even a quarter empty.

REVISED FOR CONSISTENT TENSE

She'd attached herself to Fred the moment he arrived at the party and saw to it that his glass was filled with punch whenever it was even a quarter empty.
JOHI MAURA AND JACKIE SUTHERLAND, *If It Moves, Kiss It*

SWITCHING VOICE

Switching from Personal to Impersonal

The rule is to be consistent. Switching from personal *I* to impersonal *one*, for no apparent reason, sounds as though the writer has forgotten who he/she is.

VOICE SWITCH

When I came back, she had the pillow off her head all right—one could have predicted it—but she still wouldn't look at me, even though she was laying on her back.

REVISED FOR CONSISTENT VOICE

When I came back, she had the pillow off her head all right—I knew she would—but she wouldn't look at me, even though she was laying on her back.
J. D. SALINGER, *The Catcher in the Rye*

VOICE SWITCH

Later that evening, one walked through a hotelroom door and there they were—all lazing around drinking up the evening's profits, laughing and jiving with the assembled multitudes and being generally happy. . . .

REVISED FOR CONSISTENT VOICE

Later that evening, I walked through a hotelroom door and there they were—all lazing around drinking up the evening's profits, laughing and jiving with the assembled multitudes and being generally happy. . . .
BEN EDWARDS, "Bastard Children of Gordon Sinclair," *Creem*, Apr. 1974

The same fault sounds equally inconsistent the other way around—switching from impersonal *one* to personal *I;* some readers feel *one* is too impersonal and vague to be used at all. To avoid the choice between *I* and *one*, writers sometimes substitute the editorial *we* or the all-purpose *you:*

The changes, we may notice, had to be made by the state.
C. B. MACPHERSON, *The Real World of Democracy*

If your credit card is only good for charging things it's only half a card.
Advertisement, *Time*, Sept. 1975

Other voices include the *invisible* writer: "The experiment was conducted under difficult conditions" (by a phantom? See Passive

Sentence in Chapter 7); and the *masked writer:* "This researcher believes the evidence will show . . ." "This reporter was present when . . ." "The present writer is of the opinion . . ."

Each of these voices has its uses as long as the writer is consistent in presenting that voice. What voice you use depends on what, to whom, and why you are writing. The question of voice is closely related to the degree of formality of your writing.

Switching from Formal to Informal

In the following pairs, consider the effect of the switch from formal to informal or from informal to formal:

VOICE SWITCH

The prospect of being left alone with the young man seemed all of a sudden like a bummer.

REVISED FOR CONSISTENT VOICE

The prospect of being left alone with the young man seemed suddenly unendurable.

MARY McCARTHY, *Cruel and Barbarous Treatment*

VOICE SWITCH

I pictured a noisy all-night blast . . . a lot of drinking and inordinate amounts of inebriated discourse.

REVISED FOR CONSISTENT VOICE

I pictured a noisy all-night blast . . . a lot of drinking and tons of drunken conversation.

ROBERT H. RIMMER, *The Harrad Experiment*

Choosing a Stance

Stance refers to the author's point of view, a complex of attitudes toward self, subject, and audience (see Chapter 1). The author may be serious, humorous, sarcastic; personal or impersonal; formal or informal. The range of stances in English is very broad, covering everything from the hip, cool, half-secret lingo of the streets to the difficult, technical jargon of scholarly writing. For most writers, the best stance is somewhere in the middle between very personal and very impersonal, very formal and very informal. Whatever stance you choose, your reader will expect you to stick with it. Switching back and forth is a fault except when done for humor or irony.

Why might a writer choose one stance over another? You will be able to answer that question for yourself if you can determine what each of the following writers achieves with stance:

A WRITER CHOOSING THE MOST FORMAL ENGLISH

Russian physiologists, including Lebeden, have emphasized an interac-

tive relationship with visceral pathology and cortical centers.

JAMES C. COLMAN, *Abnormal Psychology and Modern Life*

A WRITER CHOOSING INFORMAL ENGLISH

The boomerang is a neat weapon for streetfighting and is as easy to master as a Frisbee.

ABBIE HOFFMAN, *Steal This Book*

A WRITER CHOOSING A MIDDLE LEVEL, ON THE FORMAL SIDE

British colonial rule varied greatly from colony to colony, partly depending on the interest of Europeans in settlement.

R. HARPER AND T. SCHMUDDE, *Between Two Worlds*

A WRITER CHOOSING A MIDDLE LEVEL, ON THE INFORMAL SIDE

Quite frankly, we don't know what is happening in the so-called Bermuda Triangle.

ADI-KENT THOMAS JEFFREY, *The Bermuda Triangle*

A WRITER DELIBERATELY MIXING DICTION

If the other parts of the books aren't so great, here's where the real value lies—every picture tells a story, don't it?

UNCONSCIOUS ECHOES

People who "read with their ears" often pick up things that others miss, such as the jingle-jangle noise of unconscious rhymes and alliterations and other echoes.

UNCONSCIOUS ECHOES

The payroll plans are prepared on punched cards each pay period for each person.

REVISED FOR MORE EFFECTIVE DICTION

The payroll data are prepared on punched cards each week for each employee.

DONALD H. SANDERS, *Computers in Society*

UNCONSCIOUS ECHOES

His arm is still sound; it is the Namath knees that are bound.

REVISED FOR MORE EFFECTIVE DICTION

His arm is still sound; it is the Namath knees that are gone.

"Limping for Life," *Time*, 24 Nov. 1975

UNDERSTATEMENT

Understatement is the fine art of restraint in language. The good writer knows when to restrain the impulse to hammer home a point. The more the point seems worthy of heavy emphasis, the more it achieves by understatement. A famous example is attributed to

Mark Twain: "The reports of my death have been much exaggerated."

What does the understated sentence achieve in each of the following pairs?

WEAK

She had been trying to read, though she was really too anxious to concentrate, and when she heard Paula's car rattle to a stop out back, she closed the book and darted joyfully toward the door.

REVISED FOR UNDERSTATEMENT

When she heard Paula's car rattle and pop out back, she closed the book she hadn't really been reading and darted joyfully toward the door.
ARTHUR LAURENTS, *The Way We Were*

WEAK

Mumbles taught us to drive in a '65 Nova which was pretty much stripped down to bare necessities and showed its use.

REVISED FOR UNDERSTATEMENT

Mumbles taught us to drive in a '65 Nova which had only two options—an AM radio and an overflowing ashtray.
"Drive He Said," *CM Life*, 12 Nov. 1975

WORD PLAY

In informal essays and personal-experience stories, you may have the opportunity to play with words. A cleverly turned phrase can be highly effective—as the world of advertising has discovered.

WEAK

Try the light, smooth whiskey that's becoming America's favorite import from Canada.

REVISED WITH WORD PLAY

Try the light, smooth whiskey that's becoming America's favorite Canadian.
Advertisement, *Time*, 22 Sept. 1975

WEAK

Not long ago, most people dismissed vegetarians as weird people who just drank juice and ate nuts, but now, no-meat cookbooks are selling very well and vegetarian restaurants are opening for business all over.

REVISED WITH WORD PLAY

Not long ago, most people dismissed vegetarians as weird people who just drank juice and ate nuts, but now, no-meat cookbooks are selling very well and vegetarian restaurants are sprouting up all over.
CLAIRE HENDRICKS

In each of the following pairs, one sentence is better than the other in some aspect of diction. Which is the better sentence?

1[1] A The hoses were attached at water pipes that stood out of the brick bases of the houses.
   B The hoses were attached at spigots that stood out of the brick foundations of the houses.

2[2] A He was placed in a drunk tank with two other men, neither of whom he has ever seen before in his life.
   B He was placed in a drunk tank with two other men, neither of whom he had ever seen before in his life.

3[3] A A district's sports programs may be ripe for a penalty call from the courts if those programs deny participation to an individual because of dress or hair styles, marital status, or sex.
   B It is possible that judicial intercession may be required where there is a conflict between the requirements of athletic activities and the civil liberties of participants.

4[4] A I don't suppose anybody ever deliberately attunes a watch or a clock.
   B I don't suppose anybody ever deliberately listens to a watch or a clock.

5[5] A It's really happening, Serpico thought, and identified himself as a police officer.
   B It's really happening, Serpico thought, and nommed himself as a police officer.

6[6] A That spring when I had a great deal of potential and no money at all, I took a job as a janitor.
   B That spring when I had a great deal of potential and was living from hand to mouth, I took a job as a janitor.

7[7] A Those who own the land shall govern it.
   B Government is the prerogative of ownership.

8[8] A She pulled on her overshoes, wrapped a large tartan shawl around her, put on a man's felt hat, and ventured out along the causeways of the first yard.
   B She put on her overshoes, put a large tartan shawl around her, put on a man's felt hat, and went out along the causeways of the first yard.

9[9] A As soon as the seat-belt sign goes off and people began to move about the cabin, I glanced around nervously to see who's on board.
   B As soon as the seat-belt sign goes off and people begin to move about the cabin, I glance around nervously to see who's on board.

10[10] A We were going to The Cabin when Bernie suddenly doubled over with a cramp.

B We were going to The Cabin when Bernie suddenly doubles over with a cramp.

11[11] A I knew she was guilty; I could feel it in my bones.

B I knew she was guilty; one could feel it in his bones.

12[12] A There's not much better you can call the color of an orange than orange.

B It is likely that the best description available for the color of the orange fruit is simply that which is customarily given it, namely, and simply, orange.

13[13] A He had sort of reddish hair and a kind of cute face and I couldn't help but keep on looking at him.

B He had deep dark red hair falling in waves into a face that was pure elf, and I couldn't do anything but stare love-struck at him.

14[14] A As the P.M. walked very slowly to the aircraft, there was a grey look on his face that I did not like, and when he came at last to this house, he collapsed wearily into the first chair.

B As the P.M. dragged himself to the aircraft, there was a grey look on his face that terrified me, and when he came at last to this house, he keeled over with exhaustion into the first chair.

15[15] A He was laughing, and he took a gulp of whiskey and handed the bottle to Muldoon.

B He was consumed with mirth and permitted himself to imbibe of whiskey and extended the decanter to Muldoon.

16[16] A He got off the trunk and leads the way across the clinking cinders into the dark, and the others followed.

B He got off the trunk and led the way across the clinking cinders into the dark, and the others followed.

17[17] A The faces blow past in the fog like confetti.

B The faces blow past in the fog like shredlings.

18[18] A Just as ghastly were the illegal tortures, which included smoking the suspect's head in a cylinder, or burning the skin off his torso by winding a soft pewter pipe around it like some great serpentine musical instrument and then pouring boiling water through its convolutions.

B Just as bad were the tortures, which included smoking the person's head, or burning the skin off his torso with hot water running through a pipe around his body.

19[19] A Bowling Green was well fortified, and Johnson thought he could hold the place if Buell made a frontal assault, but there was little chance that Buell would do anything so foolish.

B It was certainly true that Bowling Green was a well-fortified place, and Johnson was pretty sure that if he had to he could probably hold it if it should happen that Buell would make an assault from the front, but it was rather unlikely that Buell would do such a thing since it was so foolish.

20[20] **A** Her normally peach-blush pink cheeks were blazing-fire red from the early morning wind; her hands were ugly lobster claws as if they had just been burned in harsh chemicals, and she had the foul reek of sheep-dip about her.

B Her normally pink cheeks were polished pippin by the early-morning breeze; her hands were wrinkle-red as if they had just been washed in strong soap, and she smelled of sheep.

21[21] **A** She would step out of her shoes and kick them into a corner, step out of her flimsy frock and expose her long bony legs in their short pink pants and flesh-colored stockings.

B She would step out of her shoes and kick them into a corner, step out of her light as a feather frock and expose her bony legs in their short pink pants and flesh-colored stockings.

22[22] **A** She couldn't decide whether she shouldn't go or not.

B She couldn't decide whether she should go.

23[23] **A** There is little reason not to doubt that your watch is not keeping correct time, that is, correct sun time.

B The chances are excellent that your watch is not keeping correct time, that is, correct sun time.

24[24] **A** He put a handful of coffee in the pot and was putting a lump of grease out of a can and was making it slide across the hot skillet.

B He put a handful of coffee in the pot and dipped a lump of grease out of a can and slid it sputtering across the hot skillet.

25[25] **A** Carla was brave as a lion and spoke right up to the dean.

B Carla was scared but stubborn and spoke right up to the dean.

[1] JAMES AGEE, *A Death in the Family*

[2] CARYL CHESSMAN, *Cell 2455 Death Row*

[3] DAVID L. MARTIN, "Schoolboy Sports a Bone-Crushing Financial Problem," *Los Angeles Times*, 9 July 1972

[4] WILLIAM FAULKNER, *The Sound and the Fury*

[5] PETER MAAS, *Serpico*

[6] JAMES ALAN McPHERSON, "Gold Coast"

[7] JOHN JAY, in Michael Parenti, *Democracy for the Few*

[8] D. H. LAWRENCE, "The Blind Man"

[9] ERICA JONG, *Fear of Flying*

[10] SANDRA DROTT

[11] KATHY SMITH

[12] TONY HARMON

[13] JULIE MASTERSON

[14] LORD MORAN, "Churchill," from *The Diaries of Lord Moran*

[15] JOHN O'HARA, *From the Terrace*

[16] WILLIAM GOLDING, *Lord of the Flies*

[17] KEN KESEY, *One Flew Over the Cuckoo's Nest*

[18] DENNIS BLOODWORTH, *The Chinese Looking Glass*

[19] BRUCE CATTON, *Terrible Swift Sword*
[20] ROBERT RUARK, *Uhuru*
[21] KATHERINE ANNE PORTER, *Ship of Fools*
[22] DONNA BLAIR
[23] MICHAEL P. McINTYRE, *Physical Geography*
[24] ERNEST HEMINGWAY, "Big Two-Hearted River"
[25] STANLEY YANKLEVITCH

PART THREE

CONVENTIONS

CHAPTER NINE

Usage

> Reading Maketh a Full Man,
>
> Conference a Ready Man,
>
> and Writing an Exact Man.

FRANCIS BACON, *On Studies*

The "rules" of English are not actually rules at all; they are customs and conventions. They grew out of the history of the English-speaking peoples, and throughout history these conventions have changed as writers have changed with the times.

Very few people worry about "mistakes" in slang or informal English. But most educated readers are concerned when they find mistakes in formal writing. Therefore, this chapter on usage will help you review those problems that sometimes come up in formal writing.

Formal English is, in general, the language used in printed works today: newspapers, magazines, books, and other writing aimed at the educated public. It is the language of schools, businesses, science, and the professions. Formal English does not mean "fancy" or pretentious language; it means having a standard *form*. It is the language you yourself use when you are conscious of *how* you are writing as well as *what*. If you scribble a telephone message for a roommate, you probably don't care whether your words are precise. But if you take a message for your employer, you may be very conscious of *how* your writing looks. For example, here is a telephone message written in three different styles:

INFORMAL
B call'd, call him back tonite, he's at joans.

FORMAL

Bruce called. Call him back tonight. He is at Joan's.

PRETENTIOUS

Mr. Bruce Watson telephoned while you were absent. He requests that you return his call at your convenience this evening. He is presently visiting at the dormitory of Miss Joan Dawkins.

Your roommate would accept either the formal or the informal message without question. But the pretentious message might cause him or her to assume that you were joking or being stuffy. The pretentious message attempts to sound more important than the situation warrants.

The rule of thumb for the usage guidelines in this chapter is not what is "right" according to some arbitrary authority, but what educated readers are accustomed to. Not every authority agrees on just what those expressions are, but this chapter presents the majority solutions to most of the common problems in formal writing.

AGREEMENT

Educated readers expect things to *agree*. Mixing singulars and plurals distracts the reader. In most cases, you just have to remember how many things you are writing about, but you must handle a few cases in agreement with special care.

1. Group Words

Words like the following are considered *singular* in form.

the army	the faculty
the band	the generation
the body (of students)	the group
the class	the majority
the company	the minority
the crowd	the part (of the group)
the enemy	the portion

Conventional Usage   Group words like these take *singular* verbs and *singular* pronouns:

The company *has its* work to do.
The band *is* playing *its* introduction.

Optional Usage   Group words *may* be given plural verbs and pronouns to emphasize the actions of each member of the group. (Although this usage is customary in British English, many Americans think it sounds strange.)

The orchestra *are* tuning *their* instruments.
The class *are* studying *their* books.

2. Confusing Singulars

anyone, everyone, no one, one	a man who
a box of, a cup of, a trainload of	none (of these students)
each (student), each of (the students)	the number of (students)
everybody, nobody, somebody	physics
either Jack or Jill, neither Jack nor Jill, either person	that she likes milk and pickles
fifteen miles	two plus six
five minus three	Jack as well as Jill
ham and eggs	Jack together with Jill
mathematics	this kind (of apple)
	that kind (of apple)

— *Conventional Usage* These expressions are confusing because they often sound plural—they are frequently followed by a plural phrase (one *of the boys*)—but they are all *singular* and take *singular* verbs and *singular* pronouns.

Each of them *has* his book.
A box of strawberries *is* all she had.
Electronics *is* her major.
Five cents *doesn't* buy as much as *it* used to.

— *Special Note: Gender-specific References* The use of masculine pronouns when *both* sexes are referred to or implied is unacceptable in modern writing. For example, when a group of students contains both men and women, "Each student should have *his* work finished on time" can be revised to "Each student should have *his or her work* finished on time" or "Students should have *their* work finished on time."

Agreement practice 1

Select suitable forms from the choices in parentheses.

1 Neither the rain nor the cold (was / were) going to keep me from that party at the lake.

2 Neither of these novels (have / has) enough adventure in (them / it) to keep your interest up.

3 One of the greatest ideas of twentieth century psychology (was / were) Freud's concept of the subconscious mind.

4 They had come thither, not as friends nor partners in the enterprise, but each, save one youthful pair, impelled by (his / their) own selfish and solitary longing for this wondrous gem.

NATHANIEL HAWTHORNE, "The Great Carbuncle"

5 Every member of this club (have / has) (his / their / his or her) unique job, and each job (is / are) challenging and rewarding.

6 Neither Senator Thomas Hart Benton nor Sam Houston (was / were) dwarfed by the towering reputation of (his / their) three colleagues.

JOHN F. KENNEDY, *Profiles in Courage*

7 Twenty dollars (is / are) a lot of money for a textbook.

8 "It is required of every man," the Ghost returned, "that the spirit within (him / them) should walk abroad among (his / their) fellow-men, and travel far and wide; and if that spirit goes not forth in life, (they / it) (is / are) condemned to do so after death."

CHARLES DICKENS, *A Christmas Carol*

9 Practically everybody who (has / have) found the place, after the switch to Stinson Beach, (is / are) far enough into the thing to know what the "acid" in the Acid Test means.

TOM WOLFE, *The Electric Kool-Aid Acid Test*

10 Anyone finding the door open that way might easily have imagined (himself / themselves / him- or herself) the victim of a robbery.

3 • Confusing Plurals

Words and phrases like the following are considered *plural* in form:

both the girls and the boy	neither the girl nor the boys
both (men), both of (the men)	a number of (students)
the boys as well as the girls	one of those who (study), one of
either the boys or the girls	those girls who (study)
eleven assignments	these kinds (of apples)
girls and boys	those kinds (of apples)
Jack and Jill	those days, those years,
men who, men and women who,	the years
people who, those who	two sixes (2 × 6)

Expressions like these are all *plural* and take *plural* verbs and *plural* pronouns.

Neither the girls nor the boys *are* ready.
These kinds of apples *are* good.

— *Note* Clauses starting with *who, which,* or *that* often function as modifiers. In the second example on page 341, *have* is plural because its subject, *who,* refers to the plural *girls.*

An odd number of girls *have their* books.

She is one of those girls who *have their* books.

Agreement practice 2

Select suitable forms from the choices in parentheses.

1 The years I spent in school (was / were) a waste of time.

2 His tunic and breeches (was / were) so thickly soaked through with Italian blood that they thought at first he had been shot through the chest.
CARLOS BAKER, *Ernest Hemingway*

3 My uncle, however, was one of those men who (is / are) always prepared with expedients.
JULES VERNE, *A Journey to the Center of the Earth*

4 Gardenias and the peerage (was / were) his only weaknesses.
OSCAR WILDE, "The Canterville Ghost"

5 Five term papers in one semester (is / are) too many.

6 Tailoring and weaving, though qualitatively different productive activities, (is / are) each a productive expenditure of human brains, nerves, and muscles, and in this sense (is / are) human labour.
KARL MARX, *Capital*

7 Now therefore why tempt ye God, to put a yoke upon the disciples, which neither our fathers nor we (was / were) able to bear?
Acts 15:10

8 Those who teach themselves a foreign language (is / are) clever.

9 The difficulties of casting and staging six Strauss operas in a dozen days (make / makes) this a rare and spectacular event.
MARCIA COLMAN MORTON, "Cities in Winter: Vienna," *Saturday Review*, 8 Jan. 1977

10 Either the students or their teachers (is / are) responsible for the so-called grade inflation.

4. Irregular Plurals

SINGULAR	PLURAL
alumna	alumnae (f)
alumnus	alumni (m)
analysis	analyses
bacterium	bacteria
cactus	cactuses, cacti
crisis	crises
criterion	criteria
curriculum	curriculums, curricula

SINGULAR	PLURAL
datum	data
formula	formulas, formulae
index	indexes, indices
medium	media
nucleus	nuclei
octopus	octopuses, octopi
parenthesis	parentheses
stimulus	stimuli
stratum	strata
thesis	theses
die	dice

As a matter of fact when data are [not *is*] of this type, all of the usual mathematical and statistical implications may be made.

N. M. DOWNIE AND R. W. HEATH, *Basic Statistical Methods*

In man, with his highly developed nervous system, emotional *stimuli are* in fact the most common stressors—and of course, *these* would be encountered most frequently in psychotic patients.

HANS SELYS, *Stress without Distress*

5. Special Problems in Agreement

Mixed Compound Subject   It is possible to write a compound subject that is part singular and part plural. The rule is, the verb agrees with the part closest to it.

Neither his sisters, his parents, nor Jack *has* the answer.
Neither the space nor the things in it *were* in the room before.
SUSANNE K. LANGER, *Problems in Art*

Some   The word *some* is either singular or plural depending on context.

We thought *some* of the *books were* too mature for children.
Some of the *oil was* used for fuel.

Separated Subject and Verb   In a long or complicated sentence, words may get between the subject and the verb, causing you to "lose" the subject. Figure out who is doing what in a sentence before you decide whether the verb should be singular or plural.

The *superiority* of stockades built by the Union Troops over those built by the Confederates *was* striking.
OTTO EISENSCHIML AND RALPH NEWMAN, *Eyewitness: The Civil War As We Lived It*

Atypical Word Order   Usually, the subject comes first in the sentence, before the verb:

¹ ²
SUBJECT VERB

The dog was young and healthy.

But writers sometimes change the order of their sentences:

² ¹
VERB SUBJECT

Young and healthy *was* **the dog.**

Put the sentence in normal order (mentally) before deciding whether the verb should be singular or plural. Why is the verb singular in each of these examples?

There *is*, so far as I know, no good *reason* for these excuses.
For the many, there *is* a hardly concealed discontent.
STUDS TERKEL, *Working*
Does each of the boys *belong* to the club?

Agreement and Logic   Because educated readers expect things to *agree* in formal writing, certain expressions sound illogical:

The sophomores are clever as foxes [not *a fox*].
The frat brothers made up their minds [not *mind*] in a hurry.

The verb agrees with its subject, not with what comes after the verb:

The best *bargain* for lunch *is* sandwiches and a cup of soup.
Sandwiches and a cup of soup are the best bargain for lunch.

Agreement review

Select suitable forms from the choices in parentheses

1 As I walked along, it occurred to me that the two children's behavior (was / were) a true reflection of all mankind.
THEODOR REIK, *Of Love and Lust*

2 A number of people (is / are) coming to the dance.

3 The number of days left till Christmas (is / are) twelve.

4 Each kind of bacterium (produce /produces) a juice that creates the kind of fermentation that is necessary to do the work.
ALAN L. BENSON, *The Story of Geology*

5 Every generation (has / have) (its / their) styles of living.
SUSANNE K. LANGER, *Problems of Art*

6 There (was / were) usually several reasons for his behavior.

7 It is the government's policies which (cause / causes) the problem.

8 Neither the atomic bomb, nor its effect (is / are) very well understood by most people.

9 The implications of this argument (has / have) been examined.

10 These (sort / sorts) of ideas are what started him thinking in the first place.

11 She is one of those girls who (enter / enters) too many activities.

12 Intellectually, these include the elements of myth, magic, empiricism, and scientific attitude. . . . Each of these (has / have) a role in helping to answer the question "Who or what is man?" and in coping with the exigencies of existence.
CARL P. SWANSON, *The Natural History of Man*

13 Neither for the Catholic, the Protestant, nor for the Jew (is / are) the world a good place in which an enduring happiness is to be expected.
NORBERT WIENER, *The Human Uses of Human Beings*

14 Every one of the guys in my dorm (has / have) different ideas about dating.

15 If anyone wants good grades (he or she / they) should stay out of bars.

PRONOUNS AS SUBJECTS AND OBJECTS

Subjects and objects can cause problems for writers using pronouns.

The typical order of the English sentence is:

1	2	3
SUBJECT	VERB	OBJECT
The man	shot	the bear.

The subject does the acting, the verb names the action, and the object receives the action.

However, sentences are not always in normal order. You must turn the sentence around in your mind before deciding which word is the subject and which is the object (see Passive Sentence in Chapter 7):

Jazz I love, but opera I hate.

SUB OB   SUB OB
I love jazz, but I hate opera.

SUBJECT PRONOUNS	OBJECT PRONOUNS
I, you, we, he,	me, you, us, him,
she, it, they, who	her, it, them, whom

Why are the object pronouns required in the following?

They have known *her* for years.

Him we have known only for a short time.

— *Objects with Prepositions* Prepositions are followed by objects: *for* him, *to* us, *with* us, *by* her, *between* them, *between* you and me, *after* him, *near* whom. Most prepositions are words of position that tell the reader where something is (see Glossary for complete list). Though not position words, *but, except, since, until,* and a few others sometimes function as prepositions and can thus take objects. When these words join with a noun or pronoun to make a modifying phrase (in the winter, for him, to the store) they are called prepositions, and the noun or pronoun after them is considered an object. But note a different use for these words: "She stepped onto the ice and fell *through*." Here *through* has no noun or pronoun after it; it acts as an independent modifier. Some of the other words function as conjunctions: "She laughed, *but* I didn't see the joke."

— *The* To Be *Exception to the Subject-Object Rule* Forms of *to be* (*am, is, are, was, were, be, being, been*) do not take objects in formal writing.

It is *I* [not *me*].

The girl who said it was *she* [not *her*].

It was *who*?

Subject-object practice 1

Select suitable forms from the choices in parentheses.

1 My wife and (I /me), on our later study of chimpanzees right inside the forest, found the same thing: noisy, mobile males and quiet, slow mothers.
VERNON REYNOLDS, *The Apes*

2 Digestion is a problem for (we / us) Americans.

3 Then, as he thought, he realized that if there was any such thing as ever meeting, both (he / him) and his grandfather would be acutely embarrassed by the presence of his father.
ERNEST HEMINGWAY, *For Whom the Bell Tolls*

4 There followed a weighty correspondence between (he / him) and the King, and the King at last relented to the change in the plan, thanking his minister for his advice. . . .
CHARLES W. FERGUSON, *Naked to Mine Enemies: The Life of Cardinal Woolsey*

5 She looked up from her notes and said that if any student wanted to try something else (he / he or she / they) should say so now.

6 Let's just keep this between you and (I / me).
BETTY TRAVEN

7 As he played, empty bottles went sailing through the gathering darkness to explode and tinkle on the cobblestones, but, so far, none were directed toward (he / him) or the girl.
BOYD UPCHURCH, *The Slave Stealer*

8 Such advocates of obfuscation apparently teach fairly well, if it is (they / them) who have instructed my graduate students.
WENDELL JOHNSON, "You Can't Write Writing," in *Language, Meaning and Maturity*

9 I'm damned if I'm going to have people walking by and seeing you sit here as if this division were a partnership between you and (I / me).
NORMAN MAILER, *The Naked and the Dead*

10 I hope they invite you and (I / me) to the party.
JANE STEIL

Who and Whom

The difference between *who* and *whom* causes more trouble than it is worth. *Whom* has almost completely disappeared from informal English. (No one asks "Whom did you see?" except those who habitually speak formal English.) But the distinction between the two forms is still important in formal writing.

Who is the subject form (it can be the subject).
Whom is the object form (it can be the object).

It is necessary to figure out who is doing what in the sentence in order to know which word is the subject and which is the object. Why is the object form required in the following?

Whom are you discussing?

Whom are you looking for?

Whom did you see?

Whom does he want to marry?

With *whom* were you dancing?

Sometimes words get between the subject and the verb, changing the appearance of the sentence but not the grammar. Treat these sentences as combining problems—break the sentences down into basic sentences to see what goes where:

WHO/WHOM PROBLEM SENTENCE	SOLUTION WITH SENTENCE COMBINING
The girl (who / whom) they think was in the car has escaped	The girl has escaped. They think *she* was in the car. She = *who* The girl *who* they think was in the car has escaped.

Laura pointed out a boy (who / whom) she said was the team captain.

Laura pointed out a boy. She said [that] *he* was the team captain.
He = who
Laura pointed out a boy *who* she said was the team captain.

He is the thief (who / whom) the police agree is the most clever.

He is the thief. The police agree [that] *he* is the most clever.
He = who
He is the thief *who* the police agree is the most clever.

A related substitution trick can help you figure out *who* or *whom* problems. Substitute some other pronoun (*he, she, they, him, her, them*) into the sentence. Remember, if *he, she,* or *they* fits, use *who,* and if *him, her,* or *them* fits, use *whom.*

I know (who / whom) phoned this morning.
I know *he* phoned this morning.
He = who [see page 344]
I know *who* phoned this morning.

Subject-object practice 2

Which is the right word? How do you know?

1 He is a man (who / whom) everyone should know.

2 (Who / Whom) does he think he is?

3 To (who / whom) did he refer?

4 Anyone (who / whom) you pick will have to work hard.

5 She is one person (who / whom) should be invited.

6 (Who / Whom) are you?

7 He might not be the one (who / whom) you think he is.

8 List the ones (who / whom) you think should come.

9 She is the kind of leader (who / whom) we want for president.

10 (Who / Whom) do you think is the best candidate?

11 (Who / Whom) shall I say called?

12 We have the man (who / whom) we were looking for.

13 I wonder (who / whom) is in there.

14 You should see (who / whom) is standing outside.

15 For (who / whom) is this intended?

16 You must be (who / whom) they think you are.

17 A student (who / whom) we all know, is failing.

18 (Who / Whom) it is, I think I know.

19 (Who / Whom) do you think she is calling?

20 Who / Whom) do you think you are fooling?

21 It was she (who / whom) we wanted to question.

22 (Who / Whom) do you think you are?

23 You are the ones (who / whom) the committee selected.

24 I have to find out (who / whom) she is.

25 (Who / Whom), they asked, did this?

PRONOUN REFERENCE

1. Ambiguous

A pronoun must not appear to refer to two words simultaneously: "The President told the vice-president *he* couldn't make the speech." What does *he* refer to? Clear up such confusing references when you revise:

AMBIGUOUS
Don't touch the dishes with your hands when *they* are dirty.

REVISED
Don't touch the dishes when your hands are dirty.
When the dishes are dirty, don't touch them.

2. Vague

It should always be *completely* clear to the reader what your pronouns refer to. The farther away the pronoun gets from its referent, the greater the possibility that the reader and perhaps the writer too will "lose" the referent:

VAGUE
Helen is giving a party, *which* is a good idea.

What is good, the fact that it is Helen who is giving the party or the fact that she is giving a party instead of a speech? Often, you'll find that the best solution for vague pronoun reference is to revise the thought, getting rid of the pronoun completely:

REVISED
Helen's decided to give a party, since we've all been studying too hard for exams.

3. Illogical

In this situation, a pronoun refers to something missing from the sentence—an implied idea that must be expressed for the sentence to be understood:

ILLOGICAL
Although my school gave much attention to reading, *they* didn't do me any good.

The reading exercises didn't do any good? The teachers didn't do any good? There is no referent for *they* in this sentence; the reader has to guess at your meaning. The best course is to revise the sentence so that you convey a precise idea to the reader:

REVISED
Although my school gave much attention to reading, even remedial classes didn't prepare me for college reading assignments.

4. Excessive

A proliferation of pronouns usually creates childish-sounding sentences:

EXCESSIVE
Science has always been my worst subject and it is hard to study it when it isn't taught very well and when it comes so early in the day and especially when it is so hard to understand it anyway!

Using the skills you learned in Chapter 7, rewrite such sentences for better clarity and emphasis:

REVISED
Science—scheduled at eight in the morning before I'm really awake, hard to understand if not taught well, and almost impossible for me to comprehend in any case—continues to be my worst subject.

Pronoun reference review

Which is the better sentence? Why?

1[1] A Cunegonde fainted; as soon as she recovered, she slapped her face; and everything was confusion in the most beautiful and agreeable of all possible castles.
   B Cunegonde fainted; as soon as she recovered, the Baroness slapped her face; and everything was confusion in the most beautiful and agreeable of all possible castles.

2[2] A His new car was my father's pride, which he polished every Sunday.
   B His new car, which he polished every Sunday, was my father's pride.

3^3 A Its front foot caught a piece of quartz and little by little the shell pulled over and flopped upright.

B Its front foot caught a piece of quartz and little by little it pulled over and flopped upright.

4^4 A Her thin musical voice died away over the water; Leon could hear the wind-blown trills pass him by like a fluttering of wings.

B Her thin musical voice died away over the water; Leon could hear it pass by him like a fluttering of wings.

5^5 A Now Gregor's sister had to cook too, helping her mother; true, it didn't amount to much, for they ate scarcely anything.

B Now Gregor's sister had to cook too, helping her mother; true, the cooking didn't amount to much, for they scarcely ate anything.

6^6 A In vain I told him in English that boys were the most dangerous creatures; and if once you begin with it, it was safe to end in a shower of stones.

B In vain I told him in English that boys were the most dangerous creatures; and if once you begin with them, it was safe to end in a shower of stones.

7^7 A I was in my room waiting for the phone to ring when suddenly it started raining.

B While I was in my room waiting for the phone to ring, the rain suddenly started.

8^8 A She pretended to make light of his genius and I took no pains to defend him.

B She pretended to make light of his genius and I took no pains to defend this.

9^9 A Subjectivity is a journalistic principle among the underground press staffers and they care much more about opinion than fact.

B Subjectivity is a journalistic principle among underground press staffers and it cares much more about opinion than fact.

10^{10} A He used the wild country as the Indians do, in cooperation and communion with it, which finds any form of noise a baneful disharmony.

B He used the wild country as the Indians do, in cooperation and communion with it, finding any form of noise a baneful disharmony.

VERBS

Every verb has four forms: *write, wrote, written, writing;* a few have alternative forms; a few have repeated forms. Check the dictionary if you have any doubts about the form of a verb. A few of the more troublesome ones are listed for you here:

PRESENT	PAST	PERFECT*	PROGRESSIVE*
awake	awoke, awaked	awaked, awoke, awaken	awaking
awaken	awakened	awakened	awakening
begin	began	begun	beginning
break	broke	broken	breaking
bring	brought	brought	bringing
buy	bought	bought	buying
dive	dived, dove	dived	diving
draw	drew	drawn	drawing
drink	drank	drunk	drinking
freeze	froze	frozen	freezing
get	got	got, gotten	getting
go	went	gone	going
know	knew	known	knowing
lay	laid	laid	laying
lie (recline)	lay	lain	lying
lie (tell a lie)	lied	lied	lying
make	made	made	making
set	set	set	setting
sing	sang	sung	singing
sink	sank	sunk	sinking
sit	sat	sat	sitting
take	took	taken	taking
wake	woke, waked	waked, woken	waking
wear	wore	worn	wearing

*The perfect and progressive forms are used with forms of *to be* (*am, is, are, was, were, be, being, been*) and with forms of *to have* (*have, has, had*): *am writing, was beginning, has begun, had known, have been singing,* and so on.

1. Slang Verbs

In informal writing and personal-experience stories, slang may be both appropriate and desirable, but in formal writing, slang verbs should be avoided: "We was busted by the fuzz last night. We was just sittin' around rappin', ya know, like it was so cold I nearly frosted my butt. My old lady's all busted up about it."

2. Unconventional Verb Forms

Within formal English, inexperienced writers sometimes use the wrong verb form:

It was so cold that we were *frozen* [not *froze*] by noon.
I have *woken* [not *woke*] up at eight o'clock every morning since the semester started.

The ship *sank* [not *sunk*] in minutes.

They have *gone* [not *went*] to the library together for months.

Equally unconventional, and unacceptable in semiformal or formal writing, is the creation of new forms by mixing parts of verbs:

I have *tooken* this course twice now, and I still don't get it.

He has *drunken* so many beers he can't stand up.

3, Lie and Lay

The difference between *lie* and *lay*—like the difference between *who* and *whom*—often causes trouble. The words are different in *meaning*. *To lie* (*lie, lay, lain, lying*) means to be at rest; this word only tells you *where* something is. *To lay* (*lay, laid, laid, laying*) means to put something somewhere.

The words are different in *grammar*. *Lie* never takes an object; it is usually followed by a *place* expression (lie *down*, lie *on the bed*). *Lay* always takes an object: lay *the book* down; lay *it* on the bed.

The problem is in the past tense of *lie*.

Today I lie down; yesterday I *lay* down [not *laid*].

To decide which verb is needed, you must either be certain of the meaning you intend, or you must check to see whether the verb has an object (lay) or not (lie). But remember that writers don't always use normal order in their sentences: subject—verb—object.

He—laid—*the book* down.

The book was laid down by him.

Remember, in a passive sentence, the object appears in the subject slot (see Chapter 7). Figure out who is doing what before you decide whether the sentence has an object in it.

Verb practice 1

Select suitable forms from the choices in parentheses.

1 Teachers should not (lay / lie) hands on students.

2 The report has been (laying / lying) there all day.

3 (Lay / Lie) the carpeting straight.

4 They (lay / laid) in bed until noon yesterday.

5 That dog has (laid / lain) there all day.

6 If you're tired, you ought to (lie / lay) down for a while.

7 The letter is (lying / laying) right there in front of you.

8 They have (laid / lain) tracks right across our field.

9 I (lie / lay) here daydreaming all through yesterday's test.

10 Better let sleeping dogs (lie / lay).

11 The treasure (lies / lays) buried six feet under.

12 They (lay / laid) the child on the back seat when they went shopping.

13 The leaves were (lying / laying) all over the yard.

14 She (lay / laid) awake all night worrying.

15 You need to (lie / lay) aside your fears.

16 The ship (lay / laid) at anchor all week.

17 The book has (laid / lain) on the shelf for weeks.

18 She is (lying / laying) on the cot.

19 (Lie / Lay) the towels on the counter.

20 Could it have (lain / laid) there all this time?

21 By tomorrow, it will have (laid / lain) there a month.

22 Can you (lay / lie) brick in your spare time?

23 Time (lays / lies) heavily when you're bored.

24 The laws were (lain / laid) down by Moses.

25 They will (lie / lay) there for hours if you let them.

4. Double Past Tense

Much prose is written in the past tense, and this sometimes makes a problem for writers. How do you refer to a past or prior event when you are already writing in the past? Use the past perfect:

He *said* that he *had seen* her.

"He said that he *saw* her" and "He said that he *seen* her" are both unacceptable in this case.

He knew that he *had passed* [not *passed*] the test when he saw his mark.

Putting both verbs in simple past sounds all right in informal spoken English, but doing so fails to make the distinction in time clear for readers.

5. Conditional Statements

USAGE

People sometimes use a redundant conditional ("If you *would* do it, you *would* be sorry"). Use the *will* (*would*) verb forms to express only the consequences, not the condition. (The *if* statement is the condition.) Formal writing requires the following:

If you *do* it, you *will be* penalized.
If you *did* it, you *would be* penalized.
If you *hadn't done* it, you *wouldn't have been* penalized.

Statements of Doubts, Wishes, Probability, Conditions Contrary to Fact

The rule on *was* and *were* for statements of doubt, probability, and so on, is changing. It is disregarded by many modern writers; but the distinction is still important to many educated readers.

I wish I *were* [not *was*] dead.
If it *were* [not *was*] true, I could forgive her.
Would you do it if it *were* [not *was*] possible?
Were [not *If he was*] he a foot taller, he might make the team.

Verb review

Select suitable forms from the choices in parentheses.

1 It (sits / sets) pretty well back from the road, in a lawn gone sparse and rusty in the late season.
ROBERT PENN WARREN, *All the King's Men*

2 The jailors fed us in the morning, and it tasted good because some of us hadn't (ate / eaten) in twenty-four hours.
DICK GREGORY, WITH ROBERT LIPSTYE, *Nigger: An Autobiography*

3 We all (lay / lie) there, my mother, my father, my uncle, my aunt, and I too am (laying / lying) there.
JAMES AGEE, *A Death in the Family*

4 He said, if it (was / were) possible that there could be any country where Yahoos alone were endued with reason, they certainly must be the governing animal, because reason will always in time prevail against brutal strength.
JONATHAN SWIFT, *Gulliver's Travels*

5 At daylight, Rainsford (lying / laying) near the camp, was awakened by a sound that made him know that he had new things to learn about fear.
RICHARD CONNELL, "The Most Dangerous Game"

6 **Gurov (lay / laid) awake all night, raging, and went about the whole of the next day with a headache.**

ANTON CHEKOV, "The Lady with the Dog"

7 **If he (would break / broke) into a run, they'd chase him.**

JOHN DOS PASSOS, *Forty-Second Parallel*

8 **Unless there is a remarkable biological breakthrough in geriatrics, we have (gone / went) just about as far as we can go in raising life expectancy.**

ISAAC ASIMOV, *Of Time and Space and Other Things*

9 **The cries of the dying were (drownded / drowned) in the martial music of trumpets and drums.**

WILL DURANT, *The Reformation*

10 **And even if it (was / were) possible to devise a method for maintaining an innocent vacuity of mind, the wisdom of such a policy is surely questionable.**

LUCIUS GARVIN, *A Modern Introduction to Ethics*

11 **One event that (takes / taken) me by surprise every year is the announcement of a new Miss Rheingold.**

WILLIAM K. ZINSSER, "There Are Smiles," *The Haircurl Papers*

12 **If a modern-day Rip Van Winkle (would go / went) to sleep and didn't wake up for 100 years, how well would he be able to understand an American of 2061?**

MARIO PEI, "English 2061: A Forecast," *Saturday Review*, 14 Jan. 1961

13 **A series of tests which gave this kind of interesting evidence was (undertook / undertaken) by the well-known American author Upton Sinclair.**

SUSY SMITH, *ESP for the Millions*

14 **The people who have (manage / managed) to get off the block have only got as far as a more respectable ghetto.**

JAMES BALDWIN, *Nobody Knows My Name*

15 **The world in twenty or forty years—let us say thirty-six—has (come / came) to the point where without an atomic war, without even a hard or furious shooting war, it has (gave / given) birth nonetheless to a fearful condition.**

NORMAN MAILER, "The Last Night: A Story"

DANGLING PARTS

Some modifiers seem to "dangle" when they do not modify anything in the sentence. Often these modifiers produce humor by accidentally attaching to something unintended: "Riding my bike through the woods, the bear suddenly appeared in front of me." The modifier attaches to the *nearest* noun, and therefore *the bear* is *riding my bike*. To avoid the problem, move modifiers next to what you intend them to modify or supply an appropriate subject: "Riding my bike through the woods, *I* suddenly saw the bear in front of me."

Practice

Which is the better sentence in the following pairs?

1[11] **A** Reading carefully through the text, several concepts appeared.
    B As I read carefully through the text, several concepts began to appear.

2[12] **A** Seeing him beside his wife, I understood why people said he came from a good family and had married beneath him.
    B Seeing him beside his wife, he looked like he had come from a good family and had married beneath him.

3[13] **A** Having departed from my friend, some remote spote in Scotland was selected where I could finish my work in solitude.
    B Having departed from my friend, I determined to visit some remote spot in Scotland, and finish my work in solitude.

4[14] **A** Reaching the boulevard, the desire to run was overcoming him.
    B By the time he reached the boulevard, he was fighting the desire to run.

5[15] **A** Long and tangled and hanging down, his eyes were shining through his hair like he was behind vines.
    B His hair was long and tangled and hung down, and you could see his eyes shining through like he was behind vines.

6[16] **A** They spread the skin out and trimmed the fat from it, and then they were faced with the question of what to do with the tail.
    B Spreading the skin out and trimming the fat from it, the tail posed a question.

7[17] **A** Holding the bolts with a wrench, the plate will slowly rotate to the left.
    B Holding the bolts with the wrench, you can slowly rotate the plate to the left.

8[18] **A** As he swept his long arms, as though brushing aside some impalpable object, the wolves fell back and back further still.
    B Sweeping his long arms, as though brushing aside some impalpable object, the wolves fell back and back further still.

9[19] **A** Watching Dr. Ferris watch him, the sudden twitch of anxiety appeared, the look that precedes panic, as if a clean card had fallen on the table from a deck Dr. Ferris had never seen before.
    B Watching Dr. Ferris watch him, Rearden saw the sudden twitch of anxiety, the look that precedes panic, as if a clean card had fallen on the table from a deck Dr. Ferris had never seen before.

10^{20} A Squealing and kicking in his father's arms with all his might, his yells redoubled when he carried him upstairs and lifted him over the bannister.

B Poor Hareton was squealing and kicking in his father's arms with all his might, and redoubled his yells when he carried him upstairs and lifted him over the bannister.

MISPLACED PARTS

1. Movable Modifiers

Movable modifiers (*only*, *just*, *almost*) usually come before the verb. But in some cases an ambiguity can arise. For example, "I only lost the money" can be interpreted "I only lost the money [I didn't steal it]" or "I lost only the money [I still have the receipts]." Avoid ambiguity by placing the modifier next to the word it modifies and, when necessary, giving the reader additional information to make your meaning clear:

AMBIGUOUS	REVISED FOR CLARITY
I just earned three dollars.	I earned just three dollars [not four or five dollars.]
	I earned three dollars just now.
I only looked at the shirt.	I only looked at the shirt; I didn't buy it.
	I looked at only the shirt [not at slacks, shoes, or socks].
School begins after the summer vacation in September.	School begins again in September, after the summer vacation.

2. Negatives

Informally, many people accept the movable *not*, as in "Everyone can't [cannot] be rich." But formally, you gain greater precision by placing the *not* next to the word it negates. "*Not everyone* can be rich."

INFORMAL	REVISED FOR FORMAL ENGLISH
Everyone doesn't have to hold the same opinion.	Not everyone has to hold the same opinion.
Everybody doesn't own a Cadillac	Not everybody owns a Cadillac.

3. Squinting Modifiers

"Squinting" modifiers seem to modify in two directions at once, modifying two words at once. To clear up any doubts in the reader's mind, move the squinting modifier next to the word you intend it to modify.

The coach told them often to jog.

The coach told them to jog often.
The coach often told them to jog.

4. Awkward Split Infinitives

An infinitive is the word *to* plus a verb (to run, to go, to think). Putting a word or words between *to* and its verb is called "splitting the infinitive" (to quickly run, to slowly go, to really think). Often the split infinitive sounds perfectly natural, but sometimes it can sound unnecessarily awkward.

AWKWARD

You have to usually read with care in his class.
They liked to seldom dance together at parties.

REVISED

You usually have to read with care in his class.
They seldom liked to dance together at parties.

Practice

Which is the better sentence?

1[21] **A** Brandy tasters tell almost as much from bouquet as from taste that are professional.
  B Professional brandy tasters tell almost as much from bouquet as from taste.

2[22] **A** And now there are gas water heaters with double-density insulation and improved utilization that save gas.
  B And now there are gas water heaters that save gas with double density insulation and improved utilization.

3[23] **A** She liked to before dinner read in the evening and she drank Scotch and soda while she read.
  B She liked to read in the evening before dinner and she drank Scotch and soda while she read.

4[24] **A** At the end of the corridor a door stood open, down which M. Chasle made his way on stumbling feet.
  B A door stood open at the end of the corridor, down which M. Chasle made his way on stumbling feet.

5[25] **A** Apart from "Super Fly" midi-coats and the like, there is little tangible evidence so far that life on the street has begun to imitate art.
  B There is little tangible evidence so far that life has begun to imitate art on the street apart from "Super Fly" midi-coats and the like.

6[26] **A** We sat and listened while the professor droned on with our eyes on his face.
  B With our eyes on his face, we sat and listened while the professor droned on.

7²⁷ **A** But as time went on, he manifested some anxiety and surprise, glancing at the clock more and more frequently, and at the window less hopefully than before.

B But as the time went on glancing at the clock more frequently and at the window less hopefully than before, he manifested some anxiety and surprise.

8²⁸ **A** I travel not to go anywhere, but to go, for my part.

B For my part, I travel not to go anywhere, but to go.

COMPARISONS

1. Illogical

"She is taller than any girl in the class" is illogical since it seems to imply either that she is taller than herself, or that she is not part of the class. "She is the tallest girl in the class" or "She is taller than any other girl in the class" both solve this problem.

ILLOGICAL
Corky was faster than anyone on the team.

REVISED FOR CLARITY
Corky was the fastest runner on the team.

2. Incomplete

A comparison is meaningful only if its terms are fully expressed. For example, in "She is young, if not younger, than you are," the parenthetic phrase "if not younger," not only interrupts, it disconnects the first part of the sentence from the rest (She is young . . . than you are). The full comparison requires "She is *as young as*, if not younger than, you are."

INCOMPLETE
You need math more than Jim.

REVISED
You need math more than Jim does.

You need math more than you need Jim.

-*LY* WORDS

Much informal writing, especially in advertising, dispenses with the -*ly* on modifiers, and thus it is easy to drop the -*ly* from your own writing: "His trouble is that he can't think logical." Most verbs, however, express action (*drive* slowly) and require -*ly* modifiers:

Think *carefully* [not *careful*] before you answer.

The grand major domo, white plumes on his head, knocked *loudly* [not "loud"], but there was no response.
TROUP AND GREENE, *The Patient, Death and the Family*

Select the formal English alternative in the following sentences.

1[29] Everyone wants to surround (himself / theirself) and (his / their) family with objects of lasting beauty, meaning and value—objects to be owned now with pride and passed on as valuable heirlooms to future generations.

2[30] Rushed by ambulance to Harlem Hospital, I (lay / laid) in bed for hours while preparations were made to remove the keen-edged knife from my body.

3[31] *A* "The Alteration" starts out far better than it ends.
B "The Alteration" starts out well, if not better than, it ends.

4[32] I am being (make / made) witness to matters no human being may see.

5[33] You're one of those charming women with (who / whom) it's nice to talk, and nice to be silent.

6[34] American blacks had (become / became) recognized as a species of human being by amendments to the Constitution shortly after the Civil War.

7[35] You have to adjust your scope extra (careful / carefully) or you won't see anything but your own eye.

8[36] If man (was / were) forced to demonstrate for himself all the truths of which he makes daily use, his task would never end.

9[37] They find so often that instead of having (laid / lain) an egg, they have (laid / lain) a vote, or an empty ink-bottle, or some other absolutely unhatchable object, which means nothing to them.

10[38] A modern poet has characterized the personality of art and the impersonality of science as follows: Art is (I / me); Science is (we / us).

11[39] Hail, Emperor, we (who / whom) are about to die salute you.

12[40] It was one of those swift dramas which (is / are) played only in Italy or Paris.

13[41] *A* Coming down the slope, my skis suddenly started to ripple.
B As I was coming down the slope, my skis suddenly started to ripple.

14[42] Each of their friends (was / were) going to bring part of the dinner.

15[43] The fact is that the number of officials and the quantity of the work (is / are) not related to each other at all.

16[44] *A* Whistling bravely, the dark didn't scare me at all.
B By whistling bravely, I tried to keep from being scared of the dark.

17[45] (Who / Whom), then, was the forger?

18[46] It is even possible that the first genuine thinking machines may be (growed / grown) rather than constructed; already some crude but very stimulating experiments have been carried out along these lines.

19[47] Jesus may have expressed the feeling that, if this Temple made with hands (was / were) destroyed, real religion might not lose much.

20[48] It's better to (answer quickly / quickly answer) even if you don't know the question.

21[49] But if the open air and adventure mean everything to Defoe (it / they) (mean / means) nothing to Jane Austen.

22[50] I am apt to fancy I have contracted a new acquaintance (who / whom) it will be no easy matter to shake off.

23[51] The only difference between (he / him) and (they / them) was that he had lost his all.

24[52] Professor Smile ought to retire; he's (older than any / the oldest) professor in the department.

25[53] The gate itself, or what remained of it, (lay / laid) unhinged to one side, the interstices of the rotted palings choked with grass and weeds like the ribs of a forgotten skeleton.

26[54] In this real world his horse danced as if it (were / was) wild or crazy and this is the reason why he called himself Crazy Horse.

27[55] But Henry James and Mrs. Wharton (was / were) our most interesting novelists, and most of the young writers followed their manner, without having their qualifications.

28[56] One of my fondest recollections (is / are) of an outhouse in Virgina.

29[57] One of the biggest problems of the Carter advisors (has / have) been how to sort out all the widely varying estimates of the number of people in the affected categories.

30[58] Perhaps she pitied most not those (who / whom) she aided in the struggle, but the more fortunate (who / whom) were preoccupied with themselves and cursed with self-deceptions of private success.

DICTIONARY OF USAGE PROBLEMS

a, an   Use *a* before words beginning with a consonant sound (*a cat, a union, a historical nove*l). Use *an* before words beginning with a vowel sound or silent *h* (*an experiment, an onion, an hour, an honor*).

abbreviations   In general, avoid abbreviations in formal writing. Except for some scientific papers, in which abbreviations are common, avoid abbreviations other than for names and titles (*Mrs., Mr., Dr.,* and so on); do not abbreviate words like pound [x *lb*.], ounce [x *oz*.], inch [x *in*.] in an essay or term paper, for example. See Capitalization in Chapter 10.

accept, except   *Accept* means "to receive" or "to take." "I accept the responsibility." *Except* means "to exclude" or "but." "Everyone left except Bill."

A.D.   A.D. means "Anno Domini," in the year of the Lord, and therefore it is redundant to write "in the year A.D. 750." Note that A.D. usually precedes the number. Write it without underlining or spaces between the letters.

advice, advise   *Advice* is a suggestion, a recommendation. "They give us good advice." *Advise* means "to make a recommendation; to give a suggestion." "They advise us to take the shorter road."

affect, effect   *Affect* means "to influence." "Your health affects your personality." It also means "to pretend or take on airs." "He affects indifference to his critics." As a noun, *an affect* is a nonphysical aspect of emotion (pronounced with the emphasis on first syllable). *Effect* means "to bring about directly, make happen." "We will effect the changes in your directions as soon as they arrive." To *put into effect* is to make happen. "The changes will be put into effect as soon as the plans arrive." As a noun *an effect* is a result or outcome: "One effect of not studying is poor grades."

allude, refer   *Refer* is the more direct word; *allude* means "to make indirect reference." "She alluded to the President when she spoke of 'whoever is responsible for the mistake,' but she did not refer to him by name."

all of a sudden   *Suddenly* is more concise. *All of the sudden* is oral English.

allusion, illusion   *Allusion* means "a reference to something." "Your allusion to Shakespeare should be documented." *Illusion* means "ghost, imaginary vision, false appearance." "He created the illusion of prosperity by living on credit."

alot   Not recognized in formal writing as a spelling of *a lot*. Compare with *a little*.

already, all ready   *Already* means "previously." "You have already explained the answer." *All ready* means "everything is ready." "They are all ready for the exam."

alright   Not recognized in formal writing as a spelling of *all right*. Compare with *all wrong*.

A.M., P.M.   *Ante meridiem, post meridiem*. Do not add redundant *morning, evening,* or *o'clock* with these designators of time. "It was 9:00 A.M. [x 9:00 A.M. *in the morning*] when she arrived." Do not use them as synonyms of *morning* or *night*. "We finished at four in the morning [x *in the A.M.*]." By tradition, midnight is 12:00 P.M. and noon is 12:00 A.M. Publishers use small capital letters, but on your typewriter use lower case: *a.m., p.m.*

among, between   Use *among* when you are writing about more than two things. "We note minute differences among several plants." Use *between* for two items. "We found no differences between pre- and posttest results."

amount, number   *Number* is used for things that can be counted (number of trees). *Amount* is used for things that are measured by volume (amount of corn, amount of noise). Formal usage suggests "amount of money" and "number of dollars," but some writers use "amount of dollars," particularly where large sums of money are involved. "When the amount of dollars held in foreign banks exceeds foreign imports, we have an exchange imbalance."

and which, and who   Use only to connect with a preceding *who* or *which* clause. "This is an experiment which interests us and which we would like to try [x *This is an interesting experiment, and which we would like to try*]."

anymore   Not recognized in formal writing as a spelling of *any more*.

anyplace   Not recognized as a spelling of *any place*.

anyways   Oral English, not used in formal writing.

anywheres   Oral English, not used in formal writing.

as good as, as much as   Oral English for *virtually*. "They virtually [x *as good as*] admitted their calculations were wrong."

authored   Informal for *wrote*.

at this point in time   Pretentious for *now* or *at this time*. Such wordy phrases are falsely legalistic, and distracting to many readers.

a while, awhile   *While* is a noun. "We sat for a while to think about our plans." *Awhile* is an adverb. "We sat awhile and then left."

bad, badly   Use *bad* to describe emotions and state of health. "She felt bad about the tests. The child looked bad." Use *badly* as an adverb to describe actions. "He typed badly, but he got the work done."

B.C.   B.C. means "before Christ." It is unnecessary to use *in the year* or *in the year of* with B.C. dates. "Britain was invaded in 55 B.C." Note that B.C., unlike A.D., customarily follows the date. It is typed in lower-case letters without space between the letters and without underlining.

being, being as, being that   Oral English for *since* or *because*. "Since [x *Being as*] I knew the way, I drove."

between you and I   Oral English for *between you and me*.

bias   Oral English for *biased*. "They were biased [x *bias*] in favor of their own interests.

bored of   Oral English for *bored by, bored with, tired of*. "She was bored by [x *bored of*] long hours of reading statistical abstracts."

both . . . and   Use *both . . . and* to emphasize a pair, not *both . . . as well as*. "Both the government and [x *as well as*] private industry have projects involving environmental protection."

can, may   Not considered interchangeable. "You can pass the test" is not the same as "You may pass the test." But in making requests, the distinction between *can* and *may* is often ignored; you can use either, depending on how polite you want to sound. "Can I visit you soon? May I visit you soon?"

cause is due to   Redundant. "The cause of the long lines was [x *was due to*] a gasoline shortage."

censor, censure   To *censor* means "to deny permission to publish or broadcast." To *censure* means "to express disapproval of an action."

cite, site   *Cite* means "to refer to." "Your paper cites Hemingway." *Site* means "place." "We applied a local anesthetic to the site of the wound."

complected   Oral English for *complexioned*. Not used in formal writing. "They were a light-complexioned [x *complected*] people."

compliment, complement   To *compliment* is to flatter. "I won't compliment him for that terrible pun." To *complement* is to balance or complete. "The professor's handouts complement the textbook."

consensus of opinion   Redundant. "The consensus is that smoking is bad for you."

continuous, continual   *Continuous* means "without interruption." "A continuous supply of electricity is essential to industry." *Continual* means "happening frequently, but not without interruption." "The continual ringing of the phone kept me from studying."

contractions   Usuaully not found in the most formal writing (legal documents, doctoral dissertations), but otherwise acceptable if they serve the writing purpose—they help to alleviate a too formal tone: *I'll*, *haven't*, *don't*, *isn't*, *it's*, and so on.

contrast from, contrast to   Informal for *contrast with*. "The red end of the spectrum contrasts with [x *to*] the blue end." "In contrast with [x *from*] more advanced nations, the developing countries lack technology."

could of   Oral English. Not recognized in formal writing as a spelling for *could have*.

credible, credulous   *Credible* means "that which sounds believable, such as a witness or testimony." *Credulous* means "believing too easily, gullible." "I am so credulous I'll believe anything you tell me."

desert, dessert   *Dessert* is the last course in a meal. *Desert* means "arid land," and *to desert* means "to abandon." "She deserted him in the desert after dessert."

differ from, different from   Formal writing requires *differ from* and *different from*. "One thing differs from another. She is different from other girls." But *different than* is widely used in less formal writing.

disasterous   Not accepted as a spelling of *disastrous*.

disinterested, uninterested   Disinterested means "impartial, unbiased." "A referee must be disinterested in the outcome." *Uninterested* means "having no interest." "She was uninterested in his proposal."

double negative Oral English, not accepted in formal writing. The double negative is produced by two negatives or two words whose sense is negative, in the same sentence—*can't hardly, don't scarcely, haven't got none, can't get no,* and so forth.

emigrate, immigrate To *emigrate* is to leave your country. To *immigrate* is to enter a foreign country.

eminent, imminent *Eminent* means "well-known, outstanding" (*eminent physican*). *Imminent* means "approaching, soon to arrive" (*imminent danger*).

enthuse, enthused, enthusing Informal derivatives of *enthusiasm*.

etc. Do not use the abbreviation *etc.* Instead, use *and so on* or *and so forth*. It is often better to list the additional items. Note that *and etc.* is redundant; *and* is already contained in *et cetera*.

farther, further In formal writing, *farther* is used for progress in space, physical distance. "Her room is farther down the hall." *Further* is used for degree or progress in time. "We were able to get further with these procedures than any other." Less formally, the words are interchangeable, except when you mean *additional*. "No further applications can be accepted."

few, less *Few* should be used with countable items: *few people*. *Less* should be used with items measured by volume or degree: *less milk, less noise*.

flunk Oral English for *fail*.

former, latter In referring to two items, the first is the *former*, and the second is the *latter*. "Oak and pine—the former is strong, and the latter is soft." Use *former* and *latter* instead of *first* and *last*.

fun Not accepted as a modifier in formal writing. "Waterskiing is a thrilling [x *fun*] sport." "She is an enjoyable [x *fun*] person to be with."

hanged, hung *Hanged* means "executed by hanging." "He was hanged by a mob of racists." For any other kind of hanging, use *hung*. "The stockings were hung by the chimney with care. . . ."

hopefully Weak substitute for *maybe* or *I hope*. "I hope [x *Hopefully*] this report will get done on time. *Hopefully* is correct when used to mean "with hope." "Despite her problems, she faced the future hopefully."

how Oral English for *that* or *the fact that*. "This book shows that [x *how*] crime does not pay. We were impressed by the fact that [x *how*] they had the reports done quickly."

if, whether, whether or not Use *whether* to express doubt. "She wondered whether [x *if*] she should go." *Or not* is redundant in such cases.

in back of *Behind* is less wordy.

in, into Most educated readers believe "He fell *in* the closet" means he fell while in the closet. "He fell *into* the closet" means he fell while outside the closet. The distinction is often ignored in less formal writing.

in the area of   Vague, wordy, and imprecise. "We are working in chemical reactions [x *in the area of chemical reactions*]."

in this day and age   Wordy for *now* or *today*.

infer, imply   *Imply* means "to suggest." *Infer* means "to deduce." "We infer that you are implying our statistics are faulty."

inside of   *Inside* is less wordy. "She is inside [x *inside of*] the house."

incidence, incidents   An *incident* is a happening, an event. "Several incidents of unrest have been reported." *Incidence* means "rate of occurrence." "The incidence of these disturbances is rising."

irregardless   Not recognized in formal writing. "Regardless [x *irregardless*] of the criticism, we intend to proceed. The project looks unpromising but we intend to proceed regardless [x *irregardless*]."

its, it's   *It's* is a contraction of *it is*, not to be confused with the possessive form of *it: its*. "It's time to give the dog its annual bath."

like, as   Formal usage avoids using *like* in place of *as*. "They did things as [x *like*] their ancestors had done them." Less formally the two words are interchangeable.

lots of   Informal for *many, much*. "There are many [x *lots of*] reasons for going to high school."

mad   Not recognized in formal writing as a substitute for *angry*. Less formally, *mad* and *angry* are interchangeable.

might of   Oral English for *might have*.

monsterous, monsterosity   Not recognized as spellings of *monstrous, monstrosity*.

most every   Oral English for *almost* or *nearly*. "Nearly everyone [x *most everyone*] approves of charity. He hits the ball almost [x *most*] every time."

must of   Oral English for *must have*.

not too distant future   Wordy for *soon*.

nowheres   Oral English for *nowhere, anywhere*.

numbers   In general, any number that can be expressed in one or two words should be written out (*ninety-nine, two thousand, five million*), especially in literary essays. But in technical reports, informal writing, and any other writing in which numbers are a significant component, numerals are usually preferred (*99; 2,000; 5 million*). Avoid starting a sentence with a numeral; revise so that the numeral does not come first.

off of, off from   Redundant. "Send whatever you can take off [x *off of*] the shelves."

ourself   Not recognized in formal writing, except for royalty. "We voted ourselves [x *ourself*] a pay raise."

OK, O.K., okay All are accepted spellings, but the word itself should be restricted to informal writing. "Everything seemed ready [x *okay*] for the next day's tryout."

particular Redundant in the presence of *this*, *that*, *these*, or *those*. "This type [x *this particular type*] of chemical reaction is very common."

predominate, predominant *Predominant* is an adjective; *Predominate* is a verb. "The predominant [x *predominate*] rule was economy." "Southern accents predominate in New Orleans."

prejudice Oral English for *prejudiced*. "We are very prejudiced [x *prejudice*] in favor of our own interpretations of the data."

pretty Oral English for *somewhat* or *rather*. "The serum produced from the roots made them rather [x *pretty*] sick."

principal, principle The principal is the head of the school. The word can be used to designate any main or chief thing. "The principal cause of poverty is unemployment." In economics, *principal* is the sum of money on which interest is earned. *Principle* refers to ethics, theories, guidelines, moral quality. "His actions seem good, but his principles are suspect."

proceed Pretentious when the context requires *go*. "After dinner we should go [x *proceed*] to the library."

prophecy, prophesy A *prophecy* is a prediction. To *prophesy* is to make a prediction.

rarely ever Redundant. "I rarely [x *rarely ever*] go out at night."

real Oral English for *very*. "The results were very [x *real*] good."

reason is because Redundant. "The reason for the fire was that [x *because*] the wiring was faulty."

reason why Redundant. "They wanted to know the reason [x *reason why*] the engines overheated."

repeat again Redundant.

said A pretentious legalism [x *the said property; the said individual*].

shall, will The distinction between these words is seldom observed today. Some writers still use *shall* when they want to be especially formal or emphatic: "We shall surely die." But generally *shall* is no longer used except for formal requests: "Shall we do it?"

should of Oral English for *should have*.

somewheres Oral English for *somewhere*.

suppose Oral English for *supposed*. "We were supposed [x *suppose*] to receive new supplies in a week."

theirself, theirselves, themself None of these is recognized in formal writing. Use *themselves*.

today's modern world, today's modern society, modern world of today Wordy and redundant for *now* or *today*.

use to Oral English for *used to*. "We used to [x *use to*] give public demonstrations."

ways Oral English for *way*. "We have a long way [x *ways*] to go yet on this project."

when Informal for *in which*, particularly in definitions. "Inflation is a condition in which [x *when*] there is too much money for too few goods." But note: "Inflation *occurs when* there is too much money and too few goods."

where Informal for *in which*. "This is a book in which [x *where*] crime does pay, at least temporarily."

where . . . to, where . . . at Redundant. "Where are you going [x *going to*]? Where is my pencil [x *pencil at*]?"

would of Oral English for *would have*.

Usage review 2

Select the formal English alternative in the following sentences.

1 The reason is (that / because) they are overladen with ideas.
ALFRED NORTH WHITEHEAD, *The Aims of Education*

2 The old idea that the hen deliberately selects the male she thinks the most beautiful is putting the matter in human terms which certainly do not apply to a bird's mind; but it seems certain that the brilliant and exciting display does have an (affect / effect) on the hen bird, stimulating her to greater readiness to mate.
JULIAN HUXLEY, *On Living in a Revolution*

3 It is only with science that the (allusion / illusion) exists; the (allusion / illusion) of a neutral, inhuman activity separate from the world of "telegrams and anger."
JOHN H. STEELE, "The Fiction of Science," *The Listener*

4 The (amount / number) of college bulletins and adult-education come-ons that keep turning up in my mailbox convinces me that I must be on a special mailing list for dropouts.
WOODY ALLEN, *Getting Even*

5 (Suddenly / All of a sudden) the superintendent made up his mind.
GEORGE ORWELL, "A Hanging," *Shooting an Elephant and Other Essays*

6 Let's (accept / except) 115 as man's maximum age, then, and ask (whether / if) we have a good reason to complain about this.
ISAAC ASIMOV, "The Slowly Moving Finger," *Of Time and Space and Other Things*

7 I (hardly / don't hardly) remember getting (in / into) bed and to sleep, but all night in my dreams I thought I could hear a wolf calling and singing and sobbing in a voice of exquisite tenderness.
THEODORA C. STANWELL-FLETCHER, *Driftwood Valley*

8 (Already / All ready) it has created a situation where parents and children find it hard to communicate on social matters.

CHARLES W. COLE, "American Youth Goes Monogamous," *Harper's Magazine*, Mar. 1957

9 But according to the rules, it is (alright / all right) to kid him a little.

BENJAMIN SPOCK, *Baby and Child Care*

10 If she had never, from the first, regarded her marriage as a full cancelling of her claims on life, she had at least, for a number of years, (accepted / excepted) it as provisional compensation. . . .

EDITH WHARTON, "Souls Belated"

Revision practice

Revise any of the following sentences that contain a problem in usage. Some of the sentences may not require revision.

1 In our modern world of today, drugs have become quite a problem.

2 Adreen stepped into her closet.

3 They didn't know whether they shouldn't ask for permission.

4 The one who always has the answer is she.

5 Their racing shell sunk in six feet of water.

6 No one can lay around forever, Manny.

7 I knew he was guilty when I seen him look away.

8 Speak soft or she will hear you.

9 I felt so badly about missing the test that I went back to sleep.

10 Irregardless of the time it takes, you must keep hunting data.

11 I wonder whether or not it will snow by Christmas.

12 I had been reading for an hour when suddenly I find this marvelous quote.

13 It's easy to guess whom you mean.

14 At this point in time, I'm not prepared to answer the question.

15 No one understands why this data is so unusual; its totally unique.

16 This is one of those schools which provide financial aid to students.

17 The reason grammar is so hard is because it seems so arbitrary.

18 The party was quite a surprise for her and me.

19 They had recently conducted a experiment in cryogenic suspension.

20 In her last letter, Bernice had written that she hoped she would be excepted into the sorority.

21 These records showed that a man named Tortillius had lived in the year 27 A.D.

22 The affect of dropping water into the acid was a minor explosion of steam.

23 It is conceivable that alot of the chatter comes from loose bearings in the drive line.

24 Everyone assumes the bridge must be alright or the authorities wouldn't permit its use.

25 The amount of tools required to fix something as simple as an electric clock is staggering.

26 We have tracked the senator all over Washington and regret to say that we cannot find him anywheres.

27 Our old iron hoists were as good as rusted through before anyone noticed their dangerous condition.

28 Professor Peterson had authored a dozen books on anthropology and was recognized as an international authority.

29 Being as the chief of surgery was on vacation, the head resident performed the operation.

30 It was clear that they were bias against people of her race and were using excuses to keep her out of the club.

31 The far western states have been chosen as the cite for the new missile silos.

32 We have painted a dark green border along the base to compliment the pale green walls.

33 The consensus of opinion is that smoking cigars is hazardous to your health.

34 With a little more money we could of finished the project ahead of schedule and with better results.

35 *E.T.* is a film where a boy meets an alien creature, and the two of them become close friends.

[1] FRANCOISE-MARIE DE VOLTAIRE, *Candide*
[2] BETTY PIERCE
[3] JOHN STEINBECK, *The Grapes of Wrath*
[4] GUSTAVE FLAUBERT, *Madame Bovary*
[5] FRANZ KAFKA, *The Metamorphosis*
[6] ROBERT LOUIS STEVENSON, *An Inland Voyage*
[7] MARK SILVERS
[8] HENRY JAMES, *The Aspen Papers*
[9] ROBERT J. GLESSING, *The Underground Press in America*
[10] OLIVER LA FARGE, *Old Man Facing Death*

[11] HOWARD ADAMS

[12] ALBERT CAMUS, *The Stranger*

[13] MARY WOLLSTONECRAFT, *Frankenstein*

[14] NATHANAEL WEST, *The Day of the Locust*

[15] MARK TWAIN, *Huckleberry Finn*

[16] ROBERT MURPHY, *A Certain Island*

[17] DAN THOMPSON

[18] BRAM STOKER, *Dracula*

[19] AYN RAND, *Atlas Shrugged*

[20] EMILY BRONTË, *Wuthering Heights*

[21] "Choose from a World of Brandies,"*House Beautiful*, Nov. 1976

[22] Advertisement, American Gas Association

[23] ERNEST HEMINGWAY, "The Snows of Kilimanjaro"

[24] ROGER MARTIN DU GARD, *The Thibaults*

[25] CHARLES MICHNER, "Black Movies: Renaissance or Ripoff?" *Newsweek*, 23 Oct. 1972

[26] BONNIE SULLIVAN

[27] CHARLES DICKENS, *The Old Curiosity Shop*

[28] ROBERT LOUIS STEVENSON, *Travels with a Donkey*

[29] Advertisement, *Saturday Evening Post*, Jan./Feb. 1977

[30] MARTIN LUTHER KING, JR., *Why We Can't Wait*

[31] "Now and Forever," *Newsweek*, 17 Jan. 1977

[32] JAMES AGEE AND WALKER EVANS, *Let Us Now Praise Famous Men*

[33] LEO TOLSTOY, *Anna Kerenina*

[34] VINE DELORIA, JR., *Custer Died for Your Sins: An Indian Manifesto*

[35] VALLERIE ENSON

[36] ALEXIS DE TOCQUEVILLE, *Democracy in America*

[37] D. H. LAWRENCE, *Cocksure Women and Hensure Men*

[38] CLAUDE BERNARD, *Bulletin of the New York Academy of Medicine*, IV, 1928

[39] SUETONIUS, *Life of Claudius*

[40] HONORE DE BALZAC, *The Imaginary Mistress*

[41] DEANNA CROSS

[42] MAE SHIPERS

[43] C. NORTHCOTE PARKINSON, *Parkinson's Law and Other Studies in Administration*

[44] FELICIA STRAUSS

[45] RICHARD D. ALTICK, *The Scholar Adventurer*

[46] ARTHUR C. CLARKE, *Profiles of the Future*

[47] HENRY SLOANE COFFIN, *The Meaning of the Cross*

[48] GRETCHEN FUNNEL

[49] VIRGINIA WOOLF, "How Should One Read a Book?"

[50] OLIVER GOLDSMITH, *The Citizen of the World*

[51] JOSEPH CONRAD, "The End of the Tether"

[52] WHITNEY SODER

[53] WILLIAM FAULKNER, *The Hamlet*

[54] DEE BROWN, *Bury My Heart at Wounded Knee*

[55] WILLA CATHER, *Willa Cather on Writing*

[56] MARJORIE KINNAN RAWLINGS, *Cross Creek*

[57] "Pardon: How Broad a Blanket?" *Time*, 17 Jan. 1977

[58] ADLAI STEVENSON, *Looking Outward*

CHAPTER TEN

Mechanics

You have to really work at it to write.

I guess there has to be talent first;

but even with talent

you still have to *work* at it to write.

JAMES JONES, *Writers at Work*, George Plimpton, ed.

By comparison with large matters of purpose, ideas, and organization, such things as punctuation, spelling, and capitalization may seem trivial. But all these mechanics of writing are tools the writer uses to signal the reader. An occasional error may be excused, but writers cannot afford to ignore the effect of mistakes on the reader. At the least, mistakes are distracting and interrupt the train of thought; at the worst, mistakes may *change* the thought: faulty punctuation, a mistaken spelling, even a word not capitalized may create a meaning unintended by the writer. Careful writers take pains to ensure that the effect of their words is not distorted by faulty mechanics.

Beyond the mere avoidance of error, mechanics can give you greater facility and maturity of expression. Beginning writers frequently avoid all but a few marks of punctuation they know well—the end marks and the comma—or avoid words they cannot spell readily. All this has the effect of limiting the means of expression available to you as a writer. With some review and practice of the mechanics of writing, you will be able to increase your use of them and your skill with them.

PUNCTUATION GUIDE

Punctuation is an important part of writing; it is the signal system by which you tell the reader how to interpret your sentences. You know most of the marks, but some of the technical uses of punctuation may be unfamiliar, and others may need review. Then too, you will find that formal punctuation is somewhat different from that in popular writing. Most newspapers follow the *Associated Press Style Book*, which has punctuation conventions somewhat different from those used in academic books, business writing, scientific work, and so on. The punctuation guidelines in *The Writer's Work* are standard for all formal writing in typed papers.

For easy reference, the marks are presented here in alphabetical order.

APOSTROPHE

There is some disagreement about whether the apostrophe is really a punctuation mark; some authorities feel it should be considered part of spelling. But since it is in fact a "mark" used to indicate meaning, we have included it here with the other marks.

1. USE AN APOSTROPHE FOR SINGULAR POSSESSIVE

To show possession or ownership, add *'s* unless the word already ends in *s*—in which case just add the apostrophe: *man's hat, dog's tail, iris' color, Jones' work*.

2. USE AN APOSTROPHE FOR PLURAL POSSESSIVE

To show possession or ownership with a plural word, add *'s* to the *plural form* of the word, unless the plural ends in *s*—in which case just add the apostrophe: *men's hats, children's shoes, dogs' tails*.

Option   If you wish to indicate that the possessive is to be pronounced as a separate syllable, you have the option of adding an extra *s* to a word ending in *s: Jones's, James's, Lois's*.

3. USE AN APOSTROPHE FOR ABSTRACT OR INANIMATE POSSESSIVES

Abstract and inaminate terms can be more difficult to recognize as having possession or ownership, but a tree "possesses" leaves (*tree's leaves*) in a grammatical sense: *day's wages, life's troubles, investigation's conclusion, countries' citizens*.

4. USE AN APOSTROPHE TO FORM A CONTRACTION

Most contractions are acceptable in college writing, although they do tend to give a paper a less formal sound. The apostrophe takes the place of the missing letter or letters in the contracted word: *haven't* (have not), *they've* (they have), *I'm* (I am), *it's* (it is).

Reminder   Avoid using apostrophes to form plurals (avoid confusing plurals with possessives): *the three Rs, the ABCs, the 1980s*.

PLURAL

Compared to the music of the 1950s, the music of the 1980s is much more diverse.

POSSESSIVE

Our 1980's model cars are smaller and lighter.

The 1980s' students were concerned about jobs.

However, if there is any possible confusion without the apostrophe, you should go ahead and use it if you are sure the context will make your meaning clear: "Dot your *i*'s and cross your *t*'s."

BRACKETS

If your typewriter doesn't have brackets, draw them in with a pen.

1. **USE BRACKETS TO SET OFF CLARIFYING MATERIAL YOU INSERT INTO QUOTED MATTER**

"Eyes narrowing, he [the President] declared, 'The budget we propose is a line drawn in the dirt.' "

ED MAGNUSON, "A Line Drawn in the Dirt," *Time*, 22 Feb. 1982

"With Hemingway, Dos Passos, Wilder and Faulkner, he [Wolfe] was one of a group of talents for fiction such as rarely appear in a single hatching."

F. SCOTT FITZGERALD, "My Generation"

2. **USE BRACKETS TO MAKE MINOR ALTERATIONS IN QUOTATIONS**

Sometimes when incorporating a quote into one of your own sentences (see Incorporated Quotes) you may find that you must slightly alter the grammar of the original. Such changes are acceptable as long as they are (1) few in number, (2) clearly justified by the needs of your sentence, and (3) unlikely to cause any confusion or doubt about your accuracy.

One college admissions officer assured me one day that he recognized my importance to his school precisely as derived from the fact that, after graduation, I would surely be "going back to [my] community."

RICHARD RODRIGUEZ, "Going Home Again"

3. **USE BRACKETS TO NOTE ERRORS IN SOURCE MATERIAL**

If material you quote contains an error made by the original author, you may insert *sic* in brackets immediately after the error. *Sic*, which means "thus," tells the reader that the error in language or logic appears "thus" in the original. Don't use *sic* for every minor spelling or typographical error you find (you may routinely correct such errors); use it for errors you are reluctant to change, even though you know they may cause confusion:

Lewis reports that "over 100,00 [sic] people had been afflicted."

Since you cannot be sure what number Lewis intended, it would not be wise to alter this obvious error, and thus *sic* is appropriate. Note that *sic* is not an abbreviation and does not require a period. It is usually not underlined.

4. USE BRACKETS FOR PARENTHESES WITHIN PARENTHESES

Yet Senora Casusa thinks that Castro would have accepted an invitation if he had been offered one (*Cuba and Castro* [New York: Random House, 1961], p. 207).

THEODORE DRAPER, *Castro's Revolution*

COLON

1. USE A COLON TO INTRODUCE A SERIES

Perusal of any daily paper will turn up countless examples of compounds that are new within the last few years or months: *launching pad, blast-off, jet-port, freeway, ski-tow, free loader, featherbedding, sit-in.*

W. NELSON FRANCIS, *The English Language*

Three or more items in a series should be introduced with a colon under these conditions: (1) there is a pause before the series, (2) there is a clear signal that a series is coming—*the following, as follows, namely these,* and so on. If there is no clearly stated signal, the colon should be used only if it takes the place of the signal (your sentence should be read as if the colon itself meant "such as," "namely," and so on).

CLEARLY SIGNALED

Naturally they read authors such as the following: Poe, Hemingway, Steinbeck, Emerson.

IMPLIED "SUCH AS" OR "NAMELY"

Naturally they read many different authors: Poe, Hemingway, Steinbeck, Emerson.

NO PAUSE OR SIGNAL FOR SERIES, NO COLON

Some of their favorite authors include Poe, Hemingway, Steinbeck, and Emerson.

— *No Colon After* To Be   It is not formal style to use a colon after forms of the verb *to be* (*am, is, are, was, were, be, being, been*):

INFORMAL STYLE [NOT RECOMMENDED FOR COLLEGE]

Some of their favorite authors are: Poe, Hemingway, Steinbeck, Emerson.

FORMAL STYLE [PREFERRED]

Some of their favorite authors are Poe, Hemingway, Steinbeck, Emerson.

2. **USE A COLON TO EMPHASIZE AN APPOSITIVE**

Appositives are words that identify or rename a preceding noun or pronoun.

About ten more years elapsed before investigators were able to determine its chemical identity: indolitic acid.

FULLER, CAROTHERS, ET AL., *The Plant World*

Note that appositives are usually set off with commas and can also be set off with dashes. But to call attention to the appositive at the end of a sentence, formal writing often uses the colon.

3. **USE A COLON BEFORE AN EXAMPLE, ILLUSTRATION, COMPLEMENT**

Its effect on the process was dramatic: as the pressure increased, people began to faint.

The division between the rich and the poor countries is a simple one: incomes in the poor countries are only a fraction of those in the rich.

ROBERT THEOBALD, *The Rich and the Poor*

4. **USE A COLON TO INTRODUCE A FORMAL QUOTATION**

The remark was attributed to the Queen: "Let them eat cake."

A quote given as an illustration or example should be introduced with a colon. (All quotes, of course, require documentation.)

They were given to excessively dramatic statements: "We will surely all die quickly if we continue this policy."[1]

The author's view of commerce is often cynical:

> **Along with the opportunity for managing consumer demand, there must also be a mechanism for managing it. Authority is not well regarded here. By giving him a ration card or distributing to him the specific commodities he is to use, the individual can be required to consume in accordance with plan.**

JOHN KENNETH GALBRAITH, *The New Industrial State*

5. **USE A COLON AFTER THE SALUTATION IN A FORMAL LETTER**

Dear Sir: Dear Mrs. Holland: Professor Watt:

1. USE A COMMA TO SEPARATE SENTENCES JOINED BY *AND,*
BUT, OR, NOR, SO, FOR

As a nation the United States has not yet had to acquire the fortitude exacted of Israel, and a majority of the American people remain unwilling to accept the price of liberty.
LEWIS H. LAPHAM. "Feet of Clay," *Harpers,* 1981

Without doubt the pterodactyl attracted great attention, for even the least observant could see that there was the making of a bird in him.
MARK TWAIN, "The Damned Human Race"

— *Reminder* The comma is used only when one of the connective words (coordinate conjunctions) joins two complete sentences (two independent clauses). No comma is needed in the following example.

During the day the restaurant is filled with gray-haired ladies and businessmen lunching on hamburgers.
SUZANNE GORDON, *Lonely in America*

— *Option* Two sentences can be joined by commas alone or by conjunctions alone if the sentences are (1) very short, (2) closely related, and (3) structured alike:

I can walk out of the hospital, I can leave it all behind me.
MYRA BLUEBOND-LANGER, "How I Came to Study Dying Children"

You stick to your side, I'll stick to mine!
D. H. LAWRENCE, *Lady Chatterley's Lover*

One didn't know how the idea had been presented, one didn't know just when it had been presented.
NORMAN MAILER, *The Presidential Papers*

I am 28 years old and I have cancer.
JOEL SOLKOFF, "A New Lease on Life," *New York Times,* 26 Nov. 1976

— Comma Splice (Error)

It is informal style to join two sentences with a comma only (except for the option above). For example: *The President addressed the nation, he spoke of a crisis in trust.*

Separate such spliced sentences with a period or a semicolon:

The President addressed the nation. He spoke of a crisis in trust.
The President addressed the nation; he spoke of a crisis in trust.

Or, using techniques from Chapter 7, combine the two ideas into one sentence:

379   Addressing the nation, the President spoke of a crisis in trust.

2. USE A COMMA AFTER INTRODUCTORY WORDS AND TRANSITIONAL EXPRESSIONS

In the winter, they worked on the equipment to be used in spring.

Naturally, they denied everything.

First, the money needed would be astronomical.

When it is done, they stand around congratulating themselves.

The comma emphasizes the introductory pause. Writers sometimes omit this comma, and deemphasize the introduction, when the introductory element is very short.

In seconds the mass had swollen to twice its volume.

For Frenchmen Joan of Arc has remained the purest symbol of patriotism.

ANDRÉ MAUROIS, *A History of France*

3. USE COMMAS TO SEPARATE THREE OR MORE ITEMS IN A SERIES

For dinner they had chicken, potatoes, peas, and a tossed salad.

Reminder   Do not place a comma after the final item when the series comes first in the sentence; do not separate the series from its verb. Note there is no comma after "Chippewa" here:

Mohawk, Sioux, and Chippewa were next in popularity.

VINE DELORIA, JR., *Custer Died for Your Sins*

Kale, lettuce, chard, turnips, carrots, and onions rotated in the little garden.

JOHN STEINBECK, "A Primer on the Thirties"

— *Reminder*   In formal writing, accuracy is the most important consideration. For that reason, many writers feel it is a mistake to omit the final comma in a series.

The refugee population was composed of people whose ancestry was Vietnamese, Laotian, Thai, Cambodian and Chinese.

What does the writer mean here? How many groups are identified? To avoid any misinterpretation, follow the custom of using a comma with each item in a series. If the writer really meant to identify four groups, he or she should write the sentence to make that clear:

The refugee population was composed of Vietnamese, Laotians, Thai, and Chinese Cambodians.

Note It is not absolutely necessary to use the word *and* before the last item in a series. For example: "They stored up sugar, potatoes, salt, apples, pork, fish."

Option The items in a series can be joined with conjunctions instead of commas.

She told them to bring their books and their papers and their brains.

4. USE COMMAS TO SET OFF EXPLANATORY AND PARENTHETIC ELEMENTS

But all these practical problems are, in a sense, beside the point.
ANDREW TORCHIA, "Africa Assignment," *Columbia Journalism Review*, May/June 1981

A glass-bottomed boat, or at least a glass-bottomed bucket, is a great aid in locating the best fishing grounds.
OWEN LEE, *Snorkel and Deep Diving*

5. USE COMMAS TO SET OFF NAMES AND TITLES IN DIRECT ADDRESS

He said, "Professor Titus, please clarify your position."

"You, Eduardo, have the manners of a troll," she said.

"Did you cut the telephone wire, George?"
HAROLD MACGRATH, *The Green Stone*

6. USE COMMAS TO SET OFF APPOSITIVES

Appositives are words that identify or rename a following or preceding noun or pronoun.

And this man, John Glenn, had given them an answer as sentimental as the question itself.
TOM WOLFE, *The Right Stuff*

But that couldn't happen because he, an astronaut, was supposed to be one of the most sane people in the world.
ALAN D. FOSTER, *Dark Star*

Option The effect of the appositive is to help identify a noun or pronoun, but you may omit commas from appositives when the identification is unnecessary, as in common expressions like *My friend Dr. Long* or *My partner Alice*.

Some appositives are essential (necessary to identify which one is meant) and must not be set off.

He had three sons, but only his son George continued the work.

Titles after names should be treated like appositives—set off with commas.

Ellen Hayes, treasurer, read the report.

7. USE COMMAS TO SET OFF ELEMENTS OF DATES AND ADDRESSES

This project was begun on January 12, 1982, at Los Alamos.
Send all inquiries to Prentice-Hall, Englewood Cliffs, New Jersey.

—*Reminder* Military style is becoming popular for dates; no commas are used when dates are written this way:

The project was begun on 12 January 1981 at Los Alamos.

—*Option* Modern writers sometimes give a month and year without a comma.

Most of the reports had been turned in by April 1981.

8. USE COMMAS TO SET OFF SPEAKER TAGS

Speaker tags are identifiers in dialgoue: *he said, she replied,* and so on.

"Kiss me," Louise said, "and shut up."
IRWIN SHAW, "The Eighty-Yard Run"

The church says, "If you sin, you shall be punished hereafter."
A. S. NEILL, *Summerhill*

—*Reminder* If the quoted matter ends with a question mark or exclamation point, no separating comma is necessary.

"Now what do you make of that?" said Joe Bell, satisfied with my puzzlement.
TRUMAN CAPOTE, "Breakfast at Tiffany's"

"Oh dear!" I said. "That was my station and now I have missed the bus."
MAEVE BRENNAN, *The Long-Winded Lady*

USE COMMAS TO SET OFF CONTRASTIVE ELEMENTS

To such advice some would listen, while others would not heed it.
GRINELL, *Pawnee, Blackfoot, Cheyenne*

This difference was a question of brain, not voice.
DESMOND MORRIS, *The Naked Ape*

9. USE COMMAS TO SET OFF NONESSENTIAL MODIFIERS

Nonessential modifiers (nonrestrictive) offer extra information, but do not serve to limit or specify the word they modify. Such nonessential *who, which,* or *that* modifiers should be set off with commas. Note that you can edit out these nonessential clauses without affecting the main idea of the sentence.

The cousin, who was married to a harridan and lived in Greenwich, sometimes visited the apartment with his secretary. . . .
TRUMAN CAPOTE, "Mojave"

His text, which covered more than twelve double-sided pages, concluded with a quotation from the Bingham censure case.
THEODORE C. SORENSEN, *Kennedy*

The sign was perpetuated in his descendants, a great part of whom had red beards.
SUETONIUS, *The Lives of the Twelve Caesars*

Note Cumulative modifiers, those added after the main clause of a sentence, are usually nonrestrictive and should be set off with commas.

He spoke haltingly, his voice trailing off, his sentences often grammatically incomplete.
JOE MCGINNESS, *Heroes*

They forced open the lid, slowly, steadily, with much effort.

Reminder Do not set off essential modifiers (restrictive). The essential modifier is necessary to tell the reader *how many* or *what kind* or *which one* is being discussed.

The winner was a student *who had achieved success through sheer effort.*

The same corporations and trade associations *that formed a united front behind the administration's tax budget proposals last year* are beginning to mobilize against Reagan's fiscal 1983 budget.
"Business Cools on Reaganomics," *Business Week*, 15 Mar. 1982

If you attempt to remove the *that* clause here, the main idea becomes unclear.

Note the difference between essential and nonessential:

The women who were cold put their coats on.

Only some of the women put their coats on; the *who* clause is essential to tell the reader which ones—only those who were cold.

The women, who were cold, put their coats on.

This sentence says all the women put their coats on; the *who* clause is not essential.

10. USE COMMAS IN PLACE OF *AND* BETWEEN MOVABLE ADJECTIVES

If all the adjectives describe the same word, so that you could rearrange them in some other order, separate them with commas.

The key instrument was a long, hard, cold knife.
(The key instrument was a cold and long and hard knife.)

He used his great, sad, motionless face to suggest various related things. . . .

JAMES AGEE, *Agee on Film, I*

Reminder If one or more adjectives describe the idea formed by an adjective and the noun, no comma should be used.

He began to sing an idiotic Mexican folk song.

CARLOS CASTANEDA, *Journey to Ixtlan*

11. USE A COMMA FOR CLARITY

Commas can help the reader avoid possible misreadings.

In the kitchen, sink messes are a depressing sight.
When she dressed, her dog sat on the bed.

12. USE A COMMA AFTER THE SALUTATION OF AN INFORMAL LETTER

Dear Hetty,   My Dear Francis,   Alice,   Hi Snooky,

USE A COMMA AFTER THE CLOSE OF ANY LETTER

Love,   Respectfully,   Very sincerely,   Yours truly,

DASH

1. USE A DASH TO INDICATE A SPEAKER'S WORDS ENDING ABRUPTLY OR FALTERING

In typing, make a dash with two hyphens (--) and leave no space before, between, or after them.

Note the difference between a "dash" (two hyphens) and a hyphen in the following sentence:

```
Or in still simpler terms, you've got--well, you've got to be sixty-five
```
```
and Irish and broke and angry and frustrated and mad at the world.
```
WILLIAM SAROYAN, "Little Miss Universe"

Mary took his book to hear him, and he tried to find his way through the fog:
"Blessed are the —a—a—"
"Poor—"
"Yes—poor; blessed are the poor—a—a—"

MARK TWAIN, *Tom Sawyer*

2. USE DASHES TO EMBED QUESTIONS, EXCLAMATIONS, DECLARATIONS

A question or exclamation inserted between dashes retains its question mark or exclamation point. (The period would never be appropriate.)

We all sat there—on the Hellespont!—waiting for it to get light.
RONALD BLYTHE, *Akenfield*

There is a custom in the village—I am told it is repeated in many villages—of "buying" African natives for the purpose of converting them to Christianity.
JAMES BALDWIN, *Notes of a Native Son*

3. **USE A DASH AFTER AN INTRODUCTORY SERIES**

Randomness, a lack of uniformity, basic unfairness—those were the issues.
WOODWARD AND BERNSTEIN, *The Bretheren*

Note the difference between a series that introduces a sentence (and is followed by a dash) and a series that is the subject of the sentence (and should not be separated from its verb):

Boxes, jars, napkin rings, and dishes fell from the shelves noisily.

Boxes, jars, napkin rings, and dishes—these fell noisily from the shelves.

4. **USE DASHES TO INDICATE A SUDDEN BREAK IN THE THOUGHT OF A SENTENCE**

And Gabriel loved her—if he loved her—only because she was the mother of his son, Ray.
JAMES BALDWIN, *Go Tell It on the Mountain*

Naomi somebody—a close friend of his—told him she had a worm in a thermos bottle.
J. D. SALINGER, "Down at the Dinghy"

5. **USE DASHES TO EMPHASIZE EXPLANATORY OR CLARIFYING INFORMATION**

Students of the Grail romances will remember that in many of the versions the hero—sometimes it is the heroine—meets with a strange and terrifying adventure in a mysterious chapel. . . .
JESSE L. WILSON, *From Ritual to Romance*

6. **USE A DASH FOR DRAMATIC PAUSE OR TO EMPHASIZE A POINT**

Anyway, they each entered the car through separate doors, and as soon as they were inside—wam! a tangle of rattlesnakes hit them like lightning.
TRUMAN CAPOTE, "Handcarved Coffins"

There are whole libraries of books about the Thirties—millions of feet of film, still and moving.
JOHN STEINBECK, "A Primer of the Thirties"

ELLIPSES

1. **USE AN ELLIPSIS TO SHOW THAT YOU HAVE OMITTED ONE OR MORE WORDS FROM QUOTED MATERIAL**

Use an ellipsis (three periods, or points) to indicate material omitted from quoted matter, a pause greater than a comma, or a deliberately discontinued thought (as when, for example, the thought is too obvious to require completion).

QUOTED MATTER

Tampering with another nation's satellite would be regarded as a hostile act with serious consequences, and would only be done in a wartime emergency.
FRANK TRIPPET, "Milk Run to the Heavens," *Time*, 12 Jan. 1981, pp. 10–14.

QUOTED MATTER WITH ELLIPSIS

Tampering with another nation's satellite . . . would only be done in a wartime emergency.

Note An ellipsis has a space before and after each of the three periods. If the ellipsis comes at the end of the sentence, the sentence period becomes the fourth point.

```
Tampering with another nation's satellite would be regarded as a hostile

act with serious consequences . . . .
```

An ellipsis can be used at the start of a quoted sentence but is seldom required at the beginning of an incorporated quote. Such quotes are frequently shortened to fit into the incorporating sentence, and it is not necessary to signal this fact to the reader.

It is certain that such interference "would be regarded as a hostile act with serious consequences," consequences that we would accept only if the payoff from satellite disruption made the risk worth taking.

Whether an ellipsis should be used at the end of an incorporated quote is a decision for the writer. Distortion or misinterpretation is possible without the ellipsis if the reader mistakenly believes that an incorporated quote ends as it appears in your paper. An ellipsis can be used to show that there is more to the original sentence.

To indicate the omission of more than a word or two, up to as much as an entire sentence or two, use a line of periods.

AS IT APPEARS IN THE ORIGINAL

Just as serious is public broadcasting's perceived lack of purpose. ABC, CBS, and NBC are in business to make money. What is public television in business for?

```
Just as serious is public broadcasting's perceived lack of

purpose . . . . . . . . . . . . . . . . . . . . . . . . . . . . .

What is public television in business for?¹


     ¹ Stuart Alan Shorenstein, "Does Public Television Have a

Future?" The Wilson Quarterly, 5, No. 1 (Winter 1981), 67.
```

If you are omitting more than a sentence or two between quotes, you need a signal to the reader. That is, you must avoid stitching together ideas from different places in your source material as if it were all found close together.

He calls the program "a great embarrassment to the government." Later in the same essay he refers to it as "a colossal error."

2. USE AN ELLIPSIS FOR A PAUSE LONGER THAN A COMMA

Quality . . . you know what it is, yet you don't know what it is.
ROBERT PIRSIG, *Zen and the Art of Motorcycle Maintenance*

"Some of my family name was English," I said—Wilkins is an English name—"and the rest of it came from . . . Egypt." Egypt!
ROGER WILKINS, "Confessions of a Blue-Chip Black," *Harpers*, Apr. 1982

3. USE ELLIPSES TO INDICATE BREAKS IN DIALOGUE AND INTERRUPTED OR UNFINISHED THOUGHTS

The 10:35 express stops at Galesville, Selby, and Indiana City, except on Sundays and holidays, at which time it stops at . . . and so it goes.
RALPH ELLISON, "Repent Harlequin"

"Don't," uttered Shock with difficulty. "If there was something that I . . . please, forgive . . . ."
VLADIMIR NABOKOV, "The Potato Elf"

EXCLAMATION POINT

1. USE EXCLAMATION POINTS FOR EMPHASIS

The exclamation point indicates surprise or strong emotion. The mark should be used sparingly (doubling up the marks [!!] is never appropriate) in formal writing.

"My God!" he would exclaim, fairly beaming with admiration. "That man's got the heart of a tiger!"
BRENDAN GILL, *The New Yorker*

— *Option* Any statement can become an exclamation with the addition of an exclamation point.

It is twelve o'clock!
The guests will be here any minute!

HYPHEN

Also see Spelling for uses of and rules about hyphens.

1. USE A HYPHEN TO DIVIDE A WORD AT THE END OF A LINE

```
    The outcome of so much delay and indecision was that they under-

stood nearly nothing on the test.
```

2. USE A HYPHEN IN COMPOUND WORDS

Vice-president   brother-in-law   well-written essay

3. USE A HYPHEN TO INDICATE A COMMON ROOT FOR TWO OR MORE PREFIXES

In two recent instances in Georgia, parents have objected to their eighth-
and ninth-grade children's reading assignment in modern fiction.
FLANNERY O'CONNOR, "Total Effects and the Eighth Grade"

They even carried a little feeling of holiday with them almost like the
hops- and strawberry-pickers from London and the Midland cities of England.
JOHN STEINBECK, *Travels with Charley*

PARENTHESES

1. USE PARENTHESES TO SET OFF CLARIFYING INFORMATION AND INFORMATION NOT GRAMMATICALLY CONNECTED TO THE SENTENCE

The square of the time of the revolution of a planet about the sun (expressed in years) is equal to the cube of its average distance from the sun
(expressed in astronomical units).
MILES, SHERWOOD, AND PARSON, *College Physical Science*

Note   It is possible to have one parenthetical element within another. Use dashes for the first break and parentheses for the second.
(See also Brackets.)

These conditions—graphed in government publications (see appendix
B)—exist mainly in the Northwest.

2. USE PARENTHESES FOR RUN-IN LISTS OR OUTLINES

This view does not take into account (1) the possibility of redundant function; and (2) the fact that some human behavior is subtle.
CARL SAGAN, *The Dragons of Eden*

There are three possibilities: (a) the father retires to his bedroom and
slams the door, (b) the daughter retires to her bedroom and slams the

door, (c) both retire to their respective bedrooms and slam the doors.
ERIC BERNE, *Games People Play*

See pages 390–391 for lists arranged vertically.

— Other Punctuation with Parentheses

If the parenthetical material is less than a full sentence, the sentence period falls outside the parentheses. Even if the parenthetic material should be a full sentence, you do not need either a capital letter to begin it or a period to end it:

The white kids were going to have a chance to become Gallileos and Madame Curies and Edisons and Gauguins, and our boys (the girls weren't even in on it) would try to be Jesse Owenses and Joe Louises.
MAYA ANGELOU, *I Know Why the Caged Bird Sings*

If it should happen that the parenthetic material is a question or exclamation, you must still provide an end-of-sentence period:

Hearing that the new faith had made converts in Damascus, he obtained authorization from the high priest to go there, arrest all "who belonged to the way," and bring them in chains to Jerusalem (A.D. 31?).
WILL DURANT, *Caesar and Christ*

The end-of-sentence period (or end-of-sentence question mark or exclamation point) falls within the parentheses only when the entire sentence is written as a separate, parenthetic sentence:

We usually find that feelings connected with transference originate in the patient's childhood and were subsequently directed towards persons whom the analyst now represents for various reasons. (We shall return later to a discussion of positive transferences.)
ANGEL GARMA, *The Psychoanalysis of Dreams*

— *Reminder*   Punctuation is not used before an opening parenthesis, but it is sometimes necessary after the closing parenthesis:

If the lens is too wide, too much light will reach the film, and the image will be *overexposed* (too light); if the lens is not opened enough, the image will be *underexposed* (too dark).
LEE R. BOBKER, *Elements of Film*

PERIOD

1. **USE A PERIOD AT THE END OF A COMPLETE SENTENCE**

We know that ours is a remarkable age of science. It is for us to use it to broaden and to liberate our culture.
JACOB BRONOWSKI, *The Common Sense of Science*

USE A PERIOD AT THE END OF AN INDIRECT QUESTION

Now what I want to know is why I should have to wait until age forty-three to get an education somewhat worse than that which any sophomore ought to have.

ROBERT HUTCHINS, *Education for Freedom*

— *Reminder*   Do not use a period or capital letter for a sentence inserted into another sentence:

The scientific team protested frequently—their methods were never questioned—that theirs had been a rigorously controlled project.

— Period Faults (Errors)

The Fragment   The fragment is an incomplete utterance written with a capital letter and a period as if it were a full sentence. Some authors use fragments, some do not. However, anything which slows or interferes with the reader's comprehension should be considered a flaw in writing. In academic writing and other formal writing situations, many readers always count the fragment as an error. The best rule for college students is this: the more formal writing becomes, the less acceptable fragments become.

EXAMPLE

In the early 1970s, the women who had been born in the postwar baby boom were in their early 20s. Their prime reproductive years.

Whether anything useful is achieved by this kind of fragmentation depends on your purpose in writing. While some readers would read the sentence without difficulty, others might stumble over the fragment—especially those who read very much academic and formal English (where fragments are less common). Such readers will prefer a more conventional treatment:

In the early 1970s, the women who had been born in the postwar baby boom were in their early 20s, their prime reproductive years.

EHRLICH AND EHRLICH, *Human Nature*

— *The Fused or Run-on Sentence*   Two or more sentences joined without any intervening punctuation create the fused sentence.

EXAMPLE

The experiment failed some of the data had been contaminated.

Revise such sentences by separating them with a period, semicolon, or other appropriate punctuation:

The experiment failed; some of the data had been contaminated.
The experiment failed: some of the data had been contaminated.
The experiment failed. Some of the data had been contaminated.

Punctuation faults sometimes appear because the writer has not analyzed the relationship of one idea to another. Such faults are best removed by rewriting the sentence to clarify the relationship:

Because some of the data had been contaminated, the experiment failed.

2. USE A PERIOD AFTER ABBREVIATIONS AND INITIALS

Mr.	Mrs.	Ms.	Dr.
Inc.	Ph.D.	N.C.T.E.	H. C. Lederer

Note When an abbreviation comes at the end of a sentence, no additional period is required.

Her real name is Harcourt Clarissa Lederer, but she is known affectionately as H. C.
Here he will hold open house for a few days, visiting hours 10 A.M. to 9 P.M.
JESSICA MITFORD, *The American Way of Death*

The initials of well-known organizations may be used without periods after the name has been given in full once.

Central Intelligence Agency (CIA)
National Broadcasting Company (NBC)
North Atlantic Treaty Organization (NATO)

Technical and familiar terms within a profession are often given as initials without periods, especially when they appear frequently in a paper.

Only socialists, communists, idealists (or the BBC) fail to realize that a mass television system cannot operate without the support of sponsors. . . .
MARYA MANNES, "The Splitting Image"

3. USE A PERIOD TO MARK DECIMAL NUMBERS

.01	.001	.10	1.0

4. USE PERIODS WITH VERTICAL LISTS OF FULL SENTENCES
There are three myths about American cars:
1. They cost too much.
2. They are badly made.
3. They are inefficient to operate.

But topical or abbreviated lists are preferred by most writers, and no periods are required after the items in such lists. (Do not mix topical items with full sentences.)

There are three myths about American cars:
1. Excessive cost
2. Faulty design
3. Inefficiency

— *Reminder*   Numbers or letters used to enumerate items in a list should be followed by periods, not half parentheses: [**x** 1), a), and so on]. See Parentheses for run-in lists and outlines.

QUESTION MARK

1. USE THE QUESTION MARK FOR DIRECT QUESTIONS

Were my teachers, perhaps, so good that they could not understand the depths of my depravity?
WILLIAM GOLDING, "Thinking As a Hobby"

Note the difference between the direct question above and the indirect question here:

The question was whether my teachers were, perhaps, so good that they could not understand the depths of my depravity.

— *Reminder*   Many statements can be changed into questions by adding question marks.

These data are accurate? The experiment was conducted under controlled conditions?

— *Note*   A question inserted into a statement retains its question mark.

Thus the question which you put to me—what is to be done to rid mankind of the war menace?—took me by surprise.
SIGMUND FREUD, "Letter to Einstein"

2. USE A QUESTION MARK TO INDICATE A QUESTION AFTER EACH ITEM IN A SERIES

Is it possible for the air pressure to remain steady at 100 feet? 1,000 feet? 5,000 feet?

Should such decisions be made by the arresting officer? the district attorney? the judge? the legislature?

3. USE A PARENTHETIC QUESTION MARK FOR UNCERTAIN INFORMATION

Caedmon served as lay brother and, later, as monk in a monastery at Strenaeshale (Whitby?) under the abbess Hild. . . .

BAUGH, *Literary History of England*

QUOTATION MARKS

1. USE QUOTATION MARKS FOR TITLES OF SHORT WORKS

Most poems, short stories, magazine and newspaper articles, book chapters, specific episodes of continuing television series and radio programs, transcripts of radio and television shows, popular songs, and specific selections on records, tapes, or cassettes require quotation marks.

"The Raven" is a well-known poem by Poe.

Note   Books within the Bible are given without quotation marks.

The first book of the Bible is Genesis.

2. USE QUOTATION MARKS AROUND ODD OR INVENTED WORDS OR WORDS USED WITH SPECIAL MEANING

I began playing a game in which I had to choose between jobs with imaginary titles like "torpist" and "varisator."

MARVIN GROSSWIRTH, "Let This Computer Plan Your Future"

Instead, applicants for teacher in New York City spend months or years learning a peculiar "correct" pronounciation that is heard nowhere on land or sea.

PAUL GOODMAN, *People or Personnel*

3. USE QUOTATION MARKS AROUND WORDS REFERRED TO AS WORDS

Your pronunciation of "nudnik," by the way, is appalling. It's "nudnik," not "noodnik."

S. J. PERELMAN, *Writers at Work*, Ed. George Plimpton

—*Reminder*   This rule also applies to numerals and symbols.

There are too many "&'s" in his work.
It was full of "5's" and "6's."

—*Option*   Where the subject of your research is language, or when there are many references to words in your paper, use underlining instead of quotes.

Philanthropist is derived from the Greek words philein and anthropos.

One late fall day the teacher gave an in-class writing problem: take the word freezing, and in one or two hundred words write an impression of freezing without using either cold or chilly.

ALAN C. PURVES, *How Porcupines Make Love*

4. USE QUOTATION MARKS AROUND ALL DIRECT QUOTES

Arthur replied, "God is total awareness."

MONTGOMERY, *A World Beyond*.

"We all live in a trailer behind the school," he said.

5. USE QUOTATION MARKS TO INDICATE DIALOGUE

Indent for each new speaker in dialogue:

"Say, Clyde, what are you doing there?"
"What?"
"I say, what are you doing there? It looks like you've got the thing all torn apart."
"Did you say something?"
"I said . . . say, what's the matter with you?"

—*Note*   Thoughts and interior monologues are usually given without quotation marks.

This is a fine mess, I thought to myself.
As she was opening the box, I kept thinking, will she like it?

6. USE QUOTATION MARKS AROUND SOURCE MATERIAL INCORPORATED INTO YOUR OWN SENTENCES

Incorporating a quote does not create the need for a comma. If the sentence would not require a comma or colon without quotation marks, it will not require one with them.

We knew she was one of our finest young artists.
We knew she was "one of our finest young artists."

— *Reminder*   The incorporated quote usually does not require ellipses either before or after the quote. You have the option of using ellipses only if you think it is important to tell the reader you have incorporated less than a full sentence. In general, avoid chopping up the original: incorporate as much of the original sentence as possible.

If you quote more than three typewritten lines (the quote would take up more than three lines of your text), indent all lines of the quotation 5 spaces on the left side, and like the rest of your paper, type the quote double-spaced. The right-hand margin may also be indented 5 spaces, but for most school work you do not need to maintain the right-hand indentation.

Do not add quotation marks: indenting takes the place of quotation marks. Copy the original exactly as you find it, including any quotation marks in the original:

INDENTED QUOTE

Our democratic society is clearly divided into elite and supporting classes, according to Packard:

> Our class system is starting to bear a resemblance to that which prevails in the military services. In the services there are, of course, status differences between a private and a corporal and between a lieutenant and a captain. The greatest division, however, is between officers and enlisted men, with only quite limited opportunities for acquiring, while in service, the training necessary to pass from one division to another.[1]

[1] Vance Packard, The Status Seekers (New York: David McKay, 1959), p. 38.

INDENTED QUOTE: QUOTATION MARKS IN ORIGINAL

> The process was described as "microwave amplification by stimulated emission of radiation," and from the initials of this phrase, the instrument came to be called a "maser."[1]

[1] Isaac Asimov, Asimov's Guide to Science

— *Note*   Triple space above and below indented quotes. Do not convert quotation marks to single quotes nor make any other changes, but copy the original exactly as you find it.

Copy the indentation of the original; that is, indent 10 spaces instead of 5 to indicate a paragraph indent in the original.

QUOTING A PARAGRAPH

> Stopping out, trying alternative ways of growing up,
> has always been a practice of the affluent, who not only can
> afford it, but some of who also have an intuitive confidence
> that they can probably make it in the world whether they
> collect credentials or not.[1]

[1] Caroline Bird, The Case Against College

Copy poetry lines exactly as you find them, except when the lines are too long for your page, in which case you may either invent your own indentations or use a solidus. (See Slash.)

QUOTING LINES OF POETRY

> Here lies a lady of beauty and high degree.
> Of chills and fever she died, of fever and chills,
> The death of her husband, her aunts, an infant of three,
> And of medicos marvelling sweetly on her ills.
> JOHN CROWE RANSOM, "Here Lies a Lady"

Quotation Marks and Other Punctuation

Commas and periods always go inside the quotation marks.

"It's been a real pleasure," she said; "we must do this again."

Colons and semicolons always go outside the quotation marks.

They "run away," they "get out of hand": they are creations inside a creation, and often inharmonious towards it. . . .
E. M. FORSTER, *Aspects of the Novel*

Question marks and exclamation points go inside or outside the quotation marks. If the matter inside the quotes is a question or an exclamation, the mark goes inside too, regardless of the rest of the sentence. If the matter inside the quotes is not a question or an exclamation but the rest of the sentence is, the mark goes outside.

I heard her ask him, "When are you coming over?"
What do you mean, "We have no money"?
Note that there is no period after "money."

7. USE SINGLE QUOTES TO INDICATE A QUOTE WITHIN A QUOTE

"I can't go," Loren pouted. "My father's exact words were, 'I forbid you to see that movie!' and there's no way to get around that."

Note   On rare occasions a third set of quotation marks may be needed. Use the third set to indicate a speaker (double quotes) quoting another speaker (single quotes) who in turn is quoting a third speaker (double quotes within the single quotes).

AS IT APPEARS IN THE ORIGINAL

"Their password was 'Victory,' " Cutlip was saying.

AS IT APPEARS IN YOUR PAPER

" 'Their password was "Victory," ' Cutlip was saying."

Note that in the example the original already had two sets of quotes in it. To quote such a sentence requires that you add your own set of quotation marks (always starting with double quotes) and then reverse the ones in the original.

Theoretically there is no limit to the number of embedded quotations. By alternating single and double marks you might have as many as four or five quotes within quotes. But practically speaking, more than three sets of marks becomes too confusing for most readers.

8. DO NOT USE QUOTATION MARKS FOR INDIRECT QUOTES

INDIRECT QUOTE

He said Izzara was made of the flowers of the Pyrennes.
HEMINGWAY, *The Sun Also Rises*

DIRECT QUOTE

He said, "Izzara is made of the flowers of the Pyrennes."

Reminder   Although indirect quotes do not need quotation marks, they do require documentation (footnotes).

SEMICOLON

1. USE A SEMICOLON TO CONNECT TWO CLOSELY RELATED SENTENCES

They often went down to the seashore for the summer; they owned a small cabin there.

But how weary he was of this mask; how tiring it was to be Disraeli!
ANDRÉ MAUROIS, *Disraeli*

Supplies of gold and land are inelastic; they cannot be easily enlarged.
GEORGE GILDER, *Wealth and Poverty*

2. **USE A SEMICOLON TO SEPARATE TWO SENTENCES JOINED WITH A CONJUNCTIVE ADVERB**

He was not the source of all wisdom; indeed, one considered him greatly open to petition and persuasion, and no man could ever have had more of both.
JOHN KENNETH GALBRAITH, *A Life in Our Times*

We knew something was wrong in the tunnel; however, piles of debris kept us from entering.

For a list of conjunctive adverbs, see the entry *conjunctive adverb* in the Glossary of Language Terms.

— *Option* The comma after the conjunctive adverb (*however* above) is used to give emphasis to contrastive and complementary statements; but this comma is optional when no emphasis is desired (*hence* below).

There is no deviation; hence the standard score is 0.
DOWNIE AND HEATH, *Basic Statistical Methods*

3. **USE A SEMICOLON IN A SERIES, BETWEEN ITEMS CONTAINING COMMAS**

Scientists arrived from such places as Nome, Alaska; Chicago, Illinois; Paris, France; and Venice, Italy.

USE A SEMICOLON IN A COMPOUND SENTENCE

Compound sentences joined by coordinate conjunctions (*and, but, or, nor, so, for*) usually need a comma before the connectives. But when the sentences are long or there are other commas in the sentences, you may substitute a semicolon for the comma before the connective.

The spoil-sport is not the same as the false player, the cheat; for the latter pretends to be playing the game and, on the face of it, still acknowledges the magic circle.
JOHN HUIZINGA, *Homo Ludens*

4. **USE A SEMICOLON FOR MULTIPLE REFERENCES IN ONE NOTE**

Whether in the text or in footnotes or endnotes, use a semicolon to separate two or more references in the same note:

Ezekiel 11: 9–13; 12: 4–5; 16: 7, 9, 25.

SLASH (SOLIDUS)

1. **USE A SLASH (SOLIDUS) TO MARK LINES OF POETRY IN RUNNING DISCOURSE**

Crane says, "I stood upon a high place, / And saw, below, many devils / Running, leaping. . . ."
HART CRANE, "I Stood Upon a High Place"

398 **2. USE A SLASH TO MARK INCLUSIVE DATES AND FRACTIONS**

(Jan./Feb. 1982)   1/2   3/4

3. USE A SLASH TO MARK GRAMMATICAL CHOICES

and/or   either/or

But use such constructions sparingly.

UNDERLINING (ITALICS)

Underlining indicates material that would be set in italic print (to make it stand out) if the material were type-set. It is a direction to the printer to set in italics.

1. USE UNDERLINING FOR TITLES OF LONG WORKS

The titles of books, booklets, pamphlets, magazines, newspapers, long poems, plays, albums, (records, tapes, cassettes), operas, films, filmstrips, works of art, legal cases, and the names of radio and television series (as distinct from the titles of individual episodes of such programs) should be underlined.

Most students have read Thoreau's nonfiction book Walden.

A surprising number of people watched Carl Sagan's Cosmos series on PBS.

That is now the prevailing legal view (according to the case of

Sullivan v. The New York Times); you can libel a person all you want

as long as you don't do it out of a mean spirit.

F. LEE BAILEY WITH JOHN GREENYA, *For the Defense*

Note   Court cases are underlined in the text of your paper (that is, in the body), but not in your footnotes. Do not underline the *v* for *versus*.

Do not underline titles of documents like the Constitution or the Declaration of Independence; such documents are not considered to be publications.

2. USE UNDERLINING FOR EMPHASIS

I'm a fair mountain man in spite of my foot, but when we head for home

it won't be that way.

ALEXANDER KEY, *The Forgotten Door*

O for a man who is a man, and, as my neighbor says, has a bone in his

back which you cannot pass your hand through!

HENRY DAVID THOREAU, "On the Duty of Civil Disobedience"

— Reminder The best way to show emphasis is by means of careful word choice and sentence structure. Underlining should be used sparingly for emphasis.

It is generally not a good idea to add underlining to quoted material (to call attention to something in the original). But you may do so on occasion if immediately after the quoted matter you give the reader a parenthetic note: (Emphasis added) or (My emphasis). Occasionally you may wish to inform the reader that the italics were in the original: (Italics in original) or (Smith's italics).

3e **USE UNDERLINING FOR THE NAMES OF SHIPS, PLANES, AND TRAINS**

> The <u>Enterprise</u> is the largest man-made vessel in space.

4e **USE UNDERLINING FOR FOREIGN WORDS AND PHRASES**

> What increased the danger was that at first we mistook their wild howls
>
> for cries of <u>Vive l'Empereur</u>!

5e **USE UNDERLINING TO INTRODUCE KEY TERMS, SPECIAL TERMS, TECHNICAL TERMS**

> One well-known attempt to answer the question is the <u>linguistic rela-</u>
>
> <u>tivity hypothesis</u> (also called the Sapir-Whorf hypothesis or the
>
> Whorfian hypothesis).

For the rule on underlining words as words, see Quotations.

Punctuation proofreading practices

Suggest a revision for any sentence whose punctuation does not follow formal writing standards

PRACTICE ONE

1 The university was forced to raise its tuition, and some students found they could no longer afford to go to college.

2 Our childrens safety is one of societys major concerns.

3 "Four score and seven (87) years ago," Lincoln's speech at Gettysburg began.

4 In their freshman year, college students usually take introductory courses like English composition, speech, history, and biology.

5 Ancient Rome was very different from any of our modern cities, the absence of newspapers was one of the significant differences.

6 When the United States argued with England about Venezuela, President Cleveland declared that the Monroe Doctrine made us the protector of this hemisphere.

7 The jumbo jets, which could carry hundreds of passengers, very often flew with half their seats empty.

8 Congress has the power whether it always uses that power is another question to chart the course of the nation and to override the President.

9 In the introductory arguments concerning those nations whose representatives were not present when the voting began again.

10 The material for the senator's speeches never varied: 1) the economy, 2) foreign affairs, and 3) the President's character.

11 Many people have wondered why the apteryx didn't survive.

12 Hitler always offered excuses when he was about to invade a country he announced that Germans were being "oppressed" in Czechoslovakia.

13 Any ideas implementation is likely to be more time consuming than the generation of the idea itself.

14 A surprising number of young men and women indicated on the survey forms that they hoped to get jobs with the C.I.A.

15 "I can think of nothing better," she said, "than sitting here on the deck of the Sea Hawk, sailing along, reading *Yachting*."

16 This problem—how can we stop the killing of endangered animals—is a good deal more complex than most people think.

17 They had covered the country in the campaign: Trenton, New Jersey; Scranton, Pennsylvania; Chicago, Illinois; and points west.

18 Carl Sandburg's "Chicago" is one of the most important poems of modern America.

19 "If it rains," said Miss Prescott, "the picnic will be postponed".

20 We protested that the engine used too much oil, that the brakes were worn out, and that the tires were dangerous.

21 You are a natural athelete but to play a good game of tennis you'll need practice.

22 Convinced of the shoddiness of American cars, Nader made others believe it.

23 Churchill ought to be remembered for his eloquence for his speeches carried Britain through her darkest hours.

24 Dale asked, "Professor Emmet, did you say, 'Shakespeare said, "All the world's a stage" '?"

25 The Constitution is our chief defense against tyranny, "he said."

PRACTICE TWO

1 It was reported that Lloyd's idea of humor was to go around saying things like floomf and perd.

2 "Alfred was not a Saxon emperor, Mr. Harris," Professor Henry said wearily.

3 "Why isn't gold a good investment?", the members of the committee asked.

4 By extending the argument to its logical conclusion, *reductio ad absurdum*, you will see how silly it is.

5 Hamlet asks us whether it is, "nobler in the mind to suffer the slings and arrows of outrageous fortune."

6 In the novel, the Princess says, "Dr. Luminal, did you say, "The Queen is innocent," when they asked for your testimony"?

7 The creature was something between an ape and a human; it was very small, had an apelike head, and walked upright.

8 First on the reading list was Steinbeck's novel, "The Grapes of Wrath."

9 "Really, André, nobody could be *that* hungry," she said as she handed him the stale bread.

10 It is possible that the character of education is changing, the costs of going to school may soon create an educated elite.

11 A homeowner feels lucky if he hits water at thirty feet, however, a sixty-foot well is not uncommon.

12 Many doctors assume that Hippocrates' oath means they cannot approve of euthanasia.

13 Of course no one can write any more no one ever could!

14 It has been reliably reported that none of these young people actually fled their country nor did they wish to.

15 When it became clear that the President had been lying the mood of the nation turned sour.

16 The experiment's conclusion depends on it's design and the implementation of it's procedures.

17 Inevitably that preciseness of mind which has for so long characterized the flavor of our best scholarship.

18 Three admirals and seven captains stared silently at the message from the President: "Proceed at once to Doo Doo [sic]."

19 "No Dinsmore you may not run your rat tonight," he said.

20 The last of the American car companies were: General Motors, Ford, Chrysler, and American Motors.

21 Nobody can put up with governmental lying for long—not even governmental apologists—without losing touch with reality or becoming very cynical.

22 At dawn the birds would suddenly shriek and squeal as if their tails were on fire.

23 "A days work for a days wages" is an American cliché.

24 Though it was called a religion, Buddhism was more a philosophy of life it had no theology, no rituals, no priests as such.

25 The truth is that "hip" isn't hip any more.

SPELLING

Misspelled words are a distraction to the educated reader. Except for people who compete in spelling bees, however, misspelling need not create an obvious problem. A poor speller's first step should be to learn to proofread compositions carefully for misspellings. If you can correct misspelled words in your finished writing, your "spelling problem" will be at least partly solved, because it won't be apparent to readers.

There is probably no more effective method for improving spelling than simply memorizing the words you can't spell. However, there are a number of things you can do to improve your proofreading abilities.

Practice

Most beginning writers do not proofread as much or as carefully as they should. Proofreading calls for careful scrutiny of each line of a composition, character by character. A quick rush-through before handing in your paper will catch only the most obvious errors. You need time to do a thorough job.

Get Someone to Help You

A roommate or classmate may not know much more than you, but a fresh pair of eyes may see things yours have missed. Sensible writers ask for help in areas where they are weak. If you and a friend regularly proofread for each other, you will both get better at it and will be able to do a more thorough job on your own manuscripts.

Let Your Manuscript Cool Off

The paper that is finished the night before it is due will almost certainly look rushed. If you can give yourself at least twenty-four hours' cooling-off time, you will have a more objective view of your writing. Mistakes that were invisible before will be easier to spot a day or so later.

Memorize the Correct Spelling of Words You Habitually Misspell

Except for careless mistakes, most people misspell only certain words. A little memory work will reduce the list of words you habitually mistake. Little tricks like remembering the *iron* in *environment* and *a rat* in *separate* may help you.

Learn to Use a Spelling Dictionary

Unlike standard dictionaries, spelling dictionaries have no definitions in them, just lists of words; thus, they are small and easy to use *quickly* when looking up words. You will still need to use a standard dictionary now and then, but most of your spelling problems can be solved with a small spelling dictionary. If there is any doubt in your mind whether *receive* or *recieve* is the correct spelling, the spelling dictionary will tell you immediately. You might also find it useful to create your own spelling dictionary. Every time you check the spelling of a word, copy the correct spelling into a notebook. Keep the words in alphabetical order. Study these words specifically; they are the ones *you* don't know.

Look for Trouble Spots in Your Words

Most people know which problems they have; with a spelling dictionary you can quickly check out things like the *-able/-ible* and the *ei/ie* combinations. If you can build the habit of checking out troublesome words, you will find yourself beginning to remember the correct spelling of more and more of these words.

Review of Trouble Spots in Spelling

ei/ie   *I* before *e* except after *c* or when pronounced as *a*, as in *neighbor* and *weigh*. This jingle used to be taught in the elementary schools. It works fairly well, but there are a number of exceptions (*leisure, seize,* and so on). Check any *ei/ie* combinations; memorize the ones that cause you trouble (*friend, fiend*).

-able/-ible   These two endings (suffixes) are generally pronounced alike, and there are no very useful rules about them. By far, *-able* is the more common spelling, and *-ible* frequently follows an *s* sound (*flexible, sensible*). However, there is no substitute for looking these words up and memorizing them.

-ant, -ance/-ent, -ence   As with *-able* and *-ible*, these endings are generally pronounced alike: *abundant, existent; abundance, existence.* Look up any word you are not certain about.

final e   Final *e* is usually dropped to avoid doubling up vowels: *hop[e]ing, scrap[e]ing*. But in some cases it is kept: *changeable, peaceable. And* it is always kept when the suffix begins with a consonant: *hopeful, bore-dom*. Check any word you are not certain about; many words today are spelled either way (*livable, liveable*), but some are not.

double consonants   Many words double the final letter (consonant) before adding a suffix: *hop-ping, scrap-ping*. But "long-vowel" words do not: *hop-ing, scraping*. And there are exceptions to the rule (*benefited*). To say it another way, doubling the last consonant has the effect of changing long vowels to short ones, so *hopping* could not be pronounced as the *-ing* form of *hope*.

pre-/per-/pro-   Check words with these beginnings (prefixes) (*perspiration, performance, prepare, protect*). Don't spell them by the way you hear them spoken. Many people pronounce them all alike; a few interchange them (*prespiration, pertect*).

plurals of -y words   Most words that end in *y* change the *y* to *ie* for the plural: *babies, families*. When the *y* follows a vowel (*monkey*), the plural is formed by adding *s* only (*monkeys*).

suffixes with -y words   Change *-y* to *i* before all suffixes (endings) except *-ing: beauty, beautiful; noisy, noisily; buy, buying*.

-ery/-ary   The more common ending, by far, is *-ary*, but a few words end with *-ery: cemetery, stationery* (paper).

-or/-er/-ar   All these endings sound alike (*author, painter, grammar*). The safest practice is to check a spelling dictionary.

-ceed/-cede/-sede   Check any words ending with the *eed* sound. *Supersede* is the only word ending in *sede; exceed, proceed*, and *succeed* are the only words ending in *ceed*. All the rest of the *eed*-sounding words are spelled *-cede: precede, secede*.

look-alikes and sound-alikes   Homonyms and near-homonyms account for a large number of spelling mistakes. Writers who "spell with their ears" are likely to mistake words like *board/bored, stare/stair*, and so on. In many cases readers feel these errors are worse than spelling errors because the writer appears to have used a wrong word, instead of having misspelled the right word. Be sure you have the right form with very common words like *there/their/they're* and *your/you're/yore*.

Hyphens in Compound Words

Check your dictionary for the spelling of any compound word. Many are spelled as two words, *high school;* others as one word, *coffeepot;* and still others as hyphenated words, *half-dollar*.

Compound-Word Modifiers Before a Noun   These compounds should generally be hyphenated: *high-school graduate, left-wing politics, round-trip ticket*. This guideline does not apply to *-ly* words, which are never hyphenated:

-LY COMPOUND

roughly cut diamond
softly spoken words

HYPHENATED COMPOUND

rough-cut diamond
soft-spoken words

Compound-Word Modifiers After a Noun   Modifiers that are hyphenated when they precede the noun do not need hyphens when they come after the noun: "She is a graduate of high school," "their politics are left wing," "his ticket was round trip."

Prefixes and Suffixes   The prefixes *all-, cross-, half-,* and *self-* and the suffix *-elect* are usually hyphenated: *all-important, ex-governor, self-pity, senator-elect.* When *self* is the root of the word, however, it is not hyphenated: *selfhood, selfish.*

The prefixes and suffixes listed below form words spelled as one word (*overburdened, substandard, reread, tenfold, animallike,* but note *gull-like*):

anti	intra	pro	super
co	like	pseudo	supra
counter	non	re	ultra
extra	over	semi	un
fold	post	sub	under
infra	pre		

Note   When you use a prefix to form a compound word that is spelled exactly like an existing word, it's necessary to hyphenate. "The new prime minister intends to re-form the cabinet" means that the prime minister is going to get rid of the people in the cabinet and start afresh. "The prime minister intends to reform the cabinet," however, means that the cabinet members aren't in imminent danger of losing their jobs.

Word Division

Dividing words at the ends of lines is primarily a printer's device for making all the lines look even. Typed papers have much less need for such uniformity, and for the most part writers can avoid dividing words. However, there are times when word division is hard to avoid; you should follow established practice when you do divide a word.

ALWAYS DIVIDE BETWEEN SYLLABLES ONLY

The syllables of English words have been established by tradition and may not correspond to the actual sound units of words the way you pronounce them: *wa-ter* is the traditional syllabication, although some people pronounce the word "wat-er." Many words seem to contradict pronunciation: "weap-on," "lim-it," "dis-sect." All standard dictionaries show syllabication.

WORDS CONTAINING DOUBLE LETTERS USUALLY DIVIDE BETWEEN THE DOUBLE LETTERS

com-mon   lit-tle   es-say

PREFIXES USUALLY FORM SYLLABLES AND CAN BE DIVIDED

ex-cite   de-fault   con-vince

COMMON PREFIXES

ab	(absent)	ob	(obtuse)
ad	(admit)	mis	(mistake)
bi	(biceps)	non	(nonsense)
com	(commit)	per	(percolate
con	(content	pre	(prevent)
de	(detour)	pro	(proceed)
dis	(discuss)	re	(return)
ex	(extend	sub	(submarine)
in	(insert)	trans	(transfer)
		un	(uncertain)

SUFFIXES STARTING WITH CONSONANTS ALWAYS FORM SYLLABLES

ful	(helpful)	tion	(action)
ness	(goodness)	wise	(crosswise)
ship	(friendship)		

Other Word-Division Guidelines   The surest guide to syllabication is the dictionary, but you can avoid most errors by remembering the following:

1 Never divide a one-syllable word or a word that is pronounced as one syllable: *through, school, width, rhythm, stretched*.

2 Never leave or carry to the next line a single letter, even if the letter forms a syllable: *a-bout, e-vict, man-y, jerk-y*.

3 Hyphenated words must be divided only at the hyphen: *pistol-whip, all-star*.

4 Avoid dividing proper names: *Robert, Carter, Rockefeller*.

5 The verb ending *-ing* is a separate syllable when it is merely added to a word: *wish-ing, sew-ing, pass-ing, sell-ing*. When *-ing* causes a doubling of consonants in the root word, the rule for double letters applies: *run—ning, step-ping, hop-ping*.

6 The suffixes *-able* and *-ible* should not be divided (*-a-ble, -i-ble*) into two syllables. Take the entire suffix to the next line.

7 Avoid dividing the last word of a paragraph or the last word of a page.

8 Avoid dividing at the end of more than two lines in succession.

Word division practice

How should these words be divided?

apologetic   differentiation   immobilizing   pacification
appreciation   do-gooder   jujitsu   punctuation
backbone   dreadful   keenness   quadrangular
baldheaded   exterminate   label   rehabilitation
clairvoyant   fearsome   Massachusetts   sissy
clergy   governmental   misapplication   thorough
contrary   grinned   nonpartisan   tyrannosaurus
decompose   heavy-duty   ownership   virtuosity

Spelling proofreading practice

Some of the following sentences contain spelling errors. Correct any misspelled words you find.

1 In our soceity some form of contack with relegion is bound to touch each of us.

2 The principle had paniced when he saw all of us staying out after the last bell.

3 With four bigger brothers to compeat with at meals, you sort of learn to eat quickly, and eat alot.

4 When I was in high school, I looked towards graduation with enthusiasm.

5 The temperture in the gym was near a hundred.

6 Most users think that there are no harmful effects from marijuana.

7 "O.K.," I said to myself, "now your on your own."

8 Well, the concert went fairly well dispite a few seemingly disasterous ocassions.

9 Before she could finish, the anger was already beginning to swell up inside me.

10 The Education Amendment Act of 1972 signaled the start of a revaluation in intercollegiate and highschool sports.

11 I was not impressed by the government's promtness.

12 The other guys were quite though restless, periodicly naping to pass time.

13 It felt strange being able to streach out in front of the T.V. and just forget everything.

14 Hurryedly I threw some water on my face and draged a comb through my hair.

15 As I moved slowly out onto the pier, which was partially damaged by weather, I could look down and view beds of seaweed.

16 Maintaining your own aquarium can be a rewarding experience if you follow certain guidelines and instructions.

17 The artical listed several ways in which people have evaded there taxes.

18 I could have walked for an age and not have lost sight of that monsterosity.

19 We desparately didn't want to get wet—that water was cold!

20 I was embarassed, my mother was embarassed, everyone was embarassed.

21 While the other branches of service are attempting to make life for there troops more liveable, the Marine Corps is maintaining its standards of disipline.

22 This summer I tried to corrupt the efforts of a committee project to revise one of the English electives.

23 With my stomache in my throat, I sat next to my window and watched the road scampering below the bus.

24 By the third day, when we went to feed the children, we had to take an armed guard with the food.

25 My roomates mean well, but I wish they would just let me go to bed.

Spelling-in-context practice

One problem in proofreading is how to avoid being carried along by what you are saying instead of attending to how you are saying it. Letting your manuscript cool off for a day or two will help, but even then you must force yourself to read slowly and carefully, looking for mistakes. Practice the technique by finding and correcting the spelling errors in the following passage.

After about an hour or so of bouncing up and down in the truck, we arrived at the mountain that we wished to assend by foot. It didn't look to steep until we began to climb it. The air was thin and our legs grew sore as Marilyn and I struggled with the big canvass back pack that contained our sandwiches and pop. Every three or four minutes we'd have to sease moving and locate a peace of ground that wasn't to rocky to rest on. As we slouched down, we noticed tiny red flowers that appeared to be bright stars in the wild green grass that grew between the pebbles. We even attemted to collect different types of rocks, but we had to empty most of them out from our pockets because they were too combersome.

CAPITALIZATION

1. CAPITALIZE THE FIRST WORD OF A SENTENCE AND THE FIRST WORD OF A DIRECT QUOTATION

Shakespeare said, "All the world's a stage."

2. DO NOT CAPITALIZE THE FIRST WORD OF AN INCORPORATED QUOTE

The Detroit studies show "increasing production of particulates" in all major atmospheric samplings.

3. CAPITALIZE ONLY THE FIRST WORD OF AN INTERRUPTED QUOTE

"The highest temperatures," they said, "could approach 5000 degrees."

— *Option*   Some writers capitalize the first word of a direct question within a sentence: "The question before us is this: Can we reduce inflation and cut taxes at the same time? What I want to know is, Who is to blame for the problem?"

4. IN CONVENTIONAL USAGE, EACH LINE OF VERSE BEGINS WITH A CAPITAL LETTER

(Some modern poets ignore this convention.)

It was many and many a year ago,
  In a kingdom by the sea,
That a maiden there lived whom you may know
  By the name of Annabel Lee—
EDGAR ALLAN POE, "Annabel Lee"

5. CAPITALIZE NAMES OF AWARDS, SCHOLARSHIPS, GRANTS

Nobel Prize; Nobel Peace Prize   National Merit scholarship
Pulitzer Prize   Rhodes scholarship

6. CAPITALIZE NAMES OF BODIES OF WATER

Lake Superior   the Great Lakes
the Red Sea   the Pacific Ocean; the Pacific
Walden Pond   the Mississippi River

7. CAPITALIZE NAMES OF BUILDINGS, STRUCTURES, MONUMENTS

Golden Gate Bridge   Riverfront Stadium
the Whitney Museum   the Capitol
Anspach Hall   the Library of Congress
the White House   the Ajax Building
the Fox Theater   the Leaning Tower of Pisa
Hammond High School   the Statue of Liberty

8. CAPITALIZE NAMES OF GEOGRAPHIC FEATURES

the Azores	Rocky Mountains	the Matterhorn
Mount Everest	Great Barrier Reef	Bay of Fundy
Fiji Islands	the Great Plains	the Gobi Desert

9. CAPITALIZE A GENERIC TERM PRECEDING MORE THAN ONE NAME

Lakes Superior and Ontario   Mounts Everest and Ranier

10. DO NOT CAPITALIZE GENERIC TERMS WHEN THEY FOLLOW THE NAMES

Atlantic and Pacific oceans   Mississippi and Ohio rivers

11. CAPITALIZE NAMES OF HOLIDAYS AND RELIGIOUS OBSERVANCES

Easter	Labor Day	Christmas
Yom Kippur	Halloween	Christmas Day
Thanksgiving	New Year's Day	Christmas Eve

12. CAPITALIZE NAMES, NICKNAMES, AND DESCRIPTIVE NAMES OF PEOPLE

Eva	John	Momo
Silas Marner	Anne R. Scopel	the Sun King

13. WHEN USED WITH A GIVEN NAME, DESCRIPTIVE NAMES ARE USUALLY SET OFF IN QUOTATION MARKS

Jenny Lind, "the Swedish Nightingale."

14. CAPITALIZE THE NAMES OF MILITARY GROUPS, ENGAGEMENTS, AWARDS

United States Army	the Fifth Army	the Pacific Fleet
the Vietnam War	World War II	Medal of Honor

15. DO NOT CAPITALIZE ARMY, NAVY, AND SO ON AS AN INFORMAL REFERENCE TO A BRANCH OF THE ARMED SERVICES

My brother joined the navy last week.

16. CAPITALIZE THE NAMES OF PLACES

Chicago	England	Pine Street
North Pole	Plunkettville	North America
the West	New York City	the Orient
the Eternal City	the Promised Land	Central Park

17. DO NOT CAPITALIZE GENERAL TERMS LIKE CITY, COUNTY, STATE WHEN PRESENTED WITHOUT A NAME OR WHEN THE GENERAL TERM PRECEDES

They live in the city.

They work in the county of Clare.

411 **18.** CAPITALIZE THE NAMES OF SHIPS, PLANES, AND TRAINS

MECHANICS

Old Ironsides	the *Super Chief*
the *El Captain*	*Air Force One*
the *Columbia*	*Apollo 13*
U.S.S. Forrestal	the *Enterprise*

19. CAPITALIZE TITLES OF ADDRESS (AND ABBREVIATIONS) WITH NAMES

Mr. and Mrs. Clay   Miss Lane   Ms. Jones

Ms. can be used for single or married women.

20. DO NOT CAPITALIZE GENERAL FORMS OF ADDRESS

sir   madam

21. CAPITALIZE TITLES OF FAMILY MEMBERS WITH NAMES OR (OPTIONAL) USED AS NAMES

Cousin Fred	Grandmother Jones	Aunt Sally
Father	Mom	Sis

22. DO NOT CAPITALIZE FAMILY TITLES USED WITHOUT A NAME

my brother   Ask your father . . .   her cousin

23. CAPITALIZE TITLES OF HIGH HONOR, EVEN WITHOUT NAMES

Excellency   Her Grace   Your Honor   His Majesty

24. CAPITALIZE TITLES OF POSITION AND RANK WITH NAMES

Archbishop Hayes	President Adams	Senator Clay
Dr. French	Professor Soo	Prof. Lawrence
Doctor Nkolo	General White	Lieutenant Jakey

25. TITLES WITHOUT NAMES ARE USUALLY NOT CAPITALIZED

the general, the professor, a doctor, the senator

The letter was sent to the governor: Mr. Mario Cuomo, governor of New York.

26. CAPITALIZE WORDS FORMED FROM PROPER NOUNS

English	Shakespearian	Indian
French	Italianate	Germanic

27. DO NOT CAPITALIZE SUCH WORDS WHEN THEY HAVE ENTERED ENGLISH AND NO LONGER CONNOTE THEIR ORIGINAL MEANINGS

arabic numerals	china dishes
roman numerals	scotch whiskey
russian dressing	dutch oven
french fries	venetian blinds

28. DO NOT CAPITALIZE SCHOOL SUBJECTS EXCEPT LANGUAGES

math	history	Latin
psychology	botany	Greek

29. CAPITALIZE THE TITLE OF A SPECIFIC SCHOOL COURSE

Psychology 101	Botany 300	Art 219

30. DO NOT CAPITALIZE SCHOOL YEARS

freshman	sophomore	junior	senior

31. DO NOT CAPITALIZE ACADEMIC DEGREES

bachelor's	master of arts	doctorate

32. CAPITALIZE THE INITIALS FOR ACADEMIC DEGREES

B.A.	A.B.	M.A.	B.S.
B.Ed.	M.B.A.	Ph.D.	A.A.

33. CAPITALIZE BRAND NAMES BUT NOT PRODUCTS

Wrangler jeans	Big Macs	Sony radio

34. CAPITALIZE TITLES FOR HEADS OF STATE

Even when the names do not follow the titles, it is acceptable to capitalize the titles of the highest state officials.

the President	the Queen	the Pope

35. CAPITALIZE THE NAMES OF ORGANIZATIONS, INSTITUTIONS, COMPANIES

United States Congress	the Census Bureau
the Senate	Sears, Roebuck and Company
Parliament	the House of Representatives
the United Nations	the House of Lords
the Department of State	the United States Supreme Court
the University of Rochester	J.C. Penney Co.

36. CAPITALIZE THE NAMES OF POLITICAL PARTIES AND ORGANIZATIONS

Republican Party	Democratic Party
Libertarian Party	North Atlantic Treaty Organization

37. DO NOT CAPITALIZE NOUNS AND ADJECTIVES FORMED FROM THE NAMES OF POLITICAL PARTIES

He is a democrat.
They were not impressed with the products of communism.

38. CAPITALIZE PERIODS OF HISTORY

the Middle Ages	the Restoration	the Age of Reason
the Dark Ages	the Stone Age	the Renaissance

39. MOST REFERENCES TO HISTORICAL OR CULTURAL PERIODS DO NOT QUALIFY AS NAMES AND ARE NOT CAPITALIZED

the nineteenth century   antiquity

the romantic period   the space age

40. CAPITALIZE HISTORICAL EVENTS

Boston Tea Party   Prohibition   the New Deal

41. CAPITALIZE FORMAL DOCUMENTS

the Constitution of the United States   the Constitution

the Declaration of Independence   the Mayflower Compact

the Monroe Doctrine   the Magna Carta

Note that such documents are not usually set in quotation marks nor italics (underlined), in contrast with most publications.

42. CAPITALIZE NAMES OF MONTHS AND DAYS OF THE WEEK

March   October   Monday   Saturday

43. DO NOT CAPITALIZE THE NAMES OF SEASONS

summer   fall   winter   spring

autumn

44. CAPITALIZE THE NAMES OF GOD, DEITIES, AND REVERED FIGURES

God   Allah   Mars   Buddha

the Lord Shiva   Jupiter   the Virgin Mary   He (God)

Jehovah   the Apostle Paul   the Prophet   Messiah

45. CAPITALIZE THE NAMES OF BIBLICAL AND RELIGIOUS EVENTS

the Creation   the Crucifixion   the Exodus

Resurrection   Diaspora   Hegira

46. DO NOT CAPITALIZE NAMES OF RELIGIOUS OBJECTS

holy water   mezuzah   rosary   stations of the cross

47. CAPITALIZE THE SCIENTIFIC NAMES OF PLANTS AND ANIMALS

Scientific names are underlined. Capitalize the genus but not the species.

Rosa caroliniana   *Styrax californica*

48. DO NOT CAPITALIZE THE COMMON NAMES OF MOST PLANTS AND ANIMALS

oak tree   petunia   cardinal   grizzly bear

49. BUT SOME NAMES HAVE ACHIEVED OFFICIAL NAME STATUS

Cooper's hawk	Virginia creeper	Golden Bantam corn

50. CAPITALIZE THE NAMES OF HEAVENLY BODIES

the Big Dipper	Jupiter	Haley's Comet

Earth increasingly appears with a capital, especially in sicentific works. But do not capitalize *sun, moon, star, galaxy,* and other generic terms.

51. DO NOT CAPITALIZE THE NAMES OF DISEASES OR MEDICAL CONDITIONS

glaucoma	cancer	diabetes	leukemia

But note that some diseases bear a proper noun as part of the name: *Hodgkins disease*.

52. CAPITALIZE THE SIGNIFICANT WORDS IN THE GREETING OF A LETTER

Dear Ed,	Dear Sir or Madam:	My Dear Mr. Ui:

53. CAPITALIZE ONLY THE FIRST WORD IN THE CLOSING OF A LETTER

Sincerely,	Yours truly,	Very truly yours,

54. CAPITALIZE THE PRONOUN *I* AND THE EXCLAMATION *O*

"O, alas, the flowers are gone," I said.

55. CAPITALIZE THE TITLES OF PUBLICATIONS

In general, capitalize the first word and the last word and all significant words in between, excluding articles (*a, an, the*); coordinate conjunctions (*and, but, or, nor, so, for*); and prepositions (*at, by, below, from, in, on, to, up, with,* and so forth).

56. CAPITALIZE THE FIRST WORD OF A SUBTITLE FOLLOWING A COLON

Hydrotherapy: A Study of Arthritis	"Camping: The First Day"

57. DO NOT CAPITALIZE *THE* AS PART OF A NEWSPAPER TITLE IN YOUR PAPER

the *New York Times*	the *Christian Science Monitor*

Note that *the* is usually dropped from footnote and bibliographic references to newspapers and journals, even when it appears as part of the title on the periodical itself.

58. CAPITALIZE HYPHENATED WORDS IN TITLES

It is customary to capitalize both elements of a hyphenated word in a title except when the second element is clearly less important or together the elements form a single word.

Proofread for capitalization

Supply capital letters where formal writing requires in the following sentences.

1 chippewa hills superintendent lavern alward has said the 20 mill request on monday's ballot is necessary.

PAM KLEIN, "It's Decision Time at the Polls Monday"

2 for instance, kikkoman's soy sauce has a very strong flavor while la choy's is more mellow.

NANCY SELIGMAN, *Homesteading in the City*

3 and on a january morning in 1945, in fifteen-inch snow in the vosges mountains, by order of the man who is now president of the united states, private slovik was marched out and bound to a post.

WILLIAM BRADFORD HUIE, *The Execution of Private Slovik*

4 Starting point of the international quasar hunt is the molonglo observatory in new south wales.

SIMON MITTON, "Mysteries of Quasar Redshifts," 1975 *Yearbook of Astronomy*

5 there were not nearly enough life boats, and for reasons never explained, several of those that got away were barely filled, and passengers who were left on board when the ship sank were frozen in the icy water before captain rostrum of the *s. s. carpathia* could come to their rescue.

PEGGY GUGGENHEIM, *Confessions of an Art Addict*

6 the city university of new york, the country's third largest university system, sits these days like a giant battered orphan amid the financial ruins of new york city.

LARRY VAN DYNE, "City University of New York," *Atlantic Monthly*, June 1977

7 either the thread has snapped, or the muscle wall has broken through, but the moment the tube was extracted there appeared an open hole and, out of it, a spurt of blood a meter high!

NIKOLAI AMOSOV, *The Open Heart*

8 as dr. winnicott has put it: "at origin, aggressiveness is almost synonymous with activity."

ANTHONY STORR, *Human Aggression*

9 about thirty years ago, miss maria ward, of huntington, with only seven thousand pounds, had the good luck to captivate sir thomas bertram, of mansfield park, in the county of Northampton, and to be thereby raised to the rank ofa baronet's lady, with all the comforts and consequences of a handsome house and large income.

JANE AUSTEN, *Mansfield Park*

10 greek wisdom, she declares in her great essay on the *iliad*, has been

taken from us because the twin roman and hebrew world views supplanted it.

EDWARD GROSSMAN, "Simone Weil: A Life," *Commentary,* June 1977

11 I can remember now, quite vividly, the eighteen months my uncle angelo, an ordained priest, spent as a special visitor to the united states, serving as an adjunct assistant pastor with a church in brooklyn.

NINO LO BELLO, *The Vatican Empire*

12 now that may look to us like a stock piece of emotional blackmail—like the woman who whimpers that if sonny doesn't do as she wants him to do, mother's going to have one of her nasty turns.

ELAINE MORGAN, *The Descent of Woman*

13 two of England's leading opinion journals—*the tablet*, catholic; *the economist*, general—have taken remarkably contrasting positions on the recent meeting in rome of the anglican archibishop of canterbury, dr. coggan, and pope paul vi.

"REUNION'S DETOUR," *Commonweal,* 10 June 1977

14 normally, sheep breed only once a year, when the autumn days begin to shorten.

BEATRICE TRUM HUNTER, *Consumer Beware!*

15 besides the hosts there was a middle-aged couple, the ralph lewins— he was a colleague of harris's at the columbia university school of architecture; and maybe to balance off adler, harris's secretary, shirley fisher, has been invited, a thin-ankled, wet-eyed divorcee in a long bright-blue skirt, who talked and drank liberally.

BERNARD MALAMUD, "Notes from a Lady at a Dinner Party"

16 gordon lightfoot comes to pine knob tuesday and wednesday, bringing with him the melodic voice and gentle, yet stirring, music that has made him one of the few folk artists to outlast the '60 s and prosper in the '70s.

"A Gentle Survivor," *Detroit Free Press,* 14 June 1977

17 in 1972, dr. harry e. simmons, director of the bureau of drugs in the fda, estimated before a senate subcommittee that "superinfections" may be killing tens of thousands of persons yearly in this country.

RUTH MULVEY HARMER, *American Medical Avarice*

18 my companion at the press drank every day a pint before breakfast, a pint at breakfast with his bread and cheese, a pint between breakfast and dinner, a pint in the afternoon about six o'clock, and another when he had done his day's work.

BENJAMIN FRANKLIN, *The Life of Benjamin Franklin*

19 the tactics of a sneak raid on pearl—crippling the formidable u.s. fleet based there and freeing the japanese navy to dominate the pacific— had been a standard part of both tokyo's and washington's strategic thinking for a decade.

This Fabulous Century, 1940–1950

20 the human species, according to the best theory I can form of it, is composed of two distinct races, *the men who borrow*, and *the men who lend*.

CHARLES LAMB, "The Two Races of Man"

TYPING GUIDELINES

The following general guidelines tell you how to prepare a paper to hand in. Specific format instructions for typed papers (line spacing, indentations, and so on) are inside the back cover.

1 Typing is required in most colleges and universities today. If you don't type or don't have a machine, it may be to your advantage to become friends with someone who does. Even if your handwriting is quite legible, most readers will prefer typewritten papers. If you must write by hand, take great care to be neat and legible. Use only dark blue or black ink. If your typewriter ribbon has gone gray, replace it.

2 Use standard typing paper only. You need not buy expensive, heavy-weight paper, nor should you use onion-skin paper, nor easy-to-erase paper (it smudges). Use inexpensive typing paper of medium weight and learn to use Liquid Paper or Correction Tape for errors. Type or write on one side of the paper only.

3 Type double-spaced. On most machines there is a setting for double space at the left end of the platen (the roller). Double-space everything, but triple-space above and below indented quotes.

4 Give yourself at least a one-inch margin on all four sides. Learn to use the margin setting on your machine. Standard paper is 8½ inches wide and 11 inches long (always use standard paper). Set your roll for eleven inches, and when you get near the bottom of the page, watch for the one-inch mark to come up. If your machine has no setting for the bottom margin, mark your paper with a light pencil dot one inch from the bottom.

5 Unless your instructor requests a title page, it is customary to put your name, the date, the assignment, and/or other identifying information in the upper right-hand corner of the first page.

6 Center the title of your paper on the first page. All papers should have a title, even if it's something like "Punctuation Practice." Capitalize the first word and all other important words in the title. Do not put quotation marks around your own title; do not underline your own title.

7 If you have more than one page, staple the pages together; it might be a good idea to invest in a stapler. Do not pin, fold, or tear corners in an effort to fasten pages together; they will come undone anyway (and anything other than a staple looks unprofessional).

8 Number your pages, starting with page two, in the upper right-hand corner.

9 Use a uniform indentation for paragraphs. Set the tab for five; or, if your machine has no paragraph setting, count five spaces in for each new indentation. Handwritten papers should have paragraph indentations of at least one-half inch.

417

10 Clean copy should have no errors, but nobody is perfect. If you find an error at the last minute, paint it out with correction fluid, put the page back into your machine, and type the correction. If there isn't time for that, make a neat correction on the clean copy. Draw one (and only one) line through the error and write the correction above it in ink.

GLOSSARY
OF LANGUAGE
TERMS

This glossary is provided as a reference to terms you may encounter in composition. Some of the terms have been used in *The Writer's Work*; others may be in dictionaries, as part of the explanations of words; in language books; in articles and essays on language and composition; and so on.

absolute degree   Words like *unique, total, incomparable* describe a condition beyond comparison; thus, they are absolute. Some readers object to expressions like "more unique," "most incomparable." See *comparison* below.

accent   In dictionaries, words are marked with primary and secondary accent marks to show which syllables to stress: *'re cord* places the accent on the first syllable; *re cord'* places the accent on the second syllable; *'dig ni fy'* places a primary accent on the first syllable and a secondary accent on the last syllable. See also *accute accent* and *grave accent* below.

acute accent   A diacritical mark (´) used in some dictionaries to show primary stress: *de terá*. The acute accent is also used in many words of foreign origin (cliché, exposé, olé, resumé).

active voice   A verb is in the active voice when its subject is the actor in the sentence: "The dog *chased* the rabbit." "Three young people *found* an apartment." "Time *dragged*." See *passive voice* below.

adjective   An adjective describes, limits, changes, or in some other way modifies a noun or pronoun: "a *red* apple"; "*young* women"; "*enthusiastic* crowds"; "He is *strong*." Adjectives identify who, which, what kind, or how many. See also *modification* and *modified* below.

419

adjective clause   A clause used like an adjective: "This is the dog *that bit the mailman.*" "Give the money to those *who need it.*" Begin an adjective clause with a relative pronoun or the subordinators *where, when, or why*: "This is a time *when we must work together.*" "There must be some reason *why these things happen.*"

adjective phrase   A phrase made up of more than one adjective: "She always seems so *cool, serene,* and *regal.*" Or, any of several other kinds of phrases used like adjectives (*prepositional phrase, participial phrase, infinitive phrase*): "The girl *on the horse* is giving the orders." "This is a day *to remember.*"

adverb   Chiefly a verb modifier, but the adverb can also modify adjectives and other adverbs: "Walk *slowly.*" "She is *very* smart." "They move *quite stiffly.*" Adverbs indicate time (*now, then, yesterday*), place (*here, there*), manner (*carefully, stupidly*), and degree (*scarcely, seldom*).

adverb clause   A clause used like an adverb: "*When the lights go out,* head for the door." In addition to time, place, manner, and degree (see *Adverb* above), adverb clauses can be used to show cause, comparison, concession, condition, and purpose: "*Because it is raining,* you must stay in." "He is older *than you are.*" "*Although it is expensive,* she uses a lot of it." "*Unless it rains,* I'll work outside." "I'll turn up the volume *so that you can hear the music.*" Start adverb clauses with subordinate conjunctions (see below).

adverb phrase   A group of words composed of several adverbs: "*Slowly, quietly, and steadily,* they eased the canoe into the river." An adverb phrase can also be a prepositional phrase used like an adverb to modify a verb, adjective, or adverb: "*In the morning,* we go fishing." "The tree stands *near the shore.*" "It is too soon *after surgery* for you to get up." "Your speech is short *on information.*"

agreement   Correspondence of singulars and plurals. If the subject of a sentence is a singular word (one item), readers expect the verb to be singular too. A pronoun referring to a singular subject should also be singular. If the subject is plural, the verb and any pronouns referring to the subject should be plural. See Agreement in Chapter 9.

antecedent   A word or words a pronoun refers to. A problem of "pronoun reference" means that the pronoun does not clearly refer to its antecedent. See Pronoun Reference in Chapter 9.

anticipatory construction   An anticipatory construction appears in an inverted sentence or clause in which the subject comes after the verb: "*There is* a dog in the garage," "*There are* several kinds of apples." "*There are* in the opera elements of drama and dance"—the verb in this sentence, *are,* anticipates the subjects, *elements of drama and dance.*

appositive   A word that identifies a following or preceding noun: "My dog, *a retriever,* brings me the newspaper each morning." "*A retriever,* my dog, brings me the newspaper each morning."

article   A kind of noun modifier. The indefinite articles are *a* and *an.* The definite article is *the.* In modern grammar, articles are sometimes called *determiners* (see below). See Dictionary of Usage in Chapter 9.

auxiliary verbs   Verbs, sometimes called *helping verbs*, used with main verbs to create tense and other aspects of verbs. The auxiliaries include all the forms of *to be* (*am*, *is*, *are*, and so on) and the forms of *do*, *have*, *shall*, and *will*. In addition, there is a group called *modal auxiliaries*, containing *can*, *could*, *may*, *might*, *must*, *should*, and *would*. With these auxiliary verbs, writers create verb phrases like *is running*, *do speak*, *may have flown*, *should have been watching*, and so on.

base clause   The main clause in a sentence. The base clause, also called the independent clause, is the part of the sentence that can stand alone: "When the sun rises, *the rooster begins to crow.*" *The rooster begins to crow* is a base clause; it could be written as a separate sentence. In sentence-combining problems, the base clause is usually the top sentence; it is the one to which all the others attach.

breve   A diaritical mark (x̄) used to indicate a "short" vowel: hĭt, măt. A vowel is "long" when it "says its own name": *i* = eye, *o* = oh, and so on. Any other pronunciation of the vowel may be considered short, as marked with the breve, unless marked with other diacritical marks (see below).

caret   A proofreader's symbol (·) for adding to a line of print. Use the caret on clean copy to insert short omissions of additional words or to make corrections. The caret goes below the line, and the insertion is added above the caret. See inside back cover for the use of the caret in typed papers.

case   Case is related to the form or function of nouns or pronouns, based on their use in a sentence. Nouns and pronouns may be subjects (*subjective case*, also called *nominative*) or objects (*objective case*), or they may show possession (*possessive case*). See Pronouns as Subjects and Objects in Chapter 9.

clause   A group of words containing a subject and a verb; every sentence must have at least one clause. A simple sentence is a clause by itself. A sentence may have more than one clause. A clause may be only part of a sentence: *They knew who she was.* This sentence has two clauses: *they knew* and *who she was.* You need to distinguish between *clauses*—which have subjects and verbs (She sleeps *as it rains*)—and *phrases*—which do not (she sleeps *as often as possible*). There are four kinds of clauses: *independent clauses*, *adjective clauses*, *adverb clauses*, *noun clauses*.

collective noun   A group noun: *army*, *generation*, *minority*, *crowd*. See Goup Words in Chapter 9.

colloquial   Language used in conversations. *Colloquial* is frequently used in dictionaries to label expressions acceptable in oral English but unsuitable for formal writing. *Colloquial* is equivalent to *conversational;* and it is a style not only acceptable but preferred for such writing today—except the most formal. See Chapter 2, Personal Writing, for examples of colloquial language.

common noun   Any noun except those that are actually names of persons, places, or things (these are called *proper* nouns). The comon noun names a class or group (*dog*); the proper noun names a specific individual (*Fido*).

comparative degree Most adjectives and adverbs can show degrees of comparison (*fast, faster, fastest; slowly, more slowly, most slowly*). The middle degree of comparison (*faster; more slowly*) is the comparative. Avoid common errors like the double comparative (*more better, more slowlier*) and the faulty comparative (*more good, more soft*) and comparing the incomparable. See **absolute degree** above and **comparison** below.

comparison Refers to the degrees of modification of adjectives and adverbs. The degrees of comparison are *positive* (*fast; slowly*) *comparative* (*faster;* more slowly), and *superlative* (*fastest; most slowly*). A few modifiers have no comparison, at least in formal writing. Some readers object to *more unique, deader, fullest,* and so forth, on the grounds that degrees of uniqueness, deadness, or fullness are illogical. See **absolute degree** and **comparative degree** above.

complement Traditionally, a term for nouns and pronouns in the object position after a *being* or linking verb: "my friend Myrna is a *surgeon.*" Another term for this kind of verb complement is *predicate nominative.* Today, language and composition books use the term *complement* loosely to mean anything that receives the action of the verb or completes the sense required by the verb. Thus, direct objects, indirect objects, and predicate adjectives may be included in the term *verb complement.*

complex sentence A sentence containing at least one subordinate clause. *Our canary sings when it feels well* is a complex sentence. *Our canary sings* is the main (independent) clause; *when it feels well* is a subordinate clause—a modifying clause, not a complete sentence.

composition The art of formulating, organizing, shaping, and developing writing. In contrast with free writing, composition presupposes that a writer has a purpose and a plan for carrying it out. *To compose* means "to put together writing (or oral language) to achieve an effect on the reader." See Chapter 1, The Composing Process, and **rhetoric** below.

compound Two or more items linked together to form a sentence element. For example, there may be *compound subjects* (*Jack and Jill*), *compound verbs* (*swimming and sailing*) *compound objects* (*to the doctor or the nurse*). When two sentences or two base clauses are joined with one of the coordinate conjunctions, the result is called a compound sentence: *He sang, and his wife applauded.*

compound noun A noun composed of more than one word: *hubcap, lay of the land, old-timer.* Some compound nouns are spelled as one word, some as more than one word, some as hyphenated words. Compound nouns may have irregular plurals: *mothers-in-law, sergeants-at-arms.*

compound-complex A sentence containing two independent clauses and one subordinate clause. See **complex sentence** above.

conjugation A list of all the possible forms of a verb in all the tenses, moods, and voices, with all the pronouns: *I sing, you sing, he sings, she sings,* and so on. The word can also be used to refer to less than a full display of the verb: a conjugation in the present tense, or a conjugation of the passive voice, for example. See the list of principal parts of troublesome verbs under Verbs in Chapter 9.

conjunction   A connecting word. There are several kinds of conjunctions: *coordinate* (*and, but, or*); *correlative* (*either-or, neither-nor*); *subordinate* (*after, if, since, when*).

conjunctive adverb   A connective. Conjunctive adverbs are similar to coordinate conjunctions because they connect full sentences: "I once had a cat; *however*, it ran away." The following are conjunctive adverbs:

also	indeed	nevertheless
besides	in fact	next
consequently	instead	otherwise
furthermore	likewise	still
however	meanwhile	then
incidentally	moreover	therefore
		thus

connective   See *conjunction* above.

coordinate   The term *coordinate* means "equal in order"; it contrasts with *subordinate*, "lower in order." Coordinate clauses are clauses of equal importance to the writer: "*Old men snore* and *babies gurgle in their sleep.*" Each of these clauses could be written as a separate sentence; both are independent clauses. Conjunctions that join coordinate clauses (*and, but, for, not, or, so*) are called *coordinate conjunctions*. In contrast, one idea is more important than the other in a subordinate construction: *The men will have to keep working until all the material is gone.* The main idea here (*The men will have to keep working*) is the important one. The other idea (*until all the material is gone*) has been reduced to a modifier. Other terms for this subordinate construction are *independent clause* for the part that could stand alone and *dependent clause* for the part that "depends on" the other for its existence. In a coordinate construction there are two independent clauses. Neither of them requires the other; each could stand alone: *The men will have to keep working; the new material will arrive soon.*

correlative conjunction   Correlative conjunctions operate in pairs: *either-or, neither-nor, not only-but also, both-and.*

cumulative modifier   See *nonrestrictive* below.

dangling modifier   See Dangling Parts in Chapter 9.

declarative sentence   A declarative sentence makes a statement of fact, "declares" an assertion: *It is raining outside. The experiment lasted a year.*

declension   A list of all the forms of a pronoun (*I, we, me, us, my, mine,* and so on). A declension shows number (singular and plural), case (subjective, possessive, objective), and person (first, second, third).

demonstrative pronouns   The demonstrative pronouns are *this, that, these,* and *those.* They are used like adjectives or definite articles: *this house, that dog.*

dependent clause   A group of words containing a subject and a verb but not a complete thought: "They don't know *where you will be tomorrow.*" Dependent clauses begin with relative pronouns and subordinate conjunctions (see below). There are three kinds of dependent clauses: *adjective clauses, adverb clauses, noun clauses*.

determiner   In modern grammar, a word that places, limits, or "slots" a noun or nominal (see below) rather than amplifying or describing it: "*a* catastrophe," "*either* alternative," "*that* hurdy-gurdy," "*their* reasons." Determiners include:

a	no	this	my
an	one	these	your
any	some	what	his
each	the	whatever	her
either	that	which	our
every	those	whichever	their
neither			

diacritical mark   A mark that shows how to pronounce a word. See *acute accent, breve, dieresis, grave accent, macron, schwa,* and *tilde* in this glossary. See also inside back cover for forms of diacritical marks in typed papers.

dialect   An oral language style differing from the so-called "standard." Dialects concern writers because regional speech patterns and "foreign" accents (the patterns and sounds of any language as spoken by someone to whom it is not native) are difficult to reproduce in writing. Caricatures of dialects are offensive. See ***standard English*** below.

dieresis   A diacritical mark (¨) used to show that a vowel is pronounced as a separate syllable: *naïve, coöperation, Brontë*.

direct object   The direct object receives the action of the verb: "I shot the *bear*." "She gave me a *dollar*." Notice that in the second example there seem to be two objects, *me* and *dollar*. In this example, *me* is an *indirect object* (see below). See also Pronouns as Subjects and Objects in Chapter 9.

double negative   See Dictionary of Usage Problems, Chapter 9.

elliptical construction   A sentence structure that omits one or more words. The "understood" subject of many sentences is an elliptical *you*: "[You] shut the door." As long as the missing element is clearly implied, there is no problem: "You may be old enough to get married but [you are] not [old enough] to drink." Elliptical constructions are a feature of impressionistic style:

Slung awry by its chain from a thin nail, an open oval locket, glassed. In one face of this locket, a colored picture of Jesus, his right hand blessing, his red heart exposed in a burst of spiky gold halo. In the other face, a picture by the same artist of the Blessed Virgin, in blue, her heart similarly exposed and haloed, and pierced with seven small swords.
JAMES AGEE AND WALKER EVANS, *Let Us Now Praise Famous Men*

epigram   An especially well-worded thought. An epigram makes a memorable saying because of its effective wording:

A foolish consistency is the hobgoblin of little minds adored by little statesmen and philosophers and divines.
RALPH WALDO EMERSON, "Self Reliance"

Epigrams are frequently based on antithesis:

Man proposes but God disposes.
THOMAS À KEMPIS, *Imitation of Christ*

They are very often satiric:

Here lies our sovereign lord the king, whose word no man relies on; he never says a foolish thing nor ever does a wise one.
EARL OF ROCHESTER

epigraph   A motto or inscription on a monument or building, or an opening or illustrative quote at the beginning of a book or chapter or essay. Each chapter of *The Writer's Work* begins with an epigraph.

etymology   The science of tracing the origin and development of a word; a branch of linguistics. The etymology of a word shows the changes in meaning and the various influences that have gone into the present meaning of a word. The best authority on word histories is the *Oxford English Dictionary*, but any good modern dictionary will give a summary etymology of a word.

expletive   In language study, either the word *there* or the word *it* in an *anticipatory construction* (see above): "*There* were several writers at the convention." "*It* is cold in here." The expletive has no grammatical function.

formal language   The language used for writing to an audience of well-educated readers. Such readers expect to see writing that conforms to the conventions and traditions of print. If writing can be thought of as a continuum, with the loosest, freest, most informal kind of writing at one end (graffiti, free writing) and the most carefully controlled, technical writing at the other end (scientific reports, legal documents), we can say that the more writing moves in the direction of this tightly controlled end of the continuum, the more formal it becomes. See *standard English* below.

fragments   See *sentence* below.

gender   Distinction according to sex or the lack of it. Many nouns and pronouns have gender; they are identified by the terms *feminine, masculine*, or *neuter*.

genitive   The Latin grammar term for *possessive*.

gerund   an *-ing* form of a verb used like a noun. "*Fishing* is fun." "What you need is more *jogging*."

gerund phrase   A phrase containing a gerund plus any modifiers or objects: "*Speaking too rapidly* is one of the signs of nervousness." "I am fond of *opening presents*." In formal writing, use possessive nouns and pronouns with gerunds: "The question at issue was the *children's praying* in school." "They want *his singing the anthem* to close the show."

grammar   The terms and concepts with which linguists describe a language, such as the eight parts of speech, are the grammar of the language. Grammar is distinct from *usage*, the conventions and traditions about words and expressions that let a writer know, for example, what language may be suitable for formal writing. *Tough guy* is a noun composed of the modifier *tough* and the root word *guy*—this is *grammatical* information. Whether you should use the term *tough guy* in a formal paper about prison inmates is a *usage* questionion requiring consideration of purpose, audience, and so on.

grave accent   A diacritical mark (`) used in English to differentiate certain words that, although spelled like other words, have different meanings and pronunciations (*learnèd* and *learned* or *belovèd* and *beloved*). The grave accent indicates that the *-ed* syllable is fully pronounced.

imperative   A sentence that orders or requests: "Shut the door." "Please turn down the heat." "Halt!" The subject (*you*) is not expressed in an imperative sentence.

indefinite   Several sentence elements are called *indefinite*, meaning "not specifying a particular person or thing." The *indefinite articles* are *a* and *an*; some of the *indefinite pronouns* are *anybody, anyone, everyone, one, someone;* some of the *indefinite adjectives* are *any, few, several, some*. See **determiner** above.

independent clause   See **base clause** above.

indirect object   An indirect object shows to or for whom or what the action of the verb is done: "We gave *her* a new car." In the example, *car* is the direct object; it directly receives the action of the verb *gave*. But *her* is the indirect object; it indicates *to whom* the car was given.

infinitive   The *to* form of a verb (*to go, to walk, to speak*). The infinitive can be used like a noun as in "*To be* or not *to be*, that is the question." It can also be used like a modifier: "These are the bicycles *to be sold* at auction."

inflection   Changes in meaning indicated by changes in the forms of words. English is not a highly inflected language, but we do have some inflections: for example, plurals, possessives, subjects and objects, verb tenses, degrees of modifiers.

informal language   See **formal language** above.

intensive pronouns   The *self* pronouns when they are used for emphasis with (to intensify) a noun or pronoun: "The dog *itself* can easily jump that fence." "You did it *yourself*." When these *-self* pronouns are used as complements, they are called *reflexive*: "He gave *himself* a shock when he touched the wires."

interjection   An exclamation: "Oh!" "Ouch!" "Wow!" An interjection need not have an exclamation point: "I thought, *oh*, if I could only get away from here. . . ."

interrogative pronoun   A pronoun that asks a question (*what, which, who, whoever, whom, whomever, whose*): "*What* are your reasons for wanting to become a writer?"

intransitive verb   A verb that cannot take an object: "He sleeps during the day." "They *left* an hour ago." Note that a verb can be intransitive in one sense (They *left* an hour ago) and transitive in another (They *left him* in the station). A transitive verb is one in which the action of the verb "transfers" or "carries over" to an object.

inverted order   See *anticipatory construction* above.

irony   Irony is a means of saying one thing while implying another, often opposite, thing: "He tried on a garish flowered shirt and iridescent walking shorts and said he hoped it would soften his corporate image. I assured him that it did." The irony is in the conflict between what is said and what is implied about the way the man looks.

irregular verb   A verb that does not form its past tenses or past participle with a suffix like *-ed*: for example, *swim* (*swam, swum*) or *drink* (*drank, drunk*). See the list of irregular verb parts under Verbs in Chapter 9.

kernel sentences   In modern grammar, those minimal, basic sentences of which our language is theoretically composed: *Dogs bark. The man sees the tree.* From these kernel or basic sentences, any sentence in our language can be generated through sentence combining (see Chapter 7).

linking verbs   Linking verbs do not express action; they "link" their subjects to predicate nouns or adjectives. The linking verbs are the forms of *to appear, to be, to become, to feel, to grow, to look, to remain, to seem, to smell, to sound, to stay.* "She *is* young." "She *appears* young." "She *seems* young." Notice the difference between a linking verb—"This *looks* good"—and an action verb—"He *looks* carefully for mistakes in proofreading."

macron   A diacritical mark (¯) used to indicate the pronunciation of a "long" vowel: *cāne, tōne cūte*. See *breve* above.

main clause   See *base clause* above.

mass noun   A noun that identifies some commodity or substance we measure by weight, volume, or degree (money, wheat, temperature). Mass nouns are sometimes called *noncount nouns* to distinguish them from *count nouns*.

merged verb   See *particle* below.

misplaced modifier   A modifier that has been accidentally placed near some word the writer does not intend to modify: "There is a pile of clothing for the children *in the basket*." See Dangling Parts in Chapter 9.

modal auxiliary   See *auxiliary* verb above.

modification   To change or alter. By means of modification, writers can describe, limit, expand, and make clear the relationships among ideas. Note that the basic idea, "I had forgotten," is expanded and clarified through modification in the following sentence:

I had forgotten, in the rage of my growing up, how proud my father had been of me when I was little.
JAMES BALDWIN, *Notes of a Native Son*

modifier   A word or group of words that describes or in some way limits another word or words. Modifiers may be single-word adjectives and adverbs, or phrases and clauses used like adjectives and adverbs. See **modification** above.

mood of verbs   The "moods" of verbs are *indicative* (for statements and questions); *imperative* (for requests or commands); and *subjunctive* (for expressions of doubt, wishes, probabilities, and conditions contrary to fact). See Conditional Statements and Statements of Doubt, Wishes, Probability . . . in Chapter 9.

nominal   Like a noun. *Nominal* is sometimes used to describe gerunds and noun clauses.

nonrestrictive   An adjective clause is nonrestrictive if it is nonessential. A restrictive clause is essential to tell *how many* individuals are meant or *which ones*. Set off nonrestrictive clauses with commas (see Punctuation in Chapter 10). Cumulative modifiers are "add-on" modifiers; they are usually nonrestrictive and should be set off with commas.

noun   The name of a person, place, thing, or idea (*woman, Irene, Texas, dog, tool, freedom*).

noun clause   A clause used like a noun: "*What you see* is *what you get*."

number   Refers to singular and plural.

object   That which receives action, the *direct object* (see above). There are other kinds of objects, such as object of a preposition, object of an infinitive, object of a participle, object of a gerund.

objective complement   A verb complement after a direct object: "We named him *our leader*." In this example, *him* is the direct object, and *our leader* is the objective complement.

participle   A progressive or perfect form of a verb used like an adjective (*laughing* clown, *broken* promises, *ruined* dreams). When the participle is part of a modifying phrase, you must avoid the problem of the dangling participle. See **dangling modifier** above.

participial phrase   See *participle* above.

particle   A preposition or adverb that has merged with a verb: "It's time to close *up* the shop." "Turn *off* the engine." The particle has become part of the verb. Note that the particle is movable: "It's time to close the shop *up*." "Turn the engine *off*."

parts of speech   In ancient times, scholars hoped to make a science of speech by naming and describing each of the "parts" of language. Traditionally, there are eight parts of speech: *noun, pronoun, verb, adjective, adverb, preposition, conjunction,* and *interjection*. The parts of speech get their definitions from *context*. In one context, for example, *punch* is a noun: "She threw a *punch* at him." In another context, *punch* is a verb: "She may *punch* him in the nose."

passive   (See Chapter 7.)

past participle The form of the verb used with *have*, *has*, *had* (*have sung*, *has drunk*, *had swum*). The past participle is used in the "perfect" tenses (present perfect, past perfect, future perfect). See list of verb parts under Verbs in Chapter 9.

perfect tense See *past participle* above.

person Refers to pronouns used to identify the speaker (*I; we*), *first person;* the audience (*you; you*), *second person;* and the subject (*he, she, it; they*), *third person.* Note that only the third person singular pronouns require *s*-form verbs: *he speaks, she drives, it barks.* All singular nouns are third person and require *s*-form verbs in the present tense: *the man speaks; Sue drives, the dog barks.*

personal pronouns The person pronouns are *I, you, he, she, it,* and their plurals and possessives (*yours, hers,* and so on); and objective forms (*me, us, them,* and so on).

phrase A group of words without a subject—in contrast with a clause. There are several kinds of phrases: *prepositional, infinitive, participial, absolute.* Informally, a phrase is any group of words or expression: "She used the phrase *God bless you* when anyone sneezed."

plural More than one.

point of view A complex of attitudes: the writer's attitude toward self, subject, and audience. Often the term *point of view* is used to mean any of these attitudes individually (the author's point of view toward his or her audience). See Chapter 1.

positive degree See *comparison* above.

possessive Possessive nouns and pronouns can be used to show ownership: "*Brenda's* car," "*my* cat." (See Apostrophe in Chapter 10.) Note that gerunds are preceded by possessive, not objective, pronouns. See *gerund* above.

predicate The predicate is the part of a sentence that makes a statement about the subject: "The President [subject] must struggle with the economy [predicate]." The subject is who or what the sentence is about (*the President*); the predicate tells the reader what you want to say about the subject (*must struggle with the economy*).

predicate adjective A modifier of the subject but appearing in the predicate after a linking verb: "She is *pretty.*" "The young woman in that position seems very *competent.*" Note the difference between a sentence with a progressive verb (She *is talking*) and one with a participle as a predicate adjective (She *is interesting*). The predicate adjective is the one that can be modified by the adverb *very* (*very interesting* but not *very talking*).

predicate nominative See *predicate noun* below.

predicate noun A noun in the object slot in a sentence with a linking verb: "The boy is a *lieutenant.*" Such nouns are not objects; linking verbs do not take objects.

prefix   A meaning unit added to the beginning of a word: *dis*cover, *re*-turn.

PREFIX	MEANING	EXAMPLE
a-	out of, not	atypical
ab-	away from	abdicate
ad-	to, toward	admit
anti-	against	antibody
auto-	self	autograph
com-	with	commit
de-	away, down	deflate
dis-	apart, not	disengage
ex-	formerly, out of	exhale
extra-	out of	extralegal
hyper-	above, very	hyperactive
hypo-	below, under	hypodermic
in-	into, within	insert
in-	not	invalid
mono-	one	monograph
ob-	against, away from	obtuse
non-	not	nonfunctional
per-	through, very	percolate
poly-	many	polygamy
pre-	before	precursor
pro-	before, in favor of	promote
re-	again, back	return
sub-	across	transport
un-	not	unconventional

preposition   Most prepositions are small words of position: *in, out, on,* and so on. A few other words are also considered prepositions, such as *during, except,* and so on. Prepositions take objects: "to *him,*" "for *her,*" "between *you* and *me.*" See Objects with Prepositions in Chapter 9. List of common prepositions:

above	behind	in	to
across	below	into	toward
after	beneath	near	under
against	beside	of	until
along	between	off	unto
amid	beyond	on	up
among	but	out of	upon
around	by	over	upon
at	except	past	with
because	for	since	within
before	from	through	without

prepositional phrase   A preposition and its object and any modifiers: *by the boat, near the great old willow.* Prepositional phrases are almost always used as modifiers.

present participle   The -*ing* form of a verb (*doing, being, seeing*).

progressive tense   The progressive tenses—past, present, and future progressive—are written with the -*ing* form of a verb (*is running, was speaking, will be going*). See *gerund* and *participle* above.

pronoun   A pronoun takes the place of a noun. There are several kinds of pronouns: *personal, demonstrative, indefinite, intensive, interrogative, reflexive, relative*. See Pronouns as Subjects and Objects and Pronoun Reference in Chapter 9.

pronoun reference   See *antecedent* above.

proper adjective   An *adjective* derived from a proper noun (*English, Indian, American*).

proper noun   The name of a specific person, place, or thing (*Jane, Canada, Fido*). See *common noun* above.

pun   A play on words. The pun is an obvious (nonsubtle) form of humor; it relies on similarities in sounds and unexpected applications of meanings:

Our spacemen, Mrs. Lamport fears, are "heading for the lunar bin."
ARTHUR KOESTLER, *The Act of Creation*

regular verbs   Regular verbs form their past and perfect forms by adding -*d* or -*ed* (*baked, earned*). See *irregular verb* above.

reflexive pronoun   See *intensive pronouns* above.

relative clause   A clause beginning with a relative pronoun: "I found the dollar *that you lost*." In this example, the relative clause is used like an adjective to modify *dollar*.

relative pronouns   The relative pronouns are *who, whose, what, that, whatever, whom, whomever,* and *which*. They may be used to start relative clauses (see above).

restrictive   See *nonrestrictive* above.

retained object   A direct object in a passive sentence: "They were given a *book* to study."

schwa   A diacritical mark (ə) indicating the pronunciation of a vowel; the schwa looks like an upside down *e*. It is pronounced "uh" like the *a* in *ago* or the *e* in *the*.

second possessive   Some pronouns have two possessive forms—the possessive used like an adjective (*my* hat, *her* house) and a second possessive used like a predicate adjective (the hat is *mine*, the house is *hers*).

rhetoric   Rhetoric is the art of effective writing. Many scholars feel that rhetoric is the same as composition (see above).

semantics   The study of meaning; the study not only of what words mean but how they acquire their meanings and even what *meaning* means. According to some modern semanticists, writers select words to express the meanings they have in mind, and therefore words do not have meanings but denotations—only people have meanings.

sentence A group of words expressing a complete thought; a completed relationship between a subject and its predicate. Contrast with *fragment*: an incomplete sentence, an incomplete thought. See **elliptical construction** above.

sentence modifier A modifier of the entire idea in a sentence: "He had always been a very excitable person, *causing others to suspect that he had been using drugs*."

series Three or more items in a list: "We ordered hamburgers, cokes, and french fries." See Use Commas to Separate Three or More Items in a Series in Chapter 10.

simple sentence A sentence that consists of one and only one independent clause and no dependent clauses. *Fish swim* is a simple sentence. Note that *simple* has nothing to do with length; the following is also a simple sentence: *Until noon each day, the young man in the sportscar cruised the streets, looking for his friends, looking for girls, looking for something to do*.

slang Any informal, nontechnical word or expression not yet accepted by educated users of the language as part of the general language. Consequently, slang terms are often not in dictionaries. Many slang words are colorful, lively, and suitable for informal writing; but the more formal your writing situation, the less appropriate slang becomes.

solidus See **virgule** below.

split infinitive Placing a word between *to* and its verb creates a split infinitive (*to quickly go*, *to really think*), a construction to avoid in formal writing.

squinting modifier A modifier that ambiguously modifies two words: "She told him *seldom* to do any of the hard work." See *Misplaced modifiers* above and Misplaced Parts in Chapter 9.

standard English Standard English is frequently defined as the English of educated speakers and writers. Since no two speakers of English speak exactly alike, such a definition creates more problems than it solves. *Standard* is often used to contrast with *nonstandard* or *substandard*. Thus, what many people really mean by standard English is language that follows the rules in their favorite grammar books. You can avoid the issue entirely by not using the term *standard English*. Instead, use the concept of *formal language*, a concept that implies audience, purpose, and the entire complex of decisions a writer must make. Writers who choose to write in formal situations should become familiar with the language expectations of the majority of educated readers (see Chapter 9). It is possible that serious writers might (and on occasion do) successfully use some "nonstandard" expressions in formal writing; in fact, all language usage is a matter of choice and judgment on the writer's part. Twentieth century writing is moving toward more informality; the question of what is standard or nonstandard may evaporate in time. But writers will always need to decide how they wish to present themselves to readers, what effect they wish to make, and how best to accomplish their writing purpose. See **formal language** above.

subject The topic of a sentence, the part of the sentence about which the predicate makes a statement: "*The rats* came in the night and attacked the children." In the example, the subject is *the rats*. See *predicate* above.

subjective case The case of pronouns (and nouns) used as subjects (*I, he, she, they, who*); contrast with the objective case (see above).

subjunctive mood See *mood of verbs* above.

subordinate Not independent. See *coordinate* above.

subordinate conjunction Subordinate conjunctions start adverb clauses (see above):

after	because	though	whenever
although	before	unless	where
as	if	until	wherever
as if	since	when	while

suffix A meaning unit attached to the end of a word: event*ful*, dur*ation*.

SUFFIX	MEANING	EXAMPLE
-able, -ible	able to, capable of	portable
-al	act, process of	removal
-ance, -ence	condition, quality of	deliverance
-ant	one who does or is	supplicant
-ate	do or have	dominate
-ful	abundant	harmful
-ism	belief, doctrine, theory	cubism
-ist	one who does or is	therapist
-ize	become, cause to be	sterilize
-ness	condition of	humanness
-ship	function, status	authorship
-tion	act, process	promotion
-wise	direction, position, manner	clockwise

superlative degree See *comparison* above.

syntax The order of words in a sentence and their relationships to each other. See *grammar* above.

tense The aspect of verbs that lets the reader know whether the discourse is in *past, present,* or *future* time.

tilde A diacritical mark (˜) indicating a sound pronounced as if merging an *n* with a *y: Doña, señor*.

transformation In modern grammar, some linguists proposed a theory that most of the sentences of a language are generated by transforming (combining) kernel sentences (see above). Thus *The dog will come in when the rain starts* is theoretically a transformation of the two kernel sentences *The dog will come in* and *the rain starts*. See Chapter 7, Sentence Combining for Effective Sentences.

transitive verb A verb that can take an object. See *intransitive verb*.

transposition symbol   A proofreader's mark (∽) for transposed letters: m(s a)t = *most*. You may mark transpositions on finished copy as long as there aren't too many of them. See inside the back cover.

usage   See *grammar* above.

verb   A part of speech usually expressing action (*go, jump, shout, think*); a few verbs, such as the linking and auxiliary verbs (see above), do not express action.

verbal   Verb forms used for other than verb functions. Verbals include *gerunds, infinitives*, and *participles* (see above).

virgule   A slash mark (/), also called a *solidus*. For use of the virgule to mark the ends of lines of poetry in typed papers, see Punctuation, Chapter 10.

INDEX

FORMAT GUIDELINES FOR TYPED PAPERS

IDENTIFICATION
If your instructor doesn't give you another format for identifying your papers, type your name, the course title, the instructor's name, and the date in the upper right-hand corner of the first page.

TRANSPOSITION SYMBOL
used here to reverse the order of words

CARET
with a handwritten insertion above it

BRACKETS
used here to enclose clarifying information the author of the paper has inserted into the direct quote.

UNDERLINING
used here to signify the use of italics in the original

PARAGRAPH SYMBOL

NOTE NUMBERS
are typed slightly above the line, with no space between the end of the quote (in this case, the period) and the note number.

5-character indentation for new paragraphs

5 character indention for all lines of displayed quotes except a new paragraph

Quadruple-space

Double-space

Triple-space

Double-space

Triple-space

1″

1″

1″

1″

TRANSPOSITION SYMBOL
used here to reverse the order of letters

Kathy Hart

English 110

Professor Mendez

October 3, 1980

The Innovative Artist Jackson Pollock

    For the sake of earning livings, and reputations, painters have always followed the popular trends of their respective periods and concealed their experimental dabblings in their studio storerooms. At some time earlier, innovators had to create the style that established the traditions. The twentieth century is a time of many such innovators, one of the most prominent being the pioneer of abstract expressionism, Jackson Pollock. His later works, hailed by some, *and ridiculed by others,* made Pollock a revolutionary figure of modern art. A look at what and how he painted, as well as at the critical reactions to it, is necessary to understand the impact of Pollock's work.

    His creations of the 1940s show not merely a deviation from the conventional rules of painting but a complete and deliberate defiance of them, behavior that amazed Marc Moiré, the earliest favorable critic of Pollock:

The most obvious evidence of this rebellion emerges through the subject matter: there appears to be none. Ten years ago, Künstler and Fañon experimented briefly with forms as devoid of extrinsic content as Pollock's, but they vitiated the effect by conferring elaborate titles on their works. Pollock simply tags his with numbers because, according to Lee Krasner [Pollock's wife], "Numbers are neutral. They make people look at a picture for what it is--pure painting." And that painting <u>should</u> be utterly pure is rebellion of an unprecedented variety.[1]

    ¶ Moiré's astonishment was perhaps to be expected in 1943, but later critics

---

LONG QUOTES
If a quote is 3 or more typed lines long, display it. That is, triple-space above the first line and below the last line of the quote and indent all lines of the quote 5 characters from the left. Indent 10 characters for each new paragraph. The quote itself is double-spaced. Note especially that QUOTATION MARKS are used only if, and exactly as, they appear in the original.